Daffodils in American Gardens
1733–1940

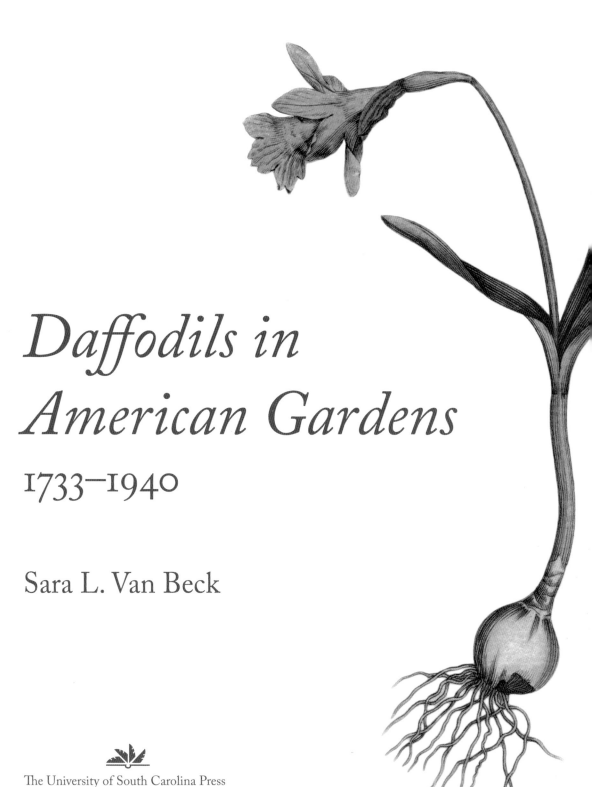

Daffodils in American Gardens

1733–1940

Sara L. Van Beck

The University of South Carolina Press

© 2015 University of South Carolina

Published by the University of South Carolina Press
Columbia, South Carolina 29208

www.sc.edu/uscpress

Manufactured in Korea

24 23 22 21 20 19 18 17 16 15   10 9 8 7 6 5 4 3 2 1

Library of Congress Cataloging-in-Publication Data

Van Beck, Sara L.
    Daffodils in American gardens, 1733–1940 / Sara L. Van Beck.
        pages cm
    Includes bibliographical references and index.
     ISBN 978-1-61117-401-4 (hardback : alk. paper) 1. Daffodils—United States—History.
     1. Title.
    QK495.A484V36 2015
    584'.34—dc23   2014011487

Contents

Preface

A common misconception holds that surviving old daffodils in landscapes, especially if hybrid cultivars, are older than they really are. The Royal Horticultural Society (RHS) introduction date misleads one to think the daffodil was in American gardens by shortly after that date, whereas for many hybrid cultivars that is very likely not the case. The rich and enthusiastic ordered out of the latest British and Dutch catalogs, but most folks ordered from American catalogs, and in the nineteenth century there is a demonstrable delay between when a flower was the rage in Britain to when it was offered in most American catalogs. The reverse of this misconception is at work simultaneously—the perception that the daffodils struggling in the garden aren't that old, maybe as old as the nearby shrub, when in reality the bulbs may be as old as the centenarian boxwood hedge.

Further, there is a blind spot in much historic landscape work regarding bulbs and daffodils in particular. The place of spring or Dutch bulbs has been often taken for granted or not given much thought, possibly in part in keeping with the general blind spot toward bulbs as a class in many modern American gardeners' worldview. More types of daffodils were grown by aficionados of their day than is generally recognized, some of which grow well in American gardens and others that will not survive for one hundred years. Conversely, gardeners without means grew only a few, passed among friends and family. Spring bulbs had their role and function in gardens high style and vernacular, and daffodils were part of the palate. Tough and dependable, early, and welcoming, they may have been dismissed as common by many nineteenth-century writers, but others commented that a few were always to be found in gardens of the day.

It is interesting to note that while tulips and hyacinths dominated the Dutch bulb gardening world for hundreds of years, and tulips still evoke great emotions in people, there are no American tulip or hyacinth societies. Within the RHS there is the daffodil and tulip committee, with snowdrops thrown in for good measure, but the interest and horticultural and botanical work is dominated by the genus *Narcissus*. The daffodil now is where the tulip and hyacinth were hundreds of years ago—experiencing a dynamism from great leaps in hybridizing, bringing new color and forms as hybridizers experiment with entirely novel "sections" within the genus and refine back-line breeding. Further, as the tulip succumbs to the American deer population explosion, the Dutch are looking for new flowers to fill the void as gardeners tire of spending good money to feed their local herd of "long-legged goats."

This is not an attempt to comprehensively review the rich and detailed history of the daffodil, nor of gardening in America; rather this book seeks to document the appearance of daffodils within American gardens by written word and planted bulb. To do so requires placing daffodils in the context of the early history of European gardening in general, as this sets the parameters for daffodils in colonial America. Detailed and entrancing histories of gardening await in Ann Leighton's pair of tomes (*American Gardens in the Eighteenth Century, American Gardens of the Nineteenth Century*); specific regional histories offer greater detail of place and time (Barbara Sarudy, *Gardens and Gardening in the Chesapeake 1700–1805;* Peter Martin, *The Pleasure Gardens of Virginia;* James Cothran, *Gardens and Historic Plants of the Antebellum South*). I relied on and drew from these works, by no means seeking to supplant any of them; these books are recommended reading for those interested in American gardening history.

There are numerous interesting tales to be told, many of which are yet to be uncovered and comprehensively explored. Surveys and oral histories are needed for many regions of the country, details on the early market for forced and cut flowers, details on small growers across the country in the 1920s, and more cemetery data are to be collected—all interesting, and all warranting more attention than is provided here.

Many examples are skewed to the South, partly because of access to resources. Travel for pleasure during a very limited window each year (daffodil season) means the researcher can't get everywhere at once and still maintain work and family. Hopefully someone will be able to do more field research for other areas of the country.

Fundamentally this is a tale of preservation by poverty, augmented by preservation by family. Historically, since the Civil War the South has not been as wealthy as the North, so property owners did not necessarily have the resources to update or modernize the landscaping. Those who did have the means to do so did, resulting in the loss of many a grand old garden in the past century. Conversely houses that have remained in family hands often retain the gardens of the grandparents, great-grandparents, and so on. Also, in some areas where northerners purchased grand old southern homes and properties for hunting plantations, money was not spent on the grounds. Regrettably the speculative housing boom from 1996 onward hastened the destruction of many a historic farmstead and house and their garden plants. The recession of 2009–2010 further wreaked havoc; in rural areas, long-fallow land was put back into production, with daffodils either sprayed off in pastures or plowed under in timber land.

Gardeners in general have discovered the intrigue, romance and durability of heirloom flowers—simple beauties that haven't had the guts (or fragrance) bred out of them, that still have some warts and issues, that have a willowy grace new hybrids have lost in a search for symmetrical perfection, new colors, new shapes, fancy foliage, extended climate tolerance, or whatever else the fad has become to keep the industry chugging along. And old daffodils are no different. Not many plants can survive being bulldozed with the house and scraped off the back of the lot, to come up from a foot or two of clay and rubble through choking vines, to bloom year after year, looking just as lovely as the day their long-dead gardener saw them their first spring. I like their twisting petals, their crinkly wonky cups, their erratic color production based on the weather, and their wacky decision to have eight petals this year instead of six. They are real, they don't look like dinner plates or fake flowers on plastic doormats, they thumb their collective nose at droughts and watering restrictions and mediocre soil, and every year someone new who wanders by my city yard says "Yours is my favorite garden in the neighborhood."

Acknowledgments

Over the course of this project, I have had the pleasure of meeting many like-minded history buffs, preservationists, and garden sleuths. Numerous individuals have provided their research expertise and opinions along the way. Thanks to: Staci Catron and the collections of the Cherokee Garden Library, Kenan Research Center at the Atlanta History Center; the late James R. Cothran; Jan Pennings; Johan von Scheeper (KAVB); Ron Fisher; Linda Van Beck; Weej Broderson; Susan Hitchcock (National Park Service); Patience Hayes; Marilyn Howe; Celia Jones; Jason Delaney (Missouri Botanical Garden); Mimi Miller (director, Historic Natchez Foundation); Dr. Elizabeth Boggess; Lawrence Griffith (Colonial Williamsburg Foundation); Mrs. Betty Nash (Chantilly); Judy Hynson and Tommy Moles (Stratford Hall); Sarah Dillard Pope (executive director, Menokin Foundation); Cherie Foster Colburn; Peter Hatch (former director of Grounds and Gardens, Monticello); Dean Norton (director of horticulture, Mount Vernon Estate and Gardens); Margo S. Stringfield (University of West Florida); Sharon McDonald and Sally Kington (Royal Horticulture Society); Ron Scamp (Quality Daffodils, Cornwall) Peter Hairston (Cooleemee Plantation); the Sand Hills Garden Club; the Peachtree Garden Club; and the Garden Club of Georgia, Inc.

I am deeply indebted to the following people for graciously allowing me access to their historic gardens: Martin Meek (Mountain Shoals); Sandra Bowles (Howard-Chafee House); the late Joanna Tilghman (Wye House); Tom Woodham (Wideman-Hanvey House); Bob and Mary Norton (Valley View); Sue Thompson and Hannah Warfield (Tuckahoe); Michelle and Tom Goodman (Oakton); Susan and Doug Abramson (Old Hill Place); Mrs. Carol Cooke (the Oaks); Mr. and Mrs. Frederick S. Fisher (Westover); and Jim Tolmach (Ward property). For those who lent assistance in sleuthing garden sites and providing introductions to property owners: Dorothy Adams; David Atkins; Sandra and Richard Frank; Ross Hotchkiss; Jim Kibler; Pelham Lyles; Mable Milner; Mackenzie Sholtz; Jerry Spencer; and Phil Wirey.

For those who lent assistance with public historic sites: Janet Henderson (Land Trust for Tennessee, Glen Leven House); Linda Eirhart (assistant director, Winterthur Museum and Country Estate); Liz Shapiro (Sharon Historical Society); Camilla Wilcox and Preston Stockton (Reynolda House and Gardens); Ann Foley (Webb-Deane-Stevens Museum); Joel Fry (curator, Bartram's Garden); Patricia Aleshire (manager,

Rosedown Plantation), Laura Keim (curator, Stenton); Gary Wetzel (landscape manager, Historic New England); Lisa Centola (site manager, Roseland Cottage, Historic New England); Kate Copsey, Janet Riggins, and Robert Winebarger (Barrington Hall); Scott McEwen and Justin Stelter (the Hermitage); Sara Henderson (Historic Oakland Foundation); Judith Kelz (director, Glebe House Museum, the Gertrude Jekyll Garden); and Mary-Beth Evans (LeConte-Woodmanston Foundation).

Thanks to the following repositories: Alabama Department of Archives and History; Barrington Hall Garden Archives; the John Bartram Association, Bartram's Garden; Colonial Williamsburg Foundation; Georgia Department of Archives and History; Halifax Historical Museum; Harvard University Herbaria and Botany Libraries; the Hermitage; Historic Natchez Foundation; Historical Society of Philadelphia; the KAVB library; Louisiana State University Libraries; Maryland Historical Society; Massachusetts Historical Society; Moravian Archives; Museum of Fine Arts, Boston; Old Salem Museums and Gardens; Reynolda House Museum of American Art; Seabury Society for the Preservation of the Glebe House; Spring Grove Cemetery and Arboretum; Swem Library, College of William and Mary; Tennessee State Library and Archives; Wilson Library, University of North Carolina, Chapel Hill; Winterthur Library—Winterthur Archives. Images are by the author or in the author's collection unless otherwise indicated.

Horticulture and Classification Basics

To talk about a flower and not actually talk about the flower ignores a critical piece of the picture—the botany of the flower itself, which is a fundamental determinant of what people can actually do with any given flower in their own garden. With daffodils this is particularly true, as there is such variety in the species and derived hybrid cultivars that this dictated what types of daffodils were ideal for what garden or indoor uses, first and foremost because of climate adaptations.

To date, there have been over twenty-eight thousand hybrid daffodils named, and most have been registered with the Royal Horticulture Society (RHS) of England. Garden daffodils began as wildflowers in the Mediterranean basin, with Spain the epicenter from which many of the species spread. Spain, Portugal, and Morocco have the greatest number of daffodil species, flourishing in both alpine and coastal environments, but the genus *Narcissus* spreads around the Levant to northern Africa.

Daffodils, true bulbs like onions, are summer dormant, bulbous perennials—an evolutionary answer to seasonal extremes of wet winters and very dry summers. The leaves and flower stalk grow from a bulb, emerging sometime from fall to early spring. Flowering occurs from fall to late spring, while foliage remains viable until late spring to early summer.

True bulbs are composed of separate layers of food storage organs (called "scales"), do not grow to full size in a single growing year, and multiply by the process of division whereby new bulbs are created as part of the original or parent bulb. The year's leaves become scales, which store the starch generated by the leaves; new scales form at the center of the bulb. Insufficient sunlight (caused by either shade, early removal of foliage after blooming, or early digging of the bulb after blooming) and/or depletion of soil nutrients will set a bulb into decline.

The original native habitat also influences the culture requirements of species and derived garden hybrids. Those daffodils derived from species daffodils growing at lower elevations in damper climates (for example coastal creeks banks and marshlands) are the ones best able to withstand "warm" winters and wet summers with high humidity. Hybrid garden daffodils derived from species daffodils adapted to alpine meadow environments are happy in evenly cool climes. Those bulbs from arid reaches require special cultivation practices (or simply to be treated as annuals). These differences in original habitat are the determinant factor in why different types of daffodils thrive in different regions of America (and Europe) and have dictated how they have been grown by Western gardeners over the past four hundred years.

In the English-speaking world, the common word for *Narcissus* genus flowers is "daffodil." "Daffodil" and "narcissus" are interchangeable in English, as "daffodil" is the English term for the flower and bulb, while "narcissus" is the Latin, botanical name for the genus. Used properly, "jonquil" applies only to those flowers having a Jonquilla "section" (or group) species (for example *Narcissus jonquilla*) in their ancestry (and evidencing a preponderance of "jonquilla" traits). "Poets" are species flowers within and hybrids derived from the Poeticus "section"; cold-dependent, these were often called narcissus, true narcissus, white narcissus or the poet's narcissus. "Tazetta" is the proper term for the old "polyanthus narcissus" class, and applies to all daffodils in the Tazetta "section," including paperwhites (paperwhites, by linguistic and botanical definition, cannot be "yellow").

The early Western garden history of daffodils is composed of three types of flowers—species and intersectional hybrids; wild sport doubles (doubles are not species flowers as they cannot maintain independent populations in nature), which were domesticated into garden flowers; and purposefully hybridized tazettas, then called "polyanthus narcissus." This latter group exploded into hundreds upon hundreds of named hybrid varieties sold in catalogs from the 1600s to the mid-1800s. Most all of these hybrid tazettas are long gone, replaced (and those replacements replaced in their turn) over the decades and centuries by showier or more robust varieties.

There have been many botanical and horticultural classification groups of daffodils over the centuries, and many of the old horticultural classification names from the 1800s still appear in catalogs and literature. The shuffling of names and groupings becomes confusing even for the knowledgeable. As many of the old horticultural names and groupings were done away with in the early 1900s, and the rest followed by 1950, the early systems are not referred to here for the sake of clarity. These old groupings were essentially signifiers of flower forms and color combinations for all the flowers derived from crossing two basic forms of flowers—trumpets and poeticus or "poets" for short.

This book follows the accepted nomenclature system as approved by the Royal Horticulture Society. Accepted correct species names are given in italics (*N. poeticus*); old species names, those set aside by the RHS, are in plain font (Narcissus orientalis). Accepted wild hybrids are signified by an "×" (*N. × odorus*). Names of hybrid flowers registered with the RHS are given in single quotes, such as 'Butter and Eggs' or 'Telamonius Plenus'. Common, vernacular names in current use are given in double quotes, such as "Albus Plenus Odoratus," "Van Sion," and "Queen Ann's Double Jonquil." Old varietal names no longer recognized by the RHS are given in plain font (Golden Era).

I.

A Brief History of Daffodils in Britain and the Netherlands

There are numerous references to daffodils in early history. While we now think of yellow trumpets as the daffodils of choice, in antiquity other types of *Narcissus* held sway—those of the *N. tazetta* (tazettas or "polyanthus narcissus") and *N. poeticus* ("poets") clans. The former is the dominant *Narcissus* group around the Mediterranean at sea level; they are adapted to balmy, wet winters and hot, baking summers. The *N. poeticus* clan is a mountainous flower, adapted to windblown alpine meadows with evenly cold climates. Later in Renaissance Europe, the *N. jonquilla* ("jonquil") clan rose to prominence—another group adapted to warm weather and dry summers, coveted for its fragrance. Jonquils were quickly followed by other delicate spring bloomers, such as triandrus, cyclamineus, and a variety of white trumpets, found on the granite grit mountainsides of the Iberian Peninsula. The soil and climate preferences of these wildflowers then determine how happy they, and their offspring, are in any given garden—European or American.

Various members of the *Narcissus* tribe were put to use by the ancients. Egyptians in the New Kingdom (sixteenth to eleventh centuries B.C.) imported tazettas from the Levant for perfume production. The Greeks planted *N. poeticus* around warriors' graves, wove tazettas into citizens' funeral wreaths, and wrote of the medicinal properties of various *Narcissus. Narcissus* appear on Roman villa murals in Italy and in a garden description from southern France in the late Roman period.

Many flowers have laid claim to the flower smothering the Plain of Sharon in the Bible (the Song of Solomon, thought to be written as early as 900 B.C.). While they are

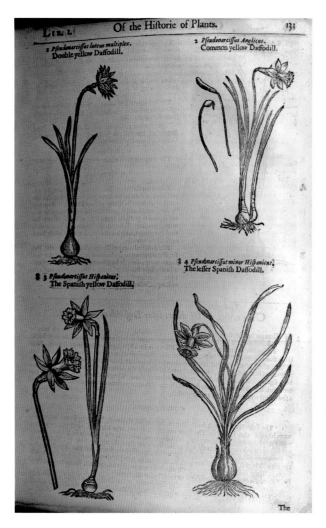

Of the Hiftorie of Plants.

1 *Pfeudonarciffus luteus multiplex.*
Double yellow Daffodill.

2 *Pfeudonarciffus Anglicus.*
Common yellow Daffodill.

3 *Pfeudonarciffus Hifpanicus.*
The Spanifh yellow Daffodill.

4 *Pfeudonarciffus minor Hifpanicus.*
The leffer Spanifh Daffodill.

Gerard, *The Herball,* 1633. Courtesy of the Cherokee Garden Library, Kenan Research Center at the Atlanta History Center, Atlanta, Georgia.

often thought to be "roses" and various bulbs come into contention, this notion was investigated in the 1870s: In the last quarterly report of the English "Palestine Exploration Fund" occurs the following interesting note by Lieutenant CONDER, on "the Rose of Sharon." Remarking that the question of the proper translation of the word *Habatstseleth,* rendered "rose" in the English version, has never been settled with certainty, he says:

> The word in Hebrew comes from the root Batzl, "bulbous," from which it has been generally concluded that some kind of Lily was intended, and a great many species have been proposed.
>
> The Targums translate the word by Narkus, the Narcissus, which is not only of the lily tribe, but also a plant very common in spring in the Plain of Sharon.
>
> Roses are not found in Palestine, though the Dog-rose flourishes on Hermon in the cooler atmosphere 6,000 feet above the sea, and in the Anti-Lebanon. It seems improbable that the climate of the lower regions can ever have been fitted for Roses.
>
> We found that the name *Buseil* was applied to one plant only in Palestine, and that plant is the Narcissus. This is confirmed by M. BERGHEIM, of Abu Shusheh, whose acquaintance with the peasant language is intimate.
>
> The agreement between the modern name and the Jewish tradition of the meaning of the word used in the Bible, seems perhaps sufficient to identify the Rose of Sharon with the beautiful white Narcissus which covers the low hills in spring, and is also found on the plain.[1]

But it is its role as a European garden flower to which our attention rightly begins.

The Narcissus and the Advent of Gardening in Europe

As Europe climbed out of the Middle Ages and broadened its intellectual horizons, so too did it expand its plant collecting and writing. Bulbs, easy to store, were collected from across the Mediterranean basin (from north Africa and the Iberian Peninsula around to southern France and Italy) and shared among interested collectors across national borders.

The botanical herbals of the 1400s and 1500s were designed to educate physicians and document the medicinal/utilitarian uses of plants. Today they also serve as the "proof of life" for many plants and bulbs—the earliest recorded date of European cultivation. For *Narcissus* these herbals reflect which plants were already well known and which were newly discovered, if not actually specifying what gardens they grew in and their sources of origin. And it is as an ornamental garden plant that *Narcissus* came to be truly valued.

Early botanists and bulb enthusiasts such as Rembert Dodoens (1517–1585), Carolus Clusius (Charles de L'Ecluse, 1526–1609), and Matthias de L'Obel, (1538–1616) were Flemish; L'Obel boasted the best gardens in Europe were in Flanders until the Civil Wars. After the Spanish invasion of the Flemish provinces in 1585, many Flemings escaped north to the Dutch provinces; others, like L'Obel, went to England—spreading their botanical knowledge and interest in bulbs.

Clusius is credited with being the first to maintain a botanical garden for ornamentals and not just medicinal plants. One of a growing group of botanists who appreciated flowers for their aesthetics alone, through his writings Clusius preached the cult of beauty. Further, Clusius is often credited with instigating the Dutch bulb industry. Upon his appointment in 1593 as professor of horticulture at the University of Leiden, Clusius established the Hortus Academicus, as well as a personal garden, into which he transplanted his prized tulips. Clusius sold his tulip bulbs but at outrageous prices; rather than pay for these bulbs (or, because Clusius refused to sell, depending on the author), local entrepreneurs instead stole them at night. Often the thefts were large; one theft in 1596 cost Clusius a hundred bulbs. Some thieves sold the bulbs illegally, a rampant problem for garden enthusiasts with rare plant collections in the late 1500s and early 1600s. Collections of rare bulbs were raided (often by servants who were familiar with the master's collection) and sold to other (unscrupulous) collectors. With Clusius' tulips, some of the stolen bulbs purportedly ended up in the hands of individuals who went into the tulip business for themselves, thus creating profit-driven tulip raising.

Exotic bulbs trickled into Europe from Turkey starting in the mid- to latter 1500s, such as the tulip, ranunculus, anemone, and muscari, among others. For *Narcissus* the star new arrival was the double tazetta of Constantinople. A few daffodils were already known in European gardens, but tazettas from the Levant were relatively new creatures, the fragrant double especially. However, unlike other genera of bulbs coming

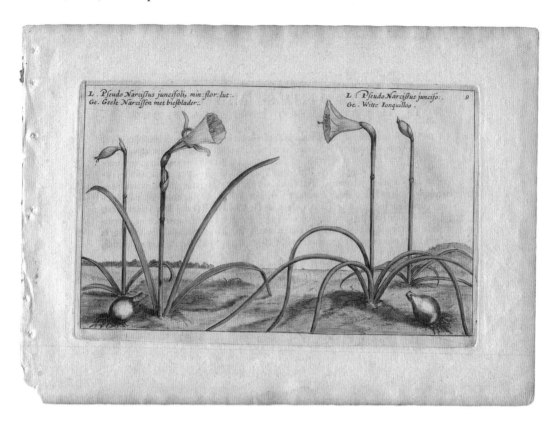

N. bulbocodium varieties. Van de Passe, *Hortus Floridus*, 1614.

from the Ottoman Empire, most daffodils are of western Mediterranean origin—so the trading of *Narcissus* was more the fruit of "backyard" explorations, which began in earnest in the late 1500s.[2]

Collecting rare, exotic flowers quickly became a status marker and passion for many wealthy Europeans beginning in the latter half of the 1500s (the Dutch dubbed members of this exclusive community *liefhebbers,* or "florists"). The wealthy patronized gardeners and botanists to create and maintain their gardens; further many of the well-known early botanists had royal or university patronage. The botanists shared plants among themselves, keeping records of what came from whom and how well it grew, and took their own collecting trips into the countryside. Many compiled texts of their plant collections, describing, illustrating, and discussing uses of the plants. And daffodils were duly noted.[3]

This new appreciation of a flower's aesthetics coincided with the spreading interest in ornamental gardening in general across the social classes. Writers began dispensing practical floriculture advice on how to grow ornamentals. The work of John Parkinson, apothecary to Charles I of England, by the close of the first quarter century is a good milestone marker for this progression—a combination of what is lovely and how to grow it, as well as a dose of herbal remedy. By the latter 1600s the transformation to "gardening" literature was complete. The sea change is well represented in England by the early florist John Rea in *Flora: seu, Du florum cultura* (1665). The Dutch also were very interested in doing ornamental growing but not so interested in writing about it, so Dutch tomes from the 1600s are scarcer than one would expect. Rather, many instructional works of the era were French.

To the dismay of some (notably Clusius), commoners rose to a perceived new job market of selling rare, novel plants. Early plant connoisseurs often traded and even bought plants among themselves, and the flow of money enticed others. One such early transaction involved the offer to pay for yellow fritillaries and double jonquils between two collectors in Amsterdam in 1601. That same year, French plant-sellers were remarked to have been selling their wares in Flanders, including hyacinths, dog-tooth violets, and narcissus. Clusius's nephew Jean de Maes went to Brussels in 1602 to visit the son of the city's postmaster, to verify that indeed he was in possession of the rare and novel double jonquil. Growing pretty flowers, and the means of supplying those flowers, transformed from a noble pursuit of the rich and educated to a monetary pursuit of the interested and able.[4] In London, one of the first "florists," (nurserymen specializing in "improved" flowers for the pleasure garden) known by name was Ralph Tuggie of Westminster, who started his nursery around 1620. Tuggie was associated with a daffodil by the time of Rea's *Flora: seu, De florum cultura;* among the doubles worthy of a place in the garden was "Tuggies great double bastard Daffodill."[5]

Early gardens of the wealthy across Europe and the florists and nurserymen who catered to them were documented by painters and engravers. In 1612 the Amsterdam painter and nurseryman Emmanuel Sweert produced *Florilegium Amplissumum et Selectissimum,* a florist's catalog for the stock he had for sale at the 1612 Frankfurt Fair. Sweert's catalog is credited for furthering the popularity of bulbs.[6]

The next year saw Basilius Besler's *Hortus Eystettensis* (1613), the garden catalog commissioned by its owner, Johann Conrad von Gemmingen, Prince-Bishop of Eich-statt, Germany. In the 367 plates depicting over one thousand plants from one of the finest gardens of the day, *Narcissus* of many forms appear. In honor of this garden and its hortus, a double daffodil is still known as 'Eystettensis'.

Crispijn van de Passe's *Hortus floridus* (1614) was essentially another plantsman's catalog, and showcased numerous *Narcissus*. Noteworthy for its very finely detailed copper-plate illustrations, his *Hortus* was organized into four books by season. Essentially leading off book 1, "Flowers of the Springe," with daffodils (Plates II and III), his *Narcissus* offerings are predominantly doubles, poets, and jonquils—commenting the double jonquil was very rare and in high esteem.[7] Interestingly he grouped two *Narcissus* in book 2 for winter—the Spanish Yellow and a dwarf trumpet (both blooming in February) and two bulbocodiums—a yellow and a white. Also of note is the dearth of tazettas, which became the florist's *Narcissus* flower of choice by the late 1600s.

The rage for new flowers spurred on ever more introductions, evidenced by Parkinson's comment as to how many more daffodils there were to describe since Gerard

Parkinson, *Paradisi in sole Paradisus terrestris*, 1629. Courtesy of the Cherokee Garden Library, Kenan Research Center at the Atlanta History Center, Atlanta, Georgia.

published his herbal in 1597. Parkinson likely had a hand in the introduction of these new daffodils, having assisted in financing William Boel's botanical expedition in Spain, Portugal, and north Africa in 1607–1608. New introductions were fashionable; those deemed readily available became "common" and so passé.

In his *Paradisi in sole Paradisus terrestris* (a pun on his own name when translated into Latin), or *A garden of all sorts of pleasant flowers* (1629), Parkinson compiled a list of ninety-two varieties of *Narcissus* growing in English gardens, the greater part of which were variants of *N. tazetta*. This was the largest gardening book published in England at the time. Parkinson even addressed the timeless question of "What's the difference between a daffodil and a narcissus?" with "Many idle and ignorant gardeners ... doe call some of these Daffodils Narcissus when as all know that know any Latine that Narcissus is the same thing, and therefore alone without any other epithite cannot properly distinguish severall things."[8]

The flow of money, and the passion for flowers, quickly established the now famous tradition of raising flowers in Flanders and the Netherlands. By 1634 the Dutch were in the grip of the tulipmania and its speculative bubble (which the government unceremoniously burst in 1637). So it is the Flemish and then Dutch who became the commercial raisers of *Narcissus,* especially the fashionable "polyanthus narcissus" (tazettas), and the English who become their classifiers and eventual preeminent hybridizers.

The Rise of the Dutch Industry

The British may have made the daffodil the garden favorite it became in modern America, but its wholesale stocks came primarily from the Dutch. Improvements in the technology of land reclamation came around 1600, so the 'polders' came to be—reclaimed marshland and sand dunes ideal for agriculture and soon thereafter bulbs.

As daffodils began to be fancied as garden flowers, the tazettas, or "polyanthus narcissus" rose to become favorites in Britain but especially in the Netherlands and the rest of Continental Europe. The earliest record of tazettas being introduced into cultivation dates to 1561 by Matthias de L'Obel, when a white petal with yellow cup tazetta was sent to him from Languedoc in France (described by him in his 1581 herbal—apparently it grew as a weed in the grass of Provence). The Dutch bulb expert J. H. Krelage noted that by the early 1630s, evidence suggests the Dutch were actively growing hybridized tazetta seedlings: "In Parkinson's well-known 'Paradisus' (1629) we find described and figured a certain number of Polyanthus Narcissi; but, after comparing his notes with those of Continental writers, we infer that at that time many more forms were cultivated on the Continent, especially in the Netherlands, than in England. It is quite certain, too, from the remarks of Petrus Lauremberg (1632, who coined the term 'tulipomania'), and from the different editions of the catalogue of the Botanic Gardens at Leiden, that already numerous Dutch seedlings were in cultivation."[9] After the tulipmania of the 1630s, Haarlem set about growing bulbs; with its superior polder sands, it quickly became synonymous with well-grown, if not the best-grown, bulbs.

Frustratingly little is written about the Dutch and Flemish hybridization of tazettas in the 1600s. Period literature focuses primarily on cataloging and wild origins and, on occasion, cultivation requirements. Moreover the French were much more inclined to write "florist's manuals" than the Dutch.[10]

One of the earliest Dutch treatises on florists' flowers and how to grow them is *The Dutch gardener: or, The compleat florist* (1700) by Leiden florist Henrik van Oosten (first English edition was printed in 1706, second edition with great amendments printed 1711). Along with sections devoted to fruit trees, shrubs, gillyflowers (carnations), the bulbs and flowers of the day are discussed primarily for propagation purposes. After lengthy discussion on tulips, van Oosten turned his attention to Narcissus and Jonquils, before hyacinths (surprising even if the work does precede the hyacinthmania or 'hyacintenhandal' of 1720–1736):

> The *Narcissus* is a pretty Flower, and there are many Sorts of them; *viz.* the Single White, called Jenet; the Double White, called the Double Spanish Jenet. There are three single yellow ones that have also their peculiar Names, the *Narcissus of Constantinople*, or *Tros Narcis*, blowing many Flowers upon one Stalk, some with single and some double Cups. These are extraordinary beautiful, every one being a Cluster or Nosegay of Flowers. The Beauty of the *Narcissus*, and the Difference that distinguishes one of them from another, consists in the Greatness of the Flowers, in their Number, and in the Variety of their Colours, but chiefly of their Cup.[11]

> The Jonquils are yellow, yet there is a single Sort that is white. This Flower has been long out of Esteem, yet lately is brought into Request again by the *French*, who are fond of them, and have brought them up wherever they could find them. They are distinguished into Single and Double; the Single are divided again into

Van Oosten, The Dutch Gardener, 1676. Courtesy of the Cherokee Garden Library, Kenan Research Center at the Atlanta History Center, Atlanta, Georgia.

four Sorts, *viz.* the little Jonquil that has many Flowers on a Stalk, and this is the best Sort; the second are those with great Flowers, and which bear but two or three on a Stalk, nor smell so sweet as the first; the third Sort bears also but two or three Flowers on a Stalk, but is of a deeper Colour; the fourth Sort is the Single White, which is esteemed for its Colour and pleasant Smell; of these there is no great Plenty, and there are Florists that will not allow them to be Jonquils, yet the Cup that is in the Leaves of the Flower shews them sufficiently to be so.[12]

The double Jonquil is a little Flower of eight or nine small Leaves, of a high yellow Colour, and a very pleasant Smell. The *French* make Sweet-waters of them for several Uses.[13]

All bulbs were subject to the fickle taste of the Renaissance gardening set. Accompanying jonquils on their slide to passé status with the Dutch were crown imperials:

"This Crown-Imperial, that was some Years ago in so great Esteem, is now so common that some will hardly afford it a Place in their Gardens, tho' it is a handsom Flower; yet none are now in Esteem but what are scarce."[14] Meanwhile, van Oosten commented some florists ("liefhebbers") put the carnation (gilly-flower or "jenoffels," 1703 Dutch edition) above all else; although van Oosten included a separate treatise on growing gillyflowers according to the French way, one senses he personally prefers other flowers (including tazettas), sniffing "some Florists prefer them before any others. Every one has his Opinion."[15]

The wealthy across Europe became interested in "gardening" as an intellectual pursuit, albeit second to their delight in a newfound vehicle for conspicuous consumption, and bulb production expanded to supply the demand. In the early mid-1600s, bulbs (tulips) were grown by citizens and traded privately, usually between socially connected individuals, or via semi-organized trading or auctions held at inns; sales transactions were recorded primarily by notaries. Van Oosten described the systems used by the Dutch and Flemish to help regulate their tulip industries after the collapse of tulipmania:

> Tulips have always been greatly esteemed, and chiefly by the *Dutch;* who in the Year 1637 intended to Traffick with them, as with Pearls and Diamonds: But the States forbade it, for a political Reason of State; and when the publick buying and selling of Tulips, was thus prohibited, they fell to trucking and private selling; but because this could not be done without Animosities, thereupon the *Flemish* Florists erected a Fraternity in the Cities; and took St. *Dorothea* to be their Patroness, and the *Syndicus* to be Judge of the Differences, that might arise by their Trucking; and he to add more Authority to it, called in four of the chief of the Brother-hood, and this was the occasion of the sweet Conversation of the Brothers, and brought them into greater Esteem. The *Dutch* keep in this Matter another Rule; they meet together on a certain Day, when Tulips are in their full Bloom, and choose, after having seen the chief Gardens of the Florists, and taken a friendly and frugal Dinner together, one of the Company to be Judge of the Diference that might arise about Flowers in that Year.[16]

By the early 1700s, bulbs were grown both by individuals and by companies or "houses," often with familial connections between the principals. No longer traded between grower and buyer on a single-bulb basis, bulb crops were sold at advertised auctions. One such auction in 1735 was announced by Lisse guild master and alderman Nicolaas Symonse de Graaff (ancestor of the famous de Graaff family), for the sale of 238 hyacinths plants of forty varieties, to be held in the presence of the sheriff and his aldermen. The stock sold for 139 guilders (roughly five months' wages for an unskilled laborer).

A lengthy catalog issued in 1739 by Nicolaas van Kampen of Haarlem illustrates the general order of things—hyacinths, tulips, ranunculus, anemones, then narcissus (with crocus, martagons, and iris bringing up the rear). Within *Narcissus,* the first thirty-six

Plate 1026, Narcissus Orientalis. Yellow Garden Narcissus. *Curtis's Botanical Magazine*, 1807. Courtesy of the Cherokee Garden Library, Kenan Research Center at the Atlanta History Center, Atlanta, Georgia.

named varieties were tazettas (eighteen of which were available in lots of one hundred), then three jonquils, rounded out by five named doubles, four of which are still grown today. This general order of desirability, entrenched by the mid- to late 1600s, continued well into the 1800s.

While spring bulbs were planted in the pleasure gardens, most tazettas were destined for indoor culture in greenhouses and parlors throughout the 1700s and 1800s. The notion of growing bulbs indoors in bottles or carafes of water is credited to Marten Triewald, a Swedish scientist and engineer. The great Scottish botanist Philip Miller (gardener of the Chelsea Physic Garden from 1722 to 1771) heard of Triewald's experiments and promptly conducted his own study, publishing his efforts in the same journal issue. Ever the gardener, Miller trialed tulips, hyacinths, and narcissus, remarking this provided a method for those without a garden to display flowers in their abodes. Special "glasses" were eventually designed, in the shape of a tea cup on top of a cone. This arrangement held the bulb just above the conical base full of water for the roots, allowing the bulb to stay dry to avoid rot. Forced bulbs of all sorts became an annual expense for the moneyed classes, and thus a recurring cash crops for the Dutch. Needless to say, this helped the tazetta market.

As early as 1733, writers noted the English never warm up to the effort of commercially raising tazettas, and so the flower remained the province of the Dutch. Philip Miller in *The Gardeners Dictionary* (1754) discussed how most *Narcissus* were imported from Holland and France, few in England having the patience to grow new varieties from seed as first flowering took five years. He also implied that a high price was maintained for the imported bulbs because of their great demand in England. Others noted that during the eighteenth century, the popularity of the polyanthus narcissus resulted in other species being neglected by gardeners.

In 1788 the premier Dutch bulb firm or "house" of Voorhelm-Schneevoogt offered 155 varieties of polyanthus narcissus. The highest price asked was 1 shilling 8 pence (a shilling equivalent to $10.00), and about a dozen cultivars were so priced. The most robust are still sold today—"Etoile d'Or" (N. bifrons now *N. × intermedius*), 'Grand Soleil d'Or,' and "Primo Citroniere."

This popularity was somewhat relative however. For as much as the British may have liked polyanthus narcissus, and those more than most other *Narcissus,* the Dutch (and other Europeans) very much liked their tazettas. Thus Londoner James Maddock, in *The florists' directory* (1792), ranks (florists') flowers as follows: Hyacinths, Tulips, Ranunculuses, Anemones, Auricula, Carnations, and Pinks. In contrast, in the *Trait*é of the Dutch florists Nicolas van Kampen et fils (1760), "Polyanthus narcissus is the first flower, after hyacinths, tulips, ranunculus and anemones, which merit our attention."[17] This relative difference in popularity of tazettas between the British and Dutch held into the early twentieth century.

In the 1600s and most of the 1700s, the florists of Haarlem obtained their seedling bulbs from towns in Flanders where even the clergy raised bulbs for sale. This early Flemish and French history is reflected in the French names of early tazettas, such as the "Belles" in Sir Thomas Hanmer's *Garden Book* (1660). Many 1700s tazettas bear

1917   **1918**

Nr.	per Stück fl.	kr
155 Cerise defleur en Citron	—	18
156 Charbon noir, ext.	—	24
157 Couleur de Jonquille	—	18
158 Cramoisie, pourpre	—	18
159 Crodus, ext.	—	24
160 Dulcinea, feuille morte	—	18
161 Elegante drieux oleur gr.	—	18
162 Erbprinz von Holland	—	18
163 Gordianus, extr.	—	45
164 Gertrude feu en or	—	18
165 Goldener Adler, ext.	—	24
166 Goldene Münze, ext.	—	30
167 Gouverneur v. Nordholl.	—	18
168 Grand Marmoisie, ext.	—	30
169 Grand Unique, ext.	—	24
170 Henry quatre, grofs	—	18
171 Jaune et noir, ext.	—	8
172 Juwel von Lisse, ext.	—	30
173 Königshof, grofs	—	18
174 La Cantique, schön	—	18
175 La Delphine noir, ext.	1	—
176 La Modeste foncé	—	18
177 L'amusante, extra	—	24
178 La village	—	18
179 La ville d'Haarlem	—	18
180 Louis d'or	—	15
181 Louise violette, en or.	—	18
182 Marmoisie, ext.	—	18
183 Maitre violet	—	18
184 Mignon de Delft, ext.	—	20
185 Mine d'or, extra	—	24
186 Miniomis, schön	—	18
187 Mereis en or, ext.	—	18
188 Namides, schön.	—	18
189 Oldenbarnefeld	—	18
190 Olivatre, en or	—	18
191 Ophir brun	—	18
192 Orange.Krone, grofs	—	18
193 Passe Tout, ext.	—	20
194 Percis en or, ext.	—	30
195 Prinz Friederich, sch.	—	18
196 Roi Salomon, extr.	—	18
197 Roi de Würtemberg	—	18
198 Staaten-General, ext.	—	24
199 Staaten v. Holland, sch.	—	18
200 Staaten von Utrecht	—	18
100 feine späte Byzarden-T. v. sehr sch. Sort. u. Farben ohne Namen		
Feine panachirte u. byzard. Tulp. in 100 der allersch. S. 50 panachirte u. 50 Byzard. mit Namen	5	30

Monströse Tulpen.   p. St

Nr.	per Stück fl.	kr
201 Admiralv.Constantinop.	—	6
202 Gelbe monströse	—	6
203 Monstreuse rouge	—	9
204 Orange Parquet	—	6
205 Perfecta, r. u. gelb gestr.	—	6
Untereinand. mel. d. 100 St.		6

Nr.	per Stück fl.	kr
206 Tulipa Persica, wohlr.	—	12

III. Abtheilung.
Frühe vielblümige gelbe und weiſſe Tazetten, doppelte und einfache Narcissen, doppelte u. einf. Jonquillen, Fritillaria imperial, Lilium, Martagon u. Amaryllis etc. etc.

Frühe gelbe Tazetten.

Nr.	per Stück fl.	kr
1 *Aigle d'or, ext.	—	10
2 *Belle Pomone, ext.	—	10
3 *Charlotte deBourbon,ex.	—	10
4 *Comte d'Artois, ext.	—	10
5 *Comte de Narcisse, sch.	—	10
6 *Flagge, extr.	—	9
7 *Grand Soleil d'or, ext.	—	10
8 *Goldene Münze, ext.	—	10
9 *Grofser Held, sch.	—	10
10 *Jaune d'or, ext.	—	10
11 *Illustre, extr.	—	10
12 *Juno, schön	—	10
13 *Libertas, ext.	—	10
14 *Lulongata, sch.	—	10
15 *Milord, ext.	—	10
16 *Ophir d'or, ext.	—	10
17 *Prinz Friedrich, ext.	—	10
18 *Prime, gelb, sch.	—	10
19 *Prime de Narcisse, ext.	—	10
20 „Vicomte, schön	—	10

Vielbl. weiſſe Tazetten.

Nr.	per Stück fl.	kr
21 *Albertine, ext.	—	10
22 *Bouquet aimable, sch.	—	10
23 *Concordia, ext.	—	10
24 *Czar v.Moscow, gfs. ext.	—	10
25 *Duc de Luxembourg, ex.	—	10
26 *Grand-Duc, sehr schön	—	10
27 *GrandMonarque,allergr.	—	10
28 *Grand Primo Citronier, grofs ext.	—	10
29 *Heldin, sehr schön	—	10
30 *Ida Triomphante, ext.	—	10
31 *Luna, schön	—	8
32 *Madame Royale, ext.	—	10
33 *Maitre blanche, sehr sch.	—	10
34 *Palestina, ext.	—	10
35 *Plena quandilus, sch.	—	8
36 *Propatria, ext.	—	10
37 *Reine du Monde, ext.	—	10
38 *Souver. d'Hollande, sch.	—	9
39 *Staaten-Generaal, ext.	—	8
40 *Frühe dopp.wohlr.Mars. Taz., z. Frührt., ext.	—	6
*100 allerb. Taz. in 25 Sort. halb gelbe u. halb weiſse mit Namen, ext.		15
*100 gelbe u .weiſse Taz. untereinander, melirt ext.		9

Doppelte Narcissen.

Nr.	per Stück fl.	kr
41 *Alba plena, odorata	—	5
42 *Incomparable	—	6
43 *Orange Phoenix	—	6
44 *Van Sion	—	5

Nr.	per Stück fl.	kr
45 *Schwefelkrone	—	6
46 *TratusCantus(centifolia)	—	6

Einfache Narcissen.

Nr.	per Stück fl.	kr
47 *Alba odorata	—	2
48 *Bifloris	—	4
49 *Maxima, Trompete	—	5
50 *Muscaris od.Silbertromp	—	5
51 *Nana major	—	3
52 *Poeticus, alba odorata	—	3
53 *Poeticus, m rothb.Kelch	—	4

Doppelte goldgelbe wohlrie-chende Jonquillen.

Nr.	per Stück fl.	kr
54 *Extra grofse Zwiebeln	—	12
55 ditto schöne	—	8
56 *ditto kleinere	—	4

Einfache Jonquillen.

Nr.	per Stück fl.	kr
57 *Jonquill. od.Campanella	—	3
58 *Jonquillen, wohlriech.	—	3

Fritillaria imperialis, oder Kaiserkronen-z. Treiben.

Nr.	per Stück fl.	kr
59 *Aurora, gelb	—	15
60 *Braut v. Haarlem, roth	—	18
61 *Coridon, roth	—	18
62 *Cupido, roth	—	18
63 *Doppelte, gelbe	—	30
64 *Doppelte, rothe	—	24
65 *Einfache, gelbe	—	18
66 *Flore rubro, fol. aureo striato	—	24
67 General,Krone auf Krone, roth	—	24
68 *Gekrönt Juwel, roth	—	18
69 *Krone auf Krone, roth	—	24
70 *Lord Mayor, roth	—	18
71 *Marechal Blücher, dklr.	—	30
72 *Marquine, roth	—	18
73 *Maxima, grofs	—	24
74 *Rouge Chateau	—	18
75 *Schlacht-Schwert	—	15
76 Tambour-Major, roth	—	18
77 *Uterbe, roth	—	18
78 *Zebra Triomphant	—	18
79 *Zinnoberroth	—	18
80 *Im Rummel	—	12

Lilien.

Nr.	per Stück fl.	kr
81 Lil. candid. aur. fol. str.	—	30
82 — fl. albo plen.	—	20
83 — fl. albo simpl.	—	15
84 — chalcedonicum	—	24
85 — canadense	—	40
86 — flore rubro maj.	—	24
87 — — min.	—	18
88 — — maculato	—	24
89 — Kamschatkense	—	40
90 — tigrinum	—	10
91 — supernum	—	40

Martagon.

Nr.	per Stück fl.	kr
92 Mart. blanche Pigette	—	20
93 — superbe	—	20
94 — bleu Pigette	—	20
95 — blüth flach	—	20

E. H. Krelage catalog for 1827 (German edition)—Tulips, Tazettas, Narcissus, Jonquils, Fritillaria, Lilies, Martagons. Courtesy of the Cherokee Garden Library, Kenan Research Center at the Atlanta History Center, Atlanta, Georgia.

the French word "bouquet" in their name, apropos for a tazetta, but are no longer in commerce. Into the 1800s Dutch names predominate. Today the oldest tazettas grown have French names and pre-date the French Revolution (1789), such as 'Soleil d'Or' (1731), 'Grand Monarque' (1759), 'Grand Soleil d'Or' (1770), and 'Grand Primo Citron-ière' (1780).

In 1774 a register of bulb auctions held in Haarlem was initiated, recording principals and buyers. But the political turmoil of the late 1700s, especially the French Revolution, changed the business practices of the Dutch. After the French Revolution, the

Dutch took on their own bulb production and no longer relied on Flemish and French sources. This coincided with the beginnings of the de Graaff family empire in 1793, in the small village of Lisse near Haarlem. Although interest in bulb growing started in Lisse in 1728, and bulb auctions occurred as early as 1735, the industry spread in earnest outward from Haarlem coinciding with this home-growing of bulbs in the 1790s.

During the Napoleonic Wars (1795–1814), the Dutch and Flemish provinces under French control were closed to British citizens. Upon restoration of the peace, the Caledonian Horticultural Society of Edinburgh, Scotland, sent members on a fact-finding mission to Flanders, Holland, and northern France in 1817 to inspect the horticultural industry. In the course of their travels they visited the leading nurserymen and their "bloemestries" or nurseries in the district around Haarlem (August 29), namely Van Eeden, Kreps, Eldering, Voorhelm, Moonen, and Schneevogt. Unfortunately they did not visit Lisse. By this time the village of Overveen was the center of bulb seedling production because of favorable soils, and Haarlem for final product show bulbs. Messrs. Veen & Co. and Mr. Eldering were the two major nurseries; when they visited Eldering, he was: "engaged in packing a very large case of bulbs for England; and he told us, that he had already dispatched about thirty similar cases, many of them for the same country. Notwithstanding the great inroads thus made on his stock, his collection is so ample, that he estimated the flowering-roots (chiefly hyacinth, tulip, and polyanthus-narcissus) still on hand, and of which he could dispose, without depriving himself of a sufficient store of breeders, as probably not fewer in number than 50,000."[18]

By the mid-1800s, the center of bulb production had shifted south from Haarlem toward Leiden and Lisse, although Haarlem remained the epicenter of the bulb auctions. In 1828 there were around a dozen first-rate florists in the Haarlem area alone. One traveler detailed the bulb raising operation of E. H. Krelage, who began raising bulbs in 1811. While his main holdings were hyacinths and tulips, Krelage raised one hundred sorts of yellow and white tazettas, on over twelve hundred square feet, with an additional six hundred square feet for all other narcissi and jonquils. By comparison Krelage was raising 914 sorts of hyacinths on over six thousand square feet, nearly half of his total land (in production) of 12,300 square feet.[19]

The Dutch sold not only to Britain and America but across Europe, issuing catalogs annually in Dutch, German, English, and French. Their comparative stocks of bulbs reflect the current market tastes for flowers, as well as (one suspects) their own preferences. Favorite flowers were hybridized, so the number of varieties cultivated were quite large. It is suspected that except for the most widely grown varieties, houses sold predominantly their own hybrid creations.

As with the previous centuries, tazettas were mostly sold for indoor forcing. Bulbs were also forced in pots or pans (wide, flat containers) of dirt. Bulbs were placed in the dark to sprout and eventually moved to the living space to enliven the winter months. After flowering, the bulbs were discarded, so each autumn new bulbs were purchased. During the Victorian age, stands became more embellished and planting schemes more elaborate. It was for this purpose that most polyanthus narcissus (tazettas) were hybridized and sold.

Wholesale Catalogue..., Flora Nurseries, 1893–1894.

The Dutch interest and cash crop may have been polyanthus narcissus/tazettas, but they did not completely ignore other daffodils. Of note, many species grown in England at the turn of the nineteenth century were credited as having come via the Dutch. In 1812 botanist Richard Anthony Salisbury detailed at great length most known narcissus species of the day, remarking on their histories of introduction, such as paperwhites being introduced at Brussels from Constantinople in 1597. Salisbury noted a number of species daffodils had been saved by the Dutch, in particular N. trilobus (grown at time of Parkinson but since lost, now called *N. × trilobus*); N. pumilus (now *N. minor* var. *pumilus*), which had been reimported in 1782 by Messrs. Lee and Kennedy; N. tenuifolius (*N. bulbocodium* subsp. *bulbocodium* var. *tenuifolius*), imported in 1760; and N. calathinus (either a form of *N. × odorus* or *N. triandrus* var. *loiseleurii*), imported around 1800. He even attributed N. bifrons (*N. × intermedius,* called "Etoile d'Or" then and "Texas Stars" now) to Dutch florists, having never found a source in the wild. Salisbury commented that the yellow trumpet Narcissus major (now considered the species *N. hispanicus* var. *spurius*) was routinely included with other Dutch bulb shipments by accident.

Brief comments are made in the British gardening literature regarding daffodils originating or being imported from France and Italy (particularly tazettas and jonquils). The Dutch apparently were never able to master the art of growing paperwhites (likely in part because of the climate), leaving production to the Italians. In the early 1800s, paperwhites and other select cold-tender tazettas were grown and imported by

Italian warehouses, dug from the sides of Mount Vesuvius. By the late 1800s, France was exporting paperwhites by the ton for the forcing market.[20]

The mid-1800s saw the ramping-up of the Dutch bulb industry into what we know today, partly in response to changes in British landscape design (which American gardeners soon fell into step with). The advent of "bedding out" and other closely related garden design tastes dictated the use of large quantities of bulbs when planted (particularly hyacinths and tulips), and the Dutch happily responded to market conditions. At first this led to questionable business practices, which proved counterproductive with the British and American gardening public. By midcentury, many Dutch houses corrected the errors of their ways. A bulb growers' association was formed in 1860, known by its acronym of KAVB (the Koninklijke Algemeene Vereening Bloembollencultuur, or the Royal General Bulb Growers' Association). By the 1870s the bulb trade was dominated by a handful of Dutch wholesalers, who bought from Dutch growers, consolidated the stocks, and resold across Europe, Britain, and North America.

Ever a culture of business, the Dutch found themselves belatedly responding to a sea change in daffodil tastes starting in the late 1880s. Tazettas fell from their pedestal as demand shifted to other kinds of daffodils. The English and Irish in the last quarter of the 1800s became enamored with other types of daffodils, such as the trumpets, that piqued cognoscenti gardeners' appetites and pocketbooks. The tazetta "Chinese Sacred Lily" (its true name of *N. tazetta* subsp. *lacticolor* is appreciated by no one) took the market by storm in the late 1880s with its ease of forcing, multiple bloom stalks, and heavenly perfume; it essentially eclipsed all other tazettas, particularly in the American market, save paperwhites.

Harsh winters in the Channel Islands in the early 1900s, combined with the devastation from World War I and two severe winters in the Netherlands, greatly decimated (true) tazetta bulb production. As a result, virtually all of the pre–World War I true tazettas are now long lost, except the core stalwart flowers still grown today and less common cultivars lurking in isolated gardens (in the Deep South and coastal South, because of the mild winters). What distinguishes this situation from that of many other historic plants is, in this case, over the centuries wild tazetta populations around the Mediterranean were so heavily harvested as to denude many original habitat locations, thus eradicating much of the original gene pool.

But the Dutch loved standard daffodils as well, and capture, hybridize, and commercially export them they did, albeit slowly. Many of the daffodils in later nineteenth-century American catalogs were Dutch introductions, one of the most enduring being 'Golden Spur'—simply found on a Dutch estate in 1885 and brought into commerce. S. A. de Graaff of the venerable de Graaff house joined British enthusiasts in hybridizing, acquiring his starter stock from Peter Barr. The firm quickly introduced 'Madame de Graaff,' the famous white trumpet, in 1888, which went on the market at over £5 per bulb.[21]

Into the twentieth century, Dutch hybridizing focused on poetaz-type tazettas (created by crossing [freeze sensitive] true tazettas with cold-hardy poets [*N. poeticus*], the resulting offspring having fewer but larger florets and much greater cold tolerance)

Hollandsche Bloemenvelden.

"Hollandsche Bloemenvelden" Dutch daffodil fields, undated.

and trumpets, with a few well-known jonquils, poets, and others created for good measure. One of today's most robust poets came from this period—'Actaea'—as well as the most robust triandrus—'Thalia'. The sensational flower of the day, however, was 'Mrs. Ernest H. Krelage'; it was a Dutch tradition to name one's best white trumpet after one's best wife. A very large flower, its creamy yellow trumpet pales over time. For many seasons after its debut in 1912, bulbs went for $250.00 a piece. While the British focused on refined show flowers, the Dutch focused on strong garden flowers, a difference that holds to the present day.[22]

The British and the Daffodil

There are two threads to trace in the British history of the daffodil as applies to daffodils in early America. The first is what was grown by the common folk who immigrated to the American colonies (along notably with Germans, who took pride in their gardens) and so were "pass-along" plants. The second is what was for sale by British (and Dutch/Flemish) florists that wealthy Americans ordered from, and, by extension, what did the gardens of the wealthy contain that aspiring Americans would have wanted to emulate.

"Narcissus," along with the poppy, acanthus, rose, lily, marigold, molis, and mandrake, was recommended for growing around a garden in twelfth-century England, in one of that country's earliest descriptions of a garden courtesy of Alexander Neckam. However, noted English garden writer Penelope Hobhouse points out that the term "narcissus" was used on the Continent for the martagon lily as well, so it cannot be clearly assumed that "narcissus" means *Narcissus*. Further, another writer noted while the daffodil was common as a wild flower, only occasionally was it cultivated in medieval English gardens.[23]

A century and a half later arrived one of the earliest writings on how to actually garden in the British Isles, namely the circa 1350 poem "The Feate of Gardening," attributed to Mayster Jon Gardener. It is generally accepted that a number of plants in the poem were actually primarily decorative, including Foxglove, Periwinkle, Cowslip, Primrose, Daffodil ("affody{?}" in the original Middle English Kent dialect), Daisy, Iris, Hollyhock, Lavender, Lily, Peony, Rose, Violet, and Waterlily.[24]

In the mid- to late 1500s, one of the best sources for information on "commoners' flowers" are the herbals and other botanical texts, and the bons mots that flow from more scholarly and erudite works. Proof of the popularity of the daffodil during the reign of Elizabeth and Shakespeare is oft cited as the Bard's references to the daffodil in *Winter's Tale.*

One of the most important such herbals is that of the Flemish botanist Rembert Dodoens (1517–1585), whose 1554 herbal was translated into English by Henry Lyte in 1578 as *A nievve herball, or, Historie of plantes,* and given

Plate 197, Narcissus Biflorus. Two-Flower'd Narcissus. *The Botanical Magazine*, 1793.

a slight English view for its audience. Dodoens echoed much of Dioscorides' medical uses in each plant's "The Vertues." Dodoens listed *N. poeticus* as beneficial for vomiting, burns, dislocations, joint pain, spots on the face, ulcers, and thorns and splinters; jonquils were used for vomiting and diseases of the bladder; and last, the bastard narcissus (the willowy yellow trumpet *N. pseudonarcissus*) was good for diseases caused by tough and clammy phlegm.

The great value in Lyte's edition of Dodoens's work today for daffodils comes from the short observations as to "The Place" where the medicinal plant in question was to be found. He addressed four kinds of daffodils, with tazettas and white trumpets mentioned only in passing. Poets and the *N. poeticus* wild hybrid known for hundreds of years as "Primrose Peerless" (*N.* × *medioluteus,* or "Twin Sisters") "grow plentifully in

Plate 1301, Narcissus Major. Large Yellow Spanish Daffodil. *Curtis's Botanical Magazine*, 1810.

diverse places in Fraunce, as Burgundie, and Languedoc, in meadowes: but in this Countrie they growe not at al saving in gardens, whereas they are sowen or planted."[25] About the jonquil: "It growth in sundrie places in Spayne, and from thence it was brought hither."[26] About the *N. pseudonarcissus:* "It groweth in moyst places in shadowey woodes and in the borders of feeldes, . . . it is also planted in gardens."[27]

The following year Clusius, while residing in England, observed in "March, 1579, that daffodils were sold in great abundance in Cheapside by country women and that all the shops were bright with them."[28] Francis Bacon, in his essay "On Gardens" (1598), directed at the aristocracy (for who else would have thirty acres for an overall plan and twelve acres specifically for the pleasure garden), recommended flower beds for every month of the year, and the Yellow Daffodil (presumably *N. pseudonarcissus*) for March and the Pale Daffodil (*N.* × *medioluteus*) for April.

Englishman John Gerard published his own herbal in 1597 (*The Herball*), albeit with a few botanical errors, that were quietly corrected by L'Obel. Gerard, true to the time, was more focused on "vertues" of a plant than on the aesthetics of its flowers, but his observations are nonetheless valuable. Gerard mentioned the same two daffodils as Dodoens as common, "the six kinde of Daffodill is that sort of *Narcissus* or Primrose peerelesse, that is most common in our country gardens, generally knowne every where. . . . The flower groweth at the top, of a yellowish white colour, with a yellow crowne or circle in the middle, and flowereth in the moneth of Aprill, and sometimes sooner."[29] About *N. pseudonarcissus* he remarked: "The common yellow Daffodilly or Daffodowndilly is so well knowne to all, that it needeth no description."[30]

In addition to the very common or vernacular daffodils, there were the less common (or more common only to the more well-to-do) daffodils. Gerard observed, "The yellow Spanish Daffodill doth likewise decke up our London gardens, where they encrease indefinitely."[31] In all Gerard describes fifteen flowers (inclusive of three non-daffodils): "we have them all, and everie of them in our London gardens in great abundance"—presumably gardens of taste, refinement, and money.[32]

Gerard indulged in plant-collecting trips as did other European botanists. On one of his excursions into the English countryside, he identified a type of daffodil growing in an old woman's garden in Wiltshire (*N. pseudonarcissus* 'Plenus'). And he swapped for the de rigueur flowers of the day. Gerard received from Robinus (Jean Robin of Paris, botanist to the King under Henri III, Henri IV, and Louis XIII) double yellow daffodils, "which he procured by means of friends, from Aurelia, and other parts of Fraunce" (along with crocus, hyacinths, cress seeds, and other plants).[33] William Cecil (advisor to Queen Elizabeth I), gave Gerard a double white daffodil from Constantinople that bloomed only once despite careful tending.[34]

Dutch, Flemish, and French Protestants, fleeing religious persecution under the Spanish Crown, fled to the protection of England under Henry VIII (1509–1547), and later in particular from the Duke of Alva (1567–1573), bringing their love of flowers and gardens with them. Before their arrival, ornamental gardening was virtually unknown in England. The English were slow to warm to the "Strangers'" love of flowers, but were quite receptive to vegetables. With industrialization in the 1600s, Dutch/Flemish weavers spread into England following the textile industry, gardening all the way. English florists began to come into their own, particularly in the North under the influence of the Dutch weavers. This was noted to be the case in Norwich, with gardens to be seen in the early 1600s and a florist's feast documented in 1637.[35]

The 1600s saw the rise of pleasure gardens and writings thereof, from translations of Continental works in the early part of the century, to English garden writers (evolving from the utilitarian herbal) at the end. *Narcissus* species listed in herbals dramatically increased, reflecting the burgeoning trade in bulbs.

At the dawn of the seventeenth century, the English took their cues from the Continent, and the leaders in gardening were the French and Italians. The early French work *L'agriculture, et Maison Rustique* (1564) by Charles Estienne was translated in the early 1600s by Gervase Markham as *Maison Rustique, or the countrey farme* (1616). Estienne's popular work guided English gardeners and garden owners in the latest/fashionable dictates on how and where to plant. Thus from the French to the English, the daffodil (including the "outlandish" ones from the eastern Mediterranean) was to be planted in the knot garden (a large, intricately patterned affair) devoted to the flowers for the nosegay—to the point of Markham dubbing it "The Nosegay Garden."

English garden writers soon struck their own path in response to their own gardening conditions and tastes. William Lawson in *The country housewifes garden* (within *A new orchard, and garden,* 1631) includes "daffodowndillies" in the "Hearbs of smallest growth," along with the pansy, coast Margeram, Savery, strawberries, saffron, and leekes.[36] He later elaborates, "Daffodowndillies have their roots parted, and set once in three or foure yeere, or longer time. They flower timely, and after *Midsummer,* are scarcely seene. They are more for ornament, then for use, so are Dasies."[37] This suggests that for many, the daffodil retained its place in the vegetable garden border as suggested

Plate IV, A. N. Pseudo-Narcissus Var. Major; B. Pseudo-Narcissus Var. Maximus. Burbidge and Baker, *The Narcissus*, 1875. Courtesy of the Cherokee Garden Library, Kenan Research Center at the Atlanta History Center, Atlanta, Georgia.

by Markham and Gardener centuries earlier.[38]

English botanists similarly responded to the explosion of plants available to European gardens from around the globe. It is their works that identify and discuss in detail the flowers recommended for the knot/nosegay gardens. The "outlandish" rare ones, the local common ones, pedigreed and wild, are all touched on. For daffodils the early benchmarks to follow Clusius and Gerard are those works by John Parkinson. Gerard described seventeen daffodils; by 1629 John Parkinson described ninety-two, quite a few being polyanthus narcissus/tazettas. In 1640 Parkinson wrote his *Theatrum Botanicum;* of its 612 pages, forty-one pages were devoted to daffodils.

Parkinson, in *Paradise in Sole paradisus terrestris* (1629), commented about "our common English wilde bastard Daffodill" that "this bastard Daffodill is so common in all England, both in Copses, Woods and Orchards, that I might well forbeare the description thereof, and, especially, in that growing wilde, it is of little respect in our Garden."[39] This notion of the commoner's flower not warranting discussion plagues the tracing of daffodils in early American colonial gardens as well. The tazettas as a florist's flower, the fragrant jonquils, the showy doubles are coveted, the common daffodils politely ignored.

Parkinson is also credited with recording and raising the first daffodil seedling. A double of 'Maximus' (a variant of *N. hispanicus,* the "Spanish Daffodil"), he called his flower "pseudonarcissus aureus hispanicus flore pleno." Everyone else called it "Parkinson's Daffodil," the "great double yellow daffodil," or the "Spanish bastard daffodil." Parkinson wrote, "I think none ever had this kind before my selfe, nor did I my selfe ever see it before the year 1618, for it is of mine own raising and flowering first in my garden."[40]

The British aristocracy was as smitten with the new exotic flowers as their European counterparts. By 1640 seeds for vegetables were imported from Europe and sold by English middlemen. This was due in part as a reflection of the English aristocracy finally deciding that vegetables were fit to eat and not just for peasants and foreigners. But the rise of the commercial or professional nurseryman occurred a little later in England than on the Continent, after the Civil War and Cromwell's Reformation.

The strife of the English Civil War and the Commonwealth (roughly from 1640–1660) saw a hiatus of sorts in gardening; even the decorating of churches was frowned on. With the Restoration of the monarchy, the English upper classes began catching up to their European counterparts in the interest of exotic plant collecting and the fashion of gardening as a means of conspicuous consumption. Further William and Mary, when invited to the English throne in the latter 1600s, were avid gardeners. This dovetailed with shifts in dietary views, and social and economic stability is always conducive to new businesses. Both new demands, for vegetables and ornamental garden flowers, eventually translated to a more educated and trained workforce. This trained workforce was then happy to launch into the nursery business to supply the plant material for the moneyed set (trees and the like).

One of the numerous English books of the latter part of the century that coincided with this newfound pastime was John Rea's *Flora: seu, De florum cultura* (1665). Rea was a noted horticulturist/florist; he rises to the fore here because of his friendship with the gardening Welsh baron, Sir John Hanmer (who was also friends with John Evelyn). Rea's book signals the final transformation from gardening for purpose to gardening for pleasure. Rea's garden designs were intended to fit within existing spaces of an estate's walled garden, with recommendations of how to change the dimensions as warranted. He expected flower beds to be raised and railed but discussed boxwood and rose hedges:

> Now for planting the Beds in the Fret, you must consider every piece, and place the Roots so as those of a kind set in several Beds may answer one another; as in the corners of each Bed the best *Crown Imperials, Lilies, Martagons,* and such tall flowers; in the middles of the Five Squares, great Tufts of best *Pionies,* and round about them several sorts of *Cyclamen;* the rest with *Daffodils, Hyacinths* and such like: The streight Beds are fit for the best *Tulips,* where account may be kept of them: *Ranunculus* and *Anemonies* also require particular Beds; the rest may be set all over with the more ordinary sorts of *Tulips, Frittillaries, bulbed Iris* and all other kinds of good Roots, in such sorts as you will find directed where they are described.[41]

Rea's introduction to his chapter "*Narcissus*" (which included a number of other bulbs) reflects the dual status codifying for daffodils. He began with a select few flowers, mostly doubles, then rolls through a handful of tazettas, to jonquils and triandrus, then to more doubles and a few singles: "The *Daffodill,* next to the *Tulips,* deserveth mention, in respect of the great variety and excellence thereof; we will begin with those called *true Daffodils,* and so proceed to the bastard kinds . . . ; but in respect many of them are now common, and of small esteem, we will insert the best in every kinde, and such onely as are fittest to be collected and entertained by all that delight in Flowers;

Rea, *Flora: Seu De Florum Cultura*, 1676. Courtesy of the Cherokee Garden Library, Kenan Research Center at the Atlanta History Center, Atlanta, Georgia.

beginning first with that best known, called *Narcissus Nonparel.*[42] No common daffodils warranted acknowledgement—no *N. pseudonarcissus, N. jonquilla,* nor *N.* × *medioluteus*—only doubles, fancy tazettas, esoteric jonquils, and delicate triandrus—everything you have to trade for, except doubles.

For such a fall in stature, Rea addressed *Narcissus* after his favorite tulips (not surprising as he was considered to have one of the best tulip collections in Britain), but before Hyacinths, which seemed to be in the same boat of small esteem, "*The Hyacinth,* or *Jacinth,* is of divers sorts, and many of them of small esteem, we will make choice of the best, and set them down in order, beginning with that so much by all Florists"—namely *Hyacinthus Indicus tuberosa radice.*[43]

Around 1660 the illustrious Sir Thomas Hanmer of Wales wrote a book on gardening, encompassing much of what he knew, which was quite extensive, given he was something of a mentor to both John Rea and John Evelyn.[44] As Rea's work was a directive to the nobility, Hanmer's is a case in point of what the most dedicated followers of *Flora* were embarking on after the strictures of the Reformation. Regrettably Hanmer's folio was never published until 1933 (part of it came to light when a descendent self-published family papers in 1876), when the folio appeared on the market. It includes the first "gardener's calendar" written, as well as the earliest cataloging of iris. A lengthy separate manuscript in the Hanmer family's papers is widely thought to have been the intended preface to the folio. Hanmer discussed the state of gardening in England, observing the English had finally begun the pursuit of rarities for the garden as peace finally descended on the country ("after our late war"; Rea referred to it as "our long Winter"), and the rich were now adorning their houses with costly garden embellishments.[45] In December of 1660, Sir Hanmer cataloged the flowers in his Great Garden at Bettisfield in Wales, the design of which was fully in keeping with the recommendations of his friend John Rea.

The book folio divides garden flowers by root type, then addressing evergreens and fruit trees and a gardener's calendar or "remembrances." All flowers of a given category are described, growing conditions specified, and other pertinent information dispensed. Hanmer begins with bulbous roots and thus with tulips, fitting for probably the greatest connoisseur of tulips in England at the time (his tulip 'Agate Hanmer' was considered one of the finest in England, a tri-colored bloom of crimson, white and 'gredeline,' a grayish-purple) followed by Narcissus or Daffodils, then hyacinths and other bulbs. Hanmer methodically describes the primary narcissus of the day complete with occasional comments if a flower is commonly found; tellingly, he begins with the two best-known doubles—Tradescant's and Wilmer's ('Plenissimus' and 'Telamonius Plenus'). While he grew many florist's tazettas in his garden per his preface manuscript, he discusses only those from specific locations (essentially species) in the book folio. Interestingly he includes what seems to be bulbocodium in with the jonquils (based on leaf morphology), illustrating their long use as garden bulbs. Further some daffodils considered common in the 1700s are absent, particularly the small trumpet *N. minor.*

Garden design plates 1 and 2. Rea, *Flora: Seu De Florum Cultura,* 1676. Courtesy of the Cherokee Garden Library, Kenan Research Center at the Atlanta History Center, Atlanta, Georgia.

Per the manuscript, the Great Garden showcased bulbs in four beds in the center of the bordered knot and in the general borders along walkways. The flowers in the beds were planted in numbered "ranks" or rows. While the garden primarily showcased his large collection of named tulips, one bed contained jonquils, double jonquils, and a number of named tazettas. His *Narcissus Constantinople* he had obtained from John Rea; his French-named tazettas suggest ordering from Flemish or French sources, as does his inclusion of the double *Robinus,* his *Narcissus* ('Eystettensis'). How Hanmer planted in ranks is typical of bulb planting for upward of two hundred years, in the seventeenth and eighteenth centuries:

1660. FLOWERS in the Great Garden, December. Bettisfield.

[First and fourth little bordered bed in the center knot are full of tulips]

The second little bed is the further of the two on the right hand. In the middle of this bed is one Double Crown Imperial. In the end are six rows of Iris raised from seed by Rea; also polyanthus and daffodils. In the four corners of this second bed are four roots of good anemones.

The third bed is the first of the four on the left hand.

First Rank—1 hyacinth of Lisle, a good watchet colour [azure, per descendent]; 6 jonquils; 1 hyacinth of Peru.

Second Rank—6 double jonquils, and 1 black fritillary in the middle.

Third Rank—1 gray fritillary; 6 red Deuscaninus; 1 gray fritillary.

Fourth Rank—2 narcissus, pale wings and yellow cups; 2 musarte oriental narcissus.

Fifth Rank—2 great white Argires; 2 Belles de Brussells.

Sixth Rank—2 Belles du Val narcissi, all yellow; 2 yellow Argires narcissus.

Seventh Rank—2 Belles Fourniere narcissi, all yellow, greater flower than the Argires; 2 Constantinople narcissi, double, bore not.

Eighth Rank—2 Belle Selmane narcissi, right dear ones; 1 Bel Del Vine narcissus, small white and yellow cup.

Ninth Rank—1 colchicum vernale; 3 iris dell' Abbaye, one died; 2 colchicum vernale.

Tenth Rank—1 gray fritillare; 6 white Deuscaninus; 1 gray fritillare.

Eleventh Rank—6 double jonquils.

Twelfth Rank—1 hyacinth of Peru; 6 jonquils; 1 hyacinth of Lisle.[46]

All the little bordered beds, besides the four little middle ones of that quarter, are full of anemones on the outside and tulips and narcissus in the midst, with some gilly-flowers and some irises at the ends of the beds, and cyclamens at the four corners.

The border under the south wall in the Great Garden is full of good anemones, and near the musk rose are two roots of daffodils of Constantinople from Rea, and a martagon pomponium.[47]

[The other border beds around the center 4 beds of the knot, along the walls, are full of roses, cowslips, tulips, anemonies, crocuses, and martagons.]

In the border under the wall within the garden by the grasse walk are several roots of fraxinellas, and Virginia spider worts, and primroses, and some anemonies and daffodils.[48]

Hanmer's roster of hybrid-named "Belle" tazettas is one of the earliest listings of florist's tazettas, supporting the contention of the Flemish hybridizing them by the 1630s. And as other dismayed gardeners found, Hanmer's 'Constantinople' was not happy in merry cold England and did not bloom. The prominence given the six double jonquils reflects both their elevated status as well as how plentiful they had become

Ld.Edwards del. Pub. by T. Curtis S.º Geo. Crescent Apr.1.1807 F. Sansom sculp

Plate 1011, Narcissus Orientalis (*var. fl. pleno*). The Cyprus or Double Roman Narcissus.
Curtis's Botanical Magazine, 1807.

since Clusius's nephew roamed the countryside looking for said illusive flower in 1605. In contrast to Hanmer's appreciation of daffodils, Leonard Meager made mention of them only in passing in *The English gardener* (1688), devoting more attention to ranunculus, anemonies, and carnations, and he evidenced a preference for hyacinths over tulips.[49] Hanmer's, Rea's and Meager's differing opinions and preferences suggest in the late 1600s there was still great variability in the fashionable flowers, as they were relatively new to the English moneyed classes.

By the close of the century, gardening as an English pursuit was in full swing. In 1691 John Aubrey reported: "But in the time of King Charles IId, Gardening was much improved and became common: I doe beleeve, I may modestly affirm, that there is now ten times as much gardning about London as there was in A° 1660: and wee have been, since that time, much improved in forreign plants, especially since about 1683, there have been exotick Plants brought into England, no lesse than seven thousand."[50] The 1700s in Britain saw two radically different views of the garden landscape vie in competition, as the new sought to usurp and supplant the old. At the same time, gardening blossomed across society, with the wealthy seeking to stay in fashion. As more of the aristocracy turned their attentions to the beautification of their properties, gardeners rose to the need. From 1691 to 1700, there were fifteen nurserymen in London; by 1730 there were thirty in "town" and another thirty in the provinces, and by 1760 there were roughly one hundred nurserymen across the country.

As with any market, some nurserymen catered to the wealthy with the latest fad and fashionable flower, while others carried more "old-fashioned" and thus inexpensive flowers for the modest gardener. Daffodils fell into both groups as reflected in the prices paid and sorts offered. Tazettas, doubles, and jonquils were offered across the board, with the best jonquils the most expensive (but still nowhere near the cost of better grade tulips). Common sorts of mixed daffodils (single and double, listed without names) were quite cheap and offered to gardeners of limited means, but still not as cheap as crocus. Daffodils that warranted being listed by name include "Campernello" jonquils, polyanthus narcissus ("Collection of 40 sorts"), "Narcissus of Constantinople," single and double jonquils, Narcissus Orientalis, and "Double White Narcissus."[51]

The high prices fetched by jonquils proved more enticing than fiddling with polyanthus narcissus seedlings. In the early 1700s, there is at least one instance of English gardeners growing jonquils as a cash crop. Under his discussion of problems in the commercial saffron production for the crocus, Philip Miller detours into the problems of growing jonquils:

> In the Parish of *Fulham* near *London,* the Gardeners us'd to drive a great Trade in the *Junquil* or *Narcissus juncifolius flore multiplici,* at which Place the greatest Quantity of those Roots was rais'd for Sale as perhaps was in any Part of *England,* and turn'd to as great Account for the Master as any Crop they could employ their ground in, till within these seven or eight Years; since which time most of their Roots have turn'd carroty, and so prov'd barren, or have produc'd only single Flowers, so that the Gardeners being hereby disheartened, have thrown them out entirely, satisfying

themselves with this Reason, that their Ground was tir'd with them.[52]

A little-known method of planting daffodils appeared in London nurseryman John Woolridge's combined horticultural treatise and commercial catalog in 1700. Rather than the formal rigidity of distinct parterres, Woolridge presaged William Robinson's "Wild Garden" movement of the 1870s: "The *Narcissus* is a Flower so well known, that it's needless to spend many words on it, but for its great variety, bright colour, and early flowring, the better kind of them deserve to be planted here and there under your *Groves* and *Avenue's* and other *Shades,* where they prosper very well, and waste no ground."[53] In the *New improvements of planting and gardening* (1718), Richard Bradley elaborated: "The Jonquil is a Flower generally admir'd for its delightful Scent; the double Kind blooms in April, and that with the Single Flower somewhat sooner . . . the Narcissus Polyanthos, whose sweet Scented Flowers are not less desirable than Jonquils. . . . Next to those I have mention'd in this Section, the double White and double Yellow Narcissus are worthy our Esteem; and even the common Daffodil is to be

Plate XXV, N. Odorus Var. Rugulosus; N. Odorus Var. Minor. Burbidge and Baker, *The Narcissus,* 1875. Courtesy of the Cherokee Garden Library, Kenan Research Center at the Atlanta History Center, Atlanta, Georgia.

admir'd for its pretty Ornament in rural Parts of the Garden."[54] Other flowers recommended for the rural parts of the garden—under hedges, along avenues of trees, and in wilderness works—were violets, primroses, cowslips, and polyanthos.

The year 1713 marks the inception of the English landscape movement emphasizing sweeping vistas, with absolutely nothing geometric tolerated (when Alexander Pope made his case that formal English gardens should be replaced with unadorned nature in his 1731 *An Epistle to Lord Burlington*). Old garden rooms and parterre gardens were swept aside as the century progressed. Fortuitously daffodils found a niche in the botanic gardens of the wealthy, which were still socially acceptable as a logical outgrowth of a learned person's interest in botany, and in general it took some time before the old way of formal compartmentalized gardening slipped away. For all bulbs the old

Frontispiece. Miller, *The Gardeners Dictionary*, 1733. Courtesy of the Cherokee Garden Library, Kenan Research Center at the Atlanta History Center, Atlanta, Georgia.

formal way was best—planting flowers along the grassy edges of the estate vistas did not gain traction—and this landscape feature is traceable through the 1700s and beginning with a French monk.

The Compleat Florist, by monk Louis Liger d'Auxerre (1658–1717) (printed in English in 1706, along with *Le Jardinier Solitaire* by François Gentil), sets the British view of gardening with bulbs for most of the century. "When you plant *Narcissus's,* whether in *Parterres,* or in Beds, be sure you set 'em at the distance of four inches from one another, and that in Rows laid out by the Line. They may be very agreeably blended with *Tulips* and *Hyacinths;* and this method is follow'd, to the end that by virtue of the number of these Plants of different sorts, which *Flower,* at different Seasons, the *Gardens* may, for several Months, be adorn'd with *flowers.*"[55] For jonquils, "Its Bulbs are generally planted in the Borders of *Parterres,* or in the other Knots of a Garden . . . and to have a like distance [four inches] between them."[56]

Liger's directions were adopted by influential Philip Miller in his 1724 edition of *The Gardeners and Florists Dictionary.* Miller became one of the ultimate horticultural authorities followed by colonial gardeners from John Bartram to Thomas Jefferson. Miller, echoing Liger, strongly admonishes against planting bulbous rooted plants with fibrous rooted ones; borders are to be three feet wide, and a grid four inches square marked out for planting. While spring and summer plants may be intermixed in a border, bulbous plants are to be always kept separate in the parterres: "Every Man may form Schemes according to his Fancy, provided they are rightly contriv'd, that is, the deep rooted *Flowers* are not mixed with those which have but ordinary Roots, and above all not with bulbous Plants; with this particular Observation, that the *Ranunculus's* and *Tulips,* must be always placed apart in particular *Decoupees,* or separate borders; and that the *Anemones* must likewise be separated from one another. This Division has a wonderful Effect; whereas the mingling of them, would produce a disagreeable Confusion."[57] Liger even instructed florists in how to prepare plants and bulbous roots for transport from foreign countries (or, how to direct bulbs' shipments when ordering), and how to handle bulbs turned moldy from long shipment.

The British newfound love of pretty flowers did not disappear as the tastemakers touted sweeping vistas of grass and a few trees and shrubs. More nurserymen offered more stock, *Narcissus* included, reflected in seminal works of the day. Philip Miller, in *The Gardeners Dictionary* (1735), listed thirty-five Narcissus (of which eleven were tazettas or N. orientalis). By the 1754 edition, he described forty-five *Narcissus* of the day, nineteen of which were polyanthus narcissus, with many doubles, poets, and jonquils as well. He recommended a number of tazettas, many still available today because of their fragrance; others, the "Eastern" sorts, were relatively new to English gardens.

Despite echoing the formality of Liger as the preferred style of growing bulbs, Miller continued to give a nod to the lingering British idea of incorporating common daffodils into the "rural" landscape in his 1754 edition: "The common Sorts of Daffodil are generally planted in large Borders of the Pleasure-garden; where being intermix'd with other bulbous rooted Flowers, they afford an agreeable Variety in their Seasons of Flowering. These Roots are very hardy, and will thrive in almost any Soil or Situation; which renders them very proper for rural Gardens, where, being planted under the Shade of Trees, they will endure several Years without transplanting, and produce annually, in the Spring, great Quantities of Flowers, which afford an agreeable Prospect."[58] This notion of daffodils and select other flowers as acceptable for the rural parts of the garden, or out along the edge of "the prospect," does not seem to have made its way into the American colonist's landscaping lexicon. As the wilderness was always close at hand in North America into the 1800s, having even more of it may not have seemed too appealing.

By his 1768 edition, owned by both Thomas Jefferson and Lady Skipwith of southern Virginia, Miller collapsed the species descriptions to nine, following more a Linnaean system of botanical description. However, he added twenty-two named florist tazettas:

The eighth sort [Narcissus Tazetta; Yellow Portugal Daffodil with many flowers, commonly called Polyanthus Narcissus] grows naturally in Portugal, and in the islands of the Archipelago; of this there are a greater Variety than of all the other Species, for as the Flowers are very ornamental, and come early in the Spring, so the Florists in Holland, Flanders, and France, have taken great Pains in cultivating and improving them; so that at present the catalogues printed by the Dutch Florists, contain more than thirty Varieties, the principal of which are these hereafter mentioned.

There are some with white petals and white cups, but these are not so much esteemed as the others, though there are two or three varieties with large bunches of small white flowers, which have a very agreeable odour, so are as valuable as any of the other, and are in later flower than most of the other sorts.[59]

Only seven of his yellow and bicolor polyanthus narcissus align with varieties in van Kampen's 1739 catalog (kindly reprinted by Dr. Ernest H. Krelage in *Drie eeuwen bloembollenexport*, 1946), indicative of the continuing hybridization of tazettas. But Miller continues to recommend the common daffodils for the rural garden as late as his 1768 edition: "These roots are very hardy, and will thrive in almost any soil or situation, which tenders them very proper for rural gardens, where, being planted under the shade of trees, they will thrive for several years without transplanting, and will produce annually in the spring, great quantities of flowers, which will make a good appearance before the trees come out in leaf."[60]

Although many parterres were banished from the manor's grounds as the wealthy sought to stay fashionable in their tastes, luckily for the daffodil, private botanical gardens came in vogue as botany became an amateur interest of the well-to-do. This interest in botany grew on the newly established American side of the Pond, and plant enthusiasts on both sides were in common communication. William Burchell, a florist from Fullam, offered seventeen *Narcissus* by their common name in his 1764 catalogue:

The common Single Daffodil	Double White Narcissus
Great Nonsuch Daffodil	White Narcissus with a purple Middle
Single Nonsuch or Mock Daffodil	White Polyanthus Narcissus
Double Daffodil	Double White Polyanthus Narcissus
Narcissus of Naples	Bossleman's Narcissus
Single Jonquil	Narcissus of the Sun
Double Jonquil	Pale Narcissus of the Sun
Mock Jonquil	Starry white Narcissus
Common Single White Narcissus[61]	

Actually, one of the "narcissus" is quite possibly a "garlic"—"The Narcissus of Naples" is possibly the Naples garlic or daffodil garlic, *Allium neapolitanium*. In the 1700s many bulbs were lumped as Narcissus, including many newly discovered in the Caribbean islands.

Period botanical works provide clues to the time frames of commercial availability of various daffodils in the mid- and late 1700s. Presumably the more esoteric bulbs were sold to those members of the aristocracy who established botanical gardens on their grounds, with the help of professional gardeners. The gardeners, in turn, often published the catalogue of said patron's garden. *Hortus Paddingtonensis: or, a Catalogue of Plants Cultivated in the Garden of J. Symmons, Esq. Paddington-house*, was compiled and published by Sir Symmons's gardener, William Salisbury (presumably with Sir Symmons's financial support), in 1797. The garden contained fourteen daffodils, only two of which were tazettas, the rest comprising jonquils, trumpets, poets, a bulbocodium, and the wild hybrid *N. × medioluteus* (then called N. biflorus). In comparison, Sir Symmons's collection of daffodils exeeded the 1796 catalogue of the Walkerian Botanic Garden at Cambridge University *Hortus Cantabrigiensis,* which grew only 7 daffodils; by the latter's 1800 catalogue, the botanic garden contained thirteen daffodils, ten held in common with Symmons's collection.

While gentlemen maintained their botanical gardens, women were regaled with the delights of gardening, including bulbs in their place in the pleasure-grounds and borders. So just because the righteously fashionable were advocating the abolition of rigid flower gardens, enough popular sentiment in their favor remained to warrant popular articles on their planting.

Lady's Magazine, in 1787, addressed all the bulbous roots of the day, from anemones to gladiolus to snowdrops to fritillaries to hyacinths to jonquils and narcissus. Interestingly fall-blooming bulbs are discussed, but not with any direction on how to incorporate them with other bulbs. Autumnal colchicums, *Narcissus serotinus* (a fall-

Plate XLII, N. poeticus. Burbidge and Baker, *The Narcissus,* 1875. Courtesy of the Cherokee Garden Library, Kenan Research Center at the Atlanta History Center, Atlanta, Georgia.

blooming white flower that looks nothing like other spring daffodils), autumn crocus, and yellow autumnal amaryllis presumably were to be planted either in bulb beds or interspersed in the borders:

> All the Narcissus are desirable garden-flowers to adorn the principal borders, beds, &c., in the flower and pleasure-garden, . . . the first species, common Daffodil, and Narcissus minor, are generally the earliest, succeeded by the common white Narcissus, Polyanthus Narcissus, and the other Narcissus kinds, Jonquils &c. and the autumn sort (Narcissus serotinus) in September or October.[62]

But all Narcissus and Jonquils, may be planted both in assemblage in the common flower borders, towards the front and middle, either singly or in rows, or in small patches, three, four, or five roots in each, three or four inches deep; and also in beds, each sort separate, in rows, five to eight or nine inches asunder, by the same distance in each row, and the depth as above.[63]

They [jonquils] may be planted both in the general flower-borders, and in beds separate, especially the best double kinds. When designed to plant them in the borders, it is most eligible to set them in small clumps, four or five roots in each, five or six inches asunder, and three deep—planting some towards the front, others more backward, in a varied order. To plant them in beds by themselves, . . . plant the bulbs, in rows six or eight inches asunder, by six inches in the lines, and three or four over the crowns of the roots.[64]

Jonquils and large Polyanthus-Narcissus for growing in "root-glasses filled with soft water" and pots for indoor blooming. Small bulbocodium are to be planted in the "towards the front of the flower border, in assemblage with other spring-blowing bulbs, . . . either singly, or three or four roots together, in little patches."[65]

Outside the gentleman's botanical and lady's bulb garden, however, "polyanthus narcissus" were the *Narcissus* of choice, and usually for indoor flowering. The reality of preference is portrayed by the catalogues produced by Richard Weston. In 1775 he published *The English Flora,* intended to be as complete a compendium of flowers available in England as possible. In it, he listed seventeen *Narcissus,* with only one tazetta (*N. tazetta*). However, in 1772 he published *The Universal Botanist and Nurseryman,* which included his 1769 *Catalogue of Curious Ranunculusses,* at the back of which were other bulbs. His listing for daffodils was thin, comprising single and double jonquils, and double white narcissus ("Albus Plenus Odoratus"). However, he carried 132 varieties of named polyanthus narcissus, namely three all-white varieties, sixty-one all-yellow varieties, and sixty-eight bicolor varieties. By comparison, he offered 208 varieties of anemones, 1,110 named ranunculus varieties, eight hundred named tulips, and roughly eight hundred named hyacinths.[66]

This state of affairs was summarized thus: "The Narcissus was a somewhat neglected plant, and the only new form that appeared was N. tenuior of Curtis, which he found in Maddock's nursery in May 1794; but Grimwood and Barrit had it in 1789. As already noted, the Polyanthus Narcissus was so popular that other species were neglected."[67]

But for a neglected plant in the latter part of the 1700s and early 1800s, its popularity was still noted in some important quarters. Miller in 1754 indicated that *N. poeticus*–type flowers were "pretty common in many of the Gardens near *London.*"[68] William Curtis at the outset of his famous *Botanical Magazine* in 1794 described a number of the better and lesser known daffodils of the day, but by no means all, complementing those written about in *Lady's Magazine.* Through the 1790s and early 1800s, daffodils appeared intermittently, some with pearls of gardening popularity. A few are hinted at as being commonly found, such as *N. minor* and *N. jonquilla* and its double form, but no definitive statements are made. After a lull daffodils appear again in the 1806 and 1810 year editions. Unfortunately these later-described flowers usually do not contain the same level of garden-specific observations, reflecting the strong focus on botany of bulbs at the time.

Of the common garden flower N. biflorus (*N. × medioluteus*):

Both Gerard and Parkinson describe and figure this plant, informing us that it was very common in the gardens in their time; the former indeed mentions it as growing wild in fields and sides of woods in the West of England; the latter says he could never hear of its natural place of growth. Clusius reports that he had been credibly informed of its growing wild in England; it probably may, but of this it remains for us to be more clearly ascertained; it undoubtedly is the plant mentioned by Ray in his Synopsis. As it grows readily, increases in a greater degree than most others and is both ornamental and odoriferous, it is no wonder that we meet with it in almost every garden, and that in abundance, flowering towards the end of April.[69]

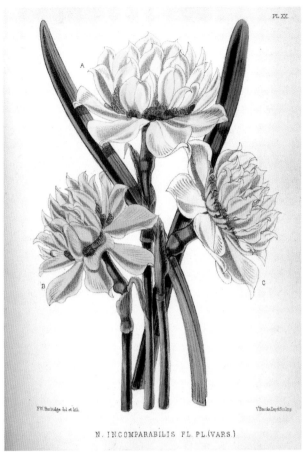

N. INCOMPARABILIS FL. PL.(VARS.)

Plate XX, N. Incomparabilis Fl. Pl. (Vars). Burbidge and Baker, *The Narcissus*, 1875. Courtesy of the Cherokee Garden Library, Kenan Research Center at the Atlanta History Center, Atlanta, Georgia.

For the Great Jonquil *N. × odorus,* Curtis noted the double form was often used for flowering in the parlor. He further commented: "We shall be thought, perhaps, too partial to this tribe of plants, this being the fifth [*Narcissus*] species now figured; but it should be remembered, that as the spring does not afford that variety of flowers which the summer does, we are more limited in our choice; the flowers of this delightful season have also greater claims, to our notice, they present themselves with double charms."[70]

While discussing the single flower N. incomparabilis (now *N. × incomparabilis*), of pale yellow petals and nectary inclined to orange, Curtis diverts onto a tangent discussing its double forms:

In its double Rate, it is well known to Gardeners, by the name of Butter and Egg Narcissus, and of this there are two varieties, both of which produce large shewy flowers, the one with colours similar to what we have above described, which is the most common, the other with petals of a pale sulphur colour, almost white, and the

Plate 51, Narcissus Major. Great Daffodil. *The Botanical Magazine*, 1788. Courtesy of the Cherokee Garden Library, Kenan Research Center at the Atlanta History Center, Atlanta, Georgia.

nectary bright orange; this, which is one of the most ornamental of the whole tribe, is named in the Dutch catalogues, the Orange Phoenix; its blossoms are so large as frequently to require supporting; its bulbs may be had of many of the Nurseries about London, and of those who, profiting by the supineness of our English Gardeners, import bulbs from abroad.[71]

Large trumpets may not have held as great a place in the English garden as one would assume. Plate 51, the Great Daffodil or N. major, suggests a less-desired status: "The present species of Daffodil is the largest of the genus, and bears the most magnificent flowers, but, though it has long been known in this country, it is confined rather to the gardens of the curious."[72] *N. moschatus* (presumably the flower now called *N. alpestris*) was known and traded, but not widely an object of desire. Meanwhile Curtis spoke favorably of *N. minor* (the Lesser or Winter daffodil) in 1793, but makes no reference to its garden inhabitance.

The dainty *N. tenuior* (now *N.* × *tenuior,* a jonquil wild hybrid) was relatively novel at the end of the 1700s; in 1794 Curtis observed it growing in the garden of the florist James Maddock, who had received it from Holland; "by the Dutch it appears to have been long cultivated."[73] It appears in the 1797 *Hortus Paddingtonensis* and the 1800 *Hortus Cantabrigiensis* (but not the 1796 catalog).

Of the delicate *N. triandrus* in 1794: "This species is found wild on the Pyrenean mountains; was an inhabitant of our gardens in the time of Parkinson (who has very accurately described it, noticing even its three stamina) to which, however, it has been a stranger for many years: it has lately been re-introduced, but is as yet very scarce. Our figure was taken from a specimen which flowered in Mr. Lee's Nursery at Hammersmith."[74] Others botanists commented occasionally on those daffodils considered to be (or possibly be) native English plants, *N. pseudonarcissus* in particular. James Sowerby noted in his *English Botany:* "The Narcissus Pseudo-narcissus, or common Daffodil, may be considered as one of the most beautiful native plants of this kingdom.... In the descriptions of rural poetry it has long been celebrated, and seldom fails to obtain an honourable mention amongst the opening beauties of the spring."[75]

N. bulbocodium appears as a minor bulb in English gardening literature; it was grown but just how widely may be debatable: "Grows spontaneously in Portugal; flowers in the open border about the middle of May, is an old inhabitant of our gardens, but, like the *triandrus,* is now become scarce, at least in the nurseries about London; in some gardens in Hampshire we have seen it grow abundantly."[76] In 1806 Curtis noted that N. bifrons (*N.* × *intermedius*) had long been cultivated in English gardens, with the leaves changing form from when they were first imported from Holland to after a few years in England.

These are the lists and sources one must rely on when speculating what daffodils were available to colonial gardeners or that were included in the general shipping lists of boxes of *Narcissus* sent in exchange for American plant material. The gardening bons mots of Curtis and others illustrate how many species known to the period were not as widely grown as often assumed. Thus many of the rarer daffodils described in the

Plate 38, Hybrid Narcissi. *Edwards's Botanical Register*, 1843. Rev. Dean Herbert provided the flowers of six crosses with respective parentage.

literature may appear in gardens of the dedicated gardener, but not much past that, while other daffodils, glossed over in period literature, were in actuality quite common.

Around the turn of the nineteenth century, botany as a scientific area of enquiry gained in popularity and credence, and many amateur and professional botanists were interested in bulbs, as evidenced by their early inclusion in *Botanical Magazine*. Some botanists sought to reclassify the genus Narcissus, and much discussion ensued as to whether many "species" were really species or in fact were (sterile) wild hybrids. It is answering this question that led to the creation of garden hybrid daffodils.

The inception of British hybridizing (or "raising") is credited to the botanist Honorable and Reverend (later Dean) William Herbert, the vicar of Chute Forest, who determined the best way to ascertain if a flower was a hybrid was to hybridize in nature's footsteps and evaluate the results. In 1837 he published his treatise *Amaryllidaceæ*, in which he reorganized and cleaned up the botanical daffodil list. He continued his contributions to the world of daffodils by publishing his results of daffodil hybridizing in *Edwards's Botanical Register* in 1843. He recounted his long experimentation with most species daffodils, and he thus was the first botanist to demonstrate hybrid *Narcissus* parentage by experimentally cross-pollinating different species daffodils, intimating that sterile hybrids are spread only by humans. Dean Herbert further encouraged the hybridizing of daffodils (conveniently omitting the fact that it takes many seedlings five to seven years to produce their first bloom): "It is desireable to call the attention of the humblest cultivators—of every labourer, indeed, or operator who has a spot of garden or a ledge in his window—to the infinite variety of Narcissi that may thus be raised, and most easily in pots, at his window, if not too much exposed to sun and wind, offering him a source of harmless and interesting amusement, and perhaps a little profit and celebrity."[77] Attracting much notice, Herbert's work encouraged the first wave of dedicated amateur hybridizers to pick up forceps and a camel-hair brush.

The first person to hybridize daffodils (other than tazettas) as a true passion was the Manchester stockbroker Edward Leeds, starting around 1843. His intention was to produce new forms of daffodils; he is credited with developing 193 cultivars until his death in 1877.[78] Leeds wrote of his obsession, "I think much remains to be done in the production of fine hybrids of this beautiful tribe of plants, and it may be mentioned, these are not ephemeral productions like many Florists' flowers, but will last for centuries with very little care, as the common kinds have done in our gardens."[79]

Leeds eventually gained company around 1855 with others amateurs, particularly the Darlington banker William Backhouse II. While a competent entomologist, Backhouse left his mark in hybridizing daffodils; he is credited with approximately 210 cultivars from 1856 to 1869. Of those, Backhouse felt only two flowers were worthy of receiving a name—'Emperor' and 'Empress'—all the rest he left with only numbers.

The critical event came in the early 1870s, as both Backhouse and Leeds were amateurs and so did not have the means to get their progeny "to market." To the rescue came Scotsman Peter Barr, a Covent Garden nurseryman with a singular passion for daffodils. Barr was utterly determined to make the British public appreciate the new daffodils just as he did.

In the 1860s and early 1870s, daffodils were decidedly not in favor with some of England's most respected garden "tastemakers," if not actually downright despised. The Duchess of Sutherland would order destroyed any found on her estate of Clivedon, much to her gardener's dismay.

But there was support for Barr's efforts in some quarters, including some British gardening magazines as well a small coterie of likeminded "daffodilians." *Floral Magazine* threw its weight behind Barr's efforts, reporting on his exhibitions at the Royal Horticulture Society in 1873:

> Amongst the oldest and most favourite of our spring flowers the Daffodil has always held a place, and although of late years it, like many other things, has had to give way to the modern system of gardening, we hope better days are in store for it. In order to give a little impetus to its growth, we have given an illustration of three varieties, and hope to add others at some future time.
>
> Mr. Barr, of the firm of Barr and Sugden, has given for years a thoughtful consideration to this family, and during last year exhibited at the Fortnightly Meeting of the Royal Horticultural Society, for nearly three months, groups of the various Narcissi as they came into bloom. Surprise at their beauty and variety was freely expressed.[80]

Barr set about collecting all the daffodils he could find. Barr had not made much progress on collecting up daffodils when he received a tip to visit a gentleman named W. P. Milner, which he did—and Milner showed him the daffodils given to him to

"Some New Daffodils." *The Garden*, 1879.

grow on by his late brother-in-law, William Backhouse. This, after a year or so, led to Barr's acquisition of some of William Backhouse's creations from his son, Charles Backhouse.

Near the end of his life, Leeds looked to sell his collection for 100 guineas. Barr sent out a letter on April 21, 1874, to parties he thought to be interested to "subscribe" for 10 guineas to the purchasing of Leeds's collection of twenty-four thousand bulbs. "We believe it will be a very good speculation and another thing, we believe that, if the collection is not very soon bought, it will be destroyed, as the old man has put it in his will, if not sold before his death, it is to be destroyed. Drop us a line."[81] Barr formed a syndicate of English amateurs and Dutch growers and asked the Dutch de Graaff Brothers firm (headed by S. A. de Graaff) to grow on his own stock.[82]

Barr took the Leeds and Backhouse collections, grew on the seedlings, and registered every good one that flowered. Barr later acquired the collection of Rev. John Gudgeon Nelson around 1882, who had collected all the old forms known in the seventeenth century, as well as some of the Leeds seedlings as he was one of Barr's original syndicate, and those Nelson raised himself. Barr thus consolidated almost all known original daffodil crosses and the stew of genetic material therein.

As Barr selected his newfound stocks of hybrids, he aggressively advertised his new daffodils in the 1870s and early 1880s. In the landmark work *The Narcissus: its history and culture with coloured plates and descriptions of all known*, respected botanist F. W. Burbidge quotes Peter Barr:

> The Narcissus is amongst the oldest and most beautiful of Spring flowering bulbous plants. It has for centuries been one of the highly-prized garden favourites, and has commanded in an unusual degree the attention of the scientific botanist. During epochs when artificial gardening has been in the ascendant, Narcissus, like many other charming flowers, has had to yield to the inexorable goddess of Fashion. At such times it has been saved from extinction by the fostering care of our Botanic Gardens, and of those enthusiastic amateurs who love flowers not for what they cost, but for their intrinsic beauty, and who, while they do not ignore new introductions, discard not their old friends, unless the new is an improvement upon the old. The Narcissus, however, like many another neglected flower, is now reasserting its position, and claiming its proper place in the general economy of border decoration, and as a cut flower for furnishing vases.[83]

While Barr addressed hybrid daffodils, the same revolution was underway botanically. While Burbidge's illustrated plates are beautiful in *The narcissus* (1875), it is the scientific review by J. G. Baker that set the new stage. Baker was keeper of the herbarium at Kew Gardens, and his scientific review of the entire genus *Narcissus* is considered the first version of the modern classification scheme. Baker arranged the genus into three main subdivisions that still stand today: magni-coronati, medio-coronati and parvi-coronati, interpreted at the time as "trumpet," "cup" and "saucer." Each division was then made up of various groups, some based on species that are still recognized and others based on hybrid daffodils resulting from specific crosses. Named in honor of various illustrious dignitaries in the world of the daffodil, some of these earlier, and no longer recognized, groups (later divisions) include Nelsoni, Incomparabilis, Barii, Leedsii, and Backhousei. However, the defining characteristics overlapped between classifications, creating dissatisfaction at the time. Even the early American daffodil enthusiast A. M. Kirby qualified his section Leedsii description with the phrase "as now understood."[84]

Supplement to THE GARDEN,
September 15th, 1906.

DAFFODILS :
PETER BARR (WHITE).
WEARDALE PERFECTION
(PALE YELLOW & WHITE).
MONARCH (DEEP YELLOW).

Hudson & Kearns, Printers, London.

"Daffodils: Peter Barr, Weardale Perfection, Monarch." *The Garden*, 1906.

The year 1884 is a watershed in the history of the daffodil. Barr and Baker's efforts resulted in the Royal Horticultural Society organizing the first Daffodil Conference. Barr felt that the public was finally seeing beauty in the heretofore despised flower, and by having F. W. Burbidge open the conference with a scientific paper, and with the influence of the RHS, success would be assured, and it was. The British daffodil craze was born.

At the conference a permanent committee was established to recognize new daffodil varieties and bestow awards on the most meritorious. Up until 1884 daffodils were given Latin names in a descriptive manner; for example "plenus" signifies the flower is a double. Unfortunately this led to confusion; there are still eight cultivars registered simply as 'Plenus' in the RHS' International Daffodil Register and Classified List, despite having very different appearances. To end some of this confusion, and make the names more sympathetic to the English ear, the RHS adopted a resolution during the Daffodil Conference that "garden varieties of narcissus, whether known hybrids or natural seedlings, should be named or numbered in the manner adopted by florists and not in the manner adopted by botanists."[85] So the new hybrid varieties were given English names, and Latin names were assigned only to species.[86]

Another singular event in 1884 was the publication of the first trade catalog devoted solely to daffodils. Published by William Baylor Hartland of Cork, Ireland, it offered eighty-four varieties of daffodils, not including polyanthus narcissus. A contemporary of Peter Barr and just as passionate about the daffodil, Hartland was considered the pioneer of the Irish daffodil, nearly making it the national flower of Ireland. His 1885 catalog provides a glimpse into the Victorian world of daffodils. *Papyraceus* (Unicolor Niveus) is noted as "most useful for bunching and wreath making, and for early forcing." Incomparabilis 'Cynosure' is "Most beautiful for wearing three blooms together in front of a dress, and one of the best on this account for cutting." Odoratus Rugulosus is "most excellent for sprays." "Double Roman" is "an excellent sort for forcing purposes, and grown in thousands by the market gardeners about London, for supplying Covent Garden market at Christmas with blooms." Moreover, "The pips of this latter [Double Roman] make excellent button-hole flowers."[87]

Hartland noted where flowers were raised, reflecting the newfound enthusiasm for daffodils in all their myriad of forms, from new hybrids to exotic species. Hartland's daffodils came from near and far, such as Gurnsey, the Scilly Isles, Cornwall, around London, southern France, Italy, the Netherlands, and Ireland. He described how forms of a given cultivar vary based on country of origin, usually Dutch, Irish or English but on occasion Scottish. One section header is "Moschatus or White Spanish Daffodils," for species and hybrid daffodils originating from Spain and Portugal. His bulbocodium species originated in Algiers, Spain, and southern France. One of Hartland's most lasting introductions is the diminutive Irish garden double 'Rip van Winkle'.

The venerable Dutchman E. H. Krelage, whom Barr called the "father of the bulb-growers," visited the Royal Horticulture Society daffodil show in 1885.[88] Reportedly he returned home and announced the daffodil to oust the hyacinth. The daffodil's position was cemented by the toast of English gardening society with the second Daffodil Conference in 1890.

Barr is credited with single-handedly putting daffodils on the gardener's list of acceptable flowers in Britain, and from there the rest of the world. Dubbed the "King," Barr made tireless efforts on behalf of the daffodil. Through Barr the daffodil came into its own. This newfound interest in daffodils and hybridizing new seedlings led to a veritable explosion in the number of cultivars available to the aficionado. The secretary of the Royal Horticulture Society, Rev. W. Wilks, marveled at how in 1879, when he set out to own every daffodil variety readily available through ordinary trade sources, he was whittling away at about fifty daffodils. By 1910 he was looking at a list of almost twenty-five hundred cultivars as issued by the RHS's Daffodil Committee, some commanding prices of £30 to £50.

These high prices were the product of an interesting development. A consortium of six wealthy daffodil lovers formed in the early 1900s, who conspired to buy up the bulbs of "any new variety of exceptional beauty and merit, . . . paying extravagant prices for the sole ownership of these coveted beauties, from $500 to $2,000 sometimes being expended by these enthusiasts for five or six bulbs. One of the compacts of this close club is that at the demise of any member, his or her bulbs are to be distributed among the remaining members of this monopoly."[89]

The late nineteenth to early twentieth century produced the next wave of hybridizing, primarily in the person of Rev. George Herbert Engleheart. Dubbed by one writer "the Father of the Modern Daffodil," with 727 introduced flowers, he was the first hybridizer to breed for the modern daffodil form now considered the standard. In 1889 he wisely predicted that the intense interest in daffodils was not a fad but would remain "an abiding habit of springtime."[90] His earliest creations emerged in the late 1890s in the forms of 'Albatross' (1891), 'Horace' (1894), 'Seagull' (1895), 'White Lady' (1897), and 'Will Scarlett' (introduced in 1895 but not in a commercial catalog until 1904), all still available today. Peter Barr reportedly stated the Engleheart flowers at the 1909 daffodil show at Birmingham, England, effectively forced those of Leeds and Backhouse into obscurity. And thus the modern daffodil was born.

2.

Daffodils in Early America, *1733 to 1820*

While everyone says in an offhanded way that the immigrants from England and Europe brought daffodils with them, it is much harder to prove. Written mention of narcissus, jonquils, and/or daffodils are few and far between. The assumption runs that because daffodils were in England, Holland, France, and Germany, then Dutch, British, French, and German colonists had them too, along with the other Dutch bulbs that warranted mention (tulips top of the list). Tantalizing evidence for daffodils in colonial gardens is found in written records of what colonists traded for, what nurserymen advertised in newspapers, and what the wealthy included in their plant orders.

By the (late) 1600s daffodils were well ensconced in the English flower repertoire, both of commoner and aristocrat, even if they weren't growing the same types of daffodils. The Dutch/Flemish were growing and selling polyanthus narcissus to the affluent, as evident from Sir Hanmer's garden, while commoners grew common daffodils in their gardens as per Parkinson (and later in the 1700s per Curtis). The French were giving special accommodation to bulbs in the pleasure garden and flower borders, so presumably French colonists had daffodils too—at least jonquils. Last, the Germans were some of the earliest avid bulb enthusiasts and so should have had daffodils as well.

In stark contrast most of America in the 1600s was a tough, or at least unpredictable, place to live. The Dutch, English, Swedish, French, and Spanish were still much at war with each other for New World land. The first three of the Anglo-Dutch Wars drug on from 1652 to 1674, and William Penn did not receive his land grant for Pennsylvania until 1681. Carolina's first settlement was founded in 1653; the province chartered in 1663; and its capital town, Charles Town (Charleston, South Carolina), established in 1670. Thus the two regions with stable populations for most of the 1600s were the Puritans in New England and Virginia. By the late 1600s, both Pennsylvania and Charleston had quickly become gardening meccas along with the great gardens of the first families of Virginia—coinciding with the widespread rise of gardening in England.

As life became more secure into the 1700s, particularly for the affluent, regional garden designs developed, while the modest in station had modest gardens. Broad, terraced gardens evolved in the mid-Atlantic colonies. Charleston, South Carolina, became known for its small urban parterre gardens of Dutch inspiration. New England developed its own version of Dutch parterre beds in its dooryard gardens (and rear gardens for the wealthy); there are two opinions as to what this garden style was. In the Chesapeake region, in first half of 1700s, intricate garden designs with intermixed plants were the preferred style, which then fell out of favor, to then return back strongly in 1790s. In eastern North Carolina, either simple rows of rectangular beds (a popular French garden design) or variations of the quincunx were the predominant garden forms. Later, as colonists cum Americans spread west into the frontier, they took their back-home gardening traditions, and flowers, with them. Meanwhile the French and Creole gardeners of Louisiana preferred rectangular or geometric parterres, often in a quincunx pattern. The raised, bordered beds facilitated drainage in the wet climate as well as helped with weed control.

The "naturalism" school of thought in garden design that swept Britain in the mid- to late 1700s (so much so that it is a plot vehicle in Jane Austen's *Mansfield Park*) started turning wealthy colonials' heads by the 1780s, but this new worldview was filtered by American realities and thus made a more modest impact on American's pleasure gardens. The New World was still plenty wild, so making one's hard-won plantation or estate more wild was not necessarily taken much to heart in some quarters. Winding roads and some curvature was acceptable, but most American pleasure gardens remained very formal, and that is where daffodils were planted.

After the Revolution and the depression of the late 1780s (which contributed to the establishment of the dollar), Americans became a bit more prosperous and looked to gardening as a way to establish their cultural independence and importance. And Europeans in the garden trade looked to create a new market to tap that newfound wealth of the emerging middle class and its sense of being. Traveling seedsmen from Europe came to hawk their wares, and not a few settled and established permanent nursery businesses. In *The American Gardener's Calendar* (1806), Bernard M'Mahon pitched the classical sensibility of Greek and Roman design to the new America, looking to gain its footing and prove its intellectual and cultural worthiness.

The year 1820 to end this period was chosen as much on economic grounds as because of changes in American gardening and the daffodils in them. The new landscape revolution from England (belatedly) was on the doorstep of America (best known in the person of Andrew J. Downing). Meanwhile the Panic of 1819, the issue of slavery, and the Monroe Doctrine of 1820 demarcated a change in American national mood as the Era of Good Feelings (marked by decrease in bitter partisanship and a rise in nationalism after the War of 1812), ended. Bankruptcies skyrocketed, and unemployment was severe. By 1823 the panic was over, and growth resumed in the national economy—and more money is always good for gardening.

Finally, after the era of Philadelphia nurseryman Bernard M'Mahon (who died in 1816), the offerings of daffodils in American catalogs underwent a profound shift, if not contraction. Many of the species daffodils offered in the late 1700s and early 1800s were never to be seen again in American catalogs until well after the Civil War, while the polyanthus narcissus (tazettas) become the dominant daffodil offering, and then primarily for parlor flowering.

Daffodils in Early America

Much of any colonist's time was spent on practical, subsistence activities. Kitchen gardens of necessity contained as many food and medicinal plants as could be accommodated. The Puritans shunned anything nonutilitarian in the garden, and while *Narcissus* had medicinal uses attributed to it in some early herbals, this apparently was insufficient to earn them a berth in the crowded New England kitchen garden as part of the medical plant repertoire.

Three herbals New England colonists relied on were the 1633 edition of John Gerard's *The Herball*, John Parkinson's *Paradisi in sole*, and Nicholas Culpeper's *The English Physician* (1653). Boston booksellers are thought to have probably sold Gerard's 1633 edition of *The Herball*; Parkinson's books are known to have been in the library of Harvard College president Leonard Hoar upon his death in 1678.

In modern daffodil lore, Gerard's "vertues" for the medicinal uses of daffodils are well recited, their uses so fanciful to today's expectations. All involve the crushing of the bulb—the leaves were not used—and most were plasters. Remedies ranged from "the root of the Narcissus, stamped with hony and applied plaister-wise, helpeth with them that are burned with fire, and joineth together fisures that are cut in sunder" and "helpeth the great wrenches of the ancles" to "helpeth Sun burning and the morphew."[1] The last use is what the daffodil is still known for today—as an emetic for inducing (violent) vomiting.

Parkinson, in his *Paradisi in sole*, paints a very different picture of the uses of the *Narcissus* genus and thus may provide a more accurate indication of the medicinal practices of 1600s England and explains why *Narcissus* are scarce in New England garden documentation: "The Vertues of Daffodils in generall.—Howsoever Dioscorides and others, doe give unto some of them speciall properties, both for inward and outward diseases, yet know I not any in these dayes with us, that apply any of them as a remedy for any griefe, whatsoever Gerard or others have written."[2] This view is supported by both Lawson's observations of "daffodowndillies" being more for ornament and by Culpeper's work, which makes no mention of any *Narcissus* in his herbal or in his subsequent *The English Physitian Enlarged* (1666) and its 369 medicines made of English herbs. This is not to say that daffodils did not appear in 1600s New England dooryard gardens but perchance explains why they are not discussed as one would expect (or rather hope), and don't appear in general until the 1700s, when gardening for pretty flowers was more socially acceptable and economically feasible.

Unfortunately the best-known earliest accounts of ornamental garden plants in 1600s America make no mention of any *Narcissus*. For all the well-known and now obscure common-named flowers Adrian van der Donck recited in his 1642 accounts of New Amsterdam, from gillyflowers to tulips and crown imperials to baredames and anemones, *Narcissus* are almost conspicuous by their absence (written 1655, see Denise Adams). Thomas Ashe, in his 1682 accounts of Carolina (primarily Charleston), noted of the inhabitants, "Their Gardens also begin to be beautified and adorned with such Herbs and Flowers which to the Smell or Eye are pleasing and agreable, viz. the *Rose, Carnation* and *Lilly*, &c."[3] One can speculate *Narcissus* were not far behind, but alas there is no proof to date. But this beginning of ornamental gardening coincides with its rise in England in the 1660s, after the Civil War, in a frontier town yet twelve years old. And while William Penn was busily planning his new town to provide gardens for his settlers, who, when they came, were inclined to garden, no mention has yet been encountered of *Narcissus* in Pennsylvania in its early decades of settlement. Jacob Bobart the Younger, keeper of the Oxford Physic Garden, sent to William Byrd I in Virginia tulips, anemones, iris, and crocus before 1684, for in that year they bloomed. Alas, even William Byrd's entry in his *London Diary* in 1721—"I went to see the Governor to beg that he spare me some bulbs for my garden"—is still not enough evidence to declare daffodils were in American gardens.[4] One tends to wonder if this isn't generally reflective of the lower status of *Narcissus* on the English totem pole as compared to Continental gardeners.

So although John Bartram remarked on the first colonists bringing the white double daffodil "Albus Plenus Odoratus" with them (presumably to Pennsylvania), suggesting back in the 1680s, this time frame is unfortunately conjecture. That "Albus Plenus Odoratus" was the flower brought across the sea is interesting, as other daffodils were reported to be more common in England, such as the two-floret "Primrose Peerless" (*N.* × *medioluteus*) or the wild/common English yellow trumpet daffodil (*N. pseudonarcissus*). It is very tempting to speculate these others were brought along but were deemed too common to warrant comment by Bartram, or anyone else (Dutch or British) for that matter. Alas, for now, the daffodils' place in American garden history begins in the 1700s, simply because this is when the earliest documentation in literature appears.

Daffodils make their appearance in colonial America in the 1730s, from Dutch-Anglo New York to Quaker Pennsylvania to English North Carolina. The early preference for doubles and polyanthus narcissus applied to colonists as well as to the British and Dutch.

Alice Morse Earle, an early American historical garden writer, may have identified the earliest colonial appearance of the genus *Narcissus* in the circa 1731 portrait of Pierre van Cortlandt (1721–1814) as a child in New Amsterdam (housed at the Brooklyn Museum). On the floor next to the child is a very large vase filled with cut spring flowers, which she identifies as "Tulip, Convolvulus, Harebell, Rose, Peony,

Plate 193, Narcissus Angustifolius. Narrow-Leaved Narcissus.
The Botanical Magazine, 1793. Courtesy of the Cherokee Garden
Library, Kenan Research Center at the Atlanta History Center,
Atlanta, Georgia.

Narcissus, and Flowering Almond." She then elaborates, "and it is the pleasure of the present mistress of the manor, to see that the garden still holds all the great-grandfather's flowers."[5] If Ms. Earle is correct, the "narcissus" would be *N. poeticus* in the center of the spray. The Van Cortlandt Manor garden survived into the early 1900s; a photograph shows small circular flower beds within the larger garden room.

Isaac Norris Sr. (1671–1735), after decades of constructing an elaborate agricultural estate near Philadelphia, turned to ornamental gardening in his waning years. In 1733 he expanded into beekeeping and noted flowers in his formal garden, making notes in his almanacs. That year he recorded tulips, daffodils, double larkspur, poppies, wall-flowers, pinks, and Persian iris.

In 1737 the North Carolina physician John Brickell published *The Natural History of North Carolina*. A member of a prominent family, he was known to be practicing medicine in Edenton around 1731. Brickell updated and expanded on a well-known earlier history of the colony, John Lawson's *History of North Carolina*, published in 1714 but based on travels dating around 1700. Although in the past Brickell was maligned as simply having copied Lawson, this is fortuitously not quite so, for Brickell's observant eye and cataloging temperament added to Lawson's account: in "Of the Corn of Carolina," he inserted the observations, "*Strawberries* are in such Plenty in the Season, that they are Feeding for Hogs; *Narcissus, Daffodil, Snow-Drops, Wall-Flowers, Bloodwort,* the red and white *Lillie, Stargrass,* which is used with good Success in most Fevers in this Country."[6]

Brickell lamented the nascent state of the pleasure garden: "The Pleasure Gardens of *North Carolina,* are not yet arrived to any great perfection, or Adorned with many beautiful fragrant Flowers; there being only some few *Rose-Trees, Bead-Trees, Orange-Trees, Clove Gilly-Flower, Pinks* of several sorts, *Sweet-William, Cowslips, Lavender-Spike,* and *Lavender-Cotton, Violets, Princess-Feather, Tres-Colores;* and such like."[7]

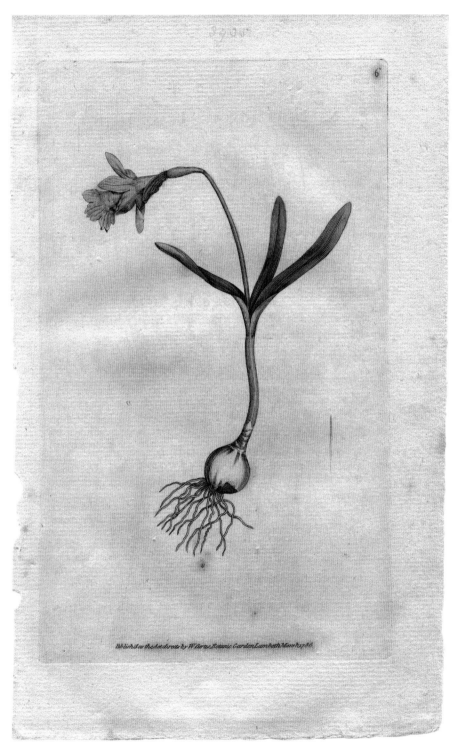

Plate 6, Narcissus minor. Least Daffodil. *The Botanical Magazine*, 1787. Courtesy of the Cherokee Garden Library, Kenan Research Center at the Atlanta History Center, Atlanta, Georgia.

These disparate descriptions tempt speculation that the former was for the commoner and the second for the wealthy landowner.

Throughout the mid-1700s American colonial plants enthusiasts maintained a steady stream of correspondence between themselves and their British and European comrades, trading bulbs, plants, seeds, and trees between gardens and continents. Glimmers of the numbers of daffodils trading about the colonies and between the continents survive in these letters, scattered among the frittilaries, hyacinths, tulips, martagons, atamasco, pancratium, and whatever else there was to be shared. These exchanges are invaluable for establishing dates of introductions for plant material when the correspondents are specific in naming the flowers at hand (or wished to be had at hand).

The best-known (and best-documented) surviving discussions are found in the letters between John Bartram in Philadelphia, Colonel John Custis of Williamsburg, and Peter Collinson of London (one of both men's English providers and coenthusiasts), starting in the mid-1730s. Another early member of this circle was Dr. Christopher Witt, who established an early botanical garden in Germantown near Philadelphia. Unfortunately little direct correspondence with Dr. Witt, or description of his garden, survives. Charlestonian gardeners join the historical daffodil-swapping record by the 1750s. While colonial plant enthusiasts maintained a steady stream of correspondence among themselves and with European comrades, the letters between these three provide the best sense of the number of *Narcissus* plying the Atlantic waters as part of the plant and tree exchanges between Europe and America.

Peter Collinson began shipping bulbs and other plants to John Bartram in 1735; his first box contained cyclamens, squills, peonies, gladiolus, snowdrops, colchicum, hyacinths, anemonies, lilies, tulips, and other flowers. The two Quakers traded plants until Collinson's death in 1768.

In Collinson's correspondence and shipment of August 12, 1737, to John Bartram, he wrote: "Root of Little Narcissus [most likely *N. minor* from Spain] will not flower freely with us because it is not hott enough plant at once as close as can be to the South side of the House or Wall & cover with Pea straw in Winter I doubt not but it will flower freely with you it is a fine flower."[8] In September 1739 Collinson shipped Bartram his allotment of Collinson's beloved polyanthus narcissus: "and some Narcis polyantris Sett them in a Warm place and protect from your Severe Cold—Cover them over very High with Dryed leaves Docr witt Loss't his by your Cold Weather so take Care and find them every protection for they are Choice flowers."[9] So Collinson had already trialed his favored tazettas with Dr. Witt and found them to be problematic from being cold-tender. This was confirmed by Bartram in November of 1761, when he complained to Collinson that neither his polyanthus nor his polyanthus narcissus bloomed well.[10]

On October 20, 1740, Collinson shipped Bartram another box of bulbous roots: "Inclosed is the Mate's Receipt for a box of Bulbs directed for thee—Make Much of them for they are such a Collection as is Rarely to be met with all att once For all the Sorts of Bulbous Roots being taken up this year, there is some of Every sort. There is above twenty sorts of *Crocus*—as many of *Narcissus*—all our sorts of Martagons and

Lilies—with *Gladiolus, Ornithogalums,* Moleys & *Irises*—with many others I now don't Remember, wch Time will show Thee."[11]

In June of 1741, Bartram shared narcissus and hyacinths with Peter Bayard of New York, so presumably his fall shipment of bulbs had multiplied sufficiently to have some to spare: "he promised to take them to Elizabeth town point & send them to thee or word where thay are left for thee thay Consist of A fine variety of double & breeding tulups of ye baget primors with curious hyacinths & Narcissus these are loos in ye box ye large round bulbs are hyacinths ye other kinds are lapt in perticular papers with thair names writ upon each respective paper; I think now I have fuly performed what I promised; thay are such a Curious collection as I never received nor can ever expect from any stranger."[12]

While the known large shipments of *Narcissus* were early in the plant swapping, it is only later that actual names appear in the correspondence, giving some inkling of what was actually in the boxes. When Collinson changed residences in England, moving to Ridgeway House in the Quaker stronghold of Mill Hill, he naturally took his garden with him but alas lost plants in the transition. But his loss is our gain, as he writes about his losses when asking for assistance purchasing replacement stock. He wrote to John Fredericus Gronovius of Leiden (a financial backer of Carl Linnaeus and the publisher of *Flora Virginica* 1739–1743) in 1751:[13]

> Pray if opportunity offers Buy the plants as under for Mee & send by any Friend:
>   4 Roots of Geele Franse Roos Narcissus
>   4 Roots of Narcis campanelle flo Luteo Reflexo
>   4 Do–of–Camp–flo Albo reflexo
>   1 D–of Moly purpureo Major
>   2 Narcisus Nana Minor–2 Stvven Stuck
>   2 Ranunculus flo plantagines
>   12 Duc Vanloe Tulips
> This I had formerly from Van Hassen but in removing my garden lost them. All the Charges I will repay with thanks.[14]

That Collinson had grown and lost both a yellow and a white strain of *N. triandrus* (Narcis campanelle flo Luteo and Albo Reflexo) by 1750, commented to be rare by Curtis in 1789, raises the question whether that is one of the *Narcissus* he sent to his colonial botanist kith and kin. Or was this one of the rare ones that he would not share? The "Narcissus Nana Minor" is likely *N. minor,* and the same flower as what Collinson sent Bartram in 1737. The "Geele Franse Roos Narcissus" sounds quite like "yellow French Rose" narcissus, and so the coveted double of Robinus of Paris—'Eystettensis'.

One of Charleston's famous lady gardeners, Martha Daniell Logan (1704–1779), provides additional glimpses of the daffodils plying the transatlantic trade in her correspondence to John Bartram. One of Charleston's many plant enthusiasts, and its second woman gardener of note after Mrs. Lamboll, she traded plants and seeds with John

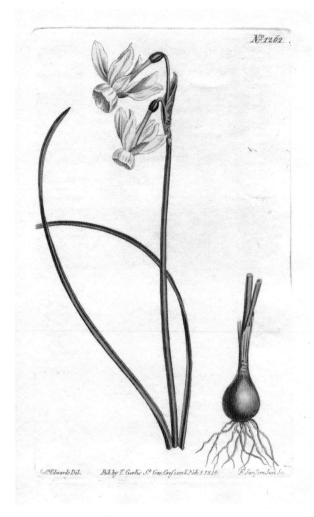

Plate 1262, Narcissus Triandrus, v. Luteus. Yellow Reflexed-Flowered Narcissus. *Curtis's Botanical Magazine*, 1810.

Bartram and other Charlestonians, even running a commercial garden and issuing her own "Gardener's Kalendar" in 1751. Logan especially liked double flowers, likely not an uncommon preference of the day. She also requested a number of white flowered bulbs; whether this was to simply get one of everything possible or a real preference for white flowers is a pleasant speculation for the likeable lady gardener. In an undated letter, written around 1760, Logan requested from Bartarm trees, shrubs, flowers, and bulbs, including:[15]

> White Crocusts
> grape Hyacinth (blue),
> Chine and Turkey pinks, Caldonian Iris
> Guise [?] Narciss, Double White. Sweet-scented Cyprus narciss, Tuby roses[16]

On December 20, 1760, Logan wrote Bartram: "I was so unluckey this Last Summer to Loose all the Roots of my Ranunculists, anemoneys, Tulips, and fine Double Hyacinths, by Laying them in a Closit to Dry after they weire taken up, for the mice Devoured them before I had a thought of it."[17] If she had dug and dried her daffodils, she would probably have not complained, as the poisonous bulbs are avoided by rodents.

Her correspondence and wish lists not only expand the list of daffodils in the colonies, but also illuminate how bulbs were obtained. In her February 20, 1761 letter, she enquired of Bartram; "When you favour me againe with a line Pray be so kinde to tell me whither the following Roots are to be Purchased with you as the Passage is so much Shorter I should Chuse it Rather than Sending to England for them Such as Tulips. Ranunculists. Anemonyes Narcissus, Hyacinths & Horsenecks, The Last named & a little Seed or Slips of the Tree you Call the Snowball is what I am particularly Desirous of & they are not to be had from England for I have Sent for them In several of my Lists but Never gott one. I find they Doe very well with us, for Doctor Garden has a good many roots Now bluming."[18]

Three days later (on February 23, 1761), the same Dr. Alexander Garden wrote to John Bartram: "N. B. I should be much obliged to you for some Hyacinths, some Narcissus with the longest Nectariums—we call these Horsenecks. I have one or two Persian irises that blossom beautifully. If you could spare some more I should be glad of them or any other bulbous root."[19] Shortly thereafter, on June 17, 1761, Garden added, "Pray remember to let me have some of your fine Bulbs especially Hyacinths, & the Daffodil with the large long pinched nectatium & whatever else you please."[20] Logan and Dr. Garden were gardening friends, and Logan had Bartram sending parcels to Dr. Garden for her, until she requested Bartram begin sending packages to her son John Logan, as "Dr. Garden has so much business he has not time to Think of me."[21] So is Dr. Garden asking Bartram for Horsenecks for Logan? And if he has so many, why isn't the good Doctor Garden sharing with poor Mrs. Logan?

The English botanist Richard Anthony Salisbury resided at Ridgeway House in Mill Hill with Collinson's garden for seven years, in the early 1800s

Plate 1300, Narcissus Moschatus. Smaller White Spanish Daffodil. *Curtis's Botanical Magazine*, 1810.

—approximately thirty years after Collinson's death (in 1768). In his marathon presentation to the Horticultural Society of London, given over three monthly meetings in 1812, Salisbury often discussed the growth habits of bulbs and plants at "Mill Hill." Occasionally he indicated if something was left from Collinson's original plantings (either in the garden proper, the terrace or in the field below the terrace), but other times he was not so specific. Parsing Salisbury's observations with some care, one begins to grasp more fully what Collinson had in his garden that he probably wasn't sharing.

According to Salisbury's comments, two different white trumpet daffodils survived in the garden from Collinson's day. Salisbury, while discussing *N. × poculiformis* (called by Salisbury Queltia Poculigera; it is a wild hybrid of *N. moschatus*), commented "I have seen it in . . . and Mr. Peter Collinson's, Mill Hill."[22] The other white trumpet harkens back to the ever-conundrum of two white trumpets—*N. cernuus* and *N. tortuosus*: "I found it in the field at Mill Hill, where the seeds ripen every year, but in the borders

PL. VIII

F.W.Burbidge del et lith   V.Brooks,Day & Son, Imp.

N. PSEUDO-NARCISSUS VAR. CERNUUS.

Plate VIII, N. Pseudo-Narcissus Var. Cernuus. *The Narcissus*, Burbidge and Baker, 1875. Courtesy of the Cherokee Garden Library, Kenan Research Center at the Atlanta History Center, Atlanta, Georgia.

of the garden, which was nearer the gravel, very seldom."[23] (Salisbury's discussion of *N. moschatus* immediately prior makes no mention of surviving flowers at Mill Hill; the Cernuus-Tortuosus flower's trumpet is straw-colored for the first day or two, then presumably pales to white.)

Harkening to Collinson's comment that his favorites were the tribe of polyanthus narcissus, Salisbury noted for Narcissus orientalis, "I found it in the borders at Mill Hill, where it had increased prodigiously, and often ripened seeds."[24] Salisbury noted the presence of *N. pseudonarcissus* at Mill Hill, but does not explicitly state these to be affiliated with Collinson's former garden or found at some other part of the village. Alas Salisbury made no indication of finding *N. triandrus, N. minor,* or any doubles.

One of the most cited and quoted exchanges regarding daffodils in colonial America is between Collinson and Bartram. In 1763 Collinson wrote to Bartram of his great delight in finally finding the white double daffodil now often known as "Albus Plenus Odoratus" (real name 'Plenus'). Collinson wrote to John Bartram, August 4, 1763:

2 years for the Double White Daffodil—Think Man & know how to Value so great a Rarity, for I waited almost all my Lifetime for to get this rare flower, I Read of It & Seen It figur'd in Books, but despaired of ever Possessing It—Butt about seven years ago Happening in a Tour forty Miles from London my Botanic Genius carried Mee into a Garden where I expected to find Nothing—on a Sudden my Eyes was ravished with the Sight of this flower & my Heart leaped for Joy—that I should find it as last—and never saw it since in any Garden but my own and I tell thee for thy Comfort—If thou had not been John Bartram, thou hadst not Possessed such a Rarity.[25]

Bartram replied on October 23, 1763: "If I had known the white double daffodil had been such A rarity with thee I could have sent thee large quantities 30 years ago our first settlers brought them with them & thay multiply so that thousands is thrown away thay rarely perfect thair flowers with us thay send forth A stalk A foot long with the appearance of A fine large flower but not one in A hundred opens but rots or disolves to A slime but last spring one or two of mine did perfect its large sweet flower which I compaired with thine."[26]

In the final exchange, Collinson wrote back Bartram on January 1, 1764: "I perceive what Thou calls the Double Sweet Daffodil—Wee call the Sweet White Narcis that indeed may be common butt yet how could I know It. remove & part the Roots, every other year & they will blow strong & fine —but Lett them grow in great Numbers together—the Roots are weaken'd & rarely bring their flowers to perfection."[27]

A likely answer to this conundrum of how a rare plant for Collinson near London was a veritable weed for Bartram in Philadelphia comes from Sir Hanmer's *Garden Book* of 1660: "*Double White*, it is sweet, and the leaves [petals] are pure white, and lye round and orderly. It is common enough in some parts of England."[28] Regrettably the Baronet does not indicate what parts of England these are, but presumably some colonists came from such locales and took their common enough double whites with them across the Atlantic.[29]

Plate XLIII, N. Poeticus Fl. Pl. (Albus Plenus Odoratus or 'Plenus'). Burbidge and Baker, *The Narcissus*, 1875. Courtesy of the Cherokee Garden Library, Kenan Research Center at the Atlanta History Center, Atlanta, Georgia.

Bartram and Dr. Witt were not always happy with their cohort in crime, as they often felt Collinson kept the best for himself and sent them the common trifles. One such exchange was more specific than others: "this puts me in mind of Doctor witts common saying that you send us all ye worst & will not let us have ye rare ones."[30] In May of 1763, Bartram complained "of the roots thee sent me two years past I had one

PL. XLI.

N. BIFLORUS.

Plate XLI, N. Biflorus (*N.* × *medioluteus*). Burbidge and Baker, *The Narcissus*, 1875. Courtesy of the Cherokee Garden Library, Kenan Research Center at the Atlanta History Center, Atlanta, Georgia.

tulip flower A pale yellow & the common double daffodil after long expectation of something curious."[31] Perchance a valid complaint after a glimpse of what Collinson ordered for his own garden. This also illustrates the trials of plant swapping in how long it took for plants to settle in and bloom, if not just survive.[32]

A lesser known document of daffodils comes from the daily gentleman's journal kept by Virginia lawyer and planter John Mercer (1704–1768, uncle of George Mason). In 1766 Mercer recorded the appearances of his garden's ornamental inhabitants at Marlborough. Members of the genus *Narcissus* appear on numerous days, indicating multiple varieties in the garden. A number of plant entries are qualified by an abbreviation for color or form, such as "Tulips early," "Hacinth dr. purp.," and so on, which lends the last *Narcissus* entry all the more import:

1766 March	April
21—Daffodil	16—Gumbogia
Hyacinths b.	Apples
Violet	Daffodil
22—Narcissus	Gooseberry
Almond	22—Jonquil
Apricot	28—Iris la.v blue
	Narcissus w.[33]

Five sorts of *Narcissus* is a great number by any colonial gardener. And a late-blooming white Narcissus is either *N. poeticus* or the elusive Primrose Peerless *N.* × *medioluteus*—now a very common flower in Tidewater Virginia, and there a later bloomer than *N. poeticus*.[34]

Parlor Gardening

Bulbs were grown indoors to brighten the winter months, extending the spring season by upward of four months until they "blowed" in the garden in the spring. Little is mentioned of colonists growing *Narcissus* per se indoors, but other tangential recounts give clues as to what Americans were doing. Of interest is that more accounts come after 1800; it may have taken some time for the fashion (or extravagance?) to spread.

While visiting in Portugal, Boston resident Sir Charles Henry (Harry) Frankland wrote copiously in his journal in the spring of 1755 on "Remarks on Flowers," emanating from Mr. Coles (from whom per one entry he received flower roots). On the page for the week of March 24–30, 1755, Sir Frankland recorded: "From Mr. Coles Remarks— When the Hyacinth is done blowing in the water, you must carefully take it out and without cutting the Pavis, put it into the Earth for about till the Leaves are dry and wither'd. Then take the root up or it will and at the proper season of the year plant it. Before you plant it in order to increase the Root, cut it spiral

Plate 1298, Narcissus Orientalis. Pale-Cupped White Garden Narcissus. *Curtis's Botanical Magazine*, 1810. *Curtis's Botanical Magazine* illustrated two versions of essentially the same flower ('Grand Primo Citronière,' Plates 946 and 1298) with slightly different petal shapes, demonstrating how subtle variations existed and (still exist) within both wild and early hybrid tazettas.

or as directed in my last year's mom book—it will not produce any flowers that year but the root will be greatly increased."[35] So contrary to usual assumption, forced bulbs were not always discarded.

In his *The American Gardener's Calendar* (1806), the great Philadelphia nurseryman Bernard M'Mahon discussed growing polyanthus narcissus, hyacinths, and other bulbs in bulb-glasses for the month of January, giving instructions on how to speed up bloom by placing in the hothouse or to retard the blooming times as desired. He also gave directions for growing in pots hyacinths, spring crocuses, snowdrops, dwarf Persian irises, and polyanthus narcissus, and for forcing earlier bloom times by placing potted bulbs in the hothouse.[36]

Boston merchant Kirk Boott emigrated from Derby, England, in 1783 and remained a bit of an Anglophile all his life, even in his love of plants. He wrote to his sister Eliza and to friends back in Derby for plants, including gooseberries, vegetables, and bulbs. He wrote Eliza on December 16, 1805, that bulbs from an English friend were already "shooting above the earth"; Boott also grew bulbs for winter blooming in his long lean-to greenhouse. On June 10, 1809, he wrote Eliza: "Our chief pleasure is in our family and among our flowering plants. Flora has decked our parlor windows for four months past in the most gay and beautiful manner. She is now about transferring her beauties to the open garden. I have more than one hundred rose trees of the best kinds just bursting into bloom. . . . From the first dawn of vegetation I have had a succession of flowers. The modest Snowdrop, the golden Crocus, Daffodils, Narcissus, Hyacinths, Cowslips, Tulips, etc. Those from Derby never blow but with the most pleasing association of ideas."[37] A more pedestrian accounting of indoor bulb growing comes from one of America's early polymaths. Around Philadelphia in 1816, C. S. Rafinesque kept a journal of "the progress of vegetation"; one entry read: "March 12. Seen in blossom, at the windows, *Narcissus tazzetta, N. janguilla* [*sic*], and several saffrons, genus *Crocus, &c.*"[38] On April 22, he observed *N. pseudonarcissus* and *Sedum ternatum* naturalized near Gray's Ferry, the site of a large public pleasure garden.

Daffodils in the Pleasure Garden

Not all *Narcissus* were created equal. Polyanthus narcissus as a florists' flower, jonquils and particularly double jonquils, and the not-so-common doubles were viewed differently by the colonial gardening world than were the common daffodils, presumably of the commoner's garden. John Bartram's complaint of waiting years for the common double reflects this multifaceted view of what we now consider a rather monolithic genus of flower. The bias against commoners' flowers (and commoners' daffodils) was longstanding in England. The disparity of comparative gardening worth of *Narcissus* was commented on in particular with the "Primrose Peerless" (*N. × medioluteus*). Clusius informs us, that in his days this species was supposed to grow wild in England; but Parkinson says he could never hear where, though "so common in all country gardens, that we scarce give it place in our more curious parks."[39] Thus Dutch florists flowers, in this case polyanthus narcissus as reflected in their popularity and dominance in catalogs, were a status symbol on one hand, while other daffodils save jonquils and (some?) doubles were commoners' flowers not worthy of mention.

The preferred florists' flower of the colonial day was of course tulips. Many a wealthy Bostonian is known to have imported Dutch bulbs, tulips top of the list. Boston merchant Thomas Hancock, uncle of John Hancock, was a garden-proud man and well known for his tulips, which he ordered through his London agent around 1740. In the 1750s Sir Charles Henry (Harry) Frankland ordered daffodils and tulips for his famous love, Agnes Surriage. Sir Harry, the royally appointed collector of the Port of Boston and a baronet of the English aristocracy, notoriously fell in love with the lowly, scruffy bar maid, in what was colonial America's closest thing to a true Cinderella story.

Syd. Edwards del. Pub. by T. Curtis, St Geo: Crescent May.1.1806. F Sansom sculp.

Plate 925, Narcissus Tazetta. Polyanthus Narcissus. *Curtis's Botanical Magazine*, 1806.

Sir Harry Frankland's journal writings reflected a view of daffodils common to educated gardeners—only jonquils and "Narcissus de Bouquet" (a French-origin tazetta) are discussed. On the page for the week of April 7–13, 1755, Frankland noted that the roots of ranunculus and anemones should be planted three inches deep, while jonquils and narcissus were to be planted at twice that depth.[40] Earlier (week March 31–April 6, 1755) Frankland entered the reminder to tie the jonquils to sticks when blooming.[41] Almost as a reminder, Frankland squeezed in the bottom of the page for April 14–20, 1755:

For Borders 3 feet wide
Persian Ranunculus, Narcissus
Jonquils   en Bouquet
Red Tansey, Yellow Do., Belladona
                    Lilly[42]

As an almost random aside, in between his invoices and a recipe for Portuguese white washing in May of 1755, Frankland jotted that the "Narcissus en Bouquet" came from the town of Caen in Normandy.[43]

A German traveler's perspective comes to us from Johann David Schöpf in 1783, evidencing again a tastemaker's preferences:[44]

The taste for gardening is, at Philadelphia as well as throughout America, still in its infancy. There are not yet to be found many orderly and interesting gardens. Mr. Hamilton's near the city is the only one deserving special mention. Such neglect is all the more astonishing, because so many of the people of means spend the most part of their time in the country. Gardens as at present managed are purely utilitarian—pleasure-gardens have not yet come in, and if perspectives are wanted one must be content with those offered by the landscape, not vary various, what with the still immense forests.[45]

The taste for garden-flowers is likewise very restricted: however, a few florists are to be found. Dr. Glentworth, formerly a surgeon in the army, has a numerous collection of beautiful bulbs and other flowers which he maintains by yearly importations from Holland. But as a rule one finds in the gardens nothing but wild jasmine, flower-gentles, globe-amaranths, hibiscus syriacus, and other common things.[46]

William Hamilton himself provides another hint of the disparate views held of daffodils—not just a florists' flower worthy of special treatment in the pleasure gardens of the wealthy, nor the "common daffodils" sniffed at by Bartram, but also as a stalwart flower that may be in the workhorse stable of basic herbaceous perennials. Hamilton was friends with his nearby neighbors William and John Bartram and traded plants with them.

In a letter to his secretary Benjamin H. Smith in 1785, Hamilton detailed his intentions for his estate the Woodlands, as he toured Europe studying the architecture and landscapes of great estates: "Nor should a plantation be neglected of the different hardy perennial plants such as yucca, corn-flag (gladiola), lilies, french honeysuckle, foxglove, Lily-of-the-Valley (Bush Hill), paeonies, columbines, hollyhocks, polyanthus, jonquils (from Bush Hill), hyacinths, &c."[47] Bush Hill (built circa 1740) was the main estate of the Hamilton family, so the implication is that Hamilton already has access to jonquils at Bush Hill and wished to transplant some to Woodlands. This also hints at a special regard given to jonquils, parallel to but distinct from polyanthus narcissus, likely due to their fragrance and greater cold tolerance/robustness in the garden. Jonquils have long tended to be held in a class apart, because of their strong, distinctive fragrance. This held into the late nineteenth century, as some American seedsmen gave jonquils their own category in their catalogs, separate from the Narcissus or Daffodil.

Jonquils

For all the species jonquils documented by botanists, a simple handful has dominated gardens from the late 1500s onward. Often, however, even these few are lumped simply as "jonquils" or "double jonquils." Single jonquils are either *N. jonquilla* or *N.* × *odorus*, albeit many forms of *N.* × *odorus* have been considered separate species over the centuries (particularly "calathinus"). The double forms of these similarly have ebbed and flowed but primarily come down to one double form of *N. jonquilla* ('Flore Pleno') and two double forms of *N.* × *odorus* ('Plenus')—and one of those much less frequently found in gardens. Further the *N. jonquilla* double was found to not be very robust in the open garden in northern climates. This is not to say that distinct strains of these species were not involved, as they most likely were—reflecting what mountainside in which country they were originally dug from.

Plate XL, N. Jonquilla. Burbidge and Baker, *The Narcissus*, 1875. Courtesy of the Cherokee Garden Library, Kenan Research Center at the Atlanta History Center, Atlanta, Georgia.

Jonquils (continued)

In an article on double daffodils, the *Narcissus* species expert Burbidge remarked that the double of *N. jonquilla* "bears two or three golden yellow fragrant flowers on a slender, deep glossy green scape, the individual blossoms being considerably smaller than those of N. odorus and more pleasing in form. It is a common and well-known plant in gardens. . . . Of this plant [N. odorus] there are two well-marked double-flowered forms not unfrequently met with in old-fashioned gardens. One has double Rose-shaped flowers, two or even three on a scape, of clear golden yellow colour, made up of coronal and periath segments. This form, which is by no means scarce, may often be seen at Covent Garden and other flower markets in the shape of cut flowers. In another form, more rarely met with, the duplication is confined almost entirely to the perianth segments, as is the case with Herbert's N. Eystettensis. . . . The double varieties of N. odorus are popularly known as Queen Anne's Jonquil"[48]

The federal era was a golden one, of sorts, for daffodils. American gardeners of taste evidence a greater savvy in their daffodil orders, choosing more esoteric and refined plants. This may be in part due to the expansion of botanical interest in Britain particularly in bulbs and then daffodils—harkening to Curtis's not very apologetic apology for showcasing so many *Narcissus* in his early issues (roughly two per issue for the first four years). Irrespective of the refined selections, tazettas, jonquils, and doubles remained the daffodils of choice.

In creating his horticultural masterpiece of Middleton Place near Charleston, South Carolina, Henry Middleton placed a seed order in the early 1800s. Included in his large order (well into the hundreds of items) of perennials, herbs, vegetables, hothouse plants, and bulbs were a few *Narcissus*. But not just the usual "polyanthus narcissus" and a handful of "double jonquils"—these are specified by botanical name:

> Narcissus tazetta
> Narcissus majolis, fl. pleno
> Narcissus incomparabiles, fl. pleno
> Narcissus major fl. pleno
> Narcissus poeticus
> Narcissus minor[49]

Three of these were in early Curtis volumes. *Narcissus minor* warranted a high place in the pantheon as Plate No. 6 in Curtis's first volume in 1790. Narcissus major flore pleno was mentioned in passing by Curtis in his entry for Narcissus Major (Volume 2, Plate 51, 1790), and the discussion of the N. incomparabilis doubles by Curtis was lengthy in volume 4 issued in 1791. Of note is the interest in N. majolis flore pleno. Narcissus majalis was a distinct poet species per Curtis in Plates 193 and 197 published in 1792, but no discussion of a double form; it is possible Middleton is looking for "Albus Plenus Odoratus" but under a new scientific name. The others—*N. tazetta* and *N. poeticus*—were well-known flowers of the day. Attesting to Middleton's gardening eye, these flowers span the daffodil blooming season with two early-season flowers (*N. minor* and *N. tazetta*), two midseason bloomers (N. incomparabiles flore pleno and N. major flore pleno), and two late bloomers (*N. poeticus* and possibly N. majolis flore pleno). Conspicuous by their absence are jonquils.

From Boston to Charleston, wealthy colonists imported Dutch bulbs to grace their gardens and impress the townsfolk, cementing their status in the process. But there was a fly in the ointment. While under British rule, the American colonies were subject to the Navigation Acts. These were passed by Parliament beginning in 1651 to ensure the wealth of the colonies remained directed to the royal coffers and was not lost to rival countries by

N. INCOMPARABILIS FL. PL (VARS.)

Plate XXI, N. Incomparabilis Fl. Pl. (Vars). Burbidge and Baker, *The Narcissus*, 1875. Courtesy of the Cherokee Garden Library, Kenan Research Center at the Atlanta History Center, Atlanta, Georgia.

direct trade. Thus all trade was to be conducted via ships under the British flag or on ships manned by a three-quarters British crew. Further trade from another country bound for British colonies was to be processed (and taxed) through Britain's home ports first. Thus any shipment from Dutch sources should have been routed through British ports, adding voyage time and taxation expense.

For daffodils English nurserymen may have been growing their own stock, but in the mid-1700s for polyanthus narcissus they were most likely just middlemen, at least per Philip Miller. While English nurserymen offered daffodils by the 1760s, period colonial writers are usually specific about the bulbs coming from Holland, an obvious statement of status. By the late 1700s to early 1800s, English florists were raising polyanthus narcissus for the cut flower trade, but to date there is no particular evidence that they were growing on tazetta seeds for the bulb trade. For bulbs, the source was

F.W.Burbidge del. et lith

V.Brooks Day & Son.Imp

N. ODORUS FL. PL.

Plate XXVI, N. Odorus Fl. Pl. (Queen Anne's double Jonquilla). Burbidge and Baker, *The Narcissus*, 1875. Courtesy of the Cherokee Garden Library, Kenan Research Center at the Atlanta History Center, Atlanta, Georgia.

still the Dutch, as noted in 1812 by botanist Sydenham Edwards: "All the different principal sorts may be procured from the seedsmen in London, who import them for sale from Holland, where they are raised in large quantities."[50] Thus, while in the literature there is often a simple blanket statement of gardens having or gardeners ordering Dutch bulbs, many specific archival references indicate gardeners ordered from British sources.

In a South Carolina/Charleston newspaper, in December 1754 Capt. Thomas Arnott advertised that he had brought a box of "*Tulip, Narcissus,* and other FLOWER ROOTS" from England, "Supposed to have been ordered by some person in this province" and that the "Person that can properly claim them, may have them."[51] Colonial merchants imported Dutch bulbs of English origin for resale, such as the Charleston dry goods firm of Lloyd & Neyle, which in January 1765 advertised their importation from London and Bristol of "Turkey ranunculus roots," Dutch tulips, fine anemones, and others.[52]

William Logan (1718–1776) resided at Stenton in Philadelphia and added to the garden of his father, James. James Logan, a friend of John Bartram and William Penn's secretary, had installed a parterre d'anglaise near the house finished in 1730. In 1749 William Logan ordered from Elias Bland in London: "roots of tulips, Ranunculus, Narcissus, Dutch poppys, Seeds of Double Larkspurs, Stocks of severall sorts, French & African marygolds, Sweet scented peas, with directions with them when to be sowed. Take care the mise don't eat them."[53] Six years later Logan ordered from Thomas Binks; along with seeds of stocks, hepatica, snap dragons, double china pinks, hollyhocks, and of course carnations, he detailed a long list of flower roots:

Flower roots to be sent—
   24 earliest Tulips sorted
   30 largest and very best hyacinths sorted
   50 double jonquils
   100 yellow and blue crocus yt bloy in ye fall of ye year
   50 snow drops
   24 Persian Iris
   12 naked ladies
   20 double anemonies (if tuberose roots are plenty and cheap send me some of
them dry also)
   8 pots of carnations
   8 pots of auriculas (Let them be Good and the Potts be put into a course Rough
Box made with a shelving lid so as it may throw ye water at sea when the weather
is bad and yet be half open when good so as the Sun may not come too Violently
on ye Auricula plants.)[54]

Henry Laurens (1723–1792) of Charleston, South Carolina, whose English gardener John Watson started an early commercial nursery (and sold to Laurens's friend William Logan), wrote on May 20, 1763, to "Sarah Nicholson and Company, London" to order seeds of colly flowers (two ounces), auriculas and carnations

PL.III.

F.W.Burbidge del et. lith.

V.Brooks.Day&Son.Imp.

N. PSEUDO-NARCISSUS.

Plate III, N. pseudonarcissus (A. A wild form. B. and C. Cultivated forms). Burbidge and Baker, *The Narcissus*, 1875. Courtesy of the Cherokee Garden Library, Kenan Research Center at the Atlanta History Center, Atlanta, Georgia.

(one-quarter to one-half ounce each), and three to half dozen each of the roots,

Pseudo Narcissus or Yellow (or white) Daffodil

Martagon–or Mountain Lilly

Double–Nasturtium

if this can be sent so as to have a tolerablechance of being propagated.

Ranunculus

Pyony

Anemone[55]

Laurens was known for his garden, a brick walled affair of 200 yards by 150 yards as reported by John Bartram after his visit in 1765. It was stocked with fruit, olive, caper, and lime trees. The larger significance of his 1763 order is it is the only colonial-era citation found to date for *N. pseudonarcissus* in the garden of a wealthy "tastemaker."

One specific discussion of ordering directly from the Dutch is rather illuminating and seems to have been regarded as a less-than-ideal endeavor. John St. Clair of Belleville remarked to John Bartram on February 27, 1761:[56]

I shall send to Holland this year for a parcel of Flower Roots: Hyacinths & Auriculass are what they run the most upon at Harlem, which far exceeds any thing of the kind at Lyden.

The Harlem florists vye wh. One another who should produce the greatest Varietys of the above flowers and when any appears that have not been seen before all curious People flock to see it.

The only way to deal with the Dutch is to give them 50 or 100 Guilders & desire them to give you Roots and Shrubs for it. the price of flowers is regulated every Year by the florists as each has a Catalogue of what the other has, and is the same as the Exchge. in Philadelphia.[57]

How to plant one's bulbs, and daffodils in particular, could be found in the widely disseminated *The Gardeners Dictionary* by Philip Miller. Over the years and editions, he expanded the *Narcissus* section, but did not substantially change the planting directions. In his 1724 *The Gardeners and Florists Dictionary* (which echoes strongly Liger's *The Solitary Gardener/The Compleat Florist*), Miller stated simply: "*Narcissus's* whether planted in Compartments or in Beds, must stand four Inches from one another. They will look very handsomely among *Hyacinths* and *Tulips*."[58]

By his 1754 edition of *The Gardeners' Dictionary,* Miller expanded his recommendations for daffodils, giving jonquils special consideration:

The common Sorts of Daffodil are generally planted in large Borders of the Pleasure-garden; where being intermix'd with other bulbous-rooted Flowers, they afford an agreeable Variety in the Seasons of Flowering. These Roots are very hardy, and will thrive in almost any Soil or Situation; which renders them very proper for rural Gardens, where, being planted under the Shade of Trees, they will endure for several Years without transplanting, and produce annually, in the Spring, great Quantities of Flowers, which afford a very agreeable Prospect.

The Jonquils should be planted in Beds, or Borders, separate from other Roots; because they require to be transplanted at least every other year. . . . These Flowers are greatly esteemed by many People for their strong sweet Scent; though there are very few Ladies that can bear the Smell of them: so powerful is it, that many times, it overcomes their Spirits, especially when confined in a Room; for which Reason they should never be planted too close to an Habitation, lest they become offensive; nor should the Flowers be placed in such Rooms where Company are entertain'd.[59]

Wealthy colonists and early Americans had access to the latest European design theory published in Britain. Miller's *The Gardeners' Dictionary* was a staple for gardening libraries of the wealthy in Maryland/Chesapeake, along with other practical gardening and garden design theory works. John Bartram wrote to Philip Miller in 1755, noting he possessed the first and second volumes of *The Gardeners' Dictionary,* and in November 1758, he wrote to Peter Collinson, "but have received A fine parcel which thee mentioned of his [Philip Miller] figures & dictionary with the Box of bulbous roots."[60]

Bartram wrote Collinson in November of 1758 that he intended to "board in A little convenient spot" for a new flower bed to contain all the curious plants he hopes to receive from his friends "to out do our Dutch in flowers pleasure."[61] Meanwhile, the practice of railed or boarded beds was abandoned at Williamsburg as too time consuming to warrant the effort. According to her husband, Thomas, in a letter to Bartram in 1761, Mrs. Lamboll of Charleston, South Carolina, planted her anemones and ranunculus in raised beds prepared months in advance, but he made no mention of edging.[62] Bartram's neighbor William Hamilton, in 1789, directed his garden laborers to plant his exotic bulbous roots six to eight inches apart, and to take care to preserve the distinctness of the sorts. The practice of those edging flower beds charged with holding more expensive bulbs with boards was still recommended into the nineteenth century in Bernard M'Mahon's *The American Gardener's Calendar* (1806) while the

Plate XXIII, N. Odorus. Burbidge and Baker, *The Narcissus,* 1875.
Courtesy of the Cherokee Garden Library, Kenan Research Center
at the Atlanta History Center, Atlanta, Georgia.

less expensive were destined for the borders:

These may be planted separately in beds, or along the borders of the flower-garden and pleasure-grounds.

In planting any of the above or other sorts in borders, observe that the lowest growing kinds are to be planted next the walks, and the larger farther back, in proportion to their respective growths, that the whole may appear to advantage and none be concealed from the view. Likewise observe to diversify the kinds and colours, so as to display, when in bloom, the greatest possible variety of shades and contrasts.

In assemblage with other flowers in the borders, these should be planted in small clumps of six, seven or eight inches in diameter, three, four, five or more roots in each, according to size and growth, and these at suitable distances from one another, say one, two, or three yards. Some of the common anemones or ranunculuses may also be planted with those roots in the borders, either in rows towards the edges, or in small clumps or patches as above.

The form of this ground may be either square, oblong, or somewhat circular; having the boundary embellished with a collection of the most curious flowering-shrubs; the interior part should be divided into many narrow beds, either oblong, or in the manner of a parterre; but plain four feet wide beds arranged parallel, having two feet wide alleys between bed and bed, will be found most convenient, yet to some not the most fanciful.

In either method, a walk should be carried round the outward boundary, leaving a border to surround the whole ground, and within this, to have the various divisions or beds, raising them generally in a gently rounding manner, edging such as you like with dwarfbox, some with trifs, pinks, sisyrinchium, &c. by way of variety, laying the walks and alleys with the finest gravel. Some beds may be neatly edged with boards, especially such as are intended for the finer sorts of bulbs, &c.

In this division you may plant the finest hyacinths, tulips, polyanthus-narcissus, double jonquils, anemones, ranunculus's, bulbous-iris's, tuberoses, scarlet and yellow amaryllis's, colchicums, fritillaries, crown-imperials, snowdrops, crocus's, lilies of various sorts, and all the different kinds of bulbous, and tuberous-rooted flowers, which succeed in the open ground; each sort principally in separate beds, especially the more choice kinds, being necessary both for distinction sake and for the convenience of giving, such as need it, protection from inclement weather; but for particulars of their culture, see the respective articles in the various months.

Likewise in this division should be planted a curious collection of carnations, pinks, polyanthus's, and many other beautiful sorts, arranging some of the most valuable in beds separately; others may be intermixed in different beds, forming an assemblage of various sorts.

In other beds, you may exhibit a variety of all sorts, both bulbous, tuberous, and fibrous rooted kinds, to keep up a succession of bloom in the same beds during the whole season.

Here I cannot avoid remarking, that many flower-gardens, &c. are almost destitute of bloom, during a great part of the season; which could be easily avoided, and a blaze of flowers kept up, both in this department, and in the borders of the pleasure-ground, from March to November, by introducing from our woods and fields, the various beautiful ornaments with which nature has so profusely decorated them. Is it because they are indigenous, that we should reject them? ought we not rather to cultivate and improve them? what can be more beautiful than our Lobelias, Orchis,' Asclepias' and Asters; Dracocephalums, Gerardias, Monardas and Ipomoeas; Liliums, Podalyrias, Rhexias, Solidagos and Hibiscus'; Phlox's, Gentianas, Spigelias, Chironias and Sisyrinchiums, Cassias, Ophrys,' Coreopsis' and Cypripediums; Fumarias, Violas, Rudbeckias and Liatris'; with our charming Limadorum, fragrant Arethusa and a thousand other lovely plants, which if introduced, would grace our plantations, and delight our senses?[63]

Early Commercial Offerings

While there are many colonial gardeners known to have established a nursery, or at least sold from their own garden, those known to have sold bulbs, and daffodils by name, are few and far between. Many businessmen sold imported garden seed from London, such as Charlestonians Charles Pickney in the 1730s and Thomas Young in the 1760s. John Watson, Henry Laurens's trained gardener turned nurseryman in Charleston, advertised for sale in the fall of 1765 "a great variety of Tulip, hiacynths, lilies, anemonies, ranocluses and double jonquils."[64] As Watson's employer, Henry Laurens, was ordering bulbs from Sarah Nickolson & Co. of London around this time, it is tempting to speculate Watson was ordering from the same sources.[65] Individual gardeners are known to have sold from their own gardens either seed or stock. Some of these early entrepreneurs were women, such as Hannah Dubree of Philadelphia, who began selling seeds in the early 1750s, and Martha Logan, who similarly sold from her garden. Logan advertised in the *South Carolina Gazette* in the fall of 1753 "seeds, flower roots and fruit stones"; she ran another newspaper advertisement in 1768, selling shrubs, including boxwood for edging beds.

After the Revolutionary War ended in 1783, American nurserymen, gardeners, florists, and seedsmen advertised far and wide to capture the more affluent gardening market. This was possible because of the establishment of the U.S. Postal Service, such as it was.[66] Nurserymen advertised their importations as coming from Holland, England, and on occasion France. The Dutch had been legally barred from direct commercial activities with the colonists under the Navigations Act, and trade was further aggravated by the Fourth Anglo-Dutch War of 1780–1784. In his comprehensive treatise on the history of the Dutch bulb industry, Dr. Krelage noted the earliest commercial activity he uncovered between Dutch companies and Americans dated to 1782, when Rosenkrantz and Son listed for sale trees and shrubs from Dr. Bartram, likely William Bartram. The Charleston Chamber of Commerce went so far as to enlisted Alexander Gillon and Thomas Jefferson in the late 1780s to increase trade with the Dutch and French. This was repaid in part by imports of Dutch florists' flowers, on top of its already robust horticultural trade with the British.[67]

Many early advertisements reflect the snob appeal and the perceived need for American gardeners to be current in fashionable flower trends. From the *Pennsylvania Packet,* February 20, 1781:

> General Philip de Baas.
>
>   Roots of flowers.
>
>   Just imported into this City, immediately from Holland a great variety of the roots of Flowers for the Pleasure Garden; of Bulbous Roots, undoubtedly the greatest variety ever imported in America, such as, Tulips, Hyacinths, Narcessus, Daffadel Lillies, and all other the most admired bulbous flowers so in esteem in the best gardens in Europe; The Bulbs are flowering roots, and in excellent condition; Likewise an excellent parcel of Ranunculus Anemones. Also a great variety of the most admired Flower Seeds, and a complete assortment of seeds for Kitchen Gardens of all sorts. All which was collected last fall out of the most famous gardens in Holland.
>
>   Enquire at General Philip De Baas, in Third Street, near Race Street.[68]

Peter Bellet first came to America from France as a traveling seedsman, before eventually becoming a settled nurseryman in Williamsburg. In December 1785 and January 1786, he posted in Baltimore newspapers his temporary stay and his offering a catalog including Dutch bulbs, with colors and names, imported from Amsterdam. He whetted his customers' appetite in January with 120 ranunculas, sixty sorts of double anemonies, twenty-two sorts of carnations, eleven sorts of rare bulbous Pyramids, eight sorts of Passetouts, eight sorts of tuberoses and "8 Sorts of double Jonquils, the most rare in all Colours," as well as hyacinths of the very best sorts.[69]

In contrast to the marketing hype, a 1791 catalog from the Dutch firm of Jean Rosenkrantz et fils, Heemstede, was printed in German, Dutch, French, and English and paints a more realistic picture of the *Narcissus* in the marketplace. As expected, tazettas were the primary offering, leading with 137 sorts of tazettas (grouped by color—yellow, white and sulphur) and then ten other daffodils—Centi Folio ("Centifolius"—the double 'Plenissimus'), Nana (*N. minor*), Albo Pleno Odorato, Incomparable ('Butter and Eggs'), 'Orange Phoenix,' Sulpher Kroon ('Sulphur Phoenix'), Van Sion ('Telamonius Plenus'), Trompet Marin (*N. bulbocodium*), Campernelle (*N. × odorus*), and Formosissimus (likely not a daffodil). While their offerings shed no light on the eight double jonquils of Bellet, these are more reasonably what was actually ending up in American gardens.

At first blush, February, never mind late March or April, seems very late in the season to sell spring-blooming bulbs. But if a seedsmen places an order in the fall, and the trip takes roughly two months one way, a request placed in October would not be delivered until February. Gardeners would then have to wait for the ground to sufficiently thaw to plant (daffodil roots begin to sprout in 55° soil temperature). Blooming occurs six to eight weeks hence, plenty of time for a good spring show. Planting in April would result in a June flowering. However, an April arrival indicates the ship left two months or so prior, in February, and likely would be whatever leftover stock the Dutch (or English) could not sell from the prior fall season.

This later shipping pattern was also, in part, in reaction to the vagaries of the high seas—bad weather would delay ship departures, and bulb shipments may have been held until the threat of freezing weather had passed. Conversely, late shipping ran the risk of bulbs sprouting in transit, and all shipping posed the threat of loss en route, from sea water soaking the crates, never mind the ship's mice and rats, as witnessed by William Logan's regular fussings in his plant orders.[70]

American nurserymen's imported stock varied from year to year. Whether this is from changes in what European wholesalers had to offer, versus what American retailers were interested in and that they knew they could sell, is undecipherable without an array of period catalogs. It is also interesting to note what was listed first to last, as presumably the choicest came first to entice the prospective customer.

Minton Collins of Richmond, Virginia, announced in the *Virginia Gazette and Richmond Daily Advertiser* on November 5, 1792, the arrival of his stock from London on the ship *Bowman*. Assuring customers a choice collection, warranted to be of last summer's growth, Collins listed after the vegetables seeds, "Animonies, Persian Iris, Mixed Tulips, Fine large hyacinths, Do. Polianthus narcissus, Do. Double white narcissus, Do. mixed ranunculus, Do. Tube roses, Mixed blue and yellow crocus, Lillies of the valley, Bella-donna lilies, Window wall flower."[71] Collins ordering for resale the presumed "common" double poet of Bartram (assuming the "Double white narcissus" to be one and the same) leads to speculation. It may suggest that to some gardeners

PL. XV.

N. TRIANDRUS

Plate XV, N. Triandrus. Burbidge and Baker, *The Narcissus*, 1875. Courtesy of the Cherokee Garden Library, Kenan Research Center at the Atlanta History Center, Atlanta, Georgia.

any double daffodil was a good double daffodil, that it was not as "common" a flower in other parts of the country as in Germantown and Philadelphia, or that it was a more esteemed flower in the eyes of London nurserymen and so on offer to their American clientele.

The new century witnessed the rise of Bernard M'Mahon's nursery business in Philadelphia and his extensive bulb offerings, daffodils included, until his death in 1816. As with Minton Collins, M'Mahon's offerings varied year to year. In his 1802 catalog M'Mahon offered: Narcissus jonquilla "Double Jonquil," Narcissus majus "Great Daffodil," and Narcissus tazetta "Polyanthus Daffodil." In an undated, but pre-1804, catalog, M'Mahon listed eighteen narcissus: nine daffodils, four jonquils, and five polyanthus narcissus. In his 1806 *The American Gardener's Calendar*, M'Mahon offered thirteen species daffodils, only two of which were tazettas and six of which are still (regularly) found in gardens. These were (are) *N. pseudonarcissus*, N. biflorus (*N. × medioluteus*), *N. × odorus*, *N. jonquilla*, *N. moschatus*, and *N. poeticus*. The rest are (quickly) recognizable: *N. bicolor, N. minor, N. triandrus* (now not quite so uncommon as discussed by Curtis?), *N. orientalis, N. tazetta, N. bulbocodium,* and *N. serotinus.* Interestingly M'Mahon offered four doubles in his pre-1804 catalog but none in his 1806 *Calendar.*

While M'Mahon was remembered for having tulip-glasses and baskets of bulbous roots in the window of his store, and large greenhouses outside of the city, it is unlikely he raised all these daffodils himself—such a collection instead being the result of import via his well-established export business network for American seeds and plants. And while he was widely respected in his day, it is unclear if M'Mahon's expanded catalog was responding to a broadening palate of his customers, or trying to create a market, or both.

Under the management of the Bartram sons John Jr. and William, Bartram's Garden expanded its business and evidently decided not to be left out of the daffodil market, for by the 1807 catalog daffodils appear. Although a sales catalog, it is thought the catalog served more as documentation of the garden's contents; thus these bulbs were presumably grown on and sold from the property. There is no evidence to date that Bartram's Gardens was importing and reselling Dutch bulbs in this period (Joel Fry, personal communication, August 27, 2009).

Narcissus poeticus
    "   pseudo-narcissus
    "   bicolor
    "   minor
    "   joquilla
    "   odorus
    "   tazetta
    "   bulbocodium
    "   triandrus
And many varieties.[72]

Presumably the "varieties" are tazettas, as they were the only ones given proper florist's names, but varieties of *N. poeticus, N. triandrus* and *N. bulbocodium* were known at that time. This list remained the same for the 1814 catalog. Logan's desired *N. moschatus* is conspicuously absent.

These named offerings thus greatly help explain the variety available to American gardeners and fill in the gaps when the broadsides or newspaper announcements are frustratingly brief. One such example is courtesy of William Booth, nursery and seedsman, near Baltimore, in his catalogue of 1810. His varieties under "Narcissus or daffodil" were "Jonquil, double and single; Double-flowered narcissus, in varieties; Polyanthus Narcissus, in varieties; Common daffodil, in varieties."[73] He offered something of everything; we just really don't know what that everything was.

Daffodils in Colonial and Federal Gardens

For all the writers writing about gardens and what they contained, few gardeners had many daffodils by name, and few actually drew their gardens' plans. Paintings and property plat maps become beacons of light in an otherwise little-illuminated sea of black ink. Two well-known sources of colonial garden illustrations are the 1769 maps of ten North Carolina towns that detailed the garden layouts of the towns' houses made by French cartographer Claude Joseph Sauthier, under the direction of Governor Tyron, and the plat maps of Charleston, South Carolina. These sources were used in the garden recreations by noted landscape architect Arthur Shurcliff at Colonial Williamsburg in the 1920s and 1930s.

Not that general observations of regional gardens are not helpful. Broad brushstroke descriptions provide their own sense of place and context, and often one of the few period sources of information remaining. In 1808 David Ramsey wrote of the

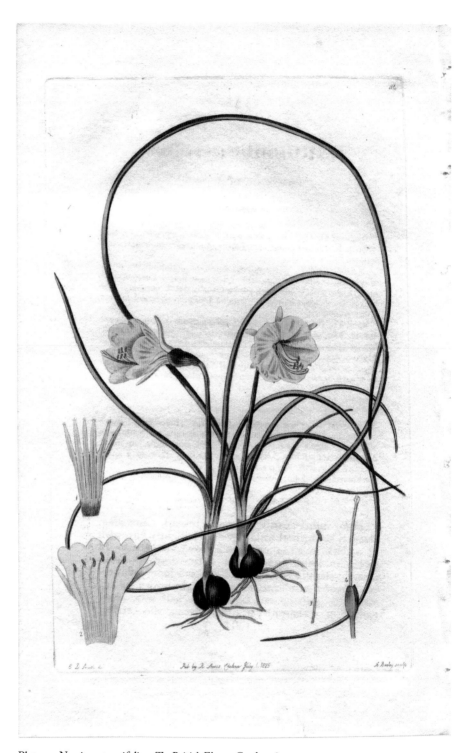

Plate 114, Narcissus tenuifolius. *The British Flower Garden*, 1825.

history of South Carolina, and he kindly recited the ornamental shrubs while describing the current natural history of the state:

> The gardenia florida or cane jasmine—the virburnumtinus—the rosa ferox, sometimes called rosa multiflora, more commonly known by the name of the nondescript—the rosa sinensis, perpetual rose—rosa moschata, musk rose—the rosa muscosa, moss rose, and many other beautiful and formerly rare kinds of roses. The olea fragrans, the hydrangea hortensis, double and single oleanders, altheas, cultivated myrtles of various descriptions, english jasmines and honeysuckles, several kinds of elegant mimosas, an abundance of hyacinths, narcissuses, daffodils, tonquills, ixias, ranunculuses, anemones, with a profusion of annuals of the most beautiful kind. Of fruit, sweet and sour oranges are raised, and, with some additional care citrons, lemons and limes, almonds and chestnuts; figs and pomegranates, red and yellow raspberries and grapes, but not in profusion.[74]

Little remains in the way of surviving eighteenth-century American gardens, much less any with original daffodils still growing in them. There are gardens re-created from the diaries and order lists of owners and family members. With great luck the descriptions of the garden's design are good, and with even better luck someone has made a drawing and maybe even included a plants list.

Grumblethorpe remained in the Wister family from its building in 1744 by John Wister until 1941, and much of that time held by active agriculturists and gardeners. John Wister (1708–1789) left Baden, Germany, for Germantown, Pennsylvania, in 1727 at the age of nineteen, joining his older brother Caspar (grandfather of the namesake for the vine *Wisteria* described by Thomas Nuttall in 1818). John became a wealthy wine merchant, and his summer home eventually became his permanent home.

Of humble beginnings, John laid out his garden beds following the European medieval tradition but bordered them with boxwood hedges. The garden was approximately 180 feet wide and 450 feet long, comprising two rows of rectangular beds, five squares each, divided by a center path.

His son Daniel J. Wister (1738–1805), a Quaker, resided all his adult life with his Welsh wife immediately next door to Grumblethorpe in the tenant house. While John stuck to vegetables and fruit trees, Daniel developed a penchant for ornamental horticulture, which his father allowed him to pursue on the family farm (where Daniel's flower beds were located awaits future archaeology). Daniel kindly recorded his ornamental gardening activities from 1771 to 1776. He had a taste for the fashionable Dutch bulbs (and carnations) and not surprisingly was particularly smitten with tulips. Daniel Wister recorded not only what he planted but approximately where he planted it. He sorted his tulips and hyacinths by color and by caliber, differentiating by "best," "good" and "middling" with separate beds for the best sorts.

In 1773 Daniel Wister noted "the round bed near the poles" was to be filled with fifteen varieties of carnations. He wrote of tulips in this year—"144 yellow, scarlet and white tulip roots" to be planted in the "Tulip bed near the cherry tree, S SE comer."

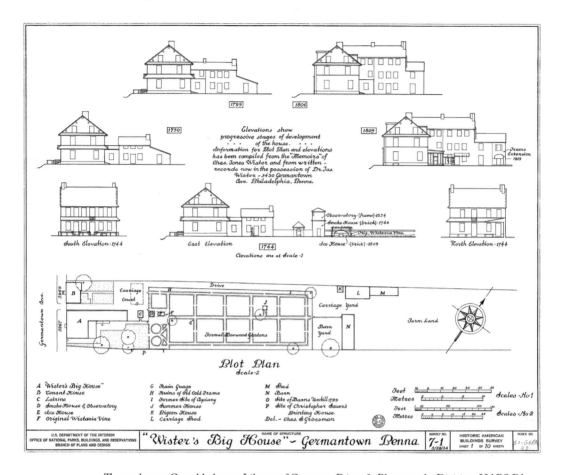

The gardens at Grumblethorpe. Library of Congress, Prints & Photographs Division, HABS PA, 51-GERM, 23- (sheet 1 of 10).

Later in October 1773, "the bed near best tulip bed" and the "bed near the garden gate" were planted with blue and white varieties of hyacinths, scarlet and white tulips, narcissus, polyanthus, and jonquils. In 1775 Daniel was growing hyacinths, eighteen tulips, and violets. Mention was made of the "bed near J. Wister's barn, bed near the summer house, and the bed near the SW fence." Wister recorded five varieties of ranunculus "in 5 rows," ninety-eight different roses, snow drops, flags, purple hyacinths, and royal-colored tulips.[75]

As Daniel's progeny were gardeners as well, his garden did not survive the tastes of his heirs. But his heirs did preserve the pattern of John's original garden, which survived into the twentieth century, albeit with a few modifications. Daniel's son Charles J. Wister Sr. (d. 1865) too grew scads of tulips; although much more involved in agricultural pursuits, Charles noted the flowers in his garden in 1813. Along with well over 138 tulips (the count for one entry), he grew crown imperials, hyacinths, jonquils, narcissus duplex, narcissus simplex, iris, ornithogalum, lilies, and roses. (Charles's son Charles

Jr. added the "goose foot" parterre by 1886).

A second documented bulb parterre planting may date to the late colonial era. Fortuitously a map from memory exists of a family-replica Williamsburg town garden, and "bulbs" are given their own parterre beds, next to the roses. (Who knows what bulbs were planted, but that they warranted their own beds, and the design thereof, is noteworthy).

The Benjamin Waller Garden at Colonial Williamsburg is a restored garden, enabled by a sketch of the Tower Hill garden in Sussex County. The Tower Hill garden was a re-creation of Benjamin Waller's (d. 1786) "town" garden by his granddaughter Eliza Waller. The sketch in question, dating to the early twentieth century, was based on the memories of Eliza's granddaughter, Miss Luty Blow. Miss Blow's sketch fit the archaeological evidence uncovered at the Waller property,

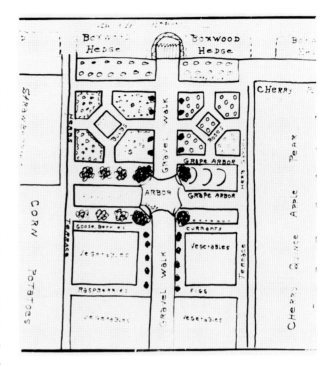

Sketch by Luty Blow of garden at Tower Hill modeled after Benjamin Waller garden, image # 79-543-2. The Colonial Williamsburg Foundation.

making the Waller House garden one of the most accurate of the re-created gardens of Colonial Williamsburg. The clipped-cornered quincunx design harkens to Philip Miller's recommendation for ease of passage around the flower beds. Although there is no indication that either grandfather or granddaughter grew daffodils, one may suppose Eliza Waller planted bulbs and roses in her parterres as did her grandfather.

Not surprisingly most known garden designs utilizing daffodils date to the federal period. A dedicated gardener, and relatively prolific writer, Lady Jean Skipwith (1748–1826) of Prestwould, on the Dan River in far southern Virginia, maintained an extensive library to stay abreast of the greater gardening world. She started with Philip Miller's *The Gardeners Dictionary* (thought to be the eighth edition, 1768, same as used by Thomas Jefferson) then moved to *Curtis's Botanical Magazine* upon its inception in 1787 and ordered from William Prince of Long Island.

To showcase her lists of bulbs and plants, Lady Skipwith designed her own flower beds. The sketches of two designs, dating to the 1790s but apparently never planted, present a very different approach to flower beds. In her circular plan, she accommodated "Annuals and Bulbous Roots" in two inner ring beds; the center circular bed is illegible; the outer ring is denoted for small shrubbery, and the triangular corner beds are denoted for annuals. The circular beds are 4½ feet wide, the paths 1½ wide, the center circular bed diameter is not written.

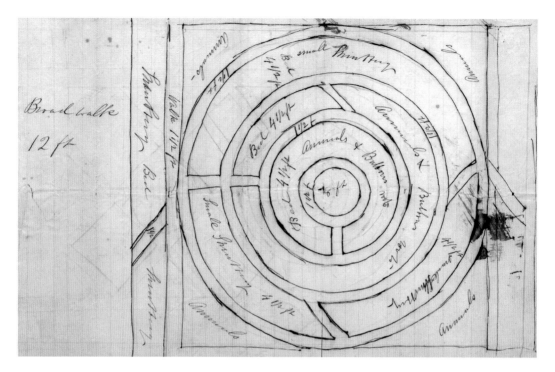

Lady Skipwith's bulb garden sketch. Skipwith Family Papers, Special Collections Research Center, Swem Library, College of William and Mary.

In *Historic Gardens of Virginia* (1923) by Edith Tunis Sale and others, a pen and ink illustration of the Prestwould gardens shows a different but still rather unconventional flower garden design, reported to have come from Lady Skipwith's journal. A flanking square (one to each side) to the traditional square vegetable plots, the flower garden squares are dominated on one side by a rectangular bed for bulbs. But her intricate and fanciful garden designs come to life with her surviving bulb order lists.

The 'Bulbous Rooted Flowers' in the garden in 1793 follow her lists of "Wild Flowers in the Garden." "Daffodil" begins the garden list, and after the blush and double blue hyacinths come "Fine double Jonquil, Polyanthus Narcissus, Single Narcissus, Double Narcissus," then tulips and the rest—but interestingly no grape or feathered hyacinths, often bulb garden staples.[76] If rank signifies importance, daffodils and hyacinths were top—with double jonquils and tazettas ranking highest, as expected, followed by doubles.

In the autumn of 1793, Lady Skipwith ordered from Minton Collins in Richmond three variegated double narcissus and single polyanthus narcissus. Whether this ordering list was made before or after the garden list is unclear; possibly she decided she was in need of more tazettas and doubles. In a separate list of flowers for Mrs. Boyd, Lady Skipwith enumerates a prodigious list of bulbs: Double blue and blush hyacinths, grape and feathered hyacinths; double, single, and polyanthus narcissus; large snow drops;

yellow autumnal amaryllis; daffodil; corn flag; double jonquil; common star flower; lily of the valley; bulbous iris; Persian iris; Florentine white iris; common blue, yellow, and tawny day lily; large white lily; Bermudian ixia; and the spotted Canada Martagon lily.

Sir Peyton Skipwith placed his own order with Collins on March 1, 1793. Among the vegetables and annuals were the bulbs—three each double variegated hyacinths, double variegated narcissus and double variegated tuberose; six tulips, twelve ranunculus, three polyanthus narcissus, and three Persian iris; and two dozen yellow and blue crocus. In an order late in the season, someone was bound and determined to lay their hands on some double variegated narcissus—particularly as Collins advertised double white narcissus only in the fall of 1792.

Likely Lady Skipwith lifted her bulbs annually as was the dictate of the day, particularly her better sorts. What she edged her beds with is more of an enigma. Her bulb choices ensured a long season of bloom, but one can only conjecture the overall color palate and its shift over time—did she mix her colors, keep all the whites together, and so on.

Annapolis innkeeper and nurseryman William Faris's garden is well documented in planting, and well re-created in plan, based on his diary spanning from 1792 to 1804. He planted his bulbs in October and lifted in early to mid-July. Faris's journal entries are interesting for what flowers warranted mention by name and what did not, which becomes apparent when comparing his daily entries to his flower bed records. Faris included a planting table in 1794 and in 1799; he grouped his bulbs by sort with tulips and hyacinths in the lead, with daffodils bringing up the rear; the first table he noted what looks to be bulb counts:

1794 Thursday May 11th   I marked the following flowers

16 John Quills 3
17 White Nercess 18
18 Yallow d°   9[77]
Munday 13th (May; 1799)
marked the Following flowers viz.
16 John Quills
17 White Narcess
18 Yallow
19 Fross Nercess from Mr. H. J. Stear[78]

Planting entry number 19 for May 1799 first appears in October 1789: "Munday 5th a fine clear day. planted 4 Fross Nercess's roots by the grape vines from Mr. H. J. Stier."[79] These went into a separate bed along his back property line; in July 1799 he noted when he "took up" the bulbs.[80]

In contrast Farris grew his "John Quills" in his mix of flowers in two different locations. All his beds were edged with boxwood. In his rectangular beds lining the paths to the "necessary," jonquils were in the mix of Dutch bulbs and perennials (tulips top of

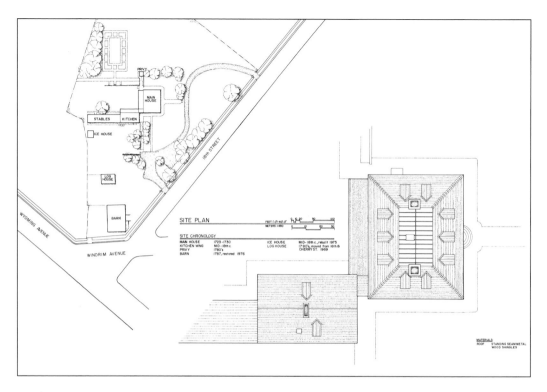

Stenton, Philadelphia, illustrating the recreated garden. Library of Congress, Prints & Photographs Division, HABS PA, 51-PHILA, 8- (sheet 1 of 10).

the list as always). In circular beds planted round canopy trees, jonquils were included. In March 1798 Faris noted his acquisition of jonquils, presumably in addition to those he had planted in 1794: "Munday April 2th—a clouded drisley morning. sow'd the Sencitive Plant seed in a pott and Planted No. 15 a root the Name for got both from Mr. Hesler & 2 of the John Quill from Mr. Leopold, in the after noon came on a good deal of bad weather. cut assparagrass this morning for the first time."[81] His last entry regarding jonquils was in 1801, when he set them out.

Interestingly, although grown for four springs, neither the White nor Yellow Narcess warranted mention by name in his diary entries. Farris's choices echo the sentiments of William Hamilton—jonquils as worthy for intermixing in the perennial borders, tazettas to be planted separately in a designated bed as a florists' flower of note, and the common daffodils silent in the background mix.[82]

There is one famous garden in the naturalistic style (its design elements rooted in *Observations on Modern Gardening* [1770] by Thomas Whately) that contained daffodils, namely Thomas Jefferson's Monticello. Although Jefferson grew *Narcissus* at his abode Shadwell in the 1760s, little is mentioned of their place in the garden. Jefferson noted on March 23, 1767, in his *Garden Book* (1944) "Purple Hyacinth & Narcissus bloom."[83] In 1766, at Shadwell, he noted "Apr. 6 Narcissus and Puckoon open."[84] In 1782

Jefferson created a blooming time line in his *Garden Book,* which lead with Narcissus blooming from March 17 to April 12, and jonquils blooming April 1 through 18.

Daffodils were similarly a background bulb in his gardens at Monticello. Along the depression for the front lawn "roundabout" walk, iris, tulips, jonquils, hyacinths, and other plants came up along on each side, assisting in the reconstruction of the roundabout walk, originally laid out by Jefferson in 1808. For all the correspondence between Jefferson and M'Mahon and the orders Jefferson placed with M'Mahon from 1807 to 1812 to stock his Monticello flower beds, no discussion of any *Narcissus* appears (although lots of tulips, anemones, tuberoses, fritillaria, hyacinth, lilies, amaryllis, and others). However in 1811, when discussing his hoped-for bulb order next year, Jefferson pointedly commented that in his extensive flower border he plants in particular flowers that are handsome or fragrant. He made no mention of any *Narcissus,* nor did he indicate his plans to order any. In April of 1812, he finally laid out his flower bed compartments along the roundabout walk; the odd compartments were reserved for bulbs requiring annual lifting, with the even numbered compartments designated for seeds and permanent bulbs.

In 1816 Jefferson asked his daughter Martha Randolph to send him at Poplar Forest by mule "daffodils, jonquils, Narcissuses, flags & lillies, of different kinds, refuse hyacinths &c. with some of the small bulbs of the hanging onion" from Monticello.[85] Thus one might hazard the assumption that the bulbs had increased to such a degree that sufficient was on hand to plant at another garden. It is tempting to speculate that Shadwell supplied the stock for Monticello—a similar situation to Poplar Grove, where the multiplied bulbs at Monticello, which did not warrant written mention, were nevertheless at some point desired.

In *Historic Gardens of Virginia* (1923), Monticello is described under its then owner Jefferson Levy prior to the site's purchase by the Thomas Jefferson Foundation and becoming a Garden Clubs of Virginia restoration project. "On the left side of this driveway was once a greensward running along the side of the quarters, or southern pavilion, and in the spring it was a mass of bulbous flowers familiar to old homes, such as jonquils, single blue Roman hyacinths and Stars of Bethlehem. The blue feathered hyacinth (Muscari comosum monstrosum) found congenial environment here. This was a rare flower in those days, and today is not generally seen here."[86]

In 1939 Hazelhurst Perkins of the Monticello Committee (of the Garden Clubs of Virginia's Restoration Committee) decided to confirm the Jefferson plan found in 1932 of the now-famous winding walk and accompanying flower beds. It was found by architect Morely Williams, who had the flash of inspiration to use oblique light from car headlights at night to determine if original features remained. He thus found clear evidence of the depression for the walk, and raised mounds on either side signifying the original narrow flower borders. Mrs. Perkins too decided to verify his findings (besides it probably sounded too good not to try): "To make doubly sure of the contour a car was driven up in the lawn at night with the lights turned on. The curves and width were even more distinctly visible. A gravel path was located by not only a definite mound and side depression, but in the early spring was outlined by clumps of bulbs (hyacinths

Syd.ª Edwards Del.   Pub. by T. Curtis St Geo Crescent Apr. 1.1809.   F. Sansom Sculp.

Plate 1187, Narcissus Bicolor. White and Yellow Garden Daffodil. *Curtis's Botanical Magazine*, 1809.

and narcissus) coming up in the sod."[87] Sadly there is no record as to what befell the bulbs.[88]

Botanic Gardens

After the war and as scientific endeavors expanded, more individuals and institutions established botanic gardens. Some were apparently partially for profit, others for purely scientific research or personal interest. Many colonial and federal-era botanists and gentlemen gardeners established botanic gardens specifically to trial new plants (or old plants in new places). One well-known botanic garden was that of Dr. David Hosack, who established the Elgin Botanic Garden in 1801 in association with his position of professor of botany at Columbia University, New York. Now the site of the Rockefeller Center in New York City, the botanic garden was contributed to by many of the leading horticulturists and botanists of the day, until its demise in 1814. The garden's 1811 catalog, *Hortus Elginensis*, was published for the benefit of the New York Assembly. In the preface, Hosack indicates that since the first edition of 1806, much had been added to the botanic garden, both foreign and native; and provides a list of plant contributors. The 1811 catalog lists seven daffodils, namely *N. bicolor, N. × medioluteus, N. jonquilla, N. × odorus, N. poeticus, N. pseudonarcissus,* and *N. tazetta.* Hosack's benefactors included William Salisbury, Proprietor of the London Botanic Garden, Bernard M'Mahon, William Prince and Louis LeConte. The striking bicolor trumpet *N. bicolor* seems to have had a short-lived period of fame in the early 1800s. (Mr. Salisbury had familiarity with daffodils from the garden of Symmons, in Paddington, and published *Hortus Paddingtonensis* in 1797 which did not contain *N. bicolor*). The *Hortus Cantabrigiensis* for the holdings of the Walkerian Botanic Garden in Cambridge, England, expanded their Narcissus collection from seven species in 1796 to thirteen in 1800, and *N. bicolor* was one of the additions. From 1800 onward saw the rise of botanical interest in Britain, including bulbs and the genus Narcissus. Bartram's Garden followed suit and offered *N. bicolor* from 1807 to 1814. Hosack's (and Bartram's Garden?) choice might have been reflective of this botanical trend across the Pond.

Established in 1805, the Botanick Garden of South-Carolina was affiliated with the Medical Society of Charleston and was a logical continuation of Charleston's horticultural predilection. For an annual subscription, persons gained admission and could take home medicinal plants not otherwise available locally. Fortuitously florists' flowers were commingled with the medicinal. An 1810 catalog, printed by the Charleston Botanic Society and Garden, boasted 494 entries of annuals, biennials, bulbs, and perennials: "The number of Plants, both exotick and indigenous, is daily augmenting, and already is so numerous as to be sufficient for the purpose of study. At the proper season, seeds, plants &c. will be distributed among the subscribers, on application to Dr. Johnson, the Treasurer. . . . From the moderate price of subscription it is placed within the means of almost every family to obtain a delightful and innocent recreation."[89]

The catalogue entries reflect this orientation to the public, as plants are listed first by "vulgar" or common name, then genera and species, class and order, and finally the location of origin. Often one of every genus is represented, so only one tulip, one hyacinth, and one crocus were present, and these were species, not florists' hybrid flowers. Of delight to a daffodil enthusiast, not one but three *Narcissus* were grown.

#132 Daffodil	Narcissus Poeticus	Europe[90]
#228 Jonquil	Narcissus jonquilla	Spain-Levant[91]
#389 Polyanthes	Narcissus tazetta	Spain-Levant[92]

Further south resided a little-known early figure important to American botany in the person of Louis LeConte (1782–1838); his dislike of the spotlight resulted in his name being less well known today than it should be. It was up to his brother John Eatton to document Louis's botanic legacy, usually mentioned in conjunction with camellias. However, Louis deserves acknowledgement in the realm of daffodils and other geophytes. Around 1810 LeConte established a botanic garden focused on bulbous roots at his familial rice plantation Woodmanston, located forty miles southwest of Savannah, Georgia.

While the personal writings of Louis LeConte disappeared into the hands of Union troops, the papers of his brother John Eatton survived. In those papers is a list of bulbous plants recording the dates of emergence, bloom, and dormancy (senescence) for forty genera and species from 1813 through 1815 in Louis's garden. Twelve narcissus head the list, which includes leucojum, iris, hyacinths, muscari, gladioli, and others. True to the day, many of his daffodils were doubles, but he also grew two types of paperwhites—well known to modern coastal South gardeners, but rarely appearing in historic gardening literature:

N. papyraceus
N. papyraceus
N. tazetta
N. jonquilla
N. odorus (*N.* × *odorus*)
N. incomparabilis (*N.* × *incomparabilis*)
N. incomparabilis (fl. pl. pal.) ('Sulphur Phoenix')
N. incomparabilis (fl. pl. lut.) ('Butter and Eggs')
N. pseudo-narcissus
N. pseudo-narcissus (fl. pl.) ('Plenus')[93]
N. minor (fl. pl.) ('Eystettensis')
N. poeticus (fl. pl.) ("Albus Plenus Odoratus" or 'Plenus')[94]

Unfortunately we do not know where he obtained his bulbs. LeConte was in communication with the botany greats of the day, including Bernard M'Mahon. However, review of the catalogues shows that M'Mahon didn't offer everything LeConte grew—harkening back to the comment in his 1806 *Calendar* that if one wanted it

M'Mahon would do his best to get it. All of LeConte's bulbs were common enough, except for the two strains of *N. papyraceus*. M'Mahon offered one *N. papyraceus* in his undated/pre-1804 catalog, so the question that begs to be answered is how LeConte knew there were two strains. The blooming times for the two strains were November 24 to December 9, and December 12 to December 31. In *Curtis's Botanical Magazine*, Plate 947 for N. papyraceus, form B, is given as having a pale yellow cup. Thus it is possible LeConte's two strains were in actuality *N. papyraceus* and the bicolor tazetta *N. italicus*. However, the usual time for *N. italicus* in the coastal South is January; so LeConte may have wanted the form B but instead got a second true strain of *N. papyraceus*.

Although some of LeConte's narcissus likely would not have survived the southern climate for long (namely "Albus Plenus Odoratus"), many did, as witnessed by a visitor and a daughter. In 1831 Alexander Gordon of Leicester, England, returned to the United States for an extensive visit and filed his report "Principal Nurseries and Private Gardens in the United States of America" with John Claudius Loudon's influen-

Plate 121, Narcissus Incomparabilis. Peerless Daffodil. *The Botanical Magazine*, 1791.

tial *Gardeners Magazine.* Gordon's tour broadened from those places he visited in 1827 and 1828; he visited the most notable seedsmen of the day, including Grant Thorburn; the Linnaean Botanic Garden of Prince Hibberti and Buist; Bartram's garden; Mr. Noisette (of rose fame) and others in Charleston; and three gardens in Savannah, including that of Woodmanston. Gordon wrote: "The Garden of Lewis le Conte, Esq., near Riceborough, in Liberty County, Georgia, forty miles south of Savannah, is decidedly the richest in bulbs I have ever seen; and their luxuriance would astonish those who have only seen them in the confined state in which we are obliged to grow them in this country. M. Le Conte has discovered many new plants; and through this kindness I have been enabled to enrich our collections with some splendid treasures."[95]

Plate 947, Narcissus Papyraceus. Italian or Paper-White Narcissus.
Curtis's Botanical Magazine, 1806.

Shortly before Louis LeConte's death in 1838, his daughter Jane married M. B. Harden. They built a home on her inherited portion of Woodmanston called Halifax or "Harden Place," and Jane established her own garden. One eyewitness wrote, "Never have I seen japonicas more beautiful—more absolutely more exquisitely perfect, and I have walked all day in the magnificent groves of japonicas in the Middleton Gardens in South Carolina."[96] Joseph LeConte's daughter, Emma, wrote of her visits to Harden Place: "a large square with a circular mound in the midst in three diminishing tiers . . . in this garden was every known variety of camellia . . . great bushes like trees . . . huge azalea bushes, not yet in bloom, but the magnolia fuscata & tea olive were, and many other shrubs and daffodils, jonquils and narcissi and many other bulbs—violets. More flowers than I can remember and this was December!"[97]

Vernacular Gardens

The actual contents of vernacular gardens from this time frame remain in the realm of educated speculation as much as in tangible written evidence. The forms of various vernacular gardens have been well established, such as the dooryard garden of New England, as well as some of the contents. Passing references such as Brickell's are often the best available for specific flowers in a general location in an approximate time frame. With daffodils this is particularly so. Evidence for their existence in common gardens of the 1700s is general and faint. Extrapolating backward in time from 1800s references broadens the palate somewhat and demonstrates the portability of flowers, bulbs included. The best known is veritable weed "Albus Plenus Odoratus," brought by colonists (before 1735) and thrown away by the 1760s.

Scientific observations of the natural world, often related to meteorology, yield small snapshots of flowers in bloom. Devoid of garden context, they instead provide recorded dates of blooming for differing regions. In 1790, the Congregationalist

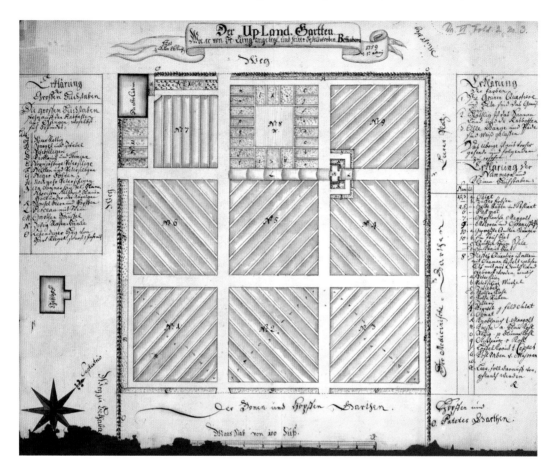

"Der Up-land Gartten. Wie er, von Br. Lung angelegt und heuer Bestelt worden, Bethabara" (Map of the upland garden in Bethabara, North Carolina, with notes on the vegetation, 1759), by Philip Christian Gotlieb Reuters. With permission from the Moravian Archives, Courtesy of Old Salem Museums and Gardens.

minister Abiel Holmes of Midway, Georgia (thirty miles south of Savannah, and roughly six miles north of LeConte's Woodmanston rice plantation), wrote in support of weather observations regarding Charleston hurricanes: "From my register, kept in Georgia, are selected the following observations: '1790. January. Mercury, highest 81°, lowest 26 above zero. Winds S.W. and N.W. Jonquils, jessamin, and woodbine in bloom.'"[98] Fortuitously, a map of a vernacular garden of a European form specifically including daffodils survives and is not English in derivation but German, coming from the Moravian settlement of Bethabara, North Carolina. In the 1730s the Moravians (originally from Moravia, now in the Czech Republic) left their sanctuary and adopted home town of Herrhut in Saxony, Germany, for the American colony of Georgia. By 1741 they departed for better climate and less political tension and settled in Bethlehem, Pennsylvania, which became the central command for all future expansion. Groups

Tazettas—Polyanthus Narcissus

Tazettas have essentially been their own world within the genus *Narcissus* almost from the beginning. Their endless variations on a narrow theme within wild species populations, coupled with very early hybridizing, created very muddy waters. Their distinct genetics has even led to a recent call for their separation once again from the genus *Narcissus* to that of Hermoine, as they were once classified in the early 1800s.

The two great conundrums in the 1700s and early 1800s were first, identifying distinct tazetta species in the wild and/or wild specimens, and second, separating the species plant from the florists' flower. The sorting and shuffling in botanical texts is made even more confusing for the modern casual reader as the terms used varied and some species names are no longer recognized by the Royal Horticulture Society.

With the advent of the Linneaean system of classification in the middle to late 1700s, tazettas went from having every flower a distinct species (a splitter's worldview) to having all flowers lumped under one species name—*N. tazetta*. This is most clearly illustrated by the change in Philip Miller's *The Gardeners Dictionary* from his 1754 to 1768 editions. In his 1768 edition, to compensate for all tazettas being listed under *N. tazetta,* he includes twenty-two popular Dutch florists' hybrids.

The universal adoption of a lumper's view did not bring the needed clarity. British botanists waded into the muddy waters in the early 1800s, attempting to sort out the species from the old hybrid florists' flowers

of the past two hundred years. But Curtis and his compatriots got only so far in contending with tazettas:

In plants that have been long cultivated in gardens, it will often be a question not readily decided, whether certain individuals are mere varieties, arising from the adventitious circumstances of culture, or originally distinct species, or hybrids deriving their origin from intermixture. . . . Hence a very long-continued existence [by human vegetative propagation] without change will often afford a strong presumption of a plant's being a real species.

Armed with such reflections, the Botanist may boldly enter the Florist's parterre, undismayed by the barbarous host of a Dutch catalogue. Here he will certainly find, that if the older botanical writers frequently raised varieties to the rank of species, the modern have sometimes confounded such as are really, and ever have been, distinct. To enable us to decide in difficult cases, it becomes necessary to study varieties as well as species; and this must be our apology for admitting several of the former into a work, in the general plan of which they are excluded. Faithful representations and accurate descriptions, when recorded, cannot fail to establish the truth in the end.[100]

The all-white (and nearly all-white) tazettas were fairly easy to tackle, coming from a limited source and never having been too popular as a florists' flower. According to *Curtis's Botanical Magazine,* they all came from Italy and were predominantly three plants—*N. papyraceus* (or "Italian Narcissus"), *N. italicus,* and 'Romanus' or "Double Roman." (A fourth Italian tazetta had yellow petals and an orange cup.) All were too cold-tender for the Dutch to have any real success with their cultivation or hybridization; "Double Roman" wouldn't properly double-up if grown by the Dutch in their cold climate. Bulbs came from around Genoa near the French Riviera (along with the tuberose), and from Mount Vesuvius.

The bicolor and yellow tazettas proved more problematic. Botanists tended to divide the rest into two groups based on which side of the Mediterranean they were thought to have originated from. Narcissus orientalis, or Narcissus of the Levant, were those species originating from the eastern end of the Mediterranean basin—these bloomed later in the spring (some said in May) and had white petals and pale yellow cups. Narcissus tazetta came to signify those flowers from the western Mediterranean of Spain, France, Portugal, and the Barbary Coast—these bloomed in early spring (February and March) and had yellow petals and orange

Plate 1188, Narcissus Italicus. Pale-Flowered Narcissus. *Curtis's Botanical Magazine,* 1809.

cups. The favorite white petal–orange cup flowers, many considered species, fell somewhere else—all suggesting the botanists of the day didn't have much success against the barbarous host of Dutch florists' tazettas in the parterres.

of Moravians left to found new settlements to fulfill their missionary goals; one such group in 1753 headed back south to found "Wachovia" in North Carolina.

On May 1, 1759, Brother Lung laid out the Upland Garden and drew up a map. The vegetable garden was laid out in squares, and a few ornamentals were planted in the borders around the beds; on the side of the map is included *N. pseudonarcissus* along with lilac and cloves. The garden bed rows were laid out on the diagonal and not the traditional perpendicular, likely to mitigate against the vagaries of the terrain. So, did the daffodils make the long treks from Germany to Georgia to Pennsylvania to North Carolina? Were they brought directly from Germany? As the Moravian communal system maintained very close ties with the hometown of Herrhut in Germany (virtually all plans were reviewed and approved by either Bethlehem or Herrhut), and the group remained fairly insular until the 1800s, it is quite plausible the *N. pseudonarcissus* came originally from Germany (as opposed to pass-alongs from other American colonists). This method of planting ornamentals to border the vegetable plot harkens back to Alexander Neckham's late twelfth-century description of flowers along the sides of the vegetable garden.[99]

Conclusion

Daffodils in colonial and federal America reflect the views of the flower held in the colonists' European homelands—a common garden flower, a florists' flower of fashion, a respectable member of the general herbaceous border palate, a species worthy of a place or three (or twelve) in the botanic garden. They appeared in vegetable gardens, perennial borders, fancy parterres, and recently settled frontier dooryards. They were brought by immigrants and imported by aristocrats.

The paucity of documentation of daffodils by name and by garden in the colonial period leaves the question of what really grew in (colonial) vernacular gardens to remain somewhat problematic. Simply that flowers were known to well-connected botanists, or were even common in early to mid-1700s English gardens, is not necessarily proof they grew in colonial gardens. The "Albus Plenus Odoratus" fracas demonstrates that: a rare flower in some parts of England (of importance, around London especially), a veritable weed around Philadelphia. Conversely it is particularly frustrating that the "Primrose Peerless," so common in English commoners' gardens, has yet to be found definitively mentioned in colonial or federal gardens, common or well-to-do, save possibly in the Virginia garden of Marlborough.

So, what were the common daffodils sent by Collinson that drove Bartram and Witt up the wall? The "common" daffodils weren't given much thought by anyone, as per Bartram's dismissive comment in 1763 and Faris's lack of mention in the 1790s. To be "common" meant to be widely grown by commoners, as well as by gardeners of taste (at least when it came to jonquils). Two doubles were obviously so, at least as far as Bartram was concerned—'Telamonius Plenus' and "Albus Plenus Odoratus." Of the two widely common English daffodils, *N. pseudonarcissus* is the "common daffodil" in early

1800s American catalogs, as offered by both Bartram's Garden and Bernard M'Mahon. It was common enough to be naturalized around Philadelphia by 1816 and was the one daffodil brought (from Germany?) by the Moravians to North Carolina in the late 1750s. Past this, all is educated conjecture.

From the minimally documented obscurity of the colonial garden, daffodils appear in federal gardens, the common, the formal, and the esoteric, representing all the social classes. Wealthy gardeners who had daffodils had a representative smattering of every sort, and the highbrow nurserymen stocked accordingly. While Bartram and LeConte the botanists (and Logan to a degree) were interested in the rare, the tasteful gardeners of the day showed their preferences through their ordering lists for polyanthus narcissus, jonquils, and doubles per Henry Middleton and Lady Skipwith—preferences that held well into the next century.

3.

Daffodils in America, 1820 to 1860

The years around 1820 are a watershed, the seminal event actually being the Panic of 1819. Newly minted America had suffered through two depressions, one in the late 1780s and another in the late 1790s, and after the War of 1812 had entered into a period of growth. The depression of 1819–1821 was a period of severe contraction; many landowners defaulted, banks failed, and unemployment skyrocketed. The change of political mood after the "Era of Good Feelings" was profound.

The subsequent period of economic expansion, created by a growing population and industrialization, meant more Americans had more leisure time and more money and thus more need to stay au currant, at least as much as possible. The first wave of American journals devoted solely to horticulture appeared in the 1830s, such as *Floral Magazine and Botanical Repository* (by D. and C. Landreth of Philadelphia, 1832), *Horticultural Register and Gardener's Magazine* (by Fessenden and Breck of Boston, 1835), and *Western Farmer and Gardener* (by Hopper and Elliot, Cincinnati, 1839). In New England, with newfound prosperity for many smaller towns, horticulture arose as a pursuit, leading to the founding of local horticulture societies.

Life in America came to a brutal halt again with the Panic of 1837, the culmination of President Andrew Jackson's bank wars with Nicholas Biddle of the Bank of the United States. Most East Coast factories closed, most magazines (including many recently founded agricultural publications) folded, and again unemployment was staggering. The depression in America lasted until 1844—in Europe it was called "the Hungry Forties"—while in the Netherlands it dragged on even longer. Once the economy regained its footing, credit flowed and growth surged anew, bringing the next wave of great house (and garden) construction. Parterre designs slowly shifted from rectilinear to curvilinear in many regions, and the English Landscape School swept in with

Andrew J. Downing Jr. in 1844. In the 1850s northern garden writers slowly adopted and promulgated a more English Victorian style as applied to bulbs, while southern garden writers were much slower to do so.

As pertains to daffodils, a shift occurred somewhere around 1820. After the expansive array of daffodils in early federal gardens came a period of contraction. Gone were the personal botanic gardens and the pursuit of the botanically esoteric. Where bulb landscaping design went, daffodils were not well adapted; where fashion tastes evolved, daffodil hybridizing was decades behind. In vernacular gardens, daffodils remained just in the mix of pass-along plants.

This loss of status, this slide to the common, is evidenced in an article on gardening written by Charlestonian Charles Fraser in 1845:

> One of the results, we might say one of the triumphs of modern horticulture, is the introduction and naturalisation, even the domestication, of foreign plants and flowers, greatly diversifying the beauty of our gardens, and enlarging the enjoyments of taste. Our vegetable population is thus greatly increased, and like that of our municipal and political communities, is fast rivalling the number of natives.... We may all remember when our gardens produced a comparative meagre display, when our roses were few, and those the descendants of the Huguenot stock: and our flower-beds confined to anemonies and stock gillyflowers—pinks, jonquils, and a few blue hyacinths (other colors being very rarely seen), as prescribed by the old-fashioned vocabulary. Whereas they now exhibit a splendid array of flowers and shrubs, contributed by every part of the globe—roses from China and Bengal, dahlias from Mexico, jessamines from Arabia, verbenas and astremerias from South America; the gardenia florida, ixia sparaxis and gladiolus from the Cape of Good Hope; mignonette from Egypt; the ice-plant (mysembryanthemum crystallinum) from Athens; the various japonicas, including the lornicera, the Italian honeysuckle; the lagerstremia from China, with its varieties, and that splendid shrub, the pittosporum, also from China. These, with many other exotics, are now familiar to us, and may be fairly enrolled in the American Flora.[1]

Uses of Dutch bulbs remain rigid, stiff, and formal in high-style gardens; for many writers daffodils didn't warrant inclusion at all. This is likely in part due to daffodils not thriving with the practice of lifting shortly after blooming to finish their season in an ignominious corner of the property in the "reserve garden," which did not impact tulips or hyacinths as much. It was well remarked daffodils did best being lifted every three years, particularly jonquils.

American fads developed for new flowers and all their newly hybridized variations, from gladiolus to dahlias to tulips to chrysanthemums, which all rose and fell in their turn. As American tastes emulated the English and changed to desire showier, flashier plants,[2] daffodils stayed the same; the plain green leaves and pale yellow flowers did not suit. No one has ever accused an old or species daffodil of being "big, bright and showy."

Pl. 38

Plate 38, Jane Loudon, *The Lady's Flower-Garden of Ornamental Bulbous Plants*, 1841. Courtesy of the Cherokee Garden Library, Kenan Research Center at the Atlanta History Center, Atlanta, Georgia.

While tastemaker gardeners in England were not favorably disposed to the daffodil, Scottish garden designer and writer John C. Loudon, followed by his wife Jane,
were. Their views, however, seemed to have made little difference to American garden
writers and nurserymen, who occasionally publicly grumbled of supply issues from
Dutch companies and on general cultivation vagaries of some *Narcissus*. The British
may have kept at collecting and classifying species *Narcissus;* a few intrepid gardeners
such as Edward Leeds were hybridizing; and the Loudons may have advocated for
them; but you can't prove it by the Americans.

Landscape Literature

Much of the landscape design published from the 1820s to 1860s does not particularly
bear on the daffodil. As a general rule, American landscape literature for the upper
classes followed the dictates and tastes of England, albeit a little slowly in the transatlantic transmittal of culture. Early antebellum American garden literature treats the
daffodil as a background plant—in its Dutch bulb niche after hyacinths and tulips.
Often daffodils did not warrant mention, and if so, it was only in passing and that they
may be treated the same as hyacinths and tulips. Further most nurserymen and florists
addressed only polyanthus narcissus and jonquils, the rest not warranting consideration.

Directives for landscaping with *Narcissus* were succinct, essentially a direct continuation of the rigid and formal colonial and federal periods. They fell into three general
planting methods: in a linear designated bulb bed, in a mixed border with other plants,
or within parterre beds. Directions for bulb bed planting varied slightly. Some were
very rigid and formal, if not downright unimaginative, while a few were more relaxed,
with slightly more inventive planting schemes, but not greatly so. Overall the rectangular bed with regimental rows held sway for decades.

In the 1820s and 1830s, bulbs were to be planted in specially designated, prepared
beds of unimaginative ubiquitous form. A posthumous edition of Charleston gardener
Robert Squibb's *The Gardener's Calendar for the States of North-Carolina, South-Carolina,
and Georgia* (1827), for September directed "the following bulbs may be set out: Snow
Drops, Polyanthus Narcissus, Iris's, Jonquills, Crocus's."[3] As a work devoted primarily
to agriculture, no "landscape" suggestions were proffered, but the implication is for
basic, designated bulb beds.[4] And as a regional guide tailored to the difficult conditions
of the South, its inclusion of polyanthus narcissus, jonquils, and crocus was in specific
rejection of tulips and hyacinths as problematic for the climate.

Roland Green of Boston published one of the earliest American works devoted
to horticulture. In *A treatise on the cultivation of ornamental flowers* (1828), he maintained the rectangular bulb bed, with narcissus and other bulbs to be planted in rows
approximately a foot apart. This echoed almost verbatim the direction from the great
nurseryman William Prince of New York in his *A Short Treatise on Horticulture* (1828).

Glimmers of gardening flair came from Philadelphia exotic nurserymen Hibbert
and Buist; in *The American Flower Directory* (1832) they instructed that polyanthus narcissus and jonquils were to be planted in raised bulb beds as with other bulbs. While

crocuses could be planted in lines by color and hyacinths in eight-inch squares of alternating colors, other bulbs could be mingled: "All of these bulbs may be advantageously planted in patches through the garden by taking out about one square foot of earth. Break it well, and if poor enrich it. Plant four bulbs in each of the same colour, and the clumps that are contiguous to contain different colours."[5] But they were the exception, not the rule.

New York florist Thomas Bridgeman, in *The young gardener's assistant* (1837), recommended planting jonquils in the border, and polyanthus narcissus in designated bulb beds in rows. "When ready, the beds may be laid out, from three to four feet wide, and they should be raised two or three inches above the level of the walks, which will give an opportunity for all superfluous moisture to run off."[6] Bridgeman allows, if not encourages, gardeners to transplant annuals into their bulb beds after the bulbs have been lifted for summer storage, to continue the gaiety of bloom. Meanwhile the same year, Thomas Fessenden of Boston varies his recommendations only slightly in *The New American Gardener,* giving no measurements for the bulb bed, but instead recommending it raised four to five inches above the walk.

For daffodils the primary alternative to the bulb bed was the mixed border. Edward Sayers, landscape and ornamental gardener, in *The American Flower Garden Companion* (1838), recommended narcissus and other bulbs for planting "indiscriminately in the flower borders,"[7] a little less rigid in effect than Green and Bridgeman. He even thoughtfully listed daffodils—eleven tazettas, four doubles and four singles.

French Louisiana too gained a gardening tome during this period. The *Nouveau Jardinier de la Louisiane* was published in 1838 by J. F. Lelièvre, who by then had been in New Orleans all of four years. Modeled extensively on Jean-Jacques Fillassier's *Dictionnaire du Jardinier Français* (1789), Lelièvre addressed only the cold-dependent *N. poeticus* under the heading of *Narcissus,* inadvertently reflecting French preferences rather than near-tropical Louisiana gardening realities. Jonquils are not completely absent, however, as Lelièvre does make passing reference to when they should be planted, suggesting van Oosten's observation of the French loving jonquils possibly lingered in Louisiana (as it does today).

Known for his revolutionary advocacy for landscapes as sweeping views, Andrew J. Downing Jr. did devote a section to the flower garden in his landmark *A treatise on the theory and practice of landscape gardening* (1844). While spring bulbs were not the top of his list, he made allowances for their presence. His most prominent treatment of them falls under his discussion of the English flower garden (no mention is made in conjunction with the other two flower-garden designs—the irregular style and the old French style) and the epitome of that style at Dropmore, in England, which for winter and spring blooming did include hyacinths, tulips, and other bulbs (but no mention of daffodils), as well as some early spring annuals. Downing accommodated spring bulbs as an acceptable preference for a specialty garden, in the manner of a botanical garden or a flower garden devoted to florists' flowers. To accomplish the Dropmore effect on an American budget, Downing suggested interplanting "the most showy herbaceous plants, perennial and biennial, alternating them with hardy bulbs and the finer species of annuals."[8] The genus *Narcissus* makes no appearance in his treatise.

The American view of Dutch bulbs and *Narcissus* in particular in the first half of the century becomes brutally apparent from two sources over almost twenty years apart. William Prince, in *A Short Treatise on Horticulture* (1828) complains bitterly:[9]

> The collections of Bulbous Flowers have been so greatly extended within these several years past, by a careful and scrutinizing selection of the most exquisite flowers of every country at all celebrated in their cultivation, that although some few collections in Europe may exceed the author's in the number of varieties, still it is believed few or none surpass it in the selection of the most choice and intrinsic flowers; and prices have been paid in many cases altogether unwarranted by the demand this country has yet afforded, but with the expectation that the increasing botanic taste evinced throughout our country, would also in time devote to this class of plants the attention which it merits. It may be well to remark, that the Bulbs which are frequently sent out on consignment to this country from Holland, and sold at our auctions, are the mere refuse, and such as are held in no esteem either by amateurs or connoisseurs, and no idea can be formed by them of the beauty of the more estimable kinds; and it is to be regretted that our citizens should have been so often duped in their purchases of these roots, under the imposition of high sounding names.[10]

The loss of status by the daffodil in America coincided with the Dutch ramping-up of production to meet market demand, and in the pursuit of cash, to a lessening of ethical business practices. According to the Dutch bulb history authority Dr. Ernest H. Krelage, Dutch bulb companies began sending shipments of bulbs on consignment for auction to America, particularly New York, Philadelphia, Boston, Washington, Baltimore, and other locales, as well as to individual nurserymen, after the cessation of European hostilities in 1815. These early shipments were admittedly of inferior quality, being basically an effort to clear out unsold and substandard stock, with no attention paid to quality nor accuracy of names. According to Krelage, it took some years before Dutch businessmen realized that dumping inferior quality merchandise was not good for long-term business, and so began improving their practices. By 1844 this attention to better business practices began paying off, as per a letter from Philadelphia nurseryman Henry A. Dreer:

> Having frequently noticed your name attached to catalogues of bulbs, sold in this country at auctions, and upon trial generally found them superior to others sold here, I am induced to address you with the view of importing directly from you yearly an invoice of Hyacinths and other bulbs suited to my sale.
>
> I am in this city in the seed and plant business, and wish to import every season from a house that I may always depend on receiving them in time and true to name and description.[11]

But issues of "loose" business practices lingered. A specific case of this sad state of affairs was commented on by garden writer Thomas Winter of Cincinnati in 1847 regarding the most common daffodil in cultivation, *N. pseudonarcissus:* "From England this bulb found its way into Holland, whence it is imported into this country under the specious name of 'Soleil d'Or,' thus disappointing those who purchase them under that name."[12] He soon continues:

> This is the "Poet's Narcissus," and an old favorite, which has been the subject of many poems by writers of old. This highly scented bulbous rooted plant bears a white flower in May. . . . It often disappoints expectation, for if the flower bud, before expanding, is pressed with the finger and thumb, it blasts the flower and prevents its expansion. Indeed it may be considered very uncertain, at the best; for sometimes it will not flower for several years.
>
> Although this flower has attracted so much attention in olden time, at this day it is hardly worth cultivation. The classic associations connected with it endeared it to many, but at the present day it hardly commands a corner in the flower garden. Such is the result of changes in the public mind. There are many of this species of bulbs at the present day enumerated in the Dutch catalogues, but whether they are really individual varieties, is a matter of doubt; cultivation alone will alter their appearance, particularly if not attended to with judgment. It requires the scrutinizing eye of the botanist to detect its real character. Care and attention would restore many to their high cultivated state, while others would retain their primitive standing as degenerated flowers. Then, again, those in a high state of culture may be crossed, such as Tazetta orientalis, the Roman Narcissus and Narcissus tazetta, which no doubt would produce some fine hybrids. When the Dutch bring forward their numerous lists, we should look on it with a suspicious eye, for we cannot depend on their statements with much assurance. We may meet with great disappointment, as in their Soleil d'Or.[13]

So added insult to injury—not only did one overpay for a bait-and-switch flower, one got a flower held in low regard, particularly when paying polyanthus narcissus prices (25 cents to 30 cents each) for a single trumpet narcissus (12 cents each, based on the William R. Prince & Co. catalog for 1842 and 1843). (One is tempted to speculate that Dutch wholesalers in the dire "straightened" economic circumstances of the Hungry Forties were not going to allow ethics to trump cash flow.)[14]

Somewhere around 1850 a subtle shift begins in landscape literature, in that daffodils are spoken of in a slightly more positive light—or at least not so dismissively. Presumably some years of better business practices (at least by some Dutchmen) eventually resulted in American gardeners and nurserymen viewing Dutch bulbs, daffodils included, in a more positive light. This also coincides with the belated recovery of the Dutch economy from the depression.

The renowned Boston nurseryman and horticulturist Joseph Breck appreciated daffodils, "many of them too well known for description; all suitable to ornament the

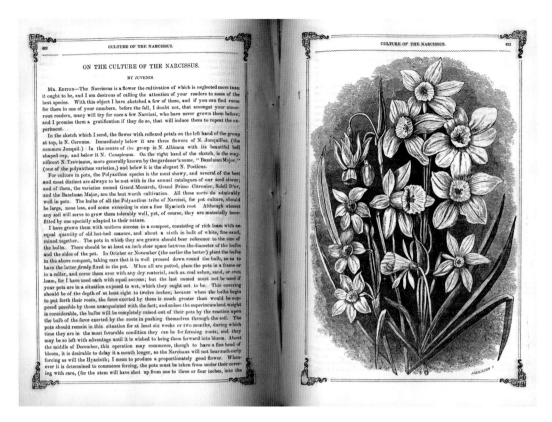

Narcissus bouquet. Juvenis, *The Horticulturist*, 1852. Courtesy of the Cherokee Garden Library, Kenan Research Center at the Atlanta History Center, Atlanta, Georgia.

garden,"[15] but proffered no specific landscape direction. Breck promulgated the aesthetic of Dutch bulbs in raised geometric beds with planted borders of box or lawn, set among broad paths. For tulips, Breck recommended a solid bed for better varieties, giving instruction on how to lay out a 36' × 4' bed with rigorous spacing. Less expensive cultivars, both tulips and hyacinths, may be planted in small groupings in the borders.

In 1852 a letter to the editor of the *Horticulturalist* (the editor being the highly influential Andrew Downing), written by "Juvenis," elaborated on growing Narcissus, " the cultivation of which is neglected more than it ought to be."[16] It is a long article, complete with an illustrative plate. The species shown in the plate are esoteric even by British standards for the day, belying a knowledge of the genus *Narcissus*. While the majority of the article focuses on various methods of parlor growing, the garden section gives a different method:

> No object amongst our early spring flowers, is more beautiful than the Narcissus, for the flower garden. Any of the varieties may be planted in the open border in the fall of the year; they should be placed deep enough in the ground for the bulbs to be covered four inches, and their situation should be a short distance from the edge

to June, and these to be succeeded by annuals or bedding plants, a combination of the two, or even bulbs, annuals, bedding plants and perennials together. When this plan of

Fig. 15. Plan of the Dropmore Flower Garden.

Scale, 32 feet to the inch.

the Dropmore garden first appeared in *Loudon's Magazine*, in 1828, the Verbena melindres, and its numerous seedlings, now so admired, were not known; the Portulacca had not

Dropmore garden illustration. Hovey, *Magazine of Horticulture*, 1854. Courtesy of the Biodiversity Heritage Library.

of the border, with Crocus or Snowdrops, or some low growing plants in the foreground. It is not necessary to lift the bulbs every year, but once in three years they will require it, to separate the offsets. With regard to soil, they will thrive very well in any tolerably good garden ground; the richer it is, the larger and more numerous will be the flowers, and they will form a most interesting contrast to the Hyacinths, which should be planted alternately with them. The effect thus produced is more pleasing to the eye, than when they are placed separately in beds, as is sometimes done.[17]

Perchance because the preferred method of planting is in a mixed border, as opposed to segregated beds, no discussion of overplanting is made. This planting formation presages an article two years later with a much more elaborate plan.[18]

A watershed seems to have been crossed by 1854. As editor of *Magazine of Horticulture, Botany and All Useful Discoveries,* Charles Mason Hovey published his own article on how to create a tasteful "Dutch flower garden."

Hovey employed the famous English Dropmore estate parterre garden as a case study. Its significance is partly in the method of scheduling the blooming of bulbs so their senescence occurred early enough to allow the overplanting of the same garden for a summer bloom, rather than implying a rectangular bed was to lie fallow through the summer. Two variants were given—in the first, the bulbs were to be removed by late June and replanted about November 1 after removing the annuals; in the second, the bulbs were to be spaced such that perennials and annuals could be interplanted, and the bulbs lifted every three years. While the dim status of daffodils is still apparent (the only acceptable *Narcissus* for this plan was an unspecified double), this article is also noteworthy for the element of encircling a parterre bed of flowers with bulbs—inside the boxwood edging. "Gardens of this kind may be rendered ornamental the whole season, from April to November. They may be so planted as to have a display of bulbous flowers from April to June, and these to be succeeded by annuals or bedding plants, a combination of the two, or even bulbs, annuals, bedding plants and perennials together."[19]

Bulbs deemed suitable were platted out in the design, with a key provided. Suggested summer flowers were lantana, heliotrope, verbena, plumbago, pansies, portulaca, petunias, geraniums, and select roses. Hovey's plan is further elaborated for its completion and continuance during the summer months:

> Another list might be made composed of bulbs, perennials, annuals and bedding plants; the bulbs to remain without removal three years; the perennials set out between them, with sufficient space to bed out plants; the annuals growing immediately among the bulbs without injuring them, unless very rare sorts, which need not be used, as the common showy ones are just as good. The only objection to this arrangement is, that for a time the dead and decaying leaves of the bulbs look bad among the green and healthy foliage of the annuals and perennials; still, if a little attention and some labor is no object, this plan will afford the most continuous bloom.

> Good taste and little judgment on the part of the amateur or gardener, will enable either to make a flower garden of this kind charmingly beautiful all the season.

> In conclusion we should add that all the beds should be edged with box, and the walks neatly gravelled.[20]

By employing the method of overplanting or interplanting, a designated bulb bed could pull double duty for both the spring and summer seasons, and thus be more palatable. The bordering of tall bulbs with lower varieties echoes back to Juvenis's article two years prior and reflects a new way of planting bulbs taking hold that would last through the end of the Victorian period.

Flower and Bulb Gardens. 327

been introduced; the Plumbàgo Larpéntæ, the beautiful lantanas, and many other fine plants, could not then be obtained. The principal plants then relied upon for summer blooming were geraniums, heliotropes, roses and annuals. How much more varied and magnificent the display now; and from the ease with which these new plants are cultivated, how much better the show can be kept up by having a reserve stock in pots ready at any time for turning into the ground!

In presenting this design, we have therefore omitted the lists of plants and bulbs which accompanied it, but in their place give two of our own, substituting the kinds now so much esteemed for bedding for those originally selected. The selection may be varied to any extent, so numerous are the varieties of verbenas, petunias, and other plants; but the same principles of grouping in colors must be attended to, or the effect will be greatly marred:—

1. THE BULB GARDEN FOR SPRING.

1. Iris of various colors, edged with crocuses.	17. Crown imperials, bordered with blue crocuses.
2, 2. Double or parrot tulips, edged with white and blue crocuses.	18. Anemones, various colors.
3. Early single tulips.	19. Anemones, various colors.
4. Early single tulips.	20. Anemones, various colors.
5, 5. Narcissus, (double.)	21. Anemones, various colors.
6, 6. Snowdrops.	22. Snowdrops.
7. Hyacinths, double blue.	23. Snowdrops.
8. Hyacinths, double white.	24. Crown imperials, bordered with crocuses.
9. Crocuses, white.	25. Hyacinths, single blue.
10. Crocuses, blue.	26. Hyacinths, single red.
11. Hyacinths, double red.	27. Crocuses, blue or mixed colors.
12. Hyacinths, double yellow.	28. Hyacinths, single yellow.
13. Snowdrops.	29. Snowdrops.
14. Snowdrops.	30. Snowdrops.
15. Tulips, single, various colors; all four beds (15) the same.	31. Hyacinths, single white.
16, 16. Crown imperials, bordered with white crocuses.	32. Crocuses, white or mixed colors.
	33, 33. Narcissus, double.

All these will be entirely out of bloom so that the bulbs may be taken up by the 20th of June, or the 30th at the latest. The ground should then be thoroughly dug over,

Dropmore garden key. Courtesy of the Biodiversity Heritage Library.

Gone was the rectangular bed of a single cultivar type; round and varied was now in, echoing larger de rigueur flower beds of the day. For a suburban gardener with limited space, an anonymous article in 1857 recommended a circular, slightly raised bed in the lawn, planted to accommodate an array of bulbs popular in the day. Bulbs were to be staggered in height, with a tall lily for the center, next encircled by six lilies each a different variety. The next row encircling would alternate six types of crown imperials with six sorts of gladiolus. The next row would be eighteen tulips, encircled then by sixteen hyacinths alternating with as many daffodils. The final encircling row, the low border, would be intermixed crocus and snowdrops. Frustrating is that there is no mention of what to do with the bed the rest of the year.[21]

Southern garden writers lagged in adopting the new fashion of round beds and the alternating of sorts. The book *Ladies' Southern Florist* (1860) by Mary Catherine Rion, of Winnsboro, South Carolina, holds the honor of the first American, and only southern, woman-authored book devoted solely to ornamental horticulture, prior to the Civil War. Her bulb beds descriptions hew to the traditional: "Daffodils, Jonquils, Iris, Crocus, Snowdrop. . . . Cultivate all of these plants in clusters, for effect. A handsome arrangement of them can be made in waves, circles, and various figures, by close and uniform planting."[22] She encouraged a more flexible use of bed design, if not the actual planting of bulbs proper, but made no suggestion for overplanting bulb beds with summer annuals. She grew bulbs in her own South Carolina garden, the descendents of which survived into the 1960s, but no types were noted (as of 2010, 'Telamonius Plenus' still appeared in the lawn).

Parlor Gardening

In 1800s America, Dutch bulbs were imported for indoor growing, often more so than for planting in the garden, as was especially the case for daffodils. Named polyanthus narcissus (tazettas) well outnumbered the named "standard" daffodils (trumpets, doubles, jonquils, poets and the like) usually grown in the garden, although these too were often potted and forced for indoor blooming. Tazettas could be brought into bloom by December, thus initiating an indoor flowering season of Dutch bulbs lasting until high spring. Polyanthus narcissus came to dominate the *Narcissus* catalog trade and hence the American view of daffodils first and foremost as a parlor plant. Once forced, daffodil bulbs take two years to recover, which most people still are not inclined to fiddle with. Bulbs were thus discarded after forcing, possibly excepting the "choice sorts." Consequently, parlor-grown daffodils were an annual expense and kept the trade in the money.

Over time, new forms and containers evolved for an ever-widening way to display and enjoy indoor plants, particularly as the Victorian styles of Britain came in vogue, such as rustic baskets, wrought iron stands, and tiered vessels. Flower displays themselves became more ornate, evolving into the "lasagna" planting style popular today. In his instructions to young florists, newspaper garden columnist Thomas Winter of Cincinnati observed jonquils were often "flowered in pots, and kept in stands with or near the Auricula; this, no doubt, is because it flowers at the same time, and the sweetness of its perfume, mixing with that of the Auricula, diffuses a most pleasing and delightful treat in the cool of the evening."[23]

Nurserymen and seedsmen often wrote articles or books educating the public on practical gardening methods, tasteful designs, and desirable flower sorts, with parlor gardening no exception. This both solidified their reputation and generated market interest. Conversely it is not uncommon for a good article to be recycled in later years in other publications, often without credit. An article in the "Ladies Department" in *American Farmer* of Baltimore in 1829 (credited as reprinted from *New England Farmer*) discusses Roman narcissus, double jonquilles, polyanthus narcissus, double narcissus, and crocuses (along with hyacinths) as suitable bulbs to bloom "in the winter season, in pots or glasses."[24]

Representative of the mid-1800s are the flower lists of Edward Sayer's

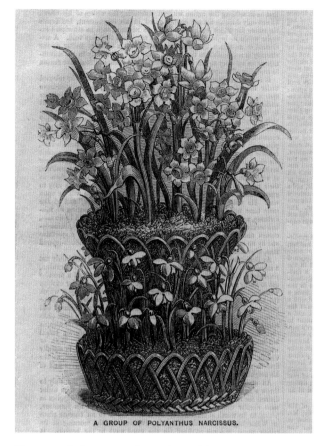

A GROUP OF POLYANTHUS NARCISSUS.

Flower stand of tazettas and snowdrops, 1858.

American Flower Garden Companion (1838) and an article by New York seedsman James Hogg for *American Farmer* (1846). Edward Sayers thoughtfully named the polyanthus narcissus offered by florists:

Bazelman Major.
Belle Legioise.
Bouquet Triumphant, *yellow.*
Dageraad, *yellow.*
Double Roman, *sweet scented.*
Glorieux, *yellow.*[25]

Grand Monarque de France.
Luna, *white and citron.*
Morgenster, *entirely white.*
Reine Blanche, *white.*
Sultan, *white and yellow.*

As his book was initially printed by two important seedsmen of the day, Joseph Breck in Boston and Grant Thorburn in New York, one could speculate these are the varieties carried by both firms at the time.[26]

Eight years later, in his 1846 article "On the Cultivation of Bulbous Roots in Pots and Glasses," Hogg's recommended list contained fewer tazettas but added doubles, jonquils, and select others. His recommended flowers were the polyanthus narcissus

Pl.39

1. Narcissus orientalis. 2. Narcissus Trewianus. 3. Narcissus Bicolor.
4. Narcissus calathinus. 5. Narcissus poeticus. 6. Narcissus viridiflora.

Plate 39. Jane Loudon, *The Lady's Flower-Garden of Ornamental Bulbous Plants*, 1841. Loudon illustrated two of the most popular tazettas of the day—Narcissus orientalis and the rarely illustrated Narcissus Trewianus, or "Bazelman Major."

'Grande Monarque de France,' "Double Roman," 'Luna,' "Morgenstern," 'Bouquet Triumphant,' and "Bazelman Major;" the doubles Double White, "Tratus Cantus," and "Orange Phoenix"; then *N. bulbocodium* and *N. poeticus* in its numerous varieties; and finally single and double jonquils. Other bulbs Hogg touted for indoor flowering were hyacinths, tulips, double and single snowdrops, double and single snowflakes, winter aconite, crocus, and Persian cyclamen. "Juvenis," in the 1852 article, named 'Grand Monarque,' 'Grand Primo Citronière,' 'Soleil d'Or' and "Bazelman Major" as the best varieties worthy of indoor cultivation, along with 'Double Roman' and *N. papyraceus,* or "the paper white of the shops."[27]

A gentlemen in the Arkansas hinterlands kept an actual gardener's diary appertaining to the tazettas grown, which reveals the reach of the East Coast nurserymen's catalogs and their influence, as well as the sway of the national agricultural journals. Jacob M. J. Smith (1799–1878), settled just outside of Fayetteville, Arkansas, in 1836, eventually establishing his own nursery. A regular subscriber to A. J. Downing's *Horticulturist,* he gained in knowledge and sophistication over the years, which even reflects in his diaries of 1844–1859 including the listings of his *Narcissus.* He planted tulips in the ground, ordered scads of hyacinths, and forced bulbs indoors. In 1844 yellow and polyanthus narcissus are as detailed as he got. By 1858 Smith noted his polyanthus narcissus by varietal name, specifically Irima, Juwel of Harlem, Papetout, 'Soleil d'Or,' "States General" ('Staaten Generaal'), and Polyanthus Narcissus Orientalis (which by this date was considered by botanists to be 'Grand Primo Citronière'). It is unclear if these were for indoor forcing or garden growing. But it suggests that as the gardening literature became more versed in tazettas by varietal name and in the importance of selecting the most robust flowers, so too did their readership.[28]

Preferred Daffodils

The preferred daffodils of this period held from colonial times. Tazettas came first, both in catalog order and in price, sold primarily for the parlor but also for the open border. Second were jonquils, single and double, for the same uses. In the garden doubles were preferred for their form but were occasionally advertised for parlor flowering. Single trumpets, poets, and others fell last, and some simply fell away altogether. Although specialty seedsmen offered a wide array of daffodils to the connoisseur, notably William R. Prince & Co. of Flushing, New York, the selections for the general gardeners were often quite limited.

Tazettas became common garden flowers in the coastal South from Charleston to Louisiana, where the mild winters were sufficiently close to their Mediterranean homelands to make them a happy winter bloomer. Garden references to "Narcissus" blooming in the winter or in January can only mean polyanthus narcissus (the earliest a trumpet or jonquil would go into bloom would be the first of February). But through the antebellum period there was a shifting and solidifying to a core group of varieties offered or touted as "preferred," although other varieties appear intermittently. As noted American horticulturists pronounced the best sorts this reinforced to the public, and thus to other seedsmen, the best varieties to purchase. Jonquils hold steady as a garden flower, the three main "sorts" of single small (*N. jonquilla*), single large (*N. × odorus*, "Campernelle" or "Great" jonquil), and double (both 'Flore Pleno' and 'Plenus'), simply lumped together.

Doubles remain popular from the colonial and federal periods, with two in particular considered common garden flowers. In 1839 Frederic Shoberl of Philadelphia remarked of the cold-dependent *N. poeticus* double, called "Albus Plenus Odoratus" or "Alba Plena Odorata": "The double variety is the most frequent in gardens."[29] In general the long-grown 'Telamonius Plenus' remained so common as to be elusive. Louisa Johnson of New Haven in 1844 listed garden flowers and led her *Narcissus* section with "*Narcissus*, or daffodil, common double yellow daffodil."[30] Elizabeth Washington Wirt of Baltimore in 1832 observed "*Narcissus major*, is a native of Spain. Common, with double flowers in garden—rarely seen single."[31]

Interestingly one double makes its first appearance in this period, remaining relatively common in American catalogs to then fade away in the mid-1880s—"Tratus Cantus" ('Plenissimus,' or "Hundred Leaved" or "Centifolius"; the old "Tradescant's Double Daffodil"). However, it was still offered in Dutch wholesale catalogs as late as 1894.[32] Conversely, the double *N. pseudonarcissus* 'Plenus' essentially disappears from view after the federal era, perhaps reflecting Burbidge's comments on the overharvesting of wild populations. The only exception is Buist's 1844 catalog, which offered "pseudo Narcissus, double flowered." It does not even appear in the Prince catalogs from 1822, the mid-1840s, or 1860.

Double tazettas shuffled about as well. The Prince catalogs for 1822 and the mid-1840s carried seven double tazettas, but the only variety widely carried in other American catalogs was 'Nobilissimus,' and then it was in the regular "Doubles" sorts. As with "Tratus Cantus," 'Nobilissimus' quietly faded from view by the mid-1880s (although still offered in the E. H. Krelage & Son 1888–1889 wholesale catalog).

After the demise of Bernard M'Mahon, the more esoteric daffodils, along, surprisingly, with some long-standing garden stalwarts, appeared only in the William R. Prince & Co. catalogs with rare exception. These were the smaller or less "showy" flowers such as *N. triandrus* and N. biflorus (*N. × medioluteus*). *Narcissus bicolor* and *N. minor* appear only sporadically in high-end catalogs, with *N. bicolor* apparently dropped altogether by Prince. Even Logan's coveted *N. moschatus* wasn't sufficiently enticing in the wholesale catalogs for most American seedsmen to pick up. Many nurserymen, especially those smaller, regional nurseries, didn't get much past polyanthus narcissus, jonquils, and doubles. It becomes a "chicken and the egg" feedback loop—daffodils were not in demand, so catalogs didn't carry them; because catalogs didn't carry them, gardeners were restricted in buying them and given the view that they weren't worth carrying—and so planting—to begin with.

While N. biflorus (*N. × medioluteus*) or "Primrose Peerless" disappears from many catalogs' lists, it remained in gardens. Joseph Breck of Boston, in *The Flower-Garden: or, Breck's Book of Flowers* (1851), described the more common daffodils too well known for description, which presumably are those found in gardens. His discussion led with the

PL.XIII.

F.W.Burbidge del et lith.

V.Brooks,Day&Son.Imp.

N. PSEUDO-NARCISSUS VAR: TELEMONIUS-PLENUS.

Plate XIII, N. Pseudo-Narcissus Var. Telamonius-Plenus. Burbidge and Baker, *The Narcissus*, 1875. Courtesy of the Cherokee Garden Library, Kenan Research Center at the Atlanta History Center, Atlanta, Georgia.

Plate X, N. Pseudo-Narcissus Fl. Pl. and Eystettensis. Burbidge and Baker, *The Narcissus*, 1875. Courtesy of the Cherokee Garden Library, Kenan Research Center at the Atlanta History Center, Atlanta, Georgia.

"Two-flowered Narcissus, Pale Daffodil, or Primrose peerless,"[33] then the many varieties of the Common Daffodil (trumpets) including a white flower and yellow cup, a yellow flower and deep golden cup, and a double form. The Great Yellow Incomparable, its double Butter and Eggs and its single form; the Great Jonquille and Common Jonquille, the many forms of the Hoop-petticoat Narcissus or Medusa's Trumpet; the White or Poet's Narcissus, and the number of double forms were all highly desirable. The most desirable of all were the Polyanthus Narcissus.

The subtle shift in the 1850s seen in garden writers toward a more favorable opinion of daffodils is reflected in some catalogs as well. The 1845 and 1846 catalogs for Mount Hope Nurseries of Ellwanger and Barry, Rochester, New York, are conspicuously devoid of *Narcissus.* Under "Bulbous Flower Roots," the bulbs offered were tulips, crocus, crown imperial, lilies, gladiolus, Iris, Tuberose, and Mexican Tiger Flower. Thus anyone subscribing to their catalogs would not even see a Narcissus to purchase and would have the notion reinforced that daffodils were not worth offering for one's garden. By 1856 Mount Hope Nurseries advertised in *Southern Cultivator* of Augusta, Georgia, their stocks of Dutch bulbs including narcissus, jonquils, polyanthus, and Early Roman narcissus. In their 1860 catalogue, more bulbs appear, such as scilla and frittilaria, as well as double and single jonquils and twenty varieties of polyanthus narcissus. Granted these likely were for indoor flowering, but they appear nonetheless.

At the other end of the spectrum, the William R. Prince & Co. nursery offered the greatest array of *Narcissus,* but the changes in its offerings again reflect changes in the marketplace. In 1822 the nursery offered sixty-four polyanthus narcissus; most of the tazettas then sold are now long gone, but a few are still well known ('Grand Monarque,' 'Grand Primo Citronière,' 'Grand Soleil d'Or,' and "Etoile d'Or" or *N.* × *intermedius*— the suspected Dutch florists' hybrid). As might be expected, very few of the 133 varieties sold by Englishman Richard Weston in his 1772 catalogue evidence any similarity to the sorts sold by Prince fifty years later. In the 1842 and 1844 catalogs, the number of tazettas offered decreased slightly to fifty-seven named sorts, the number of doubles remained the same, and singles decreased slightly from fourteen to thirteen. In the 1860 catalog however, the tazettas are greatly reduced to twenty-two, the separate section for double tazettas removed. The single narcissus lessened to ten (gone are *N. triandrus,* Sulphur Trumpet, and some small trumpets), the doubles increased from six to nine (adding "Minor pleno" and "Tenuifolius," and moving "Noblissimo" from the tazettas to "Doubles"), and notably a fourth jonquil is present, the "Sulphur White Jonquil" or *N. × tenuior.* After the Civil War, no seedsmen's catalog ever offers so many tazettas, their heyday come and gone.[34]

Ordering from Catalogs

Up to the 1860s, the wealthy are regularly cited as ordering directly from Holland, or purchasing lots of Dutch bulbs at auction. Gardeners were able to order from national or regional American seedsmen and nurserymen, but the specialty fall or autumn bulb catalog had not yet widely taken hold. Enterprising local nurserymen arose to meet the agricultural and gardening needs of the expanding population.

Plate 379, N. tenuior. *Curtis's Botanical Magazine,* 1797. Courtesy of the Cherokee Garden Library, Kenan Research Center at the Atlanta History Center, Atlanta, Georgia.

One trailblazer was Charles Minor of Montgomery Nursery in Clarksville, Tennessee. In 1835 he advertised in *Tennessee Farmer* his extensive nursery holding intending to serve the western and southern country within his reach. His nursery of nearly thirty acres, with experimental orchard and vineyard attached, was sufficient to offer fifty thousand apple trees for sale, as well as improved fruit trees recently imported from

New York and Philadelphia. Kindly, Minor offered "—100 varieties of tulips—50 of hyacinths—25 of Chrysanthemums—51 of Roses—46 of Dahlias—Paeonies, Crown Imperial, Polianthus Narcissus, Lilies, Gladiolus, Crocus, Iris, &c. in great variety."[35]

Major seedsmen and nurserymen took out advertisements in regional newspapers announcing their fall shipment arrivals to reach more customers. In the 1856 October edition of *Southern Cultivator* of Augusta, Georgia, the New York (Rochester) florists Ellwanger and Barry and James M. Thorburn & Co. of New York City advertised their stocks of Dutch bulbs including narcissus, jonquils, polyanthus, and Early Roman narcissus.[36]

They also functioned as middlemen for companies further afield lacking access to Dutch agents. On November 14, 1853, William A. Gill & Co. of Columbus, Ohio, placed an advertisement in *Ohio Cultivator* announcing: "The best assortment of bulbs ever offered in this city are now for sale . . . , received from the house of Joseph Breck & Son, Boston, and embracing a fine assortment of Hyacinths, Tulips, Narcissus, Crocuses, Jonquils, Irises, Crown Imperials, Snow Drops, Martagon Lilies, Anemones, Gladiolus, &c."[37]

The gardening connection between Louisiana and France continued into the antebellum period, even as the northern part of the state became more "Anglo." Traditional French parterre designs remained dominant as well as tastes in plants which extended to ordering of plants and spring bulbs, as illustrated by this 1825 advertisement in a New Orleans newspaper: "The French Florist Gardeners, have the honor of informing the public of their arrival in this city from Paris, with a beautiful collection of exotic plants, fruit trees of all kinds, shrubs, 150 varieties of rose, hyacinths, daffodils, jonquils, tuberoses, amaryllis (very scarce), imperial crowns, and a complete assortment of flower and kitchen vegetable seeds . . . may be seen at their store, in Mr. Andry's house, Toulouse Street. *Louisiana Courier,* February 14, 1825."[38] The wealthy across the country directly subscribed to the major East Coast seedsmen's catalogs as they did to the horticulture magazines. Martha Turnbull, mistress of Rosedown, Louisiana, maintained a garden diary from 1836 to 1896. Although she ordered Dutch spring bulbous roots (anemonies, ranunculus), tuberoses, and gladiolus from the East Coast firms of R. Buist, William R. Prince, and J. M. Thorburn (1850), alas she recorded no mention of any *Narcissus*.[39]

One of the first circuit riders sent to America from a Dutch firm was R. van der Schoot, son of J. B. van der Schoot, a major bulb grower, in 1849 (coinciding with the Dutch pulling out of the Hungry Forties depression and the potentially lucrative American market being well recovered). Van der Schoot traveled extensively from August to October, visiting individual gardeners and nurserymen alike. Stops on his tour included New York City, Philadelphia, Baltimore, Washington, D.C., Boston, Albany, and Buffalo. Van der Schoot was aiming to undercut the competition back home and thus attract new business. This did not impress Henry A. Dreer, who informed his longtime supplier E. H. Krelage that he was not about to switch his business, based on the good working relationship he had established with Krelage starting back in 1844. Van der Schoot was continuing to flood the American market with cheap bulbs into the early 1850s. John Milton Earle of Worcester, Massachusetts, in 1852 informed his usual Dutch supplier that he was not ordering that year as business was flat, and large volumes of bulbs from van der Schoot & Son were sold at auction in Boston, with hyacinths selling at as little as three and four cents a bulb.

In 1842, as Natchez Mississippi recovered first from the economic collapse pre-cipitated by the panic of 1837 and then a horrific tornado, the planter, horticulturist, and physician John Carmichael Jenkins maintained a journal of his daily activities on Elgin Plantation. His fourteen years of journals from 1840 to his death in 1855 include notations on acquisitions of ornamentals. On February 28, 1842, Jenkins wrote, "Pur-chased this morning from a Dutch (Hollander) Gardener one do. Double Hyacinths—amaryllis, iris—tazettas, one moss rose yellow & red, one doz. assorted tulips."[40] Once Natchez began to garden, as for its early decades most houses were completely unadorned, it was a status symbol to employ a European gardener who actually knew something about ornamentals, and hopefully azaleas (Dr. Boggess, personal communi-cations, February 26, 2010).

In early 1850 William Balfour of Vicksburg, Mississippi, husband of Emma, trav-eled to New Orleans and in the course of his stay purchased at auction three boxes of Dutch bulbs. His ecstatic gardening wife wrote her sister-in-law on January 28, 1850: "three boxes of bulbs from the gardens of (some hard Dutch name) near Haarlem in Holland. Hyacinths, tulips, crocuses, Narcissi, &c., and such bulbs I never saw before."[41] On March 11, 1850, Emma found her "'bon sholl' tulips . . . seem to do better here than the ordinary kind. They have very short stems, and all are double—some as double as the old 'butter-and-eggs' in the old gardens at home."[42]

In his column in *Gardener's Monthly* (1863), Walter Elder discussed how the rise of interest in Dutch bulbs and *Narcissus* continued. He visited the flower farms of Henry A. Dreer and R. Buist and Sons, admiring the spring bulbs in bloom. Regard-ing daffodils, he observed: "Although Narcissus have fewer colors the variety of the bloom, and their delightful perfume will sustain their popularity."[43] However, the most interesting overall observations opened his report: "I am much pleased to observe in my travels an increasing taste for the culture of a fine variety of flowers, and particularly of early spring bulbs. Seedsman and nurserymen have doubled their usual Importations within the past five years, and still the demand exceeds the supply. The varieties are far superior to those of late years, and yet the prices are unchanged."[44] Gardening was on the rise in America, and spring bulbs, *Narcissus* in tow, rose too.

Eyewitness Accounts: Weather Reports, Herbaria, and Travelogues

Documentation for daffodils in antebellum gardens comes from firsthand accounts published in period agriculture and horticulture journals, travelogues, diaries, and her-bariums. These preserve glimpses into gardens; they can help narrow the list of possible types of cultivars based on time of bloom, as well as offer a candid snapshot of garden flowers in a town and a year. Not surprisingly men wrote in the public sphere, often to further the agricultural sciences, whereas women wrote in private: "*The Winter in Georgia.*—The winter with us has been, thus far, mild. No very killing frosts till January 8th, when we had the thermometer down to 10°. On January 1, I noticed these in flower in the open garden;—Irish whin in full beauty; a few monthly roses and little chrysanthemums, the upper flowers and stems killed by previous frosts at 24°; two or three varieties of narcissus polyanthus; Viola odorata and tricolor; purple and pink verbena; sweet alyssum, dandelion, white and single hyacinths, Chinese pinks.—*Yours, M. A. W., Athens, Ga., Jan.* 12, 1837" (1837 is an error; all other submissions were for 1847).[45]

In 1854 Malthus A. Ward continued his observations of the weather and its effects on his garden flowers. For February 1 he reported:

> Our winter has proved to be of an anomalous character. Two snow-storms in one season has not occurred before during the 23 years I have resided here; and we have had rain and lightning in any quantity. Our extreme cold, as yet, was last Sunday morning, 16° above 0. This morning 48° 55° at noon, with a dark sky, and drizzling rain. White, single hyacinths, three sorts of narcissus, as many of violets, dandelions, daisies, (bellis,) and a few verbenas, are showing flowers in the open ground. Persian frittallary, gladioles, tulips, &c., are coming up strong; and the buds of *Paonia moutan* bursting. But they may rue it yet. I have seen the therm, at 5° in February.[46]

Andrew Gray of Savannah, Georgia, in 1855 thoughtfully wrote in to *Magazine of Horticulture,* to describe the contents of a tasteful parterre garden in the city: "The beds are planted chiefly with roses and a few of the finer varieties of shrubs, interspersed with such herbaceous and bulbous plants that we find stand the climate, viz:—Liliums, Amaryllis, Pancratiums, Hyacinth, Gladiolus, Narcissus, Phlox, Chrysanthemum, Asclepias, Carnation Pinks, Wall Flowers, Stocks, Sweet William, Alyssum, Verbenas, Violets, &c., and a good number of annuals."[47] In another report to the magazine that year, Gray reported the flowers bloom in his garden in the open ground on December 16 as "camellias, roses, chrysanthemums, alyssum and narcissus."[48]

From Eufala, Alabama, in 1846, Alexander McDonald wrote to *American Farmer* regarding the region's winter: "The winter with us has been much longer and colder than is common in this climate. I will here give you the present state of our garden, to wit: . . . Flowers out 1st of March: Yellow Jessamine, Hyacinth, the Jonquil, the Daffodils, the Narcissus, the Violet, Heart's Ease, Phlox, the Flowing Pear, and the Yellow Roses. This is the natural operation of the climate, as we have no hothouses,—the peach bloom was out on the 20th of February. I discover that we had the Pea bloom out last year on the 11th of February—we are much later the present year."[49] The blooming of flowers was not uncommonly remarked on to illustrate the weather patterns of a given year's agricultural season. Flowers as barometers were pressed into service for fruit tree management. To wit, in "Flowering of Fruit-Trees in 1857," for location reports from Vermont to Louisiana were accompanied by the observation: "At Natchez, Miss., the Purple Violet bloomed January 3d, 1857; White Hyacinth, 15th; Narcissus, 20th; Yellow Crocus, February 1st; Jonquille, 5th; Yellow Jasmine, 19th; Lilac, 20th; Locust,

March 5th."[50] In 1848 William P. Mellen, Esq., of Natchez reported to the *American Almanac* the dates of approximately thirty flowers and fruits. Noting the winter was mild, the first flowers in bloom in January were the violet on the first, the white hyacinth on the third, Narcissus on the eighth, verbena on January 18, jonquils later on January 23, and purple hyacinth on February 5, but no mention of crocus.

A wealth of garden plant material survives in an unexpected venue—herbariums that were the schoolwork of educated girls in learning the basics of botany. These volumes vividly display what were the plants of the day found in gardens of those wealthier families who could afford to send their daughters to finishing school. While it is quite possible the tazetta was a parlor plant, in Alabama it quite readily could be an open garden flower. As one might expect, the nomenclature may be a bit off.

Caroline Frances Smith, 1830–1850, labeled her flower as *N. jonquilla,* but the florets looked more like *N. × odorus* (per George Stritikus). Miss Betty Roper in 1853 pressed N. orientalis, which due to the color remaining in the cups is likely one of the long lost white-orange tazettas of the era. In 1858 Miss Fannie A. Nelms created a herbarium while a student at the Marion Female Seminary in Perry County. Her herbarium contained a plant labeled *N. jonquilla* (but looked like *N. × odorus* to Stritikus) and a poet, presumably *N. poeticus.*

Even Emily Dickinson kept a herbarium, which she began at the tender young age of fourteen in 1839. From then until 1846, she pressed plants, filling sixty-six sheets. Sheet sixty holds six *Narcissus,* of which only one was fully labeled by Miss Dickenson as *Narcissus poeticus.* The remainder—a tazetta (a paperwhite?), a double, likely *N. jonquilla,* and two undetermined flowers (*N. × odorus* and a *N. × incomparabilis*?), are labeled only by genus.

As weather reports and herbariums are specific, antebellum travelogues are often a little vague. James Stuart left England in July 1828 and returned in April 1831. Although renowned due to his cold eye taken to slavery, Stuart kindly commented on his stay in Charleston, South Carolina, in March of 1830: "The fine houses are very large, many of them enclosed like the great hotels in Paris, and all of them covered with verandas, and situated in gardens neatly dressed, and in this season not only adorned with the fairest evergreen shrubs, but with a great variety of beautiful roses, jonquils, and summer flowers."[51] Some streets were elegantly lined with Pride of India trees while those of the poor sections of town were absolutely filthy.

One of the most unexpected travelogues to mention daffodils comes from a New England clergyman traveling about America in the 1830s when he and his companions stop to pay respects at George Washington's grave. While Jefferson and Monticello are linked to early daffodils, Washington (who made no record ever of daffodils) and Mount Vernon usually are not. Unable to call on Mrs. Washington, who was not home, the party visited the old and new tombs, toured the home, and passed through the garden on the way to the decaying greenhouse. Of the garden he recalled, "Having observed all that was likely to gratify curiosity in the abode of the departed, we retraced our steps to the rear of the house, and whiled away a short time in examining the lovely daffodils and hyacinths which grew plentifully on the grounds, the luxurious box, so lofty and soft-leaved, and a strikingly beautify horse-chestnut which well nigh remained a puzzle to us all."[52]

Numerous travelers visited Mount Vernon in the 1800s, many recording their experiences. After the president's death, additional trees and shrubs were planted at Mount Vernon in the late 1810s and 1820s, but no records remain of any flowers ever being added prior to ownership by the Mount Vernon Ladies Association. So, the staff believes there is no reason to doubt the clergyman's observations, but there is no other written record to substantiate nor refute them (Dean Norton, personal communication, September 16, 2009).

High-Style Gardens

As much of the colonial documentation of daffodils tends to skew to the North, and the garden literature of this period was written by northerners, the documentation of daffodils in gardens skews to the South. Partly this is a cultural artifact of gardeners across the South looking backward in time to glorify the past, and partly an economic artifact as after the Civil War many southerners did not have access to ready cash to modernize their gardens.

Eyewitness accounts or reminiscences were collected by members of the Garden Clubs of America in the 1920s and 1930s, when historic gardens and landscapes came to the fore of national gardening consciousness (the ladies of Virginia led this charge with *Historic Gardens of Virginia* in 1923). The challenge then becomes to sift through these sources and tease out information that seems reliable. Issues arise in researching and evaluating period garden literature, ranging from veracity of sources to variations in vernacular nomenclature to the biases of the witnesses and the writers.

Color-Coordinated Gardens

Uncommon but true, some gardeners were very particular about the color combinations of their flower beds, and in one noteworthy garden, the proprietor wanted no color at all. The White Garden at Indian Hill, of West Newbury, Massachusetts, was well known for its schema of white flowers predominantly: "In this garden grew the white candytuft used for edging, the narcissus, the snowflake and the Star of Bethlehem."[53] It was laid out by James R. Lowe for Benjamin Perley Poore in 1833. The early bard of historic New England gardens Alice Morse Earle dwelled on the garden in great length in *Old Time Gardens, Newly Set Forth* (1901): "but behind the house, stretching up the lovely hillside, was The Garden, and when we entered it, lo! it was a White Garden with edgings of pure and seemly white Candytuft from the forcing beds, and flowers of Spring Snowflake and Star of Bethlehem and Jonquils; and there were white-flowered shrubs of spring, the earliest Spiraeas and Deutzias; the doubled-flowered Cherries and Almonds and old favorites, such as Peter's Wreath, all white and wonderfully expressive of a simplicity, a purity, a closeness to nature."[54]

In Virginia Mrs. Taliaferro at Belleville was known for the distinctness in colors of her fancifully shaped flower beds on the lawn. Information on the garden was provided to the contributing author by Taliaferro's granddaughter:

> Originally there was only a large vegetable garden laid off in squares defined by box-hedges and flower-borders, like many of the gardens of Colonial days. . . . The second Mrs. Taliaferro, who became the chatelaine of Belleville in 1825 [at the age of sixteen]. . . . For seventy years she remained its mistress.[55]
>
> The second feature lay in the fact that in planting her flowers, Mrs. Taliaferro massed various colors in separate beds. There was infinite variety in the coloring of the borders, but each bed displayed a mass of bloom of the same color. . . . Among the flowers were the following: snowdrops, crocus, daffodils of many varieties. The small purple and tall white and purple iris, tulips, cowslips, narcissi, violets, lilies of the valley, and the single white hyacinth grew in great profusion in the borders.[56]

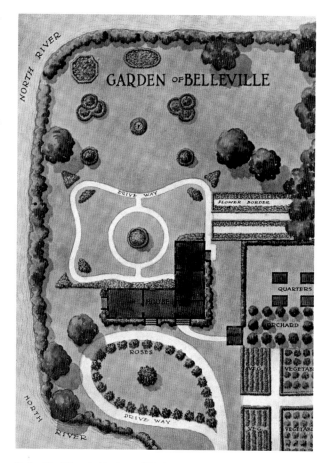

Belleville, *Historic Gardens of Virginia*, 1923.

Bulbs Lining or Bordering Parterre Beds

While the landscaping directives placed daffodils inside the sectional beds of the parterres, gardeners often planted them along the edges of the parterre beds and often in combination with other spring bulbs, with other plants inside. This harkens to the design element discussed by Hovey in his 1854 article where he lined beds of tulips, iris and crown imperials with low-growing crocus. Thus it doesn't seem surprising that many of these gardens date to the 1850s, or had long-active gardeners who may have updated their gardens with the changing styles.

This method of using bulbs appears in period descriptions of Georgia and Alabama gardens. In coastal Georgia, Mrs. King of St. Catherine's Island edged her intricate formal beds with snowdrops. Another Georgia coastal plantation garden, Elizafield Plantation on the Altamaha River, became the home of Hugh Frazier Grant in 1825, who promptly began construction. By 1933 the garden was mostly gone, as it had been acquired as a hunting plantation: "A large formal garden enclosed in a picket fence lay

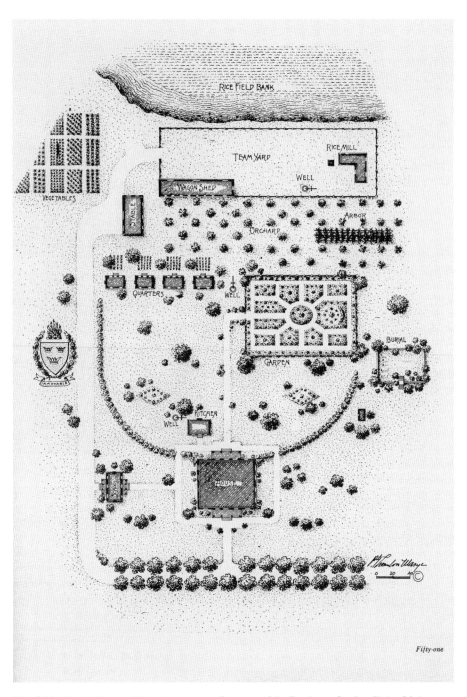

Elizafield, *Garden History of Georgia, 1733–1933*. Courtesy of the Peachtree Garden Club of Atlanta and The Garden Club of Georgia, Inc.

at the end of the right hand lawn. Roses were its pride. Here were the usual tropical plants always seen in this section; also spirea, cape jasmine, white and purple flags, gladioli, fuschias, verbenas and several kinds of lilies. The beds were outlined by narcissus, snowdrops and violets which still bloom with the coming of spring."[57]

Another Georgia garden survived long enough to be photographed. In Athens, Georgia, the 1855 home of John Thomas Grant was graced by an intricate interpretation of a quincunx pattern, the parterre beds line with boxwood. (Today it serves as the President's House for the University of Georgia). The garden's description in 1933 simply noted "bulbs" at the end of its long list of shrubs but observes the plantings are either original or careful replacements. Two images of the Grant-Hill-White-Bradshaw house illustrate the parterre garden. The 1934 image, although taken in March, documents large shrubs along one side of the garden. Fortuitously the 1940 image clearly shows daffodil foliage partially lining one bed containing roses, iris and smaller shrubs, the bulbs lining the boxwood next to the central garden walk.

In describing the high style gardens of Alabama, Thomas McAcory Owen wrote:

Old Time Flower Gardens.—The old or ante-bellum flower gardens were of two types. One of these was the garden of the wealthy and cultured slave owner modeled on the home gardens and show places of European estates. The other was that of the more modest settler. The former are numerously found about the plantation homes of the Tennessee valley, the Black Belt [referring to the rich soils], and other rich planting sections of the State. With the passing of the older homes this type of garden has disappeared also. These gardens were usually planned about the house as a center. There were winding walks, often taking the form of a maze-like labyrinth leading to a fountain, statue or a marble urn. The grounds were laid off into small flower beds which were devoted to a single plant growth and bordered with primly cut dwarf box, underneath which was always a fringe of white hyacinth. Inside of the box hedge were rows of jonquils, daffodils and giant narcissus. These plots were designed for flowers in season. In the summertime there was a blaze of color from roses, dahlias, verbenas and phlox. The odor from these and other flowers and shrubs was almost overpowering.[58]

One old garden of this form belonged to Anne Fennel Davis of Forest Home, in Trinity, north Alabama. Anne learned gardening from her mother Mary King Fennel, a true gardener, who created gardens at every home she resided in. After the death of Anne Fennel Davis in 1905, her daughter Mary Davis Henry and son-in-law resided in the house. Mary privately published a family history and biography of her mother, Anne, in 1950 and thoughtfully included a plan of her mother's garden. Under a reproduction of a plan of the house and garden layout she noted "Garden Plot designed by Ann Fennel Davis in 1858 at Forest Home. Various bulbs on all bed edges. Outside corners, tree box. All inside corners, dwarf box. One yew tree. Center of all circles, tree box. Roses, 150 varieties. Sketched from memory by M.D.H."[59]

Grant-Hill-White-Bradshaw House, 1940. Library of Congress, Prints & Photographs Division, HABS GA, 30-ATH, 4D-2.

Bulbs in Parterre Beds

As style of parterre design evolved with the changing tastes of the day, some held on to their old gardens of the old styles, such as the Bragg-Mitchell Mansion in Mobile, the Belair House in Nashville and the Richardson-Owens-Thomas House in Savannah. Another such garden was a very stubborn holdout as the entire world changed around it, and not just the tastes of parterre design. The Stryker Mansion (also called "Rosevale") in New York City, of the same family of Stryker's Bay, was one of the last holdouts of Dutch family farmsteads on Manhattan Island. Upon inheriting the property around 1818, General Garrit Hopper Striker or Stryker (d. 1868) enlarged the house and planted the extensive gardens which he continually embellished. Torn down in 1895, the circa 1751 house and gardens tenaciously clung to bucolic days of yore as tenements rose about it. Located on Eleventh Avenue, between Fifty-Second and Fifty-Fourth Streets, its remaining seven acres stretched down to the water of the North River. In the fall of 1872, the garden received an approving review: "The present appearance of the Stryker place is very pleasing, in spite of the fall season, which, however, has not changed the foliage yet to any great extent, and has permitted the flowers to linger in the garden. The parterres are very old fashioned, and the flowering bushes have usurped somewhat more space than was designed for them. But the lawns are pleasant, and the flowers are of the modern style, even including such comparative novelties as the canna, with its long leaves of dark green, and its stiff, orange flowers, and the caladium, with its huge leaves shaped like Norman shields."[60]

Later, in 1879, a *New York Times* article waxed poetically over its now three acres: "The grounds about the house are as interesting as it, and are still laid out according to the original design. In the garden, beds, arranged in squares, triangles, or other mathematical figures, bounded by rows of box, still grow such old-fashioned flowers and flowering shrubs as jonquils, daffodils, pansies, lilies of the valley, tulips, Solomon's seal, dicentra, flowering almond, papyrus Japonica, and great clumps of rose bushes and lilacs."[61]

At the other end of the parterre style spectrum were those gardeners who ardently followed the dictates of Andrew Downing. Henry C. Bowen of Roseland Cottage in Woodstock, Connecticut, was one such garden owner. His original plant order list dating to circa 1850 included the few fashionable bulbs permitted to reside in the garden—hyacinths, tulips, and grape hyacinths, but no unfashionable daffodils, nor for Downing in his opus.

In northwest Georgia the ruins of Godfrey Barnsley's home "Woodlands" and associated gardens were similarly heavily influenced by the principles of A. J. Downing and Downing's partner Calvert Vaux, possibly even down to the name of the estate. Barnsley began work improving his wilderness tract in 1842 as soon as he obtained the property and engaged in more dedicated ornamental gardening a few years later. In keeping with Downing's musings, Barnsley installed an oval parterre or "irregular" design, in the center of the drive of curved beds, which he added to over the span of many years.

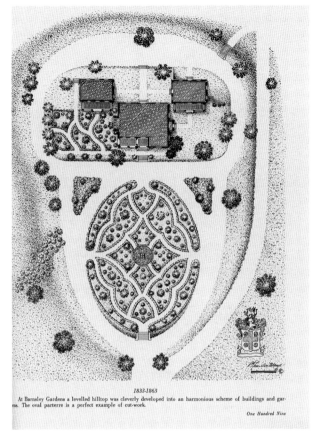

1833-1863

At Barnsley Gardens a levelled hilltop was cleverly developed into an harmonious scheme of buildings and gardens. The oval parterre is a perfect example of cut-work.

One Hundred Nine

Barnsley garden, *Garden History of Georgia, 1733–1933*. Courtesy of the Peachtree Garden Club of Atlanta and the Garden Club of Georgia, Inc.

Bulbs of any sort are not strongly represented in Barnsley's ordering lists and personal papers. Interestingly it does not appear that he ordered any spring bulbs from (Robert) Buist Nurseries in Philadelphia, from whence he ordered many of his shrubs and trees (and after 1860 he ordered regularly from Fruitland Nurseries in Augusta, Georgia). By 1845 tulips appear in reference to the oval parterre, and hyacinths are mentioned in the context of the vegetable garden. Snowdrops appear in his personal papers by 1850 in the southern side of the oval parterre. In 1857 he acquired polyanthus narcissus from New Orleans, along with Amaryllis formosissima and Gladiolus potetticina in 1859 and crocus in 1860—all mentioned for the oval parterre (but not the firm he ordered from). It tempts speculation that Barnsley broadened his palette of bulbs as their overall acceptability and popularity increased in the 1850s.

Bulbs in Mixed Borders

This straightforward flower-garden design was common across the country, as it was a continuation from the colonial and federal periods. By no means Andrew Downing's

Barnsley garden, late 1800s. Courtesy, Georgia Archives, Vanishing Georgia Collection, FLO-095.

favorite; but, being common, and commonly executed poorly in his estimation, Downing offered gentle guidance to improve the average garden. His description is valuable, as it provides more detail than otherwise found in many other works on gardening.[62]

One unexpected description of a flower border comes from a "diary" of a year in Ohio, written for a British audience but purportedly of the writer's family in Ohio, and published in 1849. The household was a well-to-do one residing at "the Cedars," the town name dutifully obscured. On April 6, an aside comment observed, "The flower-borders looked gay with hyacinths, primroses, periwinkles and daffodils, and while Willie was husking the corn, his sisters often helped their mother to weed and tie up the flowers."[63]

An interesting garden made up of box and borders was created by Dr. Francis B. Gregory and Nancy Alexander, in northern North Carolina around 1846 at Hill Airy. The boxwood served as a backdrop to flower borders planted in front, along two intersecting walks:

> A century ago Dr. Francis B. Gregory of Mecklenburg County, Virginia, and his young wife, Nancy Alexander, moved to Granville County, now Vance. In 1846, on an estate of twenty-five hundred acres, they built their house and called it Hill Airy. The house is simple, without architectural distinction, but possessing a quaint and appealing charm. From their home in Virginia they brought slips of box and made their garden, for there are some who cannot find a home without a garden. The young slips grew in the Carolina sunshine and became one of the noted gardens of Granville. The design of the garden is that of a Maltese cross and

many old-fashioned flowers bloom there, jonquils, peonies, hyacinths, bluebells, periwinkle, and roses. The broad walk leading up to the house is bordered by English box, and superb tree box stand guard on either side. This walk is intersected by another of like design. It is a peaceful and lovely spot.[64]

In eastern North Carolina, the land that became Flowery Dale Plantation was purchased in 1831 by Alfred Flowers. Two undated garden plans exist, one of the vegetable garden, the other of a formal flower garden in the traditional quincunx form. The latter is thought to have been created around 1835, by the mistress of household, Margaret Kornegay Flowers, who died in 1862. The garden was maintained by her children until the house burned in 1878. With the flower garden sketch comes lists of plants for the hedges, roses, flowering borders, and center circle; the borders flower list was "Iris, jonquils, Lily of the Valley, Phlox, Sweet William, Pinks, Poppies, Madonna lily, Peonies."[65]

Flower Garden of Flowery Dale Plantation. "Alfred and Margaret Flowers," Kennedy, Bridgers, and Flowers Family Papers #4312, Southern Historical Collection, Wilson Library, University of North Carolina at Chapel Hill.

Bordering the Vegetable Bed

Virginians often planted flowers in front of hedges around the square/rectangular vegetable gardens, and sometimes just in front of the boxwood. Numerous variations appear in *Historic Gardens of Virginia,* such as Woodbury Forrest and the Redlands. Others, like Lady Skipwith, had a designated flower bed square in the general vegetable garden area. This harkens to the European, if not medieval, practice of bordering the vegetables with more ornamentals and fragrant herbs as laid out by the Moravians in Wachovia, North Carolina.

This garden form found its way to Tennessee, and its variants became relatively widespread through the central part of the state. *The History of Homes and Gardens of Tennessee* provides a broad survey of design variations. Often a circular summerhouse was placed in the center of the four square beds. The borders could be planted with smaller flowers or larger shrubs, or both; the large center areas could be fruits,

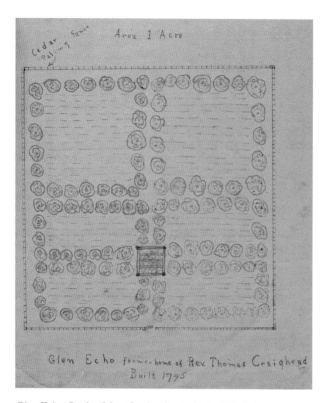

Glen Echo Garden Map, Garden Study Club of Nashville Collection, Courtesy of the Tennessee State Library and Archives.

vegetables or flowers. One variant is a central walk with multiple rectangular beds of varying sizes to totally encompass a nearly-square area (Tulip Grove). Other variants the focal center, instead of a circular summerhouse (Buena Vista, Henegar House), would be a parterre bed pattern (the Hermitage), or simply the intersection. Bulbs were noted usually in the front borders along the paths such as at the Henegar House but were noted in at least one instance as within the central square.[66]

The garden of the Barclay McGhee house in Maryville could be considered representative of the basic form. In the McGhee family from 1790 until after the Civil War, the property was then purchased by Charles T. Cates Sr., whose descendents still lived there in 1936. Interestingly the roses and box were in the front garden, while the borders to the rear vegetable garden held the bulbs:

The flower garden in the front once had its roses, its borders of box, and all the loved perennials of early days. Some of the stately old trees—elms, maples, and unusual specimens of magnolias—are still standing.

The vegetable gardens in the rear were arranged in rectangular, descending terraces, bisected by pathways bordered with narcissi, jonquils, hyacinths, and other old flowers, as well as fragrant culinary and medicinal herbs, such as sage, thyme, and lavender. The entire garden space was bordered with raspberries, currants, gooseberries, and a variety of fruit trees.[67]

Glen Echo, which stood in Nashville until 2005, when it was demolished in the name of progress for an interstate interchange, had a simple version of the bordered square pattern. The house was first built in 1794, then rebuilt in 1810 after being razed by fire. Fortuitously a pencil sketch of the garden was made during the Tennessee historic home and garden survey, a stylized version of which was published. Rather than the small plants in the borders and the large shrubs in the center squares, at Glen Echo the pattern was reversed. A buttercup is the regional term for a trumpet daffodil. "In the square garden were flower borders surrounding the beds of old-fashioned maidenblush, mycrophylla, little yellow, hundred-leaf and red velvet roses, jonquils, narcissi, and buttercups. A broad central walk, bordered with purple lilac, syringa, and flowering shrubs, bisected the garden, with other flower-filled squares placed at right angles."[68]

Planting Borders on the Terraces

Large-scale terraces as gardens predominated in the Maryland/Chesapeake area, somewhat in Virginia, and in Kentucky. Terracing contended with the terrain and run-off and erosion, as well being as a method by which to set the landscape to frame the house. Flowers would be planted around the edges of the grassy terraces, and/or along the paths connecting the terraces.

In *Old Kentucky Homes and Gardens* (1939), Elizabeth Patterson Thomas observed that the gardens laid out on hillsides were terraced, and often were bordered by flowers. Thomas indicated preferred flowers were peonies, roses, lilies, and iris. Many formal gardens were noted in the work, but not particularly described in any detail as to pattern or planting. The same plants were used in borders along walks, and vegetable squares were often bordered by flowers, but daffodils were not included when plant lists were provided.

One exception was the Hayfield garden in Louisville, once home of Dr. Charles Wilkens Short (1794–1863, a founding professor of University of Louisville medical college and a noted botanist). No historical context is provided for the garden, but the remark is made, "The old garden has three terraces of jonquils, bridal wreath and wild roses extending to Beargrass Creek."[69]

A second noteworthy anecdotal account of bulbs in terraced gardens comes from Cooleemee Plantation (built 1853–1855), near Mocksville, North Carolina. The illustrious Elizabeth Lawrence recounted finding the delicate white trumpet daffodil "Silver Bells," *N. moschatus* (or a "form" thereof), in the boxwood bordered terraces in her work *A Southern Garden* (1942). However, according to family members, no writings exist to document time frames for when the daffodils were planted in the garden.

Vernacular Gardens

Discussions of specific vernacular gardens for this time frame are few and far between; one is lucky to find diaries with firsthand accounts of such (if people could write, they wrote about the fancy things, not the mundane). As early pioneers spread across America, gardeners took favorite plants along with them, but written records of pass-along bulbs are scarce.

An interesting source of eyewitness accounts of varying degrees of reliability are the generalizations regarding places visited found in travelogues. Some are generous, others sharp. Some are very broad brush stroke, others provide a bit of nuance to place or setting. And numerous northerners published their pre–Civil War travels in the South after hostilities erupted, to better explain their adversaries (or conquered subjects).

How vernacular gardens were planted seems to be rather constant—in the front of the house, and, one would be led to believe, rather in a jumble. Frontier life was tough, and little land could be spared away from livestock, work yards, and planting fields.

Della Boswell, Hiram, Georgia, 1905. Courtesy of Georgia Archives, Vanishing Georgia Collection, PLD-2.

What was planted again was described in broad strokes, although the season of bloom at times hints as to what the daffodil was—late bloomers aren't blooming in January and February, and only tazettas bloom outdoors in December in the coastal South.

An early observer of the Mississippi Valley when it was still the newly opened "west" from roughly 1816 through the late 1820s was Presbyterian minister Timothy Flint of Alexandria, Louisiana. His dates of residency are a little fluid, as he reprinted similar material a number of times from 1826 to 1833. The first publication was his letters to his brother, also of the cloth, regarding his observations in Louisiana; he fortuitously commented in an undated letter, "The daffodil and muliflora rose are in full blossom through the winter."[70] Only tazettas bloom throughout the winter, even in the Deep South.

Later, in formal books of his travels through the Mississippi Valley or western states (presumably circuit riding; the description is identical), Rev. Flint kindly recorded his observations of the contents of the region's vernacular gardens: "The following are among the garden flowers, more particularly of the southern regions. Jessamines, white, cape, Armenian and yellow. Different kinds of sensitive plants, Spanish dagger. Primrose, Jonquils, white and yellow Iris. Blue and yellow touch-me-not. Violets. Lilies. Roses, monthly, perpetual, moss, scarlet, white, Damascus, multiflora, bell. Honeysuckle. Woodbine. Flowering pomegranate. Bamboo. Myrtle. Altheas, white and red. Daffodil. These are the common flowers, where they are not curious in choice, or varieties."[71]

Another early garden observation comes courtesy of Charles C. Wellford of Fredericksburg, Virginia: "A Nosegay in Fredewicks, in Virginia, Feb. 6—Saw, on this Sunday last, a nosegay, consisting of the following: flowers: a full-blown white hyacinth, two kinds of violets, daffodils and wallflowers. They were grown in a situation unprotected from the weather, in the garden of Mr. C. C. Welford, of this town."[72]

The diaries of women with an eye for flowers provide another glimpse of gardens of lesser means. One such anecdote pertains to the gardens of the first log cabin homes built in Leestown, Kentucky—eventually renamed Frankfort. Mary Willis Rennick Woodson (1819–1898) was the grandniece of the original surveyor of the town, Hannock Lee. Two years prior to her death, Woodson wrote down her recollections of Leestown, ostensibly before 1830. Although she spent the first thirteen or so years of her life in her grandfather Willis Atwell Lee's domicile of Glen Willis, Lee's original double log cabin built in 1793 was still standing during her childhood. In a reference to her grandfather's cabin, and possibly that of her immediate neighbors, "Aunt Willie wrote": "How vivid, even now, after long, long years, is my remembrance of the old log cabins. In my imagination I see them, perfectly embowered in wild climbing roses, lilacs and altheas, honey suckles, and cinnamon roses seeming to be clamering for possession, daffodils, jonquills, hyacinths, and star of Bethlehem, scattered everywhere, and the old great apple trees, with their ample shade."[73]

In her 1838–1839 diary, Francis Ann Kemble (the English bride of a northerner planter) wrote of her stay in coastal Georgia. Fanny Kemble delighted in jonquils and silvery narcissus blooming in January and February 1839, on St. Simons Island, at Darien, and on Butler Island. One such observation was made on February 11, 1839:

The Village of Riceborough, in John Claudius Loudon, 1835. Riceboro is about five miles from Midway (Abiel Holmes and his 1790 weather observations) and three miles from LeConte's Woodmanston plantation. Courtesy of the Cherokee Garden Library, Kenan Research Center at the Atlanta History Center, Atlanta, Georgia.

Mrs. Smith, Chechero, Georgia, late 1800s. Courtesy of Georgia Archives, Vanishing Georgia Collection, RAB-52.

"On a visit I had to make on the mainland, I saw a tiny strip of garden ground, rescued from the sandy road, called a street, perfectly filled with hyacinths, double jonquils and snowdrops, a charming nosegay for February 11."[74]

A second garden belonging to an "old, half-decayed rattling farm-house" on St. Simon's island was thus described, "close to the house itself a tiny would-be garden, a plot of ground with one or two peach-trees in full blossom, tufts of silvery narcissus and jonquils, a quantity of violets and an exquisite myrtle bush."[75] She spied this delightful site sometime around the third week of February 1839. When meeting a woman identified as "the Doctor's wife," originally from New England, Kemble was presented with violets and narcissus, already profusely blooming in January.

Information regarding vernacular gardens in Alabama tends to be reminiscences made at a much later date, and so subject to scrutiny. The following discussion of antebellum gardens was written in 1920: "The more modest type of garden was smaller and largely confined to a few plots or flower beds in the yard in front of the house, with flower beds bordering the walks and along the fence rows. Flowers were planted with little order. On the porches and trellises were clematis, cross vine, yellow Jessamine, cypress, seven sisters and Marechal Neil roses. About the yard were rosebushes, bush honeysuckle and sweet shrub. In season there were jonquils, daffodils, violets, the stately lilac, verbenas, spice pinks, hollyhocks and snowballs."[76]

Diaries are ideal. A touching diary entry belongs to Sarah R. Espy, who kept a private journal from 1859 to 1868 while living in eastern Alabama. Twice she noted flowers in the garden in 1860. On February 20, she noted the yellow jonquils were blooming, her mother's favorite flower, that she had brought with her from North Carolina over fifty years earlier.[77] Later, on April 22, she delighted in the early roses, jonquils, and pinks transforming the garden into an Eden.[78] Interestingly these cannot be the same varieties/species of jonquils blooming two months apart. One could speculate the two species referred to, but that is too fraught with peril.

One eyewitness observation of a modest Alabamian's home garden comes by way of essentially an obituary: "The Rev. Leonard Tarrant died at his home, at Mardisville, Talladega County, Alabama, February 25, 1862. The day he died the jonquils, harbingers of coming spring, were blooming in profusion in the yard before the door, and the snow, which had fallen the night before to the depth of two or three inches, in a freak of departing winter, lay upon the ground."[79]

Travelogues by northerners who toured the southern states before the Civil War gained in popularity as the northern public sought to understand their foe. Often snippets of garden landscapes were commented on, and even if somewhat unflattering are likely somewhat honest. One such work by J. Milton Mackie is vague as to when he actually made his travels, but as it was published in 1864, he likely toured in the late 1850s if not 1860:

> Before leaving Charleston, I did not fail to take a look at its environs. . . . Some of these trees were draped with grapevines climbing to their summits; and the hedges were green with the Cherokee rose, and the yellow jessamine. In a stroll through the gardens of a farmhouse, I gathered a nosegay of fragrant violets, snowdrops, jonquils, and Christmas berries, which, brought home, filled my apartment for hours with a sweet, summer perfume.[80]
>
> Nor less attractive are the gardens and courtyards invariably attached to the best houses, where, in winter, the hedges are green with pitosporum and the dwarf orange; and where blow the first fragrant violets and daffodils of spring. (In February came roses, camellias, peaches, wild oranges and strawberries.)[81]

In his observations of the town of Wilmington, North Carolina, Mackie wrote: "It contains a few moderately well-looking houses, scattered about among a great many half-painted and dilapidated ones. I saw scarcely a wall without a brick loose, or a fence without a board off, or any cement work that had not a crack in it. The yards in front of the houses, however, were pleasant with evergreens, and climbing plants; and the coming spring had here scattered in advance the first camellias, hyacinths, and daffodils."[82]

Although it is unclear whether the garden in the anecdote below was "vernacular" or "high style," this personal story written around 1903 illustrates the daffodil's long-standing role in American gardening. A simple bulb, one of many in the garden, appreciated for its showy display and sturdy constitution, and often because of its durability, a reminder:

> Narcissi and Daffodils live for generations. I know some double yellow Daffodils growing in my great-grandfather's garden, that were planted over seventy years ago. The place was sold and the house burned about thirty years since, and all this time has been entirely neglected. Some one told me that Daffodils and Narcissi still bloomed there bravely in the grass. With a cousin, one lovely day last spring, I took the train out to this old place and there found quantities of the dainty yellow flowers. We had come unprovided with any gardening implements, having nothing of the kind in town, and brought only a basket for the spoils, and a steel table-knife. We quickly found the knife of no avail, so borrowed a sadly broken coal-shovel from a tumble-down sort of a man who stood gazing at us from the door of a tumble-down house. The roots of the Daffodils were very deep, and neither of us could use a spade, so the driver of the ramshackle wagon taken at the station was pressed into service. Handling of shovel or spade was evidently an unknown art to him. The Daffodil roots were nearly a foot deep, but we finally got them, several hundreds of them, all we could carry. The driver seemed to think us somewhat mad and said "Them's only some kind of weed," but when I told him the original bulbs from which all these had come were planted by my great-grandmother and her daughter, and that I wanted to carry some away, to plant in my own garden, he became interested and dug with all his heart. The bulbs were in solid clumps a foot across and had to be pulled apart and separated. They were the old Double Yellow Daffodil and a very large double white variety, the edges of the petals faintly tinged with yellow and delightfully fragrant. My share of the spoils is now thriving in my garden. By the process of division every three years, these Daffodils can be made to yield indefinitely, and perhaps some great-grandchild of my own may gather their blossoms.[83]

Conclusion

For the disparaging comments and daffodils' lack of status, gardens had them, and gardeners trundled them about—bearing out Joseph Breck's observation of their commonality. With a few exceptions, the daffodils of the high style garden were the same as the vernacular, and these are the ones possessing the fortitude to survive in situ to the present day. This fortitude may have enticed southern gardeners all the more to accept daffodils as they found the more robust sorts to possess two valuable traits—heat and drought tolerance.

In the coastal South, some of the fancy florists' flowers crept out into the garden and stayed, primarily the paperwhites but other tazettas as well such as *N. italicus*. Happy enough in their newfound, almost-Mediterranean climate, they proliferated and joined the ranks of the common garden flower as evidenced by vernacular garden writings of the 1800s, and the familial legacy of Louis LeConte's botanic garden.

The same transpired with the doubles 'Butter and Eggs,' 'Orange Phoenix,' and 'Sulphur Phoenix,' which joined the ranks of 'Telamonius Plenus' and "Albus Plenus Odoratus." Doubles of the catalogs in the federal period, they spread into the gardens of the modest, to become firmly ensconced in the perennial palate—if only evidenced by the term "Butter and Eggs" being ubiquitous common name for whatever double daffodil is at hand.

To date no examples have been found of Americans ordering fancy single *Narcissus*, such as *N. minor, N. triandrus,* or *N. bicolor.* Yet these flowers would not have been stocked and advertised year after year (particularly by Prince & Co.) had there been no market for them—the printing ink and storage shelf space would not be wasted on a money-losing commodity. However, that their availability was limited to only the most discerning nurseries suggests these daffodils would have appeared only in the gardens of the most refined.

The slide of the tazetta by 1860 presents no ready explanation. Dutch wholesale catalogs continued to offer more tazettas than the American catalogs opted to carry well after the Civil War, implying it was a consumer-driven reaction by the seedsmen. To date no written evidence has surfaced hinting at the flowers' decline to passé status, particularly at a time when bulbs as a whole were slowly gaining favor in the American garden. The comparatively weak-kneed constitution of some of the tazettas of this era may be the key—for a less discerning market, variety for variety's sake may have been "lost," and so the nurserymen contracted their offerings to the strongest of the lot, many of which are still sold today: 'Grand Primo Citronière,' 'Grand Monarque,' "Double Roman," 'Grand Soleil d'Or,' and those "paper whites of the shops."

4.

Rise of American Daffodils, 1860 to 1940

With the rise of the industrial revolution and westward expansion, ornamental gardening came into its own as a leisure pursuit. At the same time, the daffodil began its transformation in Europe. As American gardeners found themselves in a position to grow more in their gardens, there was more on offer from Europe. As more people gardened, more people wrote about gardening, offering guidance from the mundane to the esoteric. By the early 1900s, garden magazines were exhorting their readers to convert their backyards from trash heaps to gardens. Under a photograph of a recently landscaped backyard, the caption read, "Isn't this a more pleasing sight than a yard filled with old tin cans and coal ashes?" "Reader, how is your back yard? What can you do in the way of cleaning it up and making a beauty spot of it in the coming season, instead of allowing it to be unhealthy and unsightly?"[1]

Immediately after the Civil War, economic recovery in the North was based on what was required to rebuild the South. Furthermore credit was tight, so funds via credit were not to be had to order large volumes of bulbs from Holland to await reimbursement through catalog resale. As time went on and the economy improved, seedsmen expanded their catalogs, both in caliber of printing and breadth of offerings.

In the South the Civil War halted gardening in many ways. Many of the wealthy that had relied on forced labor to maintain pleasure gardens no longer could, so some gardens were let go. A surviving daughter, Ellen Bruce Crane gave a wistful account of her father having the garden at the family plantation home of Berry Hill in Virginia removed after the Civil War: "After the war, my father, Alexander Bruce, felt it would be impossible to keep the garden as it should be kept, and so had it removed, . . .

removing all the walks and flower beds, though my mother and sister were in tears at the thought of having to give it up. But there still remain quantities of jonquils, hedges of box, and interesting flowering trees and shrubs.... Every tree had something planted beneath to come up in the spring, such as double and single jonquils, hyacinths, snowdrops, peonies or narcissi."[2] More often, the entire plantation was let go, and many had a difficult time finding buyers until the 1870s and 1880s. Then often the new owners did not invest in old gardens at all, especially if the plantation was purchased by northerners for a winter seasonal hunting retreat. For the modest, recovery after the war was slow. Thus gardeners continued their reliance on pass-along plants—those robust holdovers from better times or the excess of what a friend could afford to purchase.

Nursery catalogs hit a holding pattern for much of the 1870s—coinciding with the Long Depression of 1873–1879, kick started by the Panic of 1873. This depression hit certain sectors of the economy harder than others, railroads in particular—risky financial speculating to fund the Civil War and rampant fraud in railroad construction had eventually collapsed and taken down associated economic sectors (rather like the housing collapse)—while agriculture remained sound.

The availability of daffodils similarly changed after the Civil War—on one hand the number of seedsmen offering daffodils slowly increased, as well as the variety of what they offered, and more offered specialty fall bulb catalogs, but the varieties offered shifted, and in some sorts markedly decreased. These changes slowly gained momentum over the 1870s and then accelerated during the 1880s as the American economy recovered from the Long Depression, and modern industrialization took hold. As the seedsmen's businesses grew, more American companies, and more regional nurserymen, offered more varieties of bulbs directly to gardeners. As new landscape ideas from England gained acceptance in the late 1880s and 1890s, and new hybrid daffodils appeared on the commercial market, the daffodil as we know it came into its own.

There are two complementary but different ways to track changes in popular opinion regarding any flower—the landscape writer's tome and the seedsman's catalog. Both attempt to gauge public opinion and then steer it to their own ends, and profit as a result—both directly in terms of sales, and indirectly by enhanced reputation. And both make fascinating reading, providing windows with different views to the daffodil's coming of age in America.

Parlor Gardening

As interest in gardening in general expanded, fueled by an expanding middle class, so too did parlor gardening.[3] Numerous extensive books appeared such as Rand's *Flowers for the Parlor and Garden* (1863) and Williams's *Window Gardening* (1872), guiding the home enthusiast from soils and general culture, to conservatories, window baskets, and Wardian cases, to specifics on plants from roses, camellias, bulbs, and ferns to shrubs, vines, alpine plants, succulents, and evergreens.

In 1867, shortly after the Civil War, Fruitland Nurseries of Augusta, Georgia, announced its receipt of its annual shipment of Dutch bulbs, including jonquils and

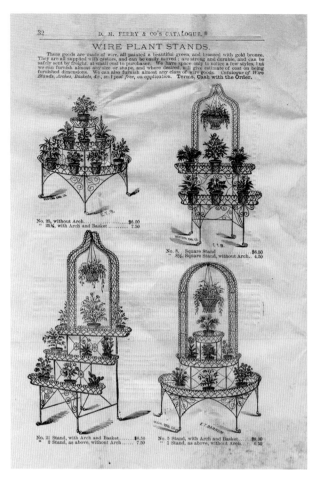

D. M. Ferry & Co., *Catalogue Dutch Bulbs and other Flowering Roots*, 1879.

polyanthus narcissus. Primarily the preferred bulbs for indoor forcing, it seems counterintuitive that some southerners were in a position to afford the luxury of winter bulbs so soon after the war.

Tazettas were still strongly marketed by the Dutch for parlor flowering. The 1872 wholesale catalog from Grube and Nieuwland touts and entices:

A splendid flower for Winter and Spring decoration, whether for the ornamentation of the conservatory, sitting room, or flower garden. In importance it ranks next to the Hyacinth, so that however limited the collection of plants may be, if there is not in it a fair proportion of this delightfully fragrant flower it will be deficient of a most essential ornament. Its perfume is that of the Jonquil, and its flower resembles the well-known Polyanthus, hence its name Polyanthus-like-Narcissus. Associated with Hyacinths and early Tulips, whatever be the style of decoration, whether on a flower stand, in a vase, or sitting-room window, it imparts a truly picturesque appearance; while in the flower-garden the display is so rich and the contrast to the Hyacinth so excellent, that once used it would become as indispensable an element in the decoration of the flower-beds and borders as either the Hyacinth or Tulip. The Double Roman planted early may be had in flower in-doors before Christmas, and a succession of bloom from the other varieties can be maintained till May.[4]

The popularity of indoor plants was such that in 1879 D. M. Ferry & Co. of Detroit, Michigan, issued a separate catalog just for wire stands, arches, baskets, and other items for the parlor and conservatory. His autumn catalogs offered not only spring-blooming bulbs but an extensive section of "plants for winter blooming" such as ferns, fuchias, geraniums, palms, caladiums, and roses.

Irrespective of the Dutch sales pitch, American nurserymen continued to slowly drop the number of tazettas varieties they carried. In 1860 William R. Prince & Co. offered twenty-two polyanthus narcissus. After the Civil War, the most extensive

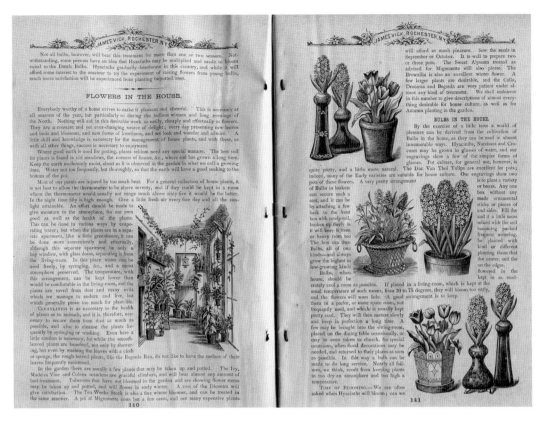

Indoor gardening. James Vick, *Vick's Catalog of Hardy Bulbs, Plants, &c.*, 1884.

offering of tazettas came from J. M. Thorburn (New York, New York) in 1882 with sixteen sorts, followed by B. K. Bliss & Sons in 1880 with fourteen sorts, and Vick's (Rochester, New York) in the late 1860s and early 1870s with twelve sorts.[5] In concert with the decrease in varieties there is a shift in the varieties offered. The Dutch house of Krelage offered twenty-five sorts for 1889, but by then most American catalogs offered only between five and ten varieties.[6]

In 1884 noted horticulturist Peter Henderson remarked that the tazettas commonly grown for forcing were "Bazelman Major," "Soleil d'Or," 'Grand Primo Citronière,' 'Grand Monarque,' "Double Roman," and others. As during the antebellum period, the preference for bicolor tazettas remained strong. But it was the "Paper White" that began taking the lion's share of the market: "N. papyraceus, is now, perhaps, more extensively forced than either of the above mentioned. It is grown in immense quantities by the florists of New York and other large cities, and, next to the Roman Hyacinth, is the bulb most extensively grown for this purpose."[7] In his fall 1883 bulb catalog, Henderson provided more detail, "The white Roman Hyacinth is largely used for forcing for winter flowers by the florists of New York and all large cities. In New York alone upward of five hundred thousand bulbs used during the winter, and the number is rapidly increasing each year."[8] By the mid-1870s, as urban florists geared up to meet the tide of rising populations, there was a demand for white flowers for the Christmas holiday season, and the white Roman hyacinth was the only bulb considered reliable to be had in bloom that early. By the early to mid-1880s, florists found the same could be done with paperwhites. That the bulbs were discarded after forcing, and the annual volume noted by Henderson, suggests the large number imported from southern Europe to supply the seasonal trade.

In Henderson's bulb catalog for autumn 1889, he promotes the new variety (the first time offered in his catalog) 'Paper White Grandiflorus,' "For forcing or early decorative purposes and for cut bloom at Christmas it will prove an invaluable plant."[9] The season prior the diminutive "Bulbocodium Monophyllus (Clusii)," or the "Algerian White Hoop Petticoat," Henderson described as "pure snow white, very early, will bloom at Christmas, if potted in August."[10] Bulbocodiums had long been grown as a parlor plant, thus expanding their allure by touting the white variety as suitable for Christmas decoration was worth a try.

By 1890 Henderson's list of most commonly forced tazettas shifted somewhat to "Soleil d'Or (yellow, with orange cup), Gloriosus (white, primrose cup), States General (white, with citron cup), Grand Primo (white, with citron cup), and Grand Monarque (white, with pale yellow cup), with the Double Roman (yellow) and Paper White."[11] That five of the seven are still in commercial cultivation also indicates these were the strongest constitution bulbs to withstand the pressures of high volume forcing, as well as some consolidation in the American market.

The fate of most tazettas in America was sealed, in large part, with the introduction of two flowers, namely 'Paper White Grandiflorus' and "Chinese Sacred Lily" (the species *N. tazetta* subsp. *lacticolor*). Both hit the American nursery trade around 1888. 'Paper White Grandiflorus' quickly displaced the old 'Paper White' due to its larger florets, larger tresses of bloom and stronger constitution. "Chinese Sacred Lily," marketed under numerous variations on its name (Joss flower, Chinese New Year Lily, Imperial Chinese Sacred, Oriental Narcissus, and so on), took the forcing market by storm once it became widely available. It became the preferred bulb for growing on pebbles in water, as it was one of the fastest to go into bloom (six weeks) and highly fragrant. Further it has the added ability to throw additional leaves and bloom stalks if one judiciously takes a knife to the bulb and cuts it into sections—with care, one can force eight to twelve flower stalks off of one bulb. Bulb carving is still practiced today in the Chinese American community, and bulb carving classes are held in conjunction with the New Year's Lunar Festival in Honolulu.[12]

Early on there was a backlash against "Chinese Sacred Lily" among some gardeners and florists. The flower was the only daffodil to come to America before Britain, brought to California by Chinese immigrants. By 1875 the Chinese immigrants in California were selling imported bulbs, which was not initially greeted with delight, and one wonders at times if the backlash wasn't a bit personal.[13] It may be a very cold-tender bulb, but it is not now considered a constitutionally weak bulb, despite this

California garden writer's complaint in 1875: "Another early flowering bulb is the Narcissus, which, unfortunately, has come into disrepute here, on account of the extremely inferior Chinese Narcissus, peddled in our streets so largely and cheaply."[14]

This grumbling was reiterated a few years later by Rochester florist and nurseryman James Vick in his 1881 catalog: "The Polyanthus Narcissus succeeds admirably in the gardens where winters are not very severe, and is prized for house culture everywhere. The Chinese, of California, brought over bulbs, and they created a great wonder on the Pacific coast and elsewhere, and were called the Chinese National Flower, though the same could be had at any respectable seed-house in America."[15] To some extent this complaint was almost true. One of the most common bicolor tazettas since the 1750s was "Bazelman Major" or "Trewianus," available from William R. Prince & Co. as late as 1860. It was once botanically classified as a subset of "Chinese Sacred Lily"—*N. tazetta* subsp. *lacticolor* var. *trewanius,* differentiated by

Chinese Sacred Lily, The Dingee & Conard Co., *Our New Guide to Rose Culture*, 1906.

its ribbed cup (whereas *N. tazetta* subsp. *lacticolor* var. *lacticolor* was distinguished by a smooth cup), but is currently not recognized by the RHS as a sufficiently distinct to warrant separation out from subsp. *lacticolor.*

Yet tazettas remained a warm-climate garden plant. Charles Howard Shinn of Alameda County (Santa Clara Valley), California, wrote: "But I must not wander so far away from the garden, in the midst of which I sit in my shirt-sleeves this warm November afternoon, and watch the men at work in that curiously confusing way incidental to California. One man is replanting daffodils and paper-white narcissuses which have become too crowded, but some of those he takes up are ready to bloom and, in fact, some which he left have been in bloom a week and more. Another is pruning cherry-trees. Still another is plowing in the orange grove. A fourth is bleaching and sacking walnuts and almonds which have been drying on wooden frames in the sunlight."[16] The forced/potted daffodil market continued to shift in the early 1900s. Daffodils were still

Window gardening, Peter Henderson & Co., *Catalogue of Bulbs, Plants and Seeds for Autumn Planting*, 1895.

grown for indoor forcing in large quantities, and florists forced potted bulbs for sale as well. More trumpets were forced by florists than tazettas. Florist preferred varieties in the early 1900s included "Spurious major," 'Emperor,' 'Golden Spur,' 'Empress,' 'Horsfieldii,' 'Victoria,' "Albicans," 'Sir Watkin,' 'Mrs. Langtry,' 'Ornatus,' 'Butter and Eggs,' 'Telamonius Plenus,' "Double Roman," and 'Paper White Grandiflorus'. Retail prices of these bulbs ranged from 25 cents to 60 cents a dozen. Florists would force large numbers of bulbs in flats, similar in dimensions to today's plant container flats, in greenhouses to protect the flowers from the elements. At peak bloom, the flowers would be cut for sale, and the bulbs discarded. Thus the bulbs were treated as annuals for a large market (florists), spurring commercial production to supply bulbs. Growing for cut flowers in fields was a later development.

One astute woman viewed home-potted bulbs as an interesting revenue opportunity. But rather than selling for personal gain, she saw forced potted flowering bulbs, particularly daffodils but hyacinths too, as a charity fund-raising opportunity. Margaret Deland of Boston, Massachusetts, was an avid "window gardener," becoming quite renowned in Boston for her jonquil sales. She went so far as to create a fund for the "Encouragement of Window Gardening" and held a February "Jonquil sale" attended by the city's prominent residents. For her 1898 sale, Deland potted twenty-five hundred Campernelle jonquils alone, augmented by the bicolor trumpet 'Princeps,' the potted flowers stacked about her house on

Photograph of woman in conservatory, Peter Henderson & Co., *Henderson's Autumn Catalog*, 1907.

tables and shelves up the walls. Deland extolled the virtues of potted jonquils as a fund-raising mechanism to a wider female audience in a 1904 article in *Good House-keeping*. She prefaced her step-by-step process of purchasing, potting, growing, and selling as thus:

> If we have to have a sale, for the kindergarten, or the new hospital, or for the hundred and one worthy objects that clamor at our doors and make our hearts ache with their pathetic needs, if neither we nor our neighbors can quite make up our minds to give our five dollars outright, and receive no equivalent for it, if we really must have a fair, then let us sell things that are at least harmless; an undesired vase is always harmful! Now, one of the most harmless things in the world is a blossoming plant. It is lovely to look upon, and when it has given its message of beauty and perfume, it vanishes, like a spoken word of love, that fills the heart, but takes up no room in the material universe. Sales of this kind have been held, here and there, with some success; and certainly with much less expenditure of nerve force (and money) than that which attends the ordinary fair for charitable purposes.

Early in September (August is even better), they give their order to a seedsman, and it may, perhaps, run something like this:

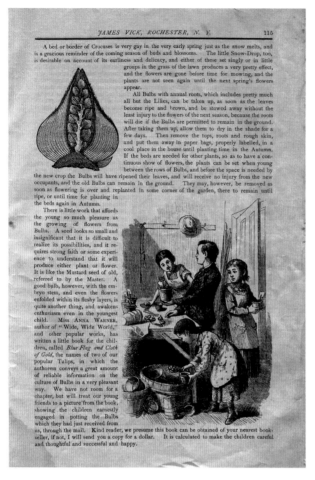

Family potting bulbs; *Vick's Floral Guide Autumn 1881.*

300 Campanile jonquils (9 or 10 bulbs to a pot, which means about 30 pots).

250 Princeps (7 bulbs to a pot, which means about 35 pots).

200 Von Zion (7 bulbs to a pot, which means about 30 pots).[17]

200 Romans (7 to a 6-inch pot, making about 25 pots).

80 Dutch (4 to 6-inch pot, making about 20 pots).

800 Grape (blue) (40 or 50 to a 6-inch pot, making about 20 pots).[18]

And how about prices? The market rate is the safest standard. In cities, six-inch pots of jonquils sell from one dollar to one dollar and twenty-five cents each; but probably lower prices must prevail in country towns. Supposing that only seventy-five cents were asked, a very fair profit will be made, for each pot costs so little—the price of ten Campanile bulbs, for instance, is about eight or nine cents; the flower pot is six cents more; the earth (if you live in town, you have to buy potting soil at the rate of about two dollars a bushel), the earth is perhaps two cents per pot, and the moss and manure another two cents; total cost, eighteen cents; and surely eighteen cents can hardly be spent in any way that will give larger returns; color, perfume, the daily joy of watching growth, and the happy toil of caring for them; and last of all, the price at the fair—whatever you can get!

And to this profit is added the moral satisfaction of knowing that the fair has not increased the number of useless and tiresome things in this dear, busy, crowded world of ours![19]

A new potting medium came on the market in the early 1900s, with nurserymen of course touting their own supply as superior, and advertising bulbs grown in their special mix as superb. The new wonder product was cocoanut fiber, to be mixed with ground oyster shells in a 6:1 ratio. Its vastly improved water retention properties over soil, manure, and sand were quite advantageous for delicate root systems such as tulips. However, its odorless, no mess, no staining, and no water drip properties were beneficial highlights—touted to keep a Victorian woman and her house clean and spotless.

Unexpectedly, tazettas staged a minor comeback in the early 1900s, but only in the catalogs of northern nurserymen catering to a wealthier gardener. Rawson of Boston, Vaughn of New York and Chicago, and to a lesser degree Henderson, all increased the number of cultivars offered to upward of ten or eleven, while Thorburn of New York offered up to eighteen varieties. These companies were also some of the earliest to offer separate sections for cold-hardy poetaz tazettas in addition to their selections of true tazettas: Rawson and Peter Henderson by 1907 and Vaughn by 1913.

Potted paperwhites, and other white flowers, flowering in the house continue today as a Christmas tradition. In an undated fall catalog dating to the 1910s, H. G. Hastings & Co. of Atlanta pitched paperwhites thus: "Here in the city one can walk along any residence street during the fall and winter and see a dish of blooming Narcissus in at least one window of almost every home, and nothing could be prettier. We want our friends who have not tried the Narcissus to do so this year. The bulbs can be bought from August to January or even later, and a little money spent in this way will repay you well. For a little Christmas or holiday remembrance, or to send to the sick room of a friend, nothing could be more pleasing or appropriate than a dishful of Narcissus just coming into bloom, and such a gift is within the reach of every one."[20]

Landscape Literature

After the Civil War, America belatedly took to the waning British landscape style of bedding out. As glass became cheaper and southern hemisphere exotics became available, a design motif of riotous colors took hold in England and Europe in the 1850s. Bed design changed to create bold swaths of single colors, or stacked bands of single colors, on the lawn, via cold-tender annuals of bright flowers or strongly variegated foliage. Peter Barr's first catalog in 1861 played *Narcissus* to this style, offering forty-four *Narcissus* for "grouping [in borders], massing, ribboning, bedding, vases, rustic baskets, and boxes on balconies,"[21] but hyacinths and tulips played better still. The use of spring bulbs allowed for overplanting, or their removal for ripening and replanting, with brilliant summer annuals.

In America the broadening planting schemes for bulbs begun in the 1850s continued in the 1860s. Edward S. Rand, author of numerous popular gardening books, wrote one of the earliest American books devoted solely to bulbs. His *Bulbs: A Treatise on Hardy and Tender Bulbs and Tubers* (1866) directed: "The mode of planting must vary according to various tastes, but generally the bulbs should be grouped as to give the most effect when in bloom. Thus small bulbs, . . . should never be planted singly, but always in clumps, the larger the better; the single bulbs about an inch apart in each way, or in triple lines as an edging to a bed. Hyacinths, narcissus and other large bulbs, may be planted singly or in lines, but are far more effective planted in threes; that is, one each at the point of a triangle, each bulb about nine inches from the others. A combination of colors may often thus be very prettily contrived."[22]

The notion of nurseryman as tastemaker, and thus driver of a market, comes in no finer form than Peter Henderson, who extolled the new "modern" European "ribbon" style of mass planting beds, both annuals and bulbs, in his highly influential book *Practical Floriculture* (1869). While he elaborated on the "promiscuous" style of intermixing plants in a single bed, he strenuously advocated a rigid planting scheme of lowest in front grading to highest in back and the use of strongly variegated foliage. But he still much preferred the ribbon method—long rows of single cultivars/colors, often stacked one atop the other, but still low. Dutch bulbs received the standard treatment: "[Holland bulbs] are best grouped in beds of each sort by itself to show to advantage. As soon as their flowering is over in spring, Verbenas or other bedding plants should be placed in the beds, as the bulbs are not sufficiently ripen to lift before June or July."[23] That daffodils were not the best-suited bulb for this extravaganza is evident in the little attention he paid to that class of bulb in even his follow-up works for home gardeners *Gardening for Pleasure* (1875) and *Henderson's Handbook of Plants* (1881). Ironically by the early mid-1880s, one of the leading catalogs for new daffodils, and lots of them, was Henderson's, demonstrating his good nose for a new market, whatever it may be.

While Henderson attempted to drive a new market by pushing a new landscape design (albeit a bit stagnant when it came to Dutch bulbs), other writers kept to the tried and true of linear borders and separate parterre flower beds. Rand continued to recommend *Narcissus* for the border. In his more general work *Seventy-Five Popular Flowers and How to Cultivate Them* (1870), Rand observed: "This genus [*Narcissus*] contains some of our handsomest and best known spring flowering plants. Beauty, delicacy, and fragrance of flower, with easy culture, combine to render them popular, and in every garden we find the daffodil [*N. pseudonarcissus*] and poet's Narcissus. More than one hundred species are enumerated, all of which are worthy a place in the flower garden, although comparatively few are in cultivation."[24] He elsewhere specified, "Narcissus should always be planted in clumps, and, except in dwarf species, in the rear of the border. The plant is a favorite of ours. We love all the species, and take more pleasure in the clumps of narcissus than in many a rarer and costlier flower."[25]

Frank Scott, in *The art of beautifying suburban home grounds of small extent* (1870), maintained the traditional dictate of formal spaces. He recommended three types or modes of planting: narrow borders along walks (fortunately falling out of favor); geometric shapes in a parterre (curlicue shapes to be avoided); and as adjuncts and embellishments to the lawn: "To make a fine display throughout the season, in beds for low flowers, it is necessary to have at least two sets of crops or plants; one for bulbs, such as snow-drops, crocuses, jonquils, hyacinths and tulips, all of which may be planted in October, to bloom the following spring; while the bedding-plants for the later bloom, such as verbenas, portulacas, phlox drummondii, etc., etc."[26] Granted these specifically were for beds of "low flowers." This is simply more of the same landscape dictates, but it was targeted for a new audience, the rising middle class, contending with smaller land lots.

While a leading proponent of the ribbon style, Scott did not see fit to use bulbs for such work; others did. Hovey, in his 1868 *Magazine of Horticulture,* recommended hyacinths in rectangular beds, planting the bulbs in rows, each its own color, and alternating the color rows to good effect. In 1865 *American Agriculturist, for the Farm, Garden and Household* also suggested ribbon-style motifs for spring bulbs: "Where there is a sufficient number of the bulbs, a very pleasing effect may be produced by planting them in circles one within another, each circle being formed of those with flowers of the same color, the colors alternating to suit the fancy."[27]

Around this time, regional horticultural journals and books targeting new rising markets and gardeners follow suit and expand their detailed recommendations for bulbs. The posthumous articles of William N. White (1819–1867), the father of Georgia horticulture, make an interesting case study. Two such articles addressing landscaping with bulbs were published in 1870 and 1871 in *Southern Farm and Home*, addressing different landscaping styles. The first to appear was a three-part

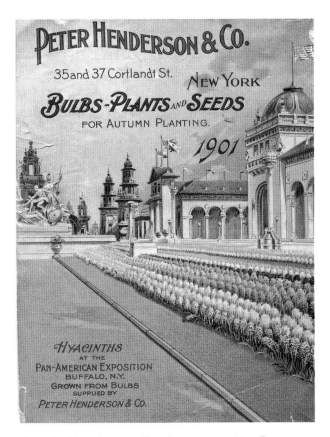

Hyacinth ribbon planting at Pan-American exposition, Peter Henderson & Co., *Autumn Bulb Catalogue*, 1901.

article on how to lay out a flower bed. While relying on a traditional bulb bed of one type per bed, its arrangement and use was less so:

> The winter garden is another department of the flower department of the flower garden second only to the Rosary in attraction. Here may be carefully arranged in a distinct locality, as great a variety of the evergreen plants, hardy enough to endure the climate, as can be conveniently obtained. Evergreens should be scattered in other departments of the flower garden, but there should be more in this than in any other portion of the grounds. The ground work of the winter garden is generally grass, though for evergreens this is not so necessary as for the Rosary or flower garden. If a sunny place is chosen, and the sides surrounded by a screen of evergreen roses, hollies, etc., and interspersed with beds of crocuses, daffodils, and other early bulbs, then a summer scene is given in the heart of winter.[28]

Regional agricultural and horticultural journals were often a bit behind the larger publications in becoming more versed in the method of overplanting bulb beds for summer beauty. Later that year, in the regular column "The Flower Garden" in the September issue of *Southern Farm,* recommendations for spring bulbs were given.

> This and the next month are the season for preparing for a fine Spring flower garden. As soon as the Fall flowering plants have been removed, fork the ground thoroughly, enrich by a liberal coating of woods-earth and ashes, and then fill the space with such bulbous roots as Tulips, Hyacinths, Narcissus, Rannucalas, Snowdrop, Crocus, and Anemone. In the spaces between the bulbs sow the seeds of hardy annuals of dwarf growth, which will thus be a sufficient start before the severe weather sets in, will shade the ground with their foliage in the Spring and present a beautiful appearance with the bulbs begin to bloom. Of the dwarf annuals the following are the most desirable, and can be easily raised: Alysum (sweet), Calliopsis, Campanula, Escholtzia (several varieties), Forget-me-not, Lupenius, Nemophila (several varieties), Phlox Dummondii, Venus' Looking-Glass.[29]

In the second posthumous article by William White, instructions were proffered for the planting and managing of circular bulb beds on the lawn, as well as for planting a ribbon-style border. White's work stands in contrast to the old the tried and true suggested by his posthumous editors:

> A very satisfactory mode of cultivating these early flowering bulbs is to mix them in the border. Take a border facing the sun, prepare the soil as directed for Hyacinths, let the outer row be composed of crocuses, the next of Hyacinths, and the third of Tulips. The crocuses will first come into bloom, and as they go out, the Hyacinths and early/Tulips will come into their prime, while the foliage of the crocus will form a pretty edging to the bed. As these bloom while the ground is still damp and cold, the border selected should be near the house where the eye can rest upon them, and they can be readily approached while in flower. Oval and circular beds planted in this manner have a beautiful effect. On each side of the approach to the house, let there be circular beds made two feet in diameter, and at regular distances from each other; alternating with them may be a bed of jonquils or narcissus, a rose bush or other choice shrub, planting the same plant or variety on the opposite side of the walk. Excavate and prepare these little beds as for Hyacinths. Round the edge of the bed, put two rows of crocuses, then spread Hyacinths equally over the bed, and fill the vacancies with early Tulips. Such a bed contains seventy-two of the crocus, six Hyacinths, and twelve Tulips. Other beds may be bordered with the crocuses and filled with Crown Imperials or other early flowering bulbs. If there are several beds, very pretty contrasts may be made by having the Hyacinths, etc., in the same bed of the same colors; but when the beds are few, the colors may be mixed in the bed. Verbenas may occupy the beds when the bulbs are removed.[30]

This ribbon style for bulb planting held in much of America into the mid-1880s, particularly in the less trendsetting regions of the country, such as this 1886 recommendation

A Boston Park. R. & J. Farquahar & Co., *Bulb Catalogue*, 1904.

for Michigan gardeners: "In planting them, do not set them out in a haphazard way, but keep each variety by itself. It is a good plan, when one has but few, to plant the tulips in the center, with the hyacinths in a circle about them, letting the crocuses and scillas edge the bed."[31]

But the American tastemakers by now were on to the next garden trend with Dutch bulbs—the formal pattern bed style. Employing either all tulips or all hyacinths, fanciful bed shapes were laid out in the lawn and striking color patterns created by careful choice of varietals. For better or worse, the daffodil with its floppy foliage and limited color palate was ill-suited for this stiff, albeit showy, planting style.[32]

Meanwhile, across the Pond, English gardeners were tiring of the garish colors and linear strictures. Two opposite lines of thought emerged—the very relaxed, and the return to the old. Both were perennial-centric, but one was of infinitely greater importance to the daffodil than the other, and both began to make inroads in American gardening in the mid- to late 1880s as the country rebounded from the Long Depression.

The daffodil truly came into its own with the second edition (and printed in America) of *The Wild Garden* (1870, 1881) and its companion, *The English Flower Garden* (1883). Englishman William Robinson's naturalistic rebellion against formalism was a sea change in 1870, but daffodils were just one of many plants. By 1881 Robinson gave spring bulbs, and the daffodil in particular, respect and detailed treatment. Naturalizing spring bulbs was prominently discussed at the front of the second edition (after the Forget-Me-Not family). Robinson was friends with Peter Barr, who was in his early years of promoting the daffodil, and this friendship and Robinson's knowledge of Barr's daffodil work and where it would lead is hinted at in the text.[33] Peter Barr

Sutton's Bulbs for 1898.

labored tirelessly to popularize the daffodil, and William Robinson lovingly gave them a home, and a showcase at that:

How many of us really enjoy the beauty which a judicious use of a profusion of hardy Spring-flowering Bulbs affords? How many get beyond the miserable conventionalities of the flower-garden, with its edgings and patchings, and taking up, and drying, and mere playing with our beautiful Spring Bulbs? How many enjoy the exquisite beauty afforded by flowers of this class, established naturally, without troubling us for attention at any time? The subject of decorating with Spring-flowering Bulbs is merely in its infancy; at present we merely place a few of the showiest of them in geometrical lines. The little we do leads to such a very poor result, that numbers of people, alive to the real charms of a garden too, scarcely notice Spring Bulbs at all, regarding them as things which require endless trouble, as interfering with the "bedding-out;" and in fact, as not worth the pains they occasion. This is likely to be the case so long as the most effective and satisfactory of all modes of arranging them is unused; that way is the placing of them in wild and semi-wild parts of country seats, and in the rougher parts of a garden, no matter where it may be situated or how it may be arranged. This way will yield more real interest and beauty than any other.[34]

But the prettiest results are only attainable where the grass need not be mown till nearly the time the meadows are mown. Then we may have gardens of Narcissi, such as men never dared to dream about a dozen years ago; such as no one ever thought possible in a garden. In grass not mown at all we may even enjoy many of the Lilies, and all the lovelier and more stately bulbous flowers of the meadows and mountain lawns of Europe, Asia, and America.[35]

Daffodil, Narcissus.—Most people have seen the common daffodil in a semi-wild state in our woods and copses. Apart from varieties, there are more than a score distinct species of daffodil that could be naturalised quite as easily as this in all parts of these islands. We need hardly suggest how charming these would be,

flowering in early spring and summer in the rougher parts of pleasure
grounds, or along wood-walks, or
any like position.[36]

At length Robinson detailed plant
material for specific landscape and soil
environments, from chalky soil to em-
bankments. For spring and early summer plants suitable for naturalization,
similar to naturalization under specimen trees and lawn, it was: iris, muscari,
hyacinth, narcissus, species tulips, leucojum, galanthus, scilla, ornithogalum,
crocus, bulbocodium vernum, aconite,
anemone, and so on.

By the 1903 edition, Robinson
pointedly states, "The most important
group of all these early flowers is the
Narcissus."[37] He proceeds to discuss at
length his personal plantings, staggering varieties for a longer season, and
so on:

Narcissi of the Poeticus Group. *The Garden*, 1880.

A very delightful feature of the
Narcissus meadow gardening is the
way great groups follow each other in the fields. When the Star Narcissi begin
to fade a little in their beauty the Poets follow, and as I write this paper we have
the most beautiful picture I have ever seen in cultivation. Five years ago I cleared
a little valley of various fences, and so opened a pretty view. Through the meadow
runs a streamlet. We grouped the Poet's Narcissus near it, and through a grove
of Oaks on a rising side of the field. We have had some beauty every year since;
but this year, the plants having become established, or very happy for some other
reason, the whole thing was a picture such as one might see in an Alpine valley!
The flowers were large and beautiful when seen near at hand, and the effect in the
distance delightful. This may, perhaps, serve to show that this kind of work will
bring gardening into a line with art, and that the artist need not be for ever divorced
from the garden by geometrical patterns which cannot possibly interest anybody
accustomed to drawing beautiful forms and scenes. I need say no more to show the
good qualities of this group of plants for wild gardening, many places having much
greater advantages than mine for showing their beauty in the rich stretches of grass
by pleasure-ground walks. Various kinds of places may be adorned by Narcissi in
this way—meadows, woods, copses, wood walks, and drives through ornamental

Horsfield's Daffodil (Narcissus Bicolor Horsfieldi). *The Garden*, 1888.

woodland and pleasure grounds, where the grass need not be mown until late in the summer.[38]

Both the daffodil and Robinson's aesthetic gained traction among America's garden elite from coast to coast. The editors of the New York–based *American Agriculturalist, for the Farm, Garden and Household,* approved of the newly expanded 1881 edition of *The Wild Garden,* just as they did the first edition in 1870: "Many an old and neglected garden, with its clumps of Poet's Narcissus, 'Daffy-Down-Dilly,' great patches of Martagon and other lilies; with Crocuses and Snow Drops, that have made their way into the grass, illustrates what we may expect from a wild garden that has been judiciously let alone."[39]

Charles Howard Shinn, a well-known California author and naturalist, published extensively to educate the public on gardening in California, informing those readers afar as to what was transpiring in the Golden State, and educating residents as to new movements in gardening and plants to be had. By 1890 he foretold of California daffodil shows in February, hyacinth shows in March, and pansy shows in April. In 1880 he wrote about how to make a "wild garden" using bulbs and perennials and supported the revolt against stiff formality of ribbon bedding in Europe, stating, "The present reaction against the ribbon-bed system contemplates the revival of an interest in old-fashioned flowers, and the use of them in new and peculiarly charming ways."[40]

But the general American disdain of daffodils was still strong into the 1890s in some quarters. An 1893 *New York Times* article, "The Day of the Daffodil," nearly sneers at the idea of the British rage over the unfashionable, if not downright despised, daffodil. The author predicts as fads move westward from England, so too would come the now overly hybridized daffodil to supplant the "overcultivated chrysanthemum" in the button holes of "the fastidious and 'quick' New-Yorker by the modest daffadowndilly of the Elizabethan poets. . . . Of course, the narcissus will be cultivated until the little garden flower will no longer be able to recognize its relatives. Many new and pretentious varieties of the narcissus have been produced in London, and high-sounding names have been bestowed upon them. The daffodil will grow in size and change its shape and take on all sorts of odd colors; and then will be supplanted by some other flower, and return to the old function fair Perdita allotted to it, to come before the swallow dares and 'take the winds of March with beauty.'"[41]

While the *New York Times* peered down its nose and sniffed, in upstate New York George Herman Ellwanger of Mount Hope Nurseries was well past having a daffodil in his button hole (this from a man relieved beyond words that the soulless and bloodless wax-flowered camellia was finally out of favor). His *The Garden's Story, or Pleasures and Trials of an Amateur Gardener,* is a garden diary of sorts written of his garden in 1888. He wrote prolifically of the new daffodils available from Peter Barr and William Baylor Hartland and traded with friends in England the trilliums from his woods for the bicolor trumpet 'Horsfieldii'. He detailed what he could and could not grow, and what he recommended of the new hybrids in American catalogs, even observing that the popular 'Sir Watkin' is not as large as described in European catalogs. Swooning

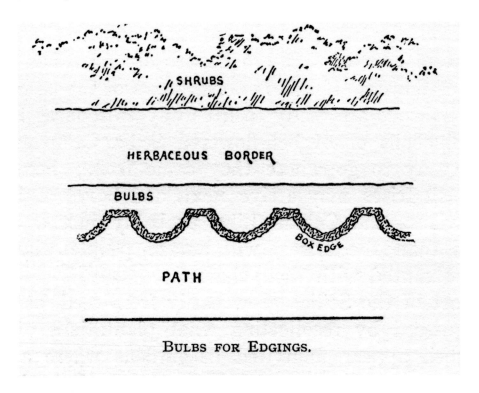

SHRUBS

HERBACEOUS BORDER

BULBS

BOX EDGE

PATH

BULBS FOR EDGINGS.

Bulbs for Edgings. Hampden, *Bulb Gardening*, 1922.

at the three hundred varieties offered in Peter Barr's catalog, marveling at the poetry in Hartland's, Ellwanger laments: "Lilies are tempting enough in the catalogues. But the lists finally come to an end, while the varieties of the daffodil are inexhaustible. The names, English and Latin, are so tempting, too, though these are nothing compared to the descriptions. To catch the daffodil-fever severely means either to break the tenth commandment or to be guilty of ruthless extravagance. You know there are swarms of varieties that will not succeed; but how are you to single them out without trying them? How artistically, how artfully devised some of the monographs are!"[42]

This is all the more entertaining when considering that thirty years prior, Mount Hope Nursery was late in carrying any *Narcissus* at all in its catalogs. Ellwanger's quips are infectious with enthusiasm: "The white daffodils generally possess a superior air of good breeding; they always seem dressed for the drawing-room. The yellow ones, even where they are superlatively handsome, look as if they preferred a romp or a game of tennis."[43] "With proper selection and intelligent cultivation, we may have in the daffodil a treasurehouse of beauty, and with this flower alone render any garden a field of the cloth of gold."[44]

Others garden writers of note with an astute ear to the new landscaping ideas emanating from Britain found the daffodil and the new mode of planting worthy of advocacy in the early 1890s. The New York City superintendent of parks Samuel

Parsons, Jr., in *Landscape Garden-ing* (1891), observed daffodils as ef-fective for naturalization among shrubs or planting in the grass. New York horticulturist C. L. Allen's *Bulbs and Tuberous-Rooted Plants* (1893) praised narcissus as border flowers but sug-gested their suitability for under trees, under fences, beside hedges, and in the shrubby border where other plants refuse to bloom, as much for simply a cutting flower bed as for brightening the corners of the property.

As the new century dawned and more gardeners bought more bulbs, more garden writers told them what to do. Some were practical and pedestrian, but most recommendations for daffo-dils fell into one of two large camps—the wild garden, or the old-fashioned garden (of which Colonial Revival gardens and Dutch bulb gardens are subsets).[45]

Poet's narcissus naturalized. *The Garden*, 1906.

There were garden writers whose books fell in the middle. Helena Rutherfurd Ely wrote a practical gardening book for practical women with smaller means or at least smaller parcels of land. *A Woman's Hardy Garden* (1903) shook its New England head at the obsession with Italian gardens and gave straightforward advice on how to plant bulbs in borders against the foundations of the house, as well as in the borders along the front walk from the sidewalk to the house—a landscape method still used to plant bulbs.

The first all-daffodil book written in the United States was published in 1907 by the New Yorker A. M. (Arthur Martin) Kirby: *Daffodils, Narcissus and How to Grow Them*. Peter Henderson acknowledged Kirby as the American daffodil expert in his 1913 catalog, which was kind, as Kirby worked for Henderson and was likely the drive behind Henderson's expanding daffodil offerings. Kirby's discussion of readily available daffodils is thus for the American market, and offers a window into what Americans could buy and plant, and on occasion discusses what cultivar was popular at the time. For example Kirby described 'Lucifer' (RHS introduction date of 1890) as "A splendid new Irish seedling."[46] Kirby advocated planting daffodils in the foreground of herba-ceous borders or mixed shrubberies, in irregular groups by variety to focus the eye, or naturalized in the lawn. For miniature species he recommended rock gardens: "Little gems that would be lost in the border—Mountain species to grow only in rock pockets and special soils."[47] These specialized gardens, basically carefully constructed rock piles

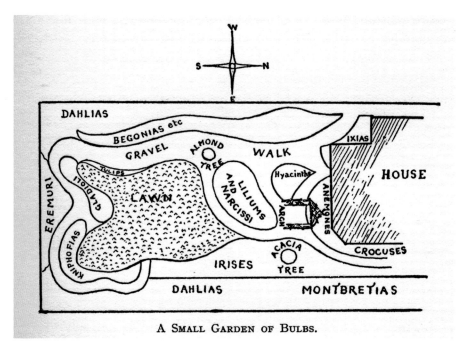

A SMALL GARDEN OF BULBS.

A Small Garden of Bulbs. Hampden, *Bulb Gardening*, 1922.

in lawn, were used to host many specialty plants; and alpine species daffodils were no different.

But Kirby strongly advocated naturalizing daffodils in grass, "the most effective method of planting daffodils,"[48] with a number of lovely photographic plates for reinforcement.[49] Repeatedly he indicates poet's narcissus for planting in heavy soils and near water, while trumpets should be planted in higher and drier situations. Later Kirby advises white trumpets to be placed on the drier, high ground of a slope, while the all-yellow and bicolor trumpets should be planted downslope in the damper locations. White trumpets, primarily derived from alpine species, require good drainage and are prone to rot. He cautioned, "the larger flowering modern hybrids are likely to 'run out'; that is to say, they may lose their size, and deteriorate toward the parental types";[50] which is also to say—they are more nutrient dependent or fertilizer needy and would do the same thing today if not carefully tended to.

Many early twentieth century women garden writers embraced the daffodil and devoted time to its use in their works. Notably some were influenced by Gertrude Jekyll, who was friends with and influenced by William Robinson. These include Grace Tabor (*Making a Bulb Garden*, 1912), Louise Beebe Wilder in particular (*My Garden*, 1916, and *Colour in My Garden*, 1918), and Mary Hampden (*Bulb Gardening*, 1922).

The competing garden design aesthetic of the time, in the rebellion against Victorian florid excess, was the return to the old-fashioned plants (perennials) and their use in the reinvented "colonial-era" garden. As houses became streamlined and "of old" so too did gardening. "Old-fashioned" plants, particularly perennials, found their turn in the sun, while exotics of foliage, form, and color were on the outs. Parterres and simple beds were the rule, often of very old, common designs. And with "old-fashioned plants" came the romance of grandmother's (or great-grandmother's) garden and its perennials. This was employed also at historic sites to recreate the original gardens, or some semblance thereof. These gardens included raised beds, lots of boxwood, and so on, not designed to be working gardens as in days of yore, but a romantic reinterpretation that, by and large, went with the pretty over the practical/utilitarian. The romance is aptly captured by Alice M. Rathbone:

> Literature has embraced the old-fashioned garden, and more and more in these days the garden gathers to itself an added charm from literature. We feel it with the primrose, the violet, and daffodil; the wallflower, whose unassuming blossoms send forth Old World memories as well as their own delightful fragrance; with the dainty columbine, and the foxglove, whose flower-stalk arrangement Ruskin likens unto the various stages of life—infancy at the top, old age withering away below. Tennyson speaks of "the foxglove spire."
>
> Rich are we in these treasures, for the flowers that a well-stocked hardy border holds may be called the classics of the garden.
>
> Compared with our short span of life, they belong to the Immortals.
>
> Year after year "the same dear things lift up the same fair faces," and we would gladly become perennial, far beyond the limit of our threescore years and ten, to longer enjoy our hardy flower friends.[51]

In formal parterre-based Colonial Revival gardens of the 1920s in important northern gardens, daffodils were often not a prominent feature. A few hardy, older daffodils may have been employed, really almost simply as "filler."

This lack of spring bulbs brings to mind the bias evidenced toward those sorts by the early historic garden writer Alice Morse Earle, in her articles and well-known book *Old Time Gardens, Newly Set Forth* (1901). She devoted four pages or so to slandering many floral scents, from opining that lilacs smell like a natural gas leak and that her cocker spaniel smelled better than Mignonette roses. She couldn't stand pear trees, old pansies, or composite flowers standing in vase water: "I dislike much the rank smell of common yellow Daffodils and of many of that family. I can scarcely tolerate them even when freshly picked, upon a dinner table. Some of the Jonquils are as sickening within doors as the Tuberose, though in both cases it is only because the scent is confined that it is cloying. In the open air, at a slight distance, they smell as well as many Lilies, and the Poet's Narcissus is deemed by many delightful."[52]

For her conspicuous lack of attention to daffodils (likely because of their fragrances), she does wax oddly poetic about the old double varieties: "In Daffodils I like the 'old fat-headed sort with nutmeg and cinnamon smell and old common English names—Butter-and-eggs, Codlins-and-cream, Bacon and eggs.' The newer ones are more slender in bud and bloom, more trumpet-shaped, and are commonplace of name

DETAILS OF PLANTING

The hyacinths in the four round beds should be of solid colors, edged with white. Pink, lavender, light blue, and yellow are good colors to use. The red may be substituted in place of the yellow.

In the four larger corner beds, double tulips should be used, in much the same color scheme as in the case of the single ones.

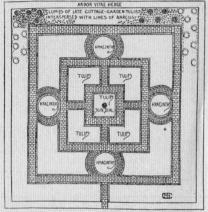

A well-arranged bulb-garden

The outer border nearest the hedge is of late-flowering Darwin and Cottage Garden tulips that do not need to be moved, but increase in number each year. From six to a dozen bulbs should be massed in each clump, and each clump should contain but one variety. Lines of narcissi, containing from fifty to five hundred bulbs in a line, according to the size of the garden and the number of varieties used, should be planted among the tulips, as shown by the diagram. Of course, only one variety should be used in a line.

Finally, a little Dutch bulb-garden is within the reach of all. It can give beauty to a tiny city lot, or can be stretched to cover a large suburban place. Its cost is not prohibitive, neither is the care of it. A few annuals sown when the bulbs are losing their beauty transform it into a little summer annual garden; or, if the family is to be away for the summer, weeds may grow and flourish unmolested, with the certainty that they will cause no harm. Winter frosts will kill them, and clear the ground for the spring's display, with only a little aid from the amateur gardener. And the spring days will bring with them a newer and livelier interest.

PLANTING TABLES

Finally, it seems best to summarize all the foregoing points, along with much other information on the planting and culture of bulbs, in a planting table. Here it is:

How to Make a Bulb Garden, 1915.

instead of common. In Virginia the name of a variety has become applied to a family, and all Daffodils are called Butter-and-eggs by the people."[53] Within the overarching umbrella of old-fashioned gardens comes the "Dutch bulb garden." Two notions of a Dutch bulb garden seem to have existed; one a very distinct garden design, the other more just a geometric flower bed planted with Dutch bulbs.

The first appears in the rarified air of important American estates, those with the space and financial ability to create one. Alice Morse Earle artfully describes this design, and then its imitator:

> I love a Dutch garden, "circummured" with brick. By a Dutch garden, I mean a small garden, oblong or square, sunk about three or four feet in a lawn—so that when surrounded by brick walls they seem about two feet high when viewed outside, but are five feet or more high from within the garden. There are brick or stone steps in the middle of each of the four walls by which to descend to the garden, which may be all planted with flowers, but preferably should have set borders of flowers with a grass-plot in the centre. On either side of the steps should be brick posts surmounted by Dutch pots with plants, or by balls of stone. Planted with

bulbs, these gardens in their flowering time are, as old Parkinson said, a "perfect fielde of delite." We have very pretty Dutch gardens, so called, in America, but their chief claim to being Dutch is that they are set with bulbs, and have Delft or other earthen pots or boxes for formal plants or shrubs.[54]

But the imitator, the pedestrian geometric flower bed with bulbs was more prevalent in gardening literature aimed at a mass market of novice gardeners, and that same group is who nurserymen pitched their bulbs to. One such example comes from *Amateur Gardencraft: A Book for the Home-Maker and Garden Lover* (1912):

I do not think it advisable to say much about plans for bulb-beds, because comparatively few persons seem inclined to follow instructions along this line. The less formal a bed of this kind is the better satisfaction it will give, as a general thing. It is the flower that is in the bed that should be depended on to give pleasure rather than the shape of the bed containing it.

I would advise locating bulb-beds near the house where they can be easily seen from the living-room windows. These beds can be utilized later on for annuals, which can be sown or planted above the bulbs without interfering with them in any respect.

I would never advise mixing bulbs. By that, I mean, planting Tulips, Hyacinths, Daffodils, and other kinds in the same bed. They will not harmonize in color or habit. Each kind will be found vastly more pleasing when kept by itself.

I would also advise keeping each color by itself, unless you are sure that harmony will result from a mixture or combination of colors. Pink and white, blue and white, and red and white Hyacinths look well when planted together, but a jumble of pinks, blues, and reds is never as pleasing as the same colors would be separately, or where each color is relieved by white.

The same rule applies to Tulips, with equal force.

We often see pleasing effects that have been secured by planting reds and blues in rows, alternating with rows of white. This method keeps the quarrelsome colors apart, and affords sufficient contrast to heighten the general effect. Still, there is a formality about it which is not entirely satisfactory to the person who believes that the flower is of first importance, and the shape of the bed, or the arrangement of the flowers in the bed, is a matter of secondary consideration.[55]

Despite all the new and improved gardening advice, many an average gardener continued to plant their daffodils (and other bulbs) in conventional, rather uninspired, ways. Frederick F. Rockwell carried on in Mary Hampden's path of innovative bulb gardening. In *The Book of Bulbs* (1927) he delighted in the surge of interest in bulb gardening by Americans in the past decade and agreed with the popularity of the daffodil. He implored his readers to broaden their landscaping uses of bulbs, and daffodils in particular—to shed the stuffy formal planting schemes preceding the development of the modern American bulb gardener and bulb garden. His uses for the daffodil first

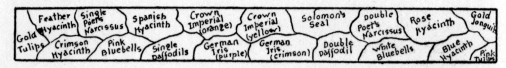

A SPRING BULB BORDER.

A Spring Bulb Border. Hampden, *Bulb Gardening*, 1922.

and foremost were in the mixed hardy border, along the front path, as foundation plantings when mixed with perennials, and as the preeminent bulb for naturalizing; it was acceptable for solid beds, and ideal for rock gardens with other alpine plants. In the general landscape section, his photographs illustrated daffodils as foundation border plantings, mixed into the "hardy border" and loosely clumped in a bed rather than in stiff rows.

Commercial Catalogs

Through the 1870s, 1880s, and 1890s, seedsmen touted the virtues of daffodils as any good salesman would, to drum up interest and revenue. Many started their own gardening periodicals to further solidify customer loyalty and ensure repeat business—more confident gardeners have a tendency to broaden their horizons. James Vick began publishing *Vick's Illustrated Magazine* in 1878; John Lewis Childs began *Mayflower* around 1884 (by 1898 he boasted a subscription rate of 294,391). Nurserymen expanded their offerings and their recommended landscape uses in tandem with the changing view of daffodils by landscapers and the general public. The *New York Times* may have sneered, but the seedsmen were smelling the money a new niche market brings, much to their delight.

Mail order catalogs reflect the slow rise in fortune of daffodils. The changing fortunes of gardening, and daffodils in particular, can be tracked in the evolution of James Vick's autumn bulb catalogs from 1868 through 1872 (during the Long Depression, his catalogs stagnate). The number of engravings increases as does the caliber of their execution, and the catalog length rises from sixteen pages to thirty-two, accommodating broader offerings both in "classes" (tulips, daffodils) as well as the number of sorts (species/cultivars) per class. In Vick's 1869 catalog, Narcissus were listed after Snow-Drops.[56] In 1870 Narcissus are bumped up to right after Crocuses, and Snow-Drops fall down the ranking. The same images, the same offerings, and exactly the same text was used in the 1870 catalog—only the order was changed. By 1871 Narcissus rise to third after hyacinths then tulips.

But bulbs in general were still a hard sell after the Civil War, despite what Walter Elder said in 1863 (or maybe bulbs simply hadn't caught on yet with the more rank-and-file gardener). James Vick, in his 1872 catalog, unhappily observed:

The treatment of Bulbs is so simple and the results so satisfactory that it seems exceeding strange that they are not far more generally cultivated. Not in one garden in a thousand, even of those of some pretensions, do we see a dozen good Tulips, and those who invest a dollar or two in good hardy Bulbs are pretty sure to eclipse all their neighbors. This is not so in Europe, for almost every little village or city garden has its Tulip bed, almost as beautiful as the rainbow every spring. Some care and skill are often required to cause flower seed to germinate, but with a little care in planting and covering after obtaining sound Bulbs of fine varieties, the most gratifying results are almost certain with Hardy Bulbs.[57]

This sentiment is obtusely reflected in a letter to the editor in *Vick's Monthly Magazine,* written by a Wisconsin gardener in support of their favorite flower, the daffodil: "The old Daffodil, though not remarkable for its sweetness, is a

Vick's Illustrated Catalog of Hardy Bulbs, 1870.

flower not to be despised, and I like it on account of early associations, for I believe it was the first flower that attracted my especial attention when a child, and the one I first cultivated."[58]

Leading nurserymen traveled to Europe to evaluate the bulb crops, and report back to general gardening magazines, thus priming the gardening public for their fall purchases. Loss of bulbs to rot during shipment was (and remains to this day) a concern. In 1869 Henry Dreer echoed the report to *Gardener's Monthly and Horticultural Advisor,* confirming the Dutch houses' representatives (E. H. Krelage & Son of Haarlem; Louis Van Houtte of Ghent), that it had been a good summer for ripening the bulbs (or, "drying off" in the current terminology), and that "a great many new varieties, of superior excellence," would be arriving.[59]

James Vick sought to reassure his catalog customers in 1872: "As these Bulbs are obtained from Holland they are somewhat expensive, and this, doubtless, tends to limit their culture. I have made the prices as low as possible, but little more than sufficient to cover the cost of importation and the expense of packing, postage or express charges.

B. K. Bliss and Sons' Autumn Catalogue and Floral Guide, 1880–1881.

Having visited the leading Bulb establishments of Holland, personally, I have no hesitation in saying that my stock is unsurpassed by any collection ever brought to this country, if ever equaled. A failure with such Bulbs is scarcely possible with any kind of decent treatment."[60]

The state of affairs bemoaned by Vick in 1872 slowly improved, as evidenced by Peter Henderson's opening remarks to his fall 1883 bulb catalog: "It is gratifying to notice a constantly increasing demand, every Fall and Winter, from amateur cultivators, for all kinds of Bulbs and Plants. To keep pace with this advancing taste, we have been gradually adding to our lists of late years, and the assortments submitted this season are larger than usual and have throughout been most artfully made up, and comprise only the most distinct and desirable varieties in their several classes."[61]

While the national and regional garden writers discussed intricate patterns for bulbs, many nurserymen stuck to the tried and true, if they offered landscaping commentary at all. James Vick's autumn bulb catalogs simply offered narcissus for the border from 1872 through 1881 (stating in 1881: "The *Single Narcissus* is extremely hardy and popular as a border flower"),[62] although by 1869 he provided directions for planting hyacinths in a red, white, and blue bull's-eye patterned circular bed on the lawn. Contrary to expectation, the early monthly magazines published by the seedsmen did not necessarily provide landscape methods, concentrating solely on cultivation. In the October 1878 *Vick's Illustrated Monthly,* illustrated with color plates of bulbs, cultivation requirements of numerous spring bulbs are discussed class by class, but not where to plant.[63]

By 1880 nurserymen B. K. Bliss & Sons were suggesting daffodils for lining walks and carriage drives, which could be viewed as an extension of ribbon planting, likely reflecting the educated tastes of the higher-end clientele he sought to woo: "Garden Narcissus. Under this head, are some remarkably showy, sweet-scented, Spring-flowering favorites, which are especially deserving of notice, on account of their easy culture, early flowering and generally effective appearance. They thrive in any soil, and are exceedingly attractive when planted in masses or long continuous lines, either in mixed borders, or along carriage drives. Narcissus albo-pleno odorato, and Narcissus Poeticus, are cultivated largely around London for Covent Garden, where the cut flowers meet with a ready sale, on account of their beauty and fragrance."[64] In the back of the B. K. Bliss & Sons catalog, Edward Sprague Rand's bulb books were advertised for sale. Peter Henderson simply directed his catalog customers to buy his own books for all the guidance they may have desired.

As the economy improved in the early 1880s after the Long Depression, the expansion in offerings began in earnest. Henry A. Dreer indicated in 1871 the doubles were very desirable, even if he only offered four sorts. Yet the double "Tratus Cantus" ('Plenissimus,' once called John Tradescant's Rose Daffodil) long offered in American catalogs (since 1822 by Prince), quietly disappeared by the early 1880s (although it was offered in Dutch wholesale catalogs up to the early 1900s). By the mid-1880s, the first listings were no longer

Plate 145, Ajax albicans. Greatest Spanish White. *The British Flower Garden*, 1832.

tazettas, and the orderings varied between seedsmen until the mid-1890s, when the general pattern caught on of singles or trumpets first, then doubles and other groups, with jonquils and tazettas at the end. The shuffling may also indicate a shift in public tastes; despite offering polyanthus first, James M. Thorburn & Co. in the 1882 catalog add the telling comment under "Single Narcissus" of "Most beautiful and fashionable Bulbs at this time."[65] This pattern mimics that of some Dutch wholesale catalogs and reflects the adoption of the classification system introduced by Peter Barr.

New varieties and actual daffodil hybrids appear in the early 1880s in higher-end catalogs, coinciding nicely with both an improved economy and Peter Barr's efforts. J. M Thorburn offers a number of early daffodil hybrids absent from his competitors' catalogs, such as the first hybrid poet 'Ornatus' and the two earliest bicolor trumpets 'Princeps' and 'Horsfieldii'—the latter known and available in Britain and Europe for decades but heretofore absent in American catalogs—and the bicolor 'Empress' introduced by Peter Barr. Peter Henderson offered the mate to 'Empress,' the yellow

Back catalog cover. Peter Henderson & Co., *Bulbs, Plants & Seeds*, 1888.

trumpet 'Emperor,' in his fall 1883 catalog. (Both 'Emperor' and 'Empress' appear in Barr's catalog for the first time in 1870.) Meanwhile, in 1886, George Park observed that in America there was but little real interest in daffodils, even while touting Narcissus as "the fashionable bedding flowers in England."[66] Demand for daffodils and other bulbs accelerated in the late 1880s, evidenced by the increasing number of firms issuing specialty autumn catalogs with expanded offerings, as well as offering landscaping advice. New species appear as well, particularly white trumpets, and were actually listed by botanic name.

The British daffodil wave began breaking on American shores in earnest by the mid- to late 1880s. George W. Park of Fannettsburg, Pennsylvania, in his 1887 fall catalog wrote, "During the past few years great attention has been given to the Narcissus in England. In the spring of 1883 a 'Daffodil Conference' was held in that country, which was addressed by eminent men who have given the subject special thought and attention, and at which a gorgeous display of all the leading kinds was to be observed. In America the genus has been comparatively neglected, because the beauty of the new and improved kinds is not generally known, and amateurs have been content to have a few of the 'Easter flowers' which have been handed down from the gardens of the pioneer settlers from generation to generation."[67] By the early 1890s, one could argue the daffodil had finally "arrived" as a flower in America. New York seedman C. E. Allen's 1890 autumn catalog commented the "admiration and demand [of daffodils] has recently sprung from hundreds to thousands."[68] He touted their suitability for rock work, in front of shrubs, and in groupings in the lawn.

Peter Henderson observed in his 1895 catalog, "The wonderful creations in the way of new varieties have awakened an interest and enthusiasm among the lovers of flowers that has placed this, 'The Flower of the Poets,' in the front rank of popularity, and they merit all the praise that can be bestowed upon them."[69] In his 1896 catalog, Dreer similarly remarked, "Within the past few years giant strides have been made in developing new and improved varieties," noting daffodils were well suited to planting among the grass, under trees, and in every vacant corner of the garden.[70]

One can judge the popularity growth of Narcissus specifically and spring bulbs generally by the customer introductions written by John Lewis Childs of Rochester, New York. In his 1891 catalog, Childs proudly wrote,

> Points For Customers. The department of Fall Bulbs is a part of our business in which we take special delight, as we are positive that no other class of flowers gives such great satisfaction. . . . For this reason we have made the Fall Bulb business a leading specialty, and for many years have exercised such care and attention that we have been enabled to procure, or have grown by special contract, in countries best suited for their development, a quality of these bulbs far superior to the usual commercial grades. This fact has been the principal cause of the enormous demand for our Fall Bulbs—a demand which gives our establishment the largest Catalogue trade in the world. The idea of the business done in our superb Fall Bulbs can be judged when we tell you that we issue 260,000 copies of this Catalogue; and of

the leading bulbs, we have in stock 225,000 Freesias, 310,000 Hyacinths, 270,000 Tulips, 160,000 Crocuses, 120,000 Narcissus, 150,000 Bermuda Easter Lilies, . . . 50,000 Chinese Sacred Lily, etc.[71]

The next year, 1892, Childs crows: "Some idea of the enormous business we do in these bulbs may be gathered from the fact that we issue and mail to our customers 400,000 copies of this Catalog, and of the leading bulbs we have stocks ready for the Fall demand as follows: 500,000 Hyacinths, 400,000 Tulips, 400,000 Narcissus, 300,000 Jonquils, 200,000 Alliums, 300,000 Crocus, 300,000 Chionodoxas, 250,000 Anemones, 300,000 Freesias, 250,000 Snowdrops, 150,000 Bermuda Easter Lilies, and other varieties in like proportion."[72] Although hyacinths and tulips retained first and second place respectively, in one season Childs less than doubled the number of bulbs of those cultivars but ordered three times the number of daffodils. And you don't order and stock what you don't think you can sell.[73]

In the early days of this British invasion, the smaller quantities of the newest hybrids as found in Peter Barr's catalogs likely restricted their ability to be exported to America in large quantities; thus only the most popular and heavily grown stocks were commonly listed in all the American nurserymen's catalogs. Smaller operations, such as B. K. Bliss, Henderson and Thorburn, served a more discerning clientele and carried more cultivars, but probably not in the volumes bragged about by Childs. Though the Dutch hadn't ramped up production on all the esoteric varieties, the Dutch wholesalers (such as E.H. Krelage's 1888 catalog) still offered more daffodils than what American nurserymen ordered.

By the early twentieth century, the British may have been paying hundreds of pounds for daffodils, but Americans were not, content to stay with the humdrum. A. M. Kirby despaired of this American state of mind but optimistically encouraged his readers to broaden their horizons:

In practical America, the daffodil fever has not, as yet, reached so acute a stage. Old, standard varieties, costing from a dollar and fifty cents to ten dollars per hundred bulbs, generally satisfy the aesthetic tastes of our flower lovers. It is noticed, however, that some of the more progressive bulb importers are cataloguing a few of the newer and better kinds, and their answers to our inquiries indicate that there is a growing demand for choicer varieties, costing from fifty cents to one dollar per bulb.

At such prices, and even for much less, hundreds of beautiful varieties, creditable representatives from all type sections, are procurable, so that worthy collections may economically be made. Indeed, it is advisable to begin with moderate-priced varieties, for the higher points of the improved and more expensive sorts may not be fully appreciated at first by the uninitiated. But in a year or two the beginner is educated to note the points of superiority in the higher grades, and is led on to other indulgences.[74]

At this other end of the spectrum was W. W. Rawson & Co. of Boston, Massachusetts—bringing to the American public "the most interesting bulb catalog ever published," catering to the aesthetic collector and botanically inclined.[75] Smitten with the new cold-hardy poetaz tazettas, the company grew a field of very new poetaz-type tazettas and entered them in a horticultural show in Boston in spring 1907. Rawson devoted the front inside catalog cover to this cutting-edge new class of flowers, of which they carried eleven sorts, and showcased one on the cover. Rawson also offered a section for the new tridymus hybrids—crosses between tazettas and yellow trumpets, offering four sorts. (Peter Henderson in 1907 also offered a new section for poetaz and tridymus hybrids; it was a number of years before either new class was regularly offered in mainstream catalogs.) They also proudly announced they were the first American company to introduce novelty Irish seedlings and new red and orange cups, some not

J. M. Thorburn & Co. was an early adopter of photography in its catalogs.

even set with their final names. Most of these were early Hartland introductions, and some never were registered with the Royal Horticulture Society.[76]

The landscaping dichotomy between daffodils and tulips and hyacinths was well entrenched by this time. Seedsmen were not particularly devoting much space to daffodil landscape recommendations, or at least the exhortations were not so pleading. Conversely tulips and hyacinths were packaged as sets for planting specific forms and patterns.[77]

Nurserymen catered to all the landscape trends, and the old-fashioned and Dutch garden trends were no exception. A 1906 advertisement, "Dreer's Old-Fashioned Hardy Garden Plants," comments, "This class of plants is one of our leading specialties. They have come into popular favor so rapidly as to astonish the most sanguine enthusiast of these gems of the garden. Their popularity is not at all surprising when we consider the many, varied and pleasant changes which take place throughout the entire growing season in a well arranged hardy border."[78] Directly below, Thomas Meehan & Sons, Inc., advertisement "Hardy Plants Worth Owning": "Among the beauties in our extensive collection you will find many an old floral friend, for our great assortment includes all the best of the old-fashioned hardy plants as well as the most worthy of the new introductions."[79] The magazine's target audience was greeted with an advertisement by Tiffany & Co. for their silverware.

In October 1921, in the *Garden Magazine,* the Julius Roehrs Co. of Rutherford, New Jersey, ran an ad enticing homeowners with a package to have their garden gay with a Dutch bulb garden, beginning with crocus, then golden shades of cheerily nodding daffodils, followed by brightly colored tulips, to be closed with Darwin tulips. These were carefully combined so the gardener would have all the major bulb types represented in one planting. The smallest package was one hundred bulbs of ten sorts, the largest was four thousand bulbs of forty different kinds.

By the 1920s regional nurserymen such as Breck's in Boston and Hastings in Atlanta were establishing company testing beds to trial daffodils suitable for their climates, and recommending varieties to their customers accordingly:

> We just wish you could see these Giants growing on the Hastings' Plantation. We are growing hundreds of thousands and experimenting with about 100 different varieties. They bloom every spring and do fine in pots, boxes and bowls of water in the house during the winter and outdoors for the early spring beds, borders and lawn or garden plots. They make beautiful cut flowers.
>
> Daffodils just naturally do well in the South, whether you care for them attentively or whether you only set them out in the lawn. They are graceful and beautiful, rich in color and delightful for all flower purposes. Many friends plant our Daffodils by the thousands and come back for more and other varieties to add to the charm of their permanent home collections.[80]

The early 1920s saw the rise of John Scheepers of New York City as the preeminent bulb merchant, issuing a weighty and gorgeous little blue book of a catalog. Looking more like a New York art auction house catalog with its aesthetic color photo plates, it was a catalog for the serious collector. And the 1920s saw the rise of daffodil shows. The Daffodil Garden Club of Washington staged the first acknowledged Georgia daffodil show on March 8, 1929. The blue ribbon flowers provide a nearly comprehensive list of the popular daffodils of the day. These were 'Glory of Leiden,' 'Empress,' "Van Sion" ('Telamonius Plenus'), jonquils, cluster narcissus (tazettas), Phoenix daffodils (doubles), 'Madame De Graaff,' and 'Sir Watkin'. All the named flowers had been sold by Hastings except 'Glory of Leiden,' which was carried by Burpee's in their 1925 catalog. They may have been rather pedestrian flowers, but the ladies loved them enough to find them worthy of competition.

Commercial Growers

As American gardeners' appreciation of bulbs expanded, so did the horticultural industry to follow the money. Enterprising farmers blazed new trails in ornamental bulb

Commercial Production of Cut Flowers. Kirby, *Daffodils, Narcissus.* 1907.

crops. They were the shrewd ones, able to spot a new moneymaker, or the astute, who knew to diversify before calamity struck. Others looked to profit from the expanding cut flower industry. But some just loved their daffodils and were able to build a business on a pretty flower near and dear to their heart.

Interestingly women were integral to this effort. As women asserted a role in business in the late 1800s, making money off of flowers was a socially acceptable avenue. On the farm, women were often able to truly control revenue only from eggs or other small efforts, and as garden flowers were viewed as part of the woman's domain, they fit in well. This section highlights a smattering of the smaller stories across the America.

Initially small entrepreneurs raised and sold bulbs to larger nurserymen for the home garden trade. One early woman in the field was the noted regional horticulturist Mrs. J. S. R. Thomson Jr., of Spartanburg, South Carolina. In the December 15, 1885, issue of the trade journal *The American Florist*, R. Thomson Jr. advertised bulbs, offering "third sized" tuberose bulbs, Z. Atamasco lily and "Southern raised Narcissus Jonquils Van Sion."[81] Earlier in the summer of that same year she went so far as to write in to *Park's Floral Magazine* offering daffodils in exchange for lilies, "I have seven one-horse wagon loads of Narcissus dug from my husband's grandmother's flower yard, planted 65 years ago. I had them planted in my kitchen garden in long rows."[82] Despite being a noted florist and garden writer, Thomson Jr. often covered the fact she was a woman by masquerading under a male nom-de-plume.[83] Another small-scale operation by a woman, Miss Margaret Oliver, flourished outside of Augusta, Georgia, in the late 1890s. After quitting her job as a teacher because the stress was ruining her health, she

'Seagull' in the cut flower field of Arthur L. Ward (Atlanta florist from 1925 to 1941), 2010.

found herself with her mother on a dreadful plot of land unfit for cow peas, but full of spring bulbs. Soliciting nurserymen, she quickly found her cash crop—double jonquils, Bermuda lilies, and gladioli. Her case was one of many in "Women Who Earn" held up as what the new southern woman was accomplishing as an entrepreneur.

While some women raised bulbs for florists and nurserymen, others began small cut flower farms, which allowed women to utilize their gardens to maintain daily existence.[84] Women picking daffodils for cash, especially in a tight economy, could be considered a long-standing tradition. Clusius's comments regarding the women of Cheapside and their *N. pseudonarcissus* reflects how long commonly grown flowers were the realm of women. While the commercial cut flower industry was the domain of men, small farms were often full of women—even if a farm was not owned by a woman, it was likely to employ women as a primary source of labor. Contrary to expectation, a cut flower stem provided a greater return on investment than a bulb (because once it was sold, you need a replacement bulb—so at some point you're buying replacement stock from Europe), so many larger operations sold both to maximize profits. Gardeners with small patches of land only sold the more profitable cut flower stems.

One of the earliest woman-owned cut flower operations is credited to Eleanor Linthicum Smith of "Toddsbury" in Gloucester, Virginia. Around 1890 she established a large daffodil bed of "Trumpet major," employing local children to pick at 10 cents per hundred stems. She then shipped the flowers packed vertically in laundry baskets covered by cheesecloth by steamer to her son William Thomas at Union Station in Baltimore, who sold the cut flowers to newsboys, who thus became street flower vendors. And so began the daffodil industry of Glouscester and Mathews Counties, Virginia.

By the late 1910s to early 1920s, small cut flower farms were popping up outside many major metropolitan areas, situated near rail lines capable of quickly delivering flowers from the field to the street vendors.[85] Early 1920s in northwest Georgia, outside Calhoun (between Chattanooga and Atlanta), the Rev. Julius Peek Jones encouraged his wife Minnie Bray to go into the cut flower business with her daffodils, as the neighbors all kept asking for some. She dubbed her enterprise Jones Floral Farm, growing more than twenty-six varieties on twenty-five acres of rolling hills. She shipped via the nearby rail line to Washington, D.C., and New York City, until her death in 1948. Still on the property are the midseason bloomers 'Ornatus,' 'Emperor,' 'Stella Superba,' 'Orange Phoenix,' 'Sulphur Phoenix,' *N.* × *odorus*/'Rugulosus,' a white-orange poetaz tazetta, and the odd Spanish bluebell and blue Roman hyacinth.

At the commercial level, by the close of the turn of the nineteenth century, American farmers saw vast sums of money leaving the country annually for imported bulbs for the florist industry. Some then determined to siphon off some of that revenue stream for themselves. One of the earliest to respond was the state of North Carolina. In 1892 the horticulturist for the North Carolina Agriculture Experiment Station in Raleigh reported on a program devised to trial bulbs such as narcissus, amaryllis, lilies, and hyacinths, to demonstrate various cultivation methods. This was partly at the behest of New York nurserymen C. L. Allen, a staunch believer that North Carolina could easily replace France as a source of Roman hyacinths and lily bulbs for florists, replacing the waning tuberose industry as that flower had fallen out of fashion in East Coast cities. Surplus stock would then be distributed to eastern North Carolina farmers to stimulate business.[86] By 1892 a number of farms in eastern North Carolina were profitably growing narcissus and tuberose, with amaryllis, tulips, hyacinths, gladiolus, and lilies being trialed for profitability.

The United States government followed suit around 1901. The new head of the U.S. Office of Foreign Seed and Plant Introduction, David Fairchild,[87] promoted the testing of new plants for commercial production. One enterprising farmer from north-central Florida, T. K. (Thomas) Godbey, promptly signed up to be a "cooperator" to test crops in the soils and climate of Florida for daffodils, namely 'Golden Spur,' 'Paper White Grandiflorus,' and "Chinese Sacred Lily," and report back his results. Godbey thus launched the commercial bulb industry in Florida.[88]

Washington state got into the bulb game in 1905. A trial program imported and distributed thirty thousand hyacinths, tulips, and narcissus to farmers in Hillyard Orchard Heights, Tacoma, and Bellingham, to ascertain if the volcanic soil was suitable for commercial production. The government provided the bulbs free of charge, with one-tenth the produce to be returned. The best farm of the three would be made a permanent experiment station. By 1908 ten acres of land had been leased at the town

Picking Paperwhites, circa 1925. Courtesy of the Halifax Historical Museum, Daytona Beach, Florida.

of Bellingham, and the eventual American industry leader in the growing and propagation of hyacinths, tulips, and narcissus was thus founded.

By 1905 the Virginia Dutch bulb industry essentially founded by Mrs. Smith was ten years old and well established. That year the U.S. Department of Agriculture received a catalog from Poat Brothers of Ettrick, Virginia, and trialed bulbs of three daffodils in their garden ('Princeps,' 'Emperor,' and *N. poeticus* var. *poetarum*) against imported Dutch stock. The Department of Agriculture found the Virginia-grown daffodils to be the same, if not superior, to the Dutch imported bulbs. As proof of the quality of the Virginia-raised daffodils, the department supplied the dinner table of President and Mrs. Theodore Roosevelt with Virginia-grown daffodils from their trial beds.[89]

Symbiotic relationships soon developed in the daffodil bulb industry with both the cut flower industry and other commercial summer bulb crops. Enterprising farmers realized they could sell both the flowers and the bulbs themselves, thus reaping two cash crops, and crop rotation practices could yield a third cash crop with summer bulbs or vegetables. These were the enterprises that ended up surviving the Depression.

In 1919 an American import quarantine against foreign plant material was instituted after the introduction of such biological disasters as Dutch elm disease. Flowering bulbs were exempted, getting a reprieve that ended on January 1, 1926, with Quarantine No. 37 applied to all bulb importations. The impact of the quarantine becomes apparent when considering that in 1924, the U.S. imported from the Netherlands alone one hundred ten million bulbs, not to mention those from France, Belgium, England, Japan, and China, representing a huge financial stake. The quarantine remained in effect until 1936, at which point World War II was looming on the horizon, which then instituted its own bulb embargo.[90]

In anticipation of the embargo, many Dutch firms began direct American operations in the early to mid-1920s, so should the American market become closed, they were not shut out. In other cases Dutch representatives partnered with American farmers already growing bulbs, providing business guidance and a guaranteed buyer. The Dutch daffodil farms were particularly concentrated in the mid-Atlantic region an in the Pacific Northwest.

On the heels of the quarantine came the Depression. These Dutch-financed operations then provided a desperately needed source of employment in rural areas. *Narcissus* bulbs were a labor intensive crop, which the abundance of cheap labor obviated as a problem (much to the workers' relief to have gainful employment). Cut flowers too were labor intensive, requiring daily picking early in the morning and quick bundling to make the first trains into the cities for sale by florists and street peddlers. Many a small cut flower operation provided "pin money," if not much-needed real income, and often to women. Women and children worked the fields as pickers and packers, while other women were able to turn small plots of land into income-producing flower fields. And cut flowers allowed many larger operations to stay in the black on the balance sheets.

The large Dutch firm of M. Van Waveren & Sons moved their American headquarters to Gloucester, Virginia, during the quarantine period, hiring George Heath as manager; the operation was five hundred to six hundred acres by its close in 1943. During the Depression years, the monthly payroll of $20,000 was a godsend to the area. Segers, long a wholesale firm selling to American clients, started an operation in Washington state, Jan de Graaff established the Oregon Bulb Farm in 1934, and John Scheepers immigrated from Holland in 1905 to New York. Other firms chased the wealthy northern gardeners, such as Van Engelen to Connecticut and Van Bourgondien Brothers which set up shop on Long Island.[91] Smaller Dutch family firms started business in coastal North Carolina (including the Van Staalduinen family of Terra Ceia Farms) and in South Carolina near Hilton Head.

Well-managed operations expanded during the 1920s and were able to stay profitable through the Depression. One such established nursery, the Gilmore Plant and Bulb Company of North Carolina, expanded its operation into Florida in the 1920s, when it bought acreage on Merritt Island. While gladioli were the primary cash crop, tuberoses and paperwhites were grown too; "old timey daffodils" like 'King Alfred' were grown back in North Carolina. Cut flowers were shipped year-round to major cities such as Boston and New York, as well as to department store chains such as McCrory, Sears, Woolworth, and W. T. Grant. Eventually the operation expanded and bought a local pottery to make the vases used in forcing crocus, narcissus, and hyacinths. The

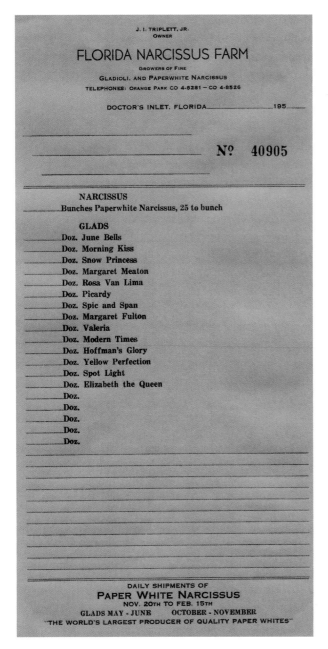

J. I. TRIPLETT, JR.
OWNER

FLORIDA NARCISSUS FARM
GROWERS OF FINE
GLADIOLI, AND PAPERWHITE NARCISSUS
TELEPHONES: ORANGE PARK CO 4-8281 — CO 4-8526

DOCTOR'S INLET, FLORIDA_____195____

N⁰ 40905

NARCISSUS
Bunches Paperwhite Narcissus, 25 to bunch

GLADS
Doz. June Bells
Doz. Morning Kiss
Doz. Snow Princess
Doz. Margaret Meaton
Doz. Rosa Van Lima
Doz. Picardy
Doz. Spic and Span
Doz. Margaret Fulton
Doz. Valeria
Doz. Modern Times
Doz. Hoffman's Glory
Doz. Yellow Perfection
Doz. Spot Light
Doz. Elizabeth the Queen
Doz.
Doz.
Doz.
Doz.
Doz.

DAILY SHIPMENTS OF
PAPER WHITE NARCISSUS
NOV. 20TH TO FEB. 15TH
GLADS MAY - JUNE   OCTOBER - NOVEMBER
"THE WORLD'S LARGEST PRODUCER OF QUALITY PAPER WHITES"

Florida Narcissus Farm Order Form, circa 1950. Courtesy of Linda Van Beck.

operation closed in 1949, as bulb prices dropped with Dutch imports, inflation rose, and hurricanes took their toll; the rise of plastics doomed the pottery operation. The land was soon thereafter purchased by the U.S. government for the creation of Cape Canaveral.

J. J. Triplett Jr. started the Florida Narcissus Farm of Doctor's Inlet near Jacksonville in 1926. In the depths of the Depression, his bulb farm was the only employment in the area. White, black, young, and old, all worked the farm. In the summer, after the bulbs were dug, everyone then worked in the drying and sorting sheds, and all were the same color at the end of the day—dirt brown. The farm eventually expanded to one hundred acres with eight hundred-foot drying sheds. Narcissus were sold from October to February, and gladiolus from May to June and October to November. Cut paperwhite stems were marketed twenty-five to the bunch in the winter to very early spring. After digging the bulbs for summer storage, the largest round bulbs were culled and sold in the fall for forcing. In the summer, the farm grew gladiolus, offering fourteen varieties.[92]

Some small-time bulb operations too generated profits during the Depression, provided they were carefully managed. Sisters' Bulb Farm in northwest Louisiana was one such farm, run by Annie Lou Holstun Jones and her adopted brother Jake Gibson. Annie Lou began planting Narcissus and other bulbs she collected from old homesteads at the start of the Depression, selling the bulbs as they multiplied as a cash crop for much-needed income. Average bulbs sold for one to three cents, choice varieties for a nickel. With careful oversight, she eventually was able to fund her son's education at Louisiana State University and Yale.[93]

At the opposite end of the spectrum was the small operation of Mrs. Drew Sherrard of Oregon, who specialized in small daffodils, namely species and miniatures. She was a prime supplier of Mrs. Elizabeth Lawrence in the garden writer's early days of small bulb collecting; Sherrard had to shutter her operation during World War II when her labor supply went to the war effort.

But while some made a killing in the business, many others did not. Untold numbers of farmers grew small acreage of bulbs, from a quarter of an acre to five acres, in an effort to diversify their crops and make more money during the 1920s and early 1930s. Many of these ventures failed; some farmers blamed the soils, while others attributed the failures to simply bad business practices. Many of these were bought up through the Depression, as farmers hit distressed times—they sold the bulbs to consolidators, kept their land, and tried planting something else. At least you could eat your vegetable crop.[94]

Few small farms survived much into or past World War II; labor and gasoline were scarce, and fertilizer was expensive. When Quarantine No. 37 was lifted in 1936, many Dutch operations closed, and those areas dependent on Dutch operations lost jobs. After the war the Dutch were desperate to ramp up commercial production to salvage their country, and many a small American farm operation could not compete. Later, as the postwar American economy recovered, new small operations started up, exploiting niche markets created by refrigeration, and these small outfits still survive, some as larger commercial horticulture ventures, and some just as "come pick your own" fields, mostly in coastal North Carolina and Virginia—as refrigerated trucks were able to replace railroad transportation in the 1950s.[95]

In retrospect Quarantine No. 37 was a double-edged sword: it gave a big boost to American production and provided a cottage industry that kept many an impoverished American with a job during the Depression, but it stifled the introduction of new European hybrid flowers and thus kept older cultivars in commerce longer than would have occurred otherwise. From 1926 onward American gardeners kept looking at the same list of varieties in catalogs for twenty years if not thirty for smaller nurseries. After the war, when the new European-hybridized varieties finally came on the market —bigger, brighter, showier—the old varieties were swept away—to the point now that many of the most common yellow trumpets from the 1910s to the early 1940s are essentially lost to even dilettante historic daffodil enthusiasts.

Daffodils in Historic Gardens

With their rise in popularity after the Civil War, daffodils were added to numerous existing old gardens. In the 1870s and early 1880s, the plantings followed a more formal schema. Some attempted to regain familial gardening glories of days long gone, and thus reimplement traditional formal gardens. Other gardeners created new gardens, keeping to the old traditional formal plans but adding new design elements on the sides. As the century drew to a close, for those with land and relative means, naturalized plantings came into vogue, leading to great sweeps of spring bulbs, daffodils prominent in many. Those without land or without means added daffodils on a more modest scale, relying on traditional pass-along flowers or new, inexpensive hybrids.

After hostilities ceased, life continued. One tale of such comes from war-ravaged Virginia courtesy of *Historic Gardens of Virginia* (1923). The estate of Annefield passed to the Renshaws in 1866, and Mrs. Annie Renshaw, originally of Hickory Hill, was an avid gardener. Annie is quoted as recollecting, "I carried many things to Annefield—cowslips, violets, snowdrops, daffodils, and dwarf iris—from Hickory Hill, and such growth I never imagined." The property eventually passed to the hands of another avid gardener, Mrs. Butler, in 1900. Edward G. Butler indicated (one presumes of his wife's endeavors), "The main walks she edged with boxwood and to the already fine collection she added numerous bulbs, peonies, and Japanese anemones."[96] The addition of boxwood as an "old fashioned" or "antebellum revival" motif is noteworthy as on occasion these boxwood plantings are now mistaken for antebellum garden remnants.[97]

The garden surveys published by the garden club ladies of the 1920s and 1930s provide numerous examples of very old properties spiffed up with daffodils in the 1880s and 1890s. A number of daffodil plantings in *Historic Gardens of Virginia* as well as *Gardens of Colony and State* (1931) are romanticized into belonging to pre–Civil War days, when in fact they were planted no earlier than the 1880s. While a bit disappointing if one is trying to discern pre–Civil War daffodil plantings, it is reassuring to find daffodils documented for posterity, if not actually a bit glamorized.

As daffodils gained in popularity, so did their plantings in naturalized settings along the edges of woodlands, creek banks, ravines, and greenswards along drives and lawns. Often these intentional naturalized plantings have not been truly recognized as distinct landscape element emanating from the "wild garden." In other cases the daffodils are thought to be older than they really are as their dates of introduction were not widely known.

One particularly ardent romanticizing comes courtesy of Colonial Williamsburg and the Burwell Bassett House (now called Bassett Hall). The house was purchased shortly after this romantic portrait in 1926 by John D. Rockefeller Jr., who owned the house until 1979; it was renovated by Colonial Williamsburg in 2002.

> The broad lawn, now cut by a long entrance lane, was once the scene of cavalry drills, but the only reminder of those stirring days is now found in the old-fashioned flowers. Violets, blue hyacinths and daffodils of many kinds—the phoenix, golden spur and Lady of Leeds in proper succession. No one knows just who it was who planted the multi-great-grandparents of this present wealth of jonquils which mantle Bassett Hall in a robe of gold in April as year follows year.
>
> So profligate have they become in number, so far-spreading have they gone, that the right has been given to the Williamsburg Civic League to take from them enough bulbs to naturalize on the esplanade which extends along Duke of Gloucester Street.[98]

The description suggests the cultivars were selected to provide for a succession of bloom to lengthen the season. And it evidences a common color palate of yellow, white, and blue/purple. However, "Lady of Leeds" as an early hybrid (even though still unidentified) was not commercially available until the late 1880s to 1890s, and so not the work of a "multi-great-grandparent" of colonial days.

An interesting history that provides the who, what, when, and why of the daffodil's addition to an existing garden may be found for Medway Plantation, near Charleston, South Carolina: "Soon after Anna Maria's death, in 1897, her bachelor son, Isaac Dwight Stoney, became the master of the house. His failing health restricted his activities to gardening. He used the garden on the slope and replanted the garden at the western end of the house, where he put flags, azaleas (indica), peonies, bulbs, and within the spicy-dark box hedge, Guernsey and lemon-lilies. Guernsey lilies in September, paper-white narcissus in December, bulbs bloom until March, the lemon-lilies until May."[99]

Northern carpetbaggers brought along their love of spring bulbs to their southern estates, at least those purchased for residence as opposed to just for the hunting season. One such well-known case of famous northern carpetbaggers was the Thomas M. Carnegie family's estate of Dungeness on Cumberland Island, Georgia. The mansion was completed 1886. Not to be dissuaded by the location of a sea island in a warm climate, spring bulbs were purchased for the estate, and daffodils were ordered from major northern seedsmen every year from 1905 to 1912. Currently it is unknown whether the daffodils were to replace the prior year's bulbs or if they were augmenting prior years' plantings. The climate would be the furthest south for most of these daffodils.

Amaryllis 1906

Allium 1908

Freesia (*Freesia refracta*) 1905, 1907, 1908, 1909, 1910

Roman hyacinths (*Hyacinthus orientalis* var. *albulus*) 1906, 1907, 1908, 1909, 1910

Hyacinths (*Hyacinthus orientalis*) 1906, 1907

Ixia

Tulips (*Tulipa* spp.) Cesneriana, Gloria Solis, La Candeur, Cottage Maid, Keiserkroon,

King of the Yellow, Mon Fresor, Prosperine, Clara Butt, Edmee, Glow, Europe

Spanish Iris (*Iris xiphium*)

Japanese Iris (*Iris ensata*) 1907

Bearded iris (*Iris germanica*) 1907

Anemone 1906, 1907, 1909, 1910, 1912

Bermuda lilies 1907, 1908

Dahlias 1909

Narcissus: Double Van Sion, Sir Watkin, Golden Spur, Incomparabilis, Cynosure, Figaro, Simplex (N. *jonquilla*), Trumpet Major, Biflorus, Emperor, Princeps, Bicolor Empress (Ordered every year 1905–1912)[100]

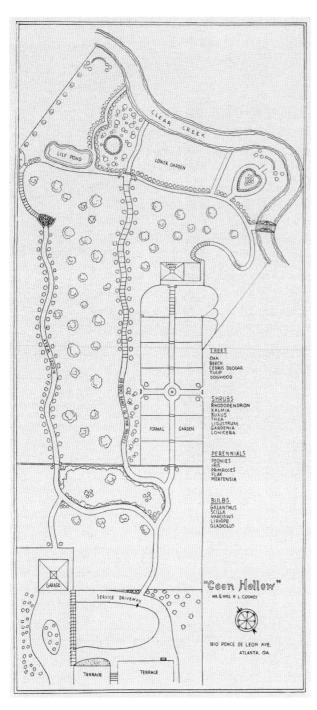

Cooney garden, c.1925. Narcissus, primroses, and mertensia lined the woodland walks with roses in the formal garden. *Garden History of Georgia, 1733–1933.* Courtesy of the Peachtree Garden Club of Atlanta and the Garden Club of Georgia, Inc.

The daffodils chosen are all early- to midseason bloomers, with the glaring exception of Biflorus (*N. × medioluteus*), which traditionally closes out the daffodil season in historic Deep South gardens. The family regularly stayed through Easter, on occasion remaining as late as Mother's Day, before departing the island. No daffodils from this list have survived, although paperwhites planted prior to 1949 by a grandson still bloom behind the cottage. Iris were holding on along a walkway until the 1970s but have since been lost (Susan Hitchcock, personal communication, January 29, 2010).

"Old fashioned gardens" came in many stripes, from traditional vernacular borders with more perennials, to formal parterre based "Colonial Revival" gardens inspired by work at Colonial Williamsburg, to the uncommon "Dutch bulb garden." For the wealthy often more than one garden design was installed on the estate—so a Colonial Revival inspired parterre was placed near the house, and a wild garden of naturalize bulb plantings complemented a vista.

As might be anticipated, since daffodils formed the backbone of the vista drift planting, they were not particularly employed in Colonial Revival parterre gardens. A number of well-known northern Colonial Revival gardens did not include spring bulbs, much less daffodils, in their design, being more of a late spring to early summer starting garden. These include the Webb-Deane-Stevens garden by Amy L. Cogswell in Connecticut (1921; specifically designed to be a summer garden for use with the commercial tea room); the Sundial Garden at Winterthur in Delaware (circa 1929; predominantly shrubbery and a few perennials) and the Kings Garden at Fort Ticonderoga (1921; iris and lilies) both by Marian Cruger Coffin; and the Hill-Stead formal garden in Connecticut by Beatrix Farrand (circa 1920; this garden plan did include Darwin tulips, the latest blooming in the tulip clan). Many of the Ellen Biddle Shipman garden designs similarly lacked early bulbs, and the few bulbs she did employ in border designs were late-season blooms (tulips especially). How much of this was some sort of view of what a colonial garden was back in the day, how much was regional systemic views, and how much just personal preference is tempting conjecture. It also could simply reflect, in part, when the owners were actually in residence. Why plant an early spring garden if the owners are still either in the city or someplace warm and balmy?

The notable exception to the rule is the first Colonial Revival garden plan for Glebe House in Woodbury, Connecticut. The plan carries the distinction of being one of the few American gardens designed by English garden designer Gertrude Jekyll, a known daffodil enthusiast. Commissioned in 1925–1926 by Annie Burr Jennings (of the Standard Oil fortune), one of the original Glebe House board members, the plan replaced a recently implemented garden by Amy Cogswell. Jekyll's garden apparently quickly fell into disarray and decline, essentially lost by the 1950s. When the Glebe House garden was rescued in the 1950s, little of Jekyll's presence survived—but the Cogswell plan was located. Following her more famous American compatriot designers, Cogswell excluded spring bulbs in her formal plan. The Jekyll plan was eventually discovered, installed in 1989–1990. Not surprisingly Jekyll's plans reflect the tried-and-true daffodils of early 1920s Britain, a much different palate than what was standard fare in America for the time—'Princeps,' 'Horsfieldii,' *N. nanus, N. minor,* N. pallidus praecox (*N. pallidiflorus*), *N. × incomparabilis, N. poeticus,* 'Ornatus,' and N. majalis patellaris (*N. poeticus* var. *majalis*).[101]

While the New England ladies geared their gardens to early summer, the southern ladies worked with a broader seasonal palate. Virginians pressed both early spring and fall-blooming bulbs into service, planting daffodils, *Hyacinthoides* (Spanish bluebells/wood hyacinths), Roman hyacinths, *Muscari*, nerines, Guernsey lilies, *Lycoris radiata*, and autumn crocus into their Colonial Revival gardens. At Oatlands, Edith (Mrs. William Corcoran) Eustis in the early 1900s revived the remains of George Carter's circa 1804 garden. Eustis added daffodils and nerines to a steep terrace slope along the lowest terrace, across the walk thus opposite to the Carter family mausoleum. In the 1920s at Belmont, Mrs. Melchers incorporated daffodils bordering the front walk, which were replenished by the Garden Clubs of Virginia when it, in turn, restored Melchers' garden (now the Gary Melchers Home and Studio at Belmont).

Westover, one of the large 1700s plantations on the James River between Williamsburg and Richmond, Virginia, has a checkered garden past. Built in the 1750s by William Byrd III, its owner prior to the Civil War, John Seldon, was an enthusiastic gardener who planted many trees. Westover's owner after the Civil War was

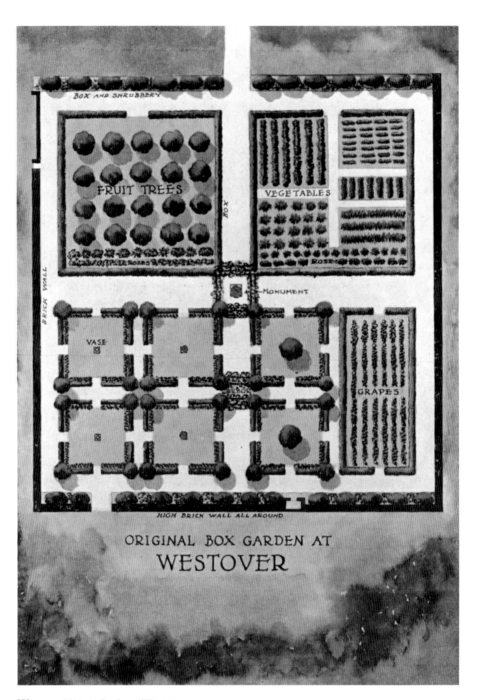

Westover, *Historic Gardens of Virginia*, 1923.

Major Drewry, an enthusiastic farmer who had no money (or use?) for a plea-sure garden, and plowed up the flower garden for vegetables and removed most of the brick wall for more utilitarian use (a horse stable). Fortuitously another enthu-siastic gardener, Clarise Sears Ramsey, took hold of Westover in 1900, and re-created a proper Virginia plantation garden around 1905. She rebuilt the brick wall on its original foundations and laid out ample squares of lawn with fruit trees and vegetable patches, all bordered by boxwood and flowers. Reportedly Sears Ramsey planted dwarf boxwood one foot on center; some of her original brick bor-ders are still visible near the center obelisk monument/tomb to William Byrd II. Clumps of daffodils, *Lycoris radiata,* Roman hyacinths and nerines remain interplanted among hostas, in front of blooming shrubs such as camellias, azaleas, and wigelia, and perennials such as roses, peonies, iris, and other flowers. The daffodils range from trum-pets to poets to 'narcissus' or *N.* × *medioluteus,* and some jonquils for good measure.

The same general plant material mix was employed by Mr. and Mrs. Robert Daniel in the restoration of Lower Brandon, located across the James River from Westover, in the late 1920s. Albeit a terraced garden and constructed on a much larger scale, a similar palate of daffodils and other bulbs again fill spots between larger flowering perennials and shrubs.

Conclusion

Taken in a long view, the rise of the daffodil coincided with not only market forces but landscape design innovations and new hybrid flowers. This mirrors what happened both with the tulip and the hyacinth in their assorted heydays—it was new forms and new colors, backed by a large horticulture industry (and important tastemakers), that propelled these flowers to the peaks of popularity. However, the tulip and hyacinth have hit their hybridizing ends, in a way, while the daffodil surges on. Its wider range of species plants allow for a much more diverse stable of forms, albeit changes in color (pinks, reds, oranges, greens) are still not as dramatic as with tulips and hyacinths. The most telling sign as to where the current excitement may be found is in the national daffodil societies in many English Commonwealth countries (all gleefully breaking the tenth commandment?), with cutthroat judged competitions and trailblazing hybridiz-ers, while there are no such societies for tulips or hyacinths—and the RHS has lumped tulips with the daffodils on its official committee and its annual yearbook. If the *New York Times* writer in 1893 thought the then-modern hybrid daffodils unrecognizable to their species progenitors, given the changes in the past century with no particular end in sight, it will be quite some time before daffodils are again relegated to a simple background flower filling an early spring hole in the mixed herbaceous border.

5.

Daffodils in Cemeteries

The rural cemetery movement began around 1835 to 1840 and lasted to around 1920—at least for daffodils. It saw the creation of community and municipal cemeteries in response to the growing populations' needs exceeding the available space in local church graveyards. These new cemeteries were meant to be inviting places for reflection and remembrance, with idyllic landscaping and winding roads. To this day many are still considered a crown jewel for its parent city.

For much of America, planting flowers in cemeteries came into widespread vogue in the late Victorian era. However, some immigrant populations brought cemetery ornamental planting traditions with them from Europe, where it had been a long-standing tradition, particularly with the Germans. A floral cemetery tradition also existed in the early nineteenth century in certain segments of Scotland and England. Prior to the Civil War, some large municipal cemeteries planted flowers as public plantings to offset their banning of ornamental clutter in family plots, while other large cemeteries did allow families to landscape their plots with shrubs and flowers. But by and large, the practice of families planting flowers with deceased loved ones did not become widespread, particularly in small cemeteries, until after the Civil War.

Some African cultures also traditionally planted cemeteries with significant plant material, often to serve a spiritual purpose. Eyewitness accounts of American slave cemeteries thus vary, the state of a given slave or freeman cemetery probably depending on local authoritarian pressures as much as old traditional customs. Until recent times small African American cemeteries in the South often were more decorated with ornamental plants than the cemeteries of their white neighbors.

The early twentieth century saw the rise of a new movement in the American design of cemeteries, namely the "lawn-park" design. The design of an open expanse

"The Cemetery at Sleepy Hollow, N.Y.," undated.

of grass lawn with orderly rows of gravestones was designed for easy maintenance. This aesthetic shunned the landscape plantings common in earlier cemeteries, and it brought in the mower. Mowing then extended to and decimated the old Victorian landscape in most smaller cemeteries. Decades of mowing have set cemetery daffodils into severe decline, making identification often impossible. In older rural cemeteries and small family burial grounds, many historic daffodil plantings (along with other ornamentals) have been lost to overzealous grounds maintenance and the general vagaries of time.

Old World Traditions

As American city leaders laid out their new municipal cemeteries in the 1830s, 1840s, and 1850s, they looked to the tastemakers and trendsetters for suggestions and guidance. Many read the leading books on the subject, while some even traveled to Europe. One such leading source consulted was John C. Loudon. His *On the Laying Out, Planting, and Managing of Cemeteries, and on the Improvement of Churchyards* (1843) provides insight as to what city leaders saw on their European fact-finding trips and what served for guidance for their own home endeavors:

> The planting of flowers in cemeteries is very general, not only in the margin of masses and belts, and in beds as in pleasure-grounds, but on graves. For our own particular taste, we would have no flowers at all, nor any portion of ground within a cemetery that had the appearance of being dug or otherwise moved for the purpose of cultivation. A state of quiet and repose is an important ingredient in the

"A German Cemetery," ca. 1900.

passive sublime; and moving the soil for the purpose of culture, even over a grave, is destructive of repose.

Nevertheless, as the custom of planting flowers on graves is common throughout Europe, and of planting them in beds is frequent in the cemeteries about London, arrangements for this purpose must be provided accordingly. We would never plant flowers or flowering shrubs in the margins of masses or belts, or in beds or patches that might be mistaken for those of a lawn or a flower-garden; but, to give them a distinctive character, we would plant them in beds of the shape of graves or coffins, raised above or sunk beneath the general surface, and only in situations and on spots where at some future time a grave would be dug.

For example, two graves are seldom dug close together, but an intervening piece of firm ground is always left of width sufficient for forming a grave at a future time; the object being to have, if possible, at all times, firm ground for the sides of a grave which is about to be excavated. Now, on these intervening spots alone would we plant beds of flowers, or of roses, or of other flowering shrubs. When flowers, shrubs, or trees are planted on occupied graves, it is done by individuals according to their own taste. The most highly ornamented cemetery in the neighbourhood of London, as far as respects plants, is that of Abney Park, in which, as already mentioned, there is a complete arboretum, including all the hardy kinds of rhododendrons, azaleas, and roses in Messrs. Loddiges's collection; and in which also dahlias, geraniums, fuchsias, verbenas, petunias, &c., are planted out in patches in the summer season.[1]

The Necropolis cemetery in Glasgow, Scotland, was similarly landscaped. Established in 1833, it was one of many municipal cemeteries in town, albeit nominally associated with a church. Its description in 1842 suggests a lovely place: "The greater portion of the graves are enclosed either by a low stone erection, or a delicate iron-railing, and each is a little flower-garden of itself, while the grounds are sprinkled over with monuments of every style of architecture, all of them graceful, and many of them gorgeous."[2]

The German tradition of planting flowers with the deceased crossed religious boundaries. In a travelogue published in 1844, a Catholic cemetery in Munich was visited, and its beauty considered a model for what ought to transpire in England: "All the grave mounds are commonly enclosed by rail or wire-work; and planted with the choicest flowers."[3]

Protestant Germans also believed the cemetery should be a pleasant place for the living to visit the deceased. The Moravians of Bethlehem, Pennsylvania, brought this notion with them from Germany, to the slight amazement of their American neighbors, who in the early 1870s were not yet inclined to personally flower up the graves of their own family:

> The Moravians have striven to make their grave-yards as attractive as possible, and they have succeeded in that in which all the rest of the world have failed; and it is very pleasant to know that it is so. Each grave is marked by a small marble slab, about a foot and a half by two feet in size, laid flat upon it; emblematic that death levels all, and that all are alike. Each stone has cut upon it the name, age, and birth-place of the departed. If a married woman, her maiden name. Sometimes a verse of a hymn, or a quotation from the Scriptures is added. Flowers are planted on many of the graves, and vases with wreaths and bouquets of flowers are common tokens of affection to be seen on the little slabs that cover the remains of some loved one, gone from the earth forever. Time soon takes oil from the marble tablets their glaring whiteness; the grass grows around them, and they are almost hidden from the sight, and the visitors see only blooming flowers, trailing vines, luxuriant grasses, waving trees, and comfortable benches to sit upon. They hear the songs of the birds, see the children playing upon the walks, and lured by the beauty and novelty of the scene, forget entirely where they are, or to be sad and mournful. And thus the Moravian grave-yard becomes a place of cheerful resort to the living, and the sweetest spot on earth in which to place the remains of the loved ones who have gone home.[4]

Traces of African funeral traditions in period observations of American slave cemeteries are scant but tantalizing. Some African cultures believe(d) the spirits of the dead remain with the living and that certain plants impacted the spirits' actions; thus, thorny yucca and cactus were planted to hold the deceased's spirit from wandering around the cemetery.

A more "expected" view of slave cemeteries as a place of neglect for the bottom of the social hierarchy may be found in *Pictures of Slavery in Church and State: Including Personal Reminiscences* (1857) by Rev. John Dixon Long. A leading Methodist Episcopal minister and abolitionist, Rev. Long made it quite clear to his audience that slaves received nothing at plantation graveyards, that their burial area was off in a corner of the plantation and that it was not a respected place.

Frederick Law Olmsted, in his observations of slave and "Negro" (presumably free persons of color) cemeteries in the 1850s, noted the paucity of plant material to be found. His comparisons of white to nonwhite cemeteries are pointedly stark. He remarked on the sad state of the Negro cemetery relegated to a vacant lot in downtown Charleston, South Carolina. A slave burial ground outside of Richmond, Virginia, was described as a "desolate place," in contrast to the white cemetery filled with stately evergreens. His lengthiest, and perchance most interesting, discussion was reserved for the Negro cemetery for Savannah:

> While riding, aimlessly, in the suburbs of Savannah, on returning from a visit to the beautiful rural cemetery of the wealthy whites, which Willis has, with his usual facility and grace, a little over-pictured, I came upon a square field, in the midst of an open pine-wood, partially inclosed with a dilapidated wooden paling. It proved to be a grave-yard for the negroes of the town. Dismounting, and fastening my horse to a gate-post, I walked in, and found much, in the monuments, to interest me. Some of these were mere billets of wood, others were of brick and marble, and some were pieces of plank, cut in the ordinary form of tomb-stones. Many family-lots were inclosed with railings, and a few flowers or evergreen shrubs had sometimes been planted on the graves; but these were generally broken down and withered, and the ground was overgrown with weeds and briars. I spent some time in examining the inscriptions, the greater number of which were evidently painted

5360. The Voyage of Life, Tis ended.

"The Voyage of Life, Tis ended," ca. 1890.

by self-taught negroes, and were curiously illustrative both of their condition and character.[5]

Despite the lack of regular care, the town's African descendents were planting flowers with deceased loved ones. And Olmsted, as an abolitionist, presumably would not have been inclined to paint a rosier picture than what he actually saw.

A floral tradition among slaves in lower Mississippi was also remarked on in the mid-1850s. Joseph Holt Ingraham published crafted "correspondence" of his travels in the South for a northern audience on the eve of war. One such letter was sent by "Katherine Conyngham" (nom de plume of Dr. J. H. Ingraham), who was residing in the suburbs of Natchez, Mississippi, at the time:

> There is here a touching custom of having burying grounds on the estates. Nearly all plantations have a private cemetery. These places of buried affection, where hope and faith wait the resurrection, are often gems of funereal beauty. Some secluded but sweet spot, not too remote from the mansion, is selected. It is enclosed by a snow-white paling, or a massive wall of brick; ivy is taught to grow over it; elms, willows, and cypresses are planted within the inclosure. White marble tombs glisten among the foliage. Perhaps over all, towers a group of ancient oaks, subduing the light beneath, and lending to the hallowed spot a mournful shade, a soft twilight even in the sultry noontide's glare.
>
> Such is the family burial-place on this estate. Not far from it, in a place scarcely less picturesque, is the cemetery for the slaves, enclosed by a neat white-washed wall. The affection of the poor Africans has planted the rose and the lily, the violet and verbena, upon many of the graves.[6]

This quickly raises the questions of how slaves were able to acquire roses, lilies, violets, and verbena, and what the ancestral traditions were that led slaves to plant flowers with the dead. (It is suspected the plantation in question was Melrose, per Dr. Elizabeth Boggess, 2010.) Thus against the backdrop of these myriad traditions came the romanticism of the Victorian era as applied to the deceased and their places of rest.

The American Victorian Cemetery

Scattered evidence indicates Americans were planting flowers on family graves prior to the Civil War in the large municipal cemeteries. Many of the major rural cemeteries across the country were of such undertaking that books regarding their establishment and early history were published. Much was made of the credentials of the various staff, such as the superintendent and head gardener, and the overarching landscape plans and governing aesthetics discussed in detail.

At Mount Auburn in the 1840s, plot owners were granted the right to "cultivate trees, shrubs and plants" within the confines of their purchased lot, but the organization made no recommendations for suitable plants.[7] The Poughkeepsie Rural Cemetery

Photograph ©2014 Museum of Fine Arts, Boston. Antonio Zeno Shindler, American (born in Bulgaria?), 1823–1899. Laurel Hill Cemetery, Philadelphia, 1850s. Opaque watercolor on paper. Sheet (rounded/cut corners): 33.8 × 44.1 cm (13 5/6 × 17 3/8 in.) Museum of Fine Arts, Boston. Gift of Maxim Karolik for the M. and M. Karolik Collection of American Watercolors and Drawings, 1800–1875, 50.3872

Association in 1854 directed plot owners to select shrubs appropriate for "their habit and character," and to be mindful of what types thrived in shade.[8]

The 1847 guidebook for the Laurel Hill Cemetery in Philadelphia educated its lot holders as to the situation needed for roses to succeed in family plot plantings, discussing the merits of many types, as well as ornamental shrubs suited to shady locations including rhododendrons, laurels, franklinia, ivy, phlox and lily of the valley.

Not surprisingly, prior to the Civil War, little is published in the way of families planting their own plots. One such early example comes by way of Forest Hills Cemetery of Boston, almost by accident in 1860:

> Spring has spread its charms over Forest Hills. With the warm south wind the soft notes of the birds have come. The black birch has hung out its pendulous blossoms, the maple is crowned with its scarlet flowers, the oak and the walnut are opening their waxen buds, and light green foliage with delicate spray clothes here and there the underwood. On the sunny slopes and in the sheltered nooks of the rugged rocks the violet lifts its blue petals to the light, and in the borders or on the cherished

grave the crocus or hyacinth has succeeded the snowdrop. The turf has grown green on the resting-places of the dead, on the hill-sides and in the valleys. Nature is awaking from its long sleep to a new and beautiful life. And here, where the dead slumber, how does this resurrection of natural life speak to the soul, of that higher resurrection which is intimated in its own longings and promised in the Divine word.[9]

Fortuitously a much more personal record of remembering deceased family and friends comes from rural eastern Alabama, courtesy of Sarah R. Espy. In March 1860 she noted in her diary that she and her daughter Olivia went to the Baptist Church, its graveyard looking much neglected, to set out flowering plants around the graves of the Brown family. Alas she offers no explanation as to why, and in the ten years spanned by her diary she makes no other mention of planting flowers for any other family. On February 22, 1861, Espy took her niece to the family grave site to beautify Espy's mother's and sister's graves, who died twenty and nineteen years prior. They planted a cedar tree at the head of the wall, and inside the wall they planted her mother's favorite flowers that she took with her to every house, namely white lily, purple-shade, yellow and white jonquils, lilac, perpetual roses, and white roses. She returned in mid-March to find the plants growing well. In February 1863 she oversaw the planting of sixteen cedar trees in two rows at the grave of her son lost to war. In late April of 1866, Espy used white jonquils and Star of Bethlehem, as both were white, to decorate a young girl in her coffin.[10]

By the 1860s horticultural guidance was being dispensed to the readerships as to tasteful and appropriate means to ornament a grave or family plot, reflecting that Espy was not alone in her gestures of remembrance. Landscaped cemeteries were now part of the American experience, resulting in more families looking for guidance, and more tastemakers wishing to influence mourners to consider plants suitable in constitution and form. One such early column to their readership in 1866 does just that, but also elucidates why white or pale flowers were preferred:

> The question is sometimes asked us, "What flowers are suitable to plant around a grave?" . . . In the first place we would avoid all gaudy colors, and in the second place, select those which need but little care. . . . A good green foliage, with white flowers, is the combination most appropriate to a funeral wreath, and is that which we prefer in floral decorations for the grave, though colored flowers are admissible, provided they be of delicate tints. . . . Among the most appropriate flowers for the cemetery are the bulbs, such as do not need lifting each year. These spring up and flower, complete their growth, and die down, and repeat this year after year, fit "emblems of our own great resurrection." White and bright colored Crocuses, and the Snowflake, are desirable, and bloom in early spring, while the Meadow Saffron—Colchicum autumnale, flowers in autumn, with lilac colored bloom.[11]

Replicating the traditional symbolism of the funerary wreath—evergreens for immortality and white for purity—is a logical extension to more permanent cemetery

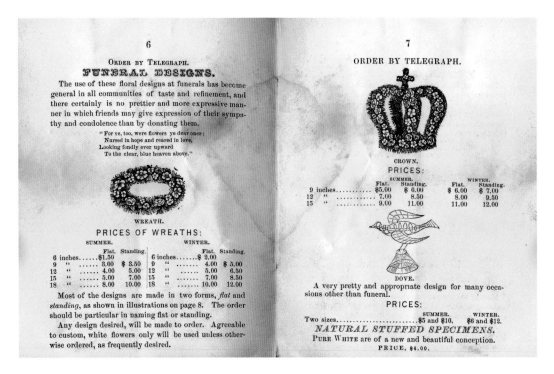

6

ORDER BY TELEGRAPH.

FUNERAL DESIGNS.

The use of these floral designs at funerals has become general in all communities of taste and refinement, and there certainly is no prettier and more expressive manner in which friends may give expression of their sympathy and condolence than by donating them.

> "For ye, too, were flowers ye dear ones;
> Nursed in hope and reared in love,
> Looking fondly ever upward
> To the clear, blue heaven above."

WREATH.

PRICES OF WREATHS:

SUMMER.			WINTER.		
	Flat.	Standing.		Flat.	Standing.
6 inches	$1.50		6 inches	$ 2.00	
9 "	3.00	$ 3.50	9 "	4.00	$ 5.00
12 "	4.00	5.00	12 "	5.00	6.50
15 "	5.00	7.00	15 "	7.00	8.50
18 "	8.00	10.00	18 "	10.00	12.00

Most of the designs are made in two forms, *flat* and *standing*, as shown in illustrations on page 8. The order should be particular in naming flat or standing.

Any design desired, will be made to order. Agreeable to custom, white flowers only will be used unless otherwise ordered, as frequently desired.

7

ORDER BY TELEGRAPH.

CROWN.

PRICES:

	SUMMER.		WINTER.	
	Flat.	Standing.	Flat.	Standing.
9 inches	$5.00	$ 6.00	$ 6.00	$ 7.00
12 "	7.00	8.50	8.00	9.50
15 "	9.00	11.00	11.00	12.00

DOVE.

A very pretty and appropriate design for many occasions other than funeral.

PRICES:

	SUMMER.	WINTER.
Two sizes	$5 and $10.	$6 and $12.

NATURAL STUFFED SPECIMENS.

PURE WHITE are of a new and beautiful conception.
PRICE, $4.00.

Illustrated Priced Catalogue of the Cut Flower Department, Floral Hill Nursery, 1870. Courtesy of the Cherokee Garden Library, Kenan Research Center at the Atlanta History Center, Atlanta, Georgia.

plantings. And while bulbs may have been viewed as symbols of resurrection, the choices suggested still played to the floral fashions of the day.[12] That family members needed chiding to stop planting garish colors leads one to speculate how brightly planted some cemeteries really were, particularly if they were planting favorite flowers of the deceased.[13]

By the 1870s larger cemeteries actually generated enough business for nurseries to be established with them. By 1873 the Allegheny Cemetery in Pittsburgh, Pennsylvania, had a small nursery with trees, shrubs, and annuals for sale to the grieving public: "The general appearance and character of the Cemetery will bear evidence of the propriety of the plan adopted by the company of keeping on the grounds a small nursery of well selected trees and shrubs suitable for ornamenting the lots. By rendering these facilities to those who may not wish to take the trouble of procuring shrubbery elsewhere, a much greater amount is planted out than would otherwise be."[14]

In addition to spruces, maples, catalpa, forsythia, deutzias, euonymus, and other trees and shrubs, the six-thousand-square-foot greenhouse was well stocked with greenhouse and hothouse plants such as azaleas, camellias, roses, phlox, verbena, pansies, daisies, and so on, but alas no bulbs. As bulbs gained in general popularity, they were introduced into public plantings. In Boston the nurseryman B. T. Wells offered a special discount to public parks and cemeteries in his fall 1882 Dutch bulbs import

St. John Lutheran Church, Charleston, South Carolina, August 31, 1886. J. K. Hillers Collection, U.S. Geological Survey.

catalog: "The City Forester of the Public Garden of the City of Boston was induced about five years ago by us to make a large planting of Hyacinths, Tulips, crocus and Lilies. The result of which was, the successful planting every fall since, of thousands of Bulbs in the same location."[15]

An isolated snippet hints at how widespread the practice of planting flowers on loved one's graves became, either as folks of traditions such as the Moravians spread across the country or as the notion took wider hold on the Victorian melancholy-prone sensibility. Miss B., of McLean County, Illinois, wrote to nurseryman James Vick (in his *Vick's Illustrated Magazine*) in the fall of 1879, asking, "I want to get a Lily, a white one, for the purpose of putting on a grave. I want one that will not spread much from year to year, and that does not grow very tall. Can you tell me of one?" Vick's succinct reply was, "We think *Lillium longiflorum* will suit your purpose."[16]

A more tantalizing tale, and frustrating for its lack of date and actual location, comes from a romanticized recollection of the old home place in 1881. Writing under the pseudonym "Lichen," the author reminisces about the family garden of old in Kentucky, and the favorite flowers of different siblings: "Here were the golden buttercups which my little sister prized, and the star of Bethlehem which the tiny brother used to gather in his little hands to take to mamma. When their graves were made in the

Unknown cemetery, undated.

beautiful cemetery just beyond the town, some of these were planted beside them."[17] The daffodil's place in the American cemetery was slower to appear, as it came more from the garden than say the rose and lily with their long-standing religious associations. Having such a history, the daffodil began in the stonework before it arose in the actual soil—as its funerary symbolism came before the daffodil's surge of popularity as a garden flower.

As with many other natural objects, the daffodil was ascribed funerary symbolism in the Victorian era. This was an outgrowth of Victorians ascribing terminology and symbolism to flowers in the garden. In the early Victorian period, the daffodil or narcissus was assigned a not-so-favorable meaning, stemming from the parable of Narcissus and his reflection. In his 1839 *The Language of Flowers*, Frederic Shoberl ascribed to the Daffodil "Self Love." His work, however, was a translation of a French work written by Charlotte de Latour in 1819. The attribution of "self-love" is supported not only by the story of Narcissus and Echo but also its appearance in Greek mythology:

Thus, too, the ancients, on account of its narcotic properties, regarded it as the flower of deceit, which, as Homer assures us, delights heaven and earth by its odour and external beauty, but, at the same time, produces stupor and even death. It was therefore consecrated to the Eumenides, Ceres, and Proserpine, on which account Sophocles calls it the garland of the great goddesses; and Pluto, by the advice of Venus, employed it to entice Proserpine to the lower world.

In the East, the Daffodil is a particular favourite. The Persians call it, by way of eminence, Zerrin, which signifies golden; and by the Turks it is denominated Zerrin Kadech, golden bowl.[18]

Meanwhile, the Jonquil was considered to represent "Desire," attributing that association to come originally from the Turks.[19]

Who assigned what meaning to a flower was rather fluid. Elizabeth Washington Wirt of Baltimore in her *Flora's Dictionary* (1832) assigned the poor Narcissus to "egotism," but interestingly the Daffodil symbolized "Chivalry," and the Jonquil was a more complex "I desire a return of affection." Bostonian Catharine H. Waterman, in her *Flora's Lexicon* (1839), specifically assigned the representation of Chivalry to *Narcissus major*. John Gierlow of Georgia provided Southern ladies a surprisingly broad lexicon for the Narcissus clan in 1856. The daffodil symbolized "be happy till life's winter," while the jonquil meant "have compassion on my love." The white narcissus was simi-

"Language of Flowers Daffodil—Regard," undated.

larly distinct, as "how can you be so cruel?"; the yellow narcissus was more typically negative, with "your associates look upon you with envious eyes."[20]

Englishman Robert Tyas in his *Language of Flowers* (1869) simplified the Jonquil to simply "Desire," kept the poets as "Egotism," and relegated the daffodil or Yellow Narcissus to "Disdain," elaborating: "Disdainful persons are for the most part exacting, and have little amiability: thus of all this genus the Yellow Narcissus is the least beautiful, most devoid of fragrance, and yet it demands more care than the rest."[21] An anonymous writer in 1854 for the London journal *Favourite* returned to the "Great Daffodil" with "Chivalry" but went one step further, pairing "Daffodil" with "Regard."

In the end, it is the Daffodil and the notion of "regard" that is taken up and broadened in American cemetery stonework symbolism. In larger and more urban cemeteries, the traditional thought is daffodils symbolize regard, longing, desire, and so on.[22] By the 1890s the desire to beautify the family burial plot had taken strong hold across the country. In 1894 an article in *Western Garden and Poultry Journal*, published in Des

Unitarian Church, Charleston, South Carolina, August 31, 1886. J. K. Hillers collection, U.S. Geological Survey.

Moines, Iowa, appeared, specifically to guide westerners in how to plant, and what to plant, at the graves of the beloved:

> There are few who are fortunate enough not to have laid any of their loved ones to rest, and nearly all try to grow flowers on the graves of their dead as a last respect they can pay to the dear departed.
>
> Few are successful in this, mainly because they do not know what to plant, and I will try to give a few hints as to this that may help someone.
>
> The most satisfactory plants that give the earliest blossoms are hyacinths and narcissus. Any white hyacinth is good, but many of the narcissus are not very hardy and are slow to bloom. However the Poeticus and Paper White are well worth the planting, and they increase so rapidly that one bulb of each soon makes a lovely bunch. These flowers bloom usually about the first of May. For blooms after these are gone plant La Candeur tulip. It is double white and a few planted in a clump make a fine showing, and they will remain in bloom a long while. A Croquette de Alps rose is hardy, with slight protection, and I have seen two-year-old plants have from thirty to forty buds and blossoms at one time. This rose will bloom till the frost kills the buds.

Achillea Alba is another hardy plant used for cemetery planting. It bears medium sized white flowers in profusion: but care must be taken with it on account of its spreading qualities. Then, as to annuals, white phlox is sure to be satisfactory: always in bloom and snowy white, it is a universal favorite. White verbenas and pinks are also good.

Alyssum is much used and is very pretty: but of all annuals for cemetery planting I admire pansies most. Any color is suitable, and the little faces seem almost to speak for the departed ones. Just a word with regard to fixing the grave ready for planting. Do not build the bed up a foot and then put a board around it to keep it in place, as I have seen people do. Plants are sure to dry out and die in such a case. Smooth off the bed until it is level with the surrounding ground, and the tendency to dry out will be much lessened.

A little care with the right kind of plants will turn a cemetery from almost a wilderness into a garden of beauty.[23]

Bulbs for Cemetery Planting, *Park's Floral Magazine*, September 1906.

This new use for flowers was not lost on the American nurseryman. The 1904 edition of Peter Henderson's *Handbook of Plants* directs: "Narcissi are well adapted for planting in the herbaceous or shrubbery border, or in the grass by the sides of woodland walks, in open spaces between trees and shrubs, in cemeteries, or in any situation where the flowers may be readily seen on their appearance in spring."[24]

Other nurserymen specifically offered cemetery bulb mixes. *Park's Floral Magazine* advertised cemetery bulb mixes from 1896 at least until 1909. The 1896 mix contained six white bulbs (double Dutch hyacinth, 'Ornatus,' crocus, *Candidum* lily, *Leucojum aestivum, Muscari botryoides alba*); the 1909 cemetery bulb mix advertised "lilies, narcissus, muscari, etc."[25]

As the cemetery business became more of a business, trade journals appeared, publishing articles on all topics of possible interest to cemetery superintendents, gardeners, and the like. And as with any other profession, employees in the field wrote letters to the editors to share best practices, crow about their successes, or warn others of potential problems. By the early 1900s, large-scale landscaping of municipal cemeteries was becoming more common. In the September 1904 issue of *Park and Cemetery and Landscape Gardening,* the "Report from Allegheny Cemetery, Allegheny PA" commented, "Last Spring the cemetery was gayer than the city parks with tulips, Narcissus and other spring flowers, tens of thousands of which were set out, and this is to be continued."[26]

New cemeteries were not the sole beneficiaries of this notion of beautification. Old cemeteries were spiffed up as well. One neglected cemetery in Watertown, Ontario, Canada, was "remodeled" in 1914 as a civic project. Fencing and headstones were repaired, a utility shed installed, flowering shrubs donated, and the first year five hundred spring bulbs of tulips, daffodils, and jonquils were planted, to be followed the next spring by peonies, iris, and roses.

Although the Victorian flowers and shrubs were being supplanted by vast sweeps of uninterrupted green lawn by 1920, in some quarters flowers for the dead held strong—no more so than in the killing fields of Europe after World War I. The Imperial War Graves Commission, for the planting of World War I cemeteries of British dead in Europe, along with commissions in other countries, drew up regulations to oversee the creation of the cemeteries. Perennial plants were permitted to be planted at the base of headstones, with daffodils, snowdrops, and crocus approved for planting atop the interments.

Daffodils in Cemeteries

The daffodil was taken up by both affluent whites and African Americans as a token of remembrance for the dead. Even members of the Cherokee Nation in Oklahoma adopted the practice. Traditionally white has been the color associated with death, such as wearing white flower corsages on Mother's Day instead of colored flowers, to signify that one's mother has passed away.

Planting daffodil bulbs seems to have been ascribed a different symbolism in the coastal Southeast. In the vernacular tradition of South Carolina, south Georgia, and north Florida, the planting of daffodils or tazettas, particularly the winter- or Christmas-blooming paperwhites, signified rebirth or resurrection. How much of this is attributable to daffodils being a spring seasonal plant; and how much due to paperwhites, first, being white, and, second, blooming in the dead of winter around Christmas, is unknown.

Few historical references actually detail how one was to plant bulbs at the family burial plot, but patterns nevertheless appear. Daffodils in historic cemetery landscapes were planted in a number of ways. These are:

- adjacent to the headstone, either front or back;
- along the top of the grave slab;
- around the interment, as a border;

"Oakland Cemetery, 1895." Courtesy of the Kenan Research Center, Atlanta History Center.

- within a stone grave border, such as for children;
- in a row along the inside of the family plot wall (often on more than one side of the plot);
- around the grave slab, or between family members' grave slabs;
- at the entrance to the family plot, when the entire plot is covered in concrete and/or gravel.

Varieties of daffodils found at cemeteries vary, generally resulting from the combination of three factors: climate, daffodils common to the town, and tree shade. The climate determines what cultivars can survive without care; those that need more cold will not survive in the South, and those that freeze will not survive in the North. While some folks had money, many did not and so simply took along what they had in their gardens already—echoing the recollection from Kentucky of the child's favorite flower being planted on their grave, the plant material coming from the home garden. So daffodils dominant in the town are what are usually found in the cemetery. Finally, daffodils dwindle under dense tree shade, so as trees grow and cast heavier shade, daffodils dwindle away. The yellow ones succumb first, being much less shade-tolerant than bicolor and white daffodils (*N.* × *medioluteus* in particular).

Oakland Cemetery was established in 1850 as the main cemetery for the city of Atlanta. In it reside many famous persons in Atlanta's and Georgia's history, such as governors, business magnets, Bobby Jones, and Margaret Mitchell. Special sections

Scene in Oakland Cemetery. Atlanta, Ga.

"Scene in Oakland Cemetery. Atlanta, Ga.," undated.

were designated for Confederate veterans, African Americans (slaves, freedmen, and descendents), Jewish residents, and the city's indigent and those without grave plots by the 1870s (a potter's field).

An early description of Oakland in 1879 as seen through an outsider's eye is as interesting for its negative comments regarding rural cemeteries of the time as it is for its comments about Oakland:

> From a consideration of her healthfulness we turn by antithesis to Oakland, the most artistic and beautifully cared for cemetery south of the oak groves. It shows a marked contrast to the decay and complete neglect of grave-yards prevailing in all the rural towns. Here lie some thousands of dead Confederate soldiers, and a plain but enduring monument watches over the graves. At this grateful season the cemetery becomes a garden of flowers, and is worth being seen for these alone. Here too, as elsewhere in Atlanta, the number and perfect growth of the hedges are very noticeable: but that finest of all Georgia's hedge plants, the historic holly, is not often seen, though abundant in a wild state in all the hilly regions of this part of Georgia.[27]

In the Atlanta newspaper the *Constitution,* on August 23, 1879, an article ran answering a reader's question. An Atlanta mother had enquired what plants are most suited for graves, presumably for her daughter's grave (age not given): "There is many a narrow home in the cemetery surrounded by beautiful flowers; . . . to make the spot look bright

N. pseudonarcissus, Confederate Section, Historic Oakland Cemetery, Atlanta, Georgia, 2009.

and cheerful, and the love which prompts us to do this to this sacred cause will usually enable us to do what is most befitting. . . . There is no more mournfully pleasant sight than to see friends cultivating flowers around the graves of relatives."[28]

Hardy plants, not all of white flower, were recommended, such as deutzia, Chinese peony, bleeding heart, perennial phlox, double daisy, anemone japonica, pansies, periwinkle (vinca), and lilies—snow drop, crocus, hyacinth, and lily of the valley. Daffodils were planted as part of the grieving process soon after burial by family and friends. As these were planted personally by family members and friends, daffodils are thus scattered throughout the cemetery. Other family-planted bulbs still growing in the cemetery included grape hyacinths (*Muscari*), *Hyacinthoides hispanicus, Ipheion uniflorum, Leucojum aestivum, Lycoris radiata* (fall-blooming red "hurricane lilies" or "surprise lilies"), *Muscari comosum* or tassel hyacinth, and then tulips in more recent plantings. In some areas the *Muscari* has perennialized, growing very low due to drought conditions and mowing. The *Ipheion* does not hold up to mowing.

Within the large Confederate cemetery, one lone clump of *N. pseudonarcissus* survives along a section wall. The bulbs are remnants from the original landscape planted by the Atlanta Ladies Memorial Association (ALMA) around 1888. The Ladies Memorial Association was founded to memorialize the Confederate dead in their home communities. (The same occurred on the Union side of the divide via women's relief aid groups affiliated with old Union posts.) Cemeteries were landscaped, obelisks were erected in courthouse squares, and so on. The ladies did the planning, the husbands did the grunt work. The Atlanta group was organized on May 7, 1868, with its primary mission to gather Confederate dead from rude graves around town, properly reinter them in Oakland, and erect a proper monument. Nearly three thousand persons were so honored. Spring bulbs were planted around the borders of the Confederate cemetery, flowering shrubs were placed in the burial plots, and a large lion statue was erected as a memorial in the center of the cemetery. From the ALMA chapter's history: "the Confederate cemetery was much improved. A new hedge, hundreds of roses, and a variety of spring flowers, magnolias and other ornamental trees were planted under the direction of Mrs. J. C. Olmstead, Mrs. W. D. Ellis and Mrs. E. P. King. Mrs. Milledge had some stone steps placed at the openings of the hedges in each lot and wire arches were set over the openings which added much beauty to the grounds which had just been sodded and put in splendid order. The sod was donated by Colonel L. P. Grant and Mr. Joe Gatins."[29]

Mowing has removed all traces of the original landscape features and the once impressive bulb borders, save for one clump of daffodils. During a multiyear survey project, of the three thousand family lots (individual burials) within Oakland Cemetery, daffodils were identified in approximately 420 lots. Plantings from before World War II far outnumbered newer. Identifying plots in the African American section was difficult because of the loss of headstones and plot demarcation stonework, but approximate thirty-five plots were so planted. Only five plots of two families in the Jewish section contained daffodils.

As often as not, only one cultivar was identified in a plot, but a few plots had three or four cultivars. The most common by far is *N. pseudonarcissus*. The other species plantings identified mirror the traditional assemblage of the most common daffodils for the region. In general order of frequency daffodils identified to date (after *N. pseudonarcissus*) include *N.* × *odorus* ("Campernelle"), 'Telamonius Plenus,' 'Orange Phoenix,' 'Sulphur Phoenix,' *N.* × *intermedius*, 'Butter and Eggs,' *N. jonquilla*, 'Emperor,' 'Golden Spur,' 'King Alfred' type, 'Empress,' unidentified all-yellow trumpets, 'Stella Superba,' 'Sir Watkin,' bicolor pre-1900 varieties (identifying daffodils after decades of neglect is difficult) and few *N.* × *medioluteus* ("Twin Sisters," "Cemetery Ladies," "April Beauties," "May Narcissus"). Daffodils in post–World War II contexts are 'Ice Follies,' 'Carlton,' 'Fortune,' and 'Tête-à-Tête'.

Planting locations follow the patterns observed at other Victorian-era cemeteries. Bulbs were planted around the edge of the plot as border, around the headstones, or around an individual grave as a border. Occasionally bulbs were planted on a grave, within the border edging stone (often thus for a child). Rarely there are husband and wife burials where a significant period of time lapsed between their deaths, from the 1920s to the 1940s. The spouse who passed away first was remembered with daffodils, while the much later burial was not. Newer plantings (1950s and later) either carpet the entire plot in daffodils or incorporate a few bulbs within a large garden-style planting. Daffodils placed in front of shrubbery occur in occasional early midtwentieth-century

Norman Chapel, photographed by Paul Briol, circa early 1930s. Courtesy of Spring Grove Cemetery and Arboretum archives.

plantings, but the bulbs are in serious decline from increasing shade and water competition from the evergreens.

Spring Grove Cemetery and Arboretum in Cincinnati, Ohio, the nation's second largest cemetery, was established in 1845. Founded as an arboretum as much as a cemetery and designed in the picturesque aesthetics of the day, its botanical holdings are diverse and multitudinous. In the annual report for 1857, two hundred varieties of trees were enumerated.

From its inception, Spring Grove was laid out to have a minimum of clutter—the landscape gardener and architect Adolph Strauch and superintendent Henry Earnshaw both recommending to the board of directors the minimal construction, if not removal of, mortuary hardscape including family plot wrought iron fences and head- and footstones. The intent was to create an open and flowing space. Families were to install a single large monument and lay out family members around it; numerous illustrations show a family monument, strategically planted trees, one or two flowering shrubs, and a single flower bed of peonies or yucca. Strauch cited Loudon and others and also gave as authority his travels to European cemeteries of note.

This was the introduction of the "lawn plan system," the genesis of the park lawn movement of cemetery design. In his 1857 report, Strauch observed:

'Paper white Grandiflorus,' Boston, Georgia, 2007.

There are burial lots in this Cemetery so crowded with trees, shrubs, and flowers, that they actually destroy each other, hide the monument, and leave hardly a place for interment, especially when such a lot is cut up with little walks and filled with the sweepings of the marble yards. Those paths are not only useless, but are also a favorite place for the growth of weeds, and the expenses of keeping them in order are more than lot holders in general are willing to pay, and yet, by right, they should be charged with the exact time devoted to the keeping them clean. In such lots economy and simple beauty is sacrificed, and the result is only an immense mosaic, unfortunately too much the case in many Cemeteries.[30]

Thus it is not a surprise that there is not much in the way of plants planted with graves. However, there are a few drifts of daffodils planted in the 1890s as specific landscape features, in keeping with Strauch's design parameters. Daffodils were planted in the Courtyard Garden in the 1890s and continue to bloom today with minimal care. Thus these daffodils may be one of the oldest representative plantings of for this style of cemetery design.

In far south Georgia are two communities lying twenty-odd miles apart, on the same county line road, each with a municipal cemetery dating to the late 1800s. The local burial tradition was for a slab atop the grave, with or without a headstone. Rarely were headstones erected without a slab.

Once the municipal Boston Cemetery was awash in paperwhites, considered to be a symbol of resurrection—its white florets bloom when little else is showing. Over a dozen family plots and single burials are still graced with 'Paper White Grandiflorus' and infrequently *Lycoris radiata*, with the earliest known burial date 1903 (a few barrel vaults are too deteriorated to date) and the latest dated to the 1950s. A very deteriorated brick vault burial was graced by one 'Paper White Grandiflorus' and the sole "Double Roman" ('Romanus'). The preponderance of bulbs were planted either inside the border of the family plot (concrete or marble rails); if the plot interior was cemented or graveled, then bulbs were planted around the outside of the plot rails. Even the less

Lycoris radiata, Church of the Holy Cross, Stateburg, South Carolina, 2011.

affluent had paperwhites; for those too poor to afford engraving (the concrete slab was written on by finger while still wet), bulbs were planted between burials and inside the concrete plot rail. A few instances of bulbs planted in a row between burials were encountered, both 'Paper White Grandiflorus' and *Lycoris radiata*. In the back fill area of the cemetery, numerous cultivars struggle in the kudzu, including Paperwhites and *Lycoris radiata*. As a few 'Paper White Grandiflorus' remain along the front entrance drive, it may be that when the drive was regraded and paved, the bulbs were scraped up and dumped with the spoil dirt behind the cemetery, where they continue to bloom.

Twenty miles north is the town of Pavo; while very few bulbs remain in the municipal cemetery, the drive to the cemetery was once lined on either side with *N. × intermedius* ("Texas Stars"). A dozen or so graves and plots (1915 to 1928) still have dwindled *N. × intermedius* and a small handful of paperwhites holding on. *N. × intermedius* survives in numerous vacant lots in town and in the ditches along the roads out of town. Of note, an early headstone without a slab (1889) was the only grave with daffodils (*N. × intermedius*) planted over it. In comparison to Boston and even the nearby town of Barwick, Pavo is noticeably low on paperwhites, while Boston does not have nearly the same quantity of *N. × intermedius*.

In Round Top, Texas, the Bethlehem Lutheran Church was founded in 1866 by German immigrants, who brought with them a floral cemetery tradition. A wide array of ornamentals grace the cemetery, including musk or starch grape hyacinths (*Muscari racemosum*), Autumn crocus (*Sternbergia lutea*), Oxblood lily (*Hippeastrum bifidum*), white spider lily (*Hymenocalis caribaea*), summer snowflakes (*Leucojum aestivum*),

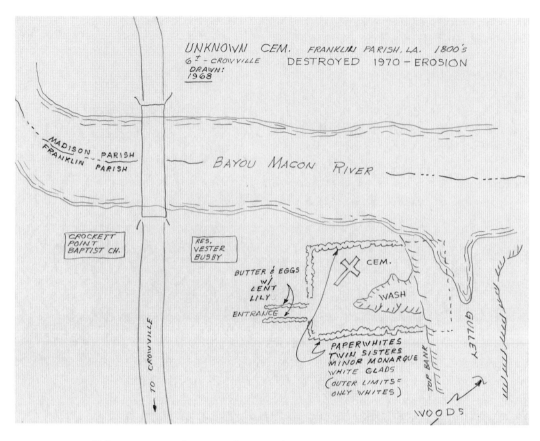

Unknown cemetery, Louisiana. Courtesy of David Atkins. Key: B&E—Doubles; Lent—
N. pseudonarcissus; Paper—Paperwhites and bicolor tazettas; Twin—*N.* × *medioluteus*; Min.M.—
N. italicus; White Glads—*Gladiolus byzantinus* 'Alba'.

crinums (*Crinum bubispernum*), "German" white iris, European and China roses, daffodils, and two species of tazettas—"Chinese Sacred Lily" and *N. italicus*. Instead of
encircling the headstones or lining the family plot, the bulbs were planted directly atop
the graves.

In the Old City Cemetery of Natchez, Mississippi, paperwhites struggle in a handful of family plots that have them, but dozens of plots are planted with *Lycoris radiata*
(locally called September lilies or spider lilies). Across the cemetery a few iris and roses
survive, along with large early-blooming camellias. As some important plots from the
1850s were planted with *Lycoris*, roses, and other ornamentals, it appears a beautification project was conducted at some point. Most family plots with bulbs date from the
1890s through to the 1920s, although some burial dates into the 1930s were observed;
some evidence suggests planting *Lycoris* continued into the 1980s or 1990s. Given the
mowing schedule, it is thought the early winter sprouting of the *Lycoris* foliage con-
tributes to their ability to survive—their foliage is green long enough into the winter
to sustain the bulbs at a minimum level, unlike the later-sprouting paperwhites.

However, a small rural cemetery associated with the Hollywood plantation of the Gillespie family and plantation church outside of Natchez had its headstones replaced. When this was done, *Lycoris radiata* were planted next to each headstone, as the color red is considered to represent "love," and seems to be a later addition to the cemetery floral lexicon. Moreover a tradition of planting bulbs near headstones rather than footstones seems to have developed in the twentieth century (David Atkins, personal communication April 10, 2012). Similarly when a small family graveyard was relocated in 1941 (to the Church of the Holy Cross) because of reservoir construction in Stateburg, South Carolina, *Lycoris radiata* were planted around the headstones and over the graves inside the rails.

Interestingly, in traditional small African American cemeteries in the Natchez area over into Louisiana, white daffodils and other white "sinless" flowers as a symbol of "purity" were allowed to be planted as a border to the cemetery proper. These were also intended to keep the dark spirits or "haints" away from the graves. At one cemetery these were 'Grand Primo Citronière,' locally referred to as "paperwhites." Yellow daffodils and other colored flowers were suitable as approach plantings, but not for the cemetery proper. Explanations for the choice of yellow varied, including that the more pleasant scent confused the haints or irritated them, but again the intention is to keep them out of the cemetery. Furthermore flowers were to be planted only at the footstone, never at the headstone, so the deceased could look down and view the flowers. In addition to daffodils, which were desired because they come up in the winter, families would plant roses, chrysanthemums, and flags (iris), but only a few in number were actually allowed close to the grave. Traces of flowers at these cemeteries are fast disappearing, as they are either raided for their flowers, or expanded and modernized for additional burials and mowing (David Atkins, personal communication, February 26, 2010; confirmed in interview with Ethel Lee Washington, aged ninety-six years, July 20, 2010).

Mobile, Alabama, has two old cemeteries. The Church Street Graveyard is small and was quickly established in 1822 to contend with the aftermath of a yellow fever epidemic. Most burials are antebellum. Bulbs survive where the weedeater doesn't easily go—against walls, in tight spaces between stones, up on raised plots. Numerous antebellum burials and family plots contained paperwhites. The walls of the antebellum Weekes family plot were bordered with crinum, with crinum also around grave slabs; 'Grand Primo Citronière' were blooming in a corner. Dwindled paperwhites were found bordering raised slab interments. Bordering inside of plots' raised walls were remnant rows of Star of Bethlehem. In the center of an overgrown walled family plot was a scatter planting of paperwhites. A few hyacinthoides (Spanish bluebells) and *Lycoris radiata* were scattered across the cemetery.

The larger Magnolia Cemetery was established in 1844, its beauty approvingly noted as early as 1883. The 1883 annual meeting of the Mississippi Valley Horticultural Society was held in New Orleans, and afterward a trip for the members was arranged to Mobile. Later they commented of the cemetery that "by the aid of the landscape gardener and the artisan's chisel, much has been done to beautify and adorn the inevitable place of rest."[31]

The city of Mobile charter and codes charged the keeper of Magnolia Cemetery with safeguarding the cemetery from predation by livestock and entry by dogs, and "to protect the cemetery from depredations, the removal or plucking of flowers and shrubbery, except by the owner or his written order."[32] By 1899 thick underbrush had grown to such an extent that prison labor was employed to clean it down.

On December 29, 1895, L. Harrison went to Magnolia Cemetery in Mobile, as a side trip on a longer sojourn:

> While waiting at Mobile, Ala., for a steamer to cross the Gulf of Mexico, to my winter home, St. Andrews Bay, Fla., I visited Magnolia Cemetery, in company with a traveling companion, Dec. 29th. The sun was shining, and the thermometer was at 55 degrees when we took an electric car. One of the inducements to visit this cemetery was the many varieties of japonicas in bloom; sweetscented violets, narcissus, sweet olives, and roses of various hues; japonicas in various hues of red, pink, and white of delicate purity. A lady at the cemetery told us that some large japonicas, that had been trained to a single stem, and were more than one foot in diameter at the base, had been brought from France by her grandfather, many years ago. His remains repose in their shade, and the beautiful blossoms pay tribute to his memory.[33]

In 2010, again dodging the mowers, *N. italicus* was found blooming in one line along a plot wall. Paperwhites were planted to line plots, around slabs, and so on. Numerous rectangular planters dating to the middle of the twentieth century are placed around the cemetery, containing white iris, crinum, paperwhites, and *Lycoris,* some with mixed plantings of crinum and paperwhites. These provide a long period of floral interest and afford some security against mowing. Other flowers holding on across the cemetery were spirea, roses, and yucca. Old 'Grand Primo Citronière' were planted around a southern magnolia in front of the maintenance building. According to the current superintendent, the ornamental plantings on family plots are thought to have been done by families and not to be the result of past beautification projects (Mark Halseth, personal communication, February 14, 2011).

Regional preferences for daffodils seem to exist. They are mostly climate driven, but other factors of desire for fragrance and local availability seem to be involved as well. In the coastal South near the Gulf, the preference is for paperwhites and "Chinese Sacred Lily" (*N. tazetta* var. *lacticolor*), both cold-tender and heat and moisture tolerant. In old cemeteries near Tallahassee, Florida, one nearly always finds a few paperwhites or *N. italicus* holding on in the dappled shade; another flower found in the old St. John's Episcopal in downtown Tallahassee is "Chinese Sacred Lily." Over in Pensacola crinums dominate St. Michael's Cemetery.

By north Alabama the still colder climes shift the palate preference to the white *N.* × *medioluteus* ("Twin Sisters"), planted by both whites and African Americans. The connection between this flower and cemeteries is reflected in their regional common name of "Cemetery Ladies." Secondary flowers used were the fragrant *N. jonquilla*

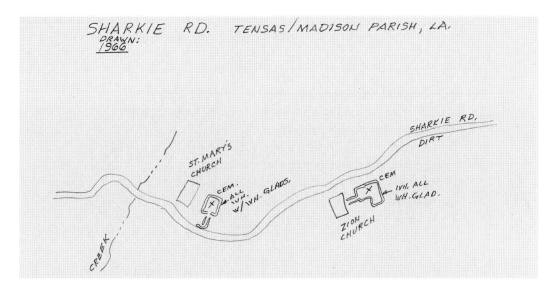

Sharkie Road, Louisiana, cemeteries. Courtesy of David Atkins.

and older, cold-tolerant white tazettas such as 'Grand Primo Citronière' and 'Grand Monarque'.

In northwest Louisiana, the winters are sufficiently colder than on the Gulf coast to shift the daffodil assemblage to slightly later blooming white tazettas, so January not December. Again the robust cultivars of 'Grand Primo Citronière,' 'Grand Monarque,' and *N. italicus* dominate. Arkansas cemeteries illustrate the two divergent desires for white flowers—*N. moschatus* (sometimes called "Silver Bells") and *N. × medioluteus* ("Twin Sisters" or "Cemetery Ladies") are the most commonly observed daffodils, and secondarily for fragrance—in *N. jonquilla* and *N. × odorus* ("Campernelle jonquil"). However, most daffodils seem to be found growing alongside the cemeteries and not within the grounds proper. As a result the soil conditions the daffodils are found in closely resemble gravel. No differences between African American and white cemetery plantings have been observed to date. *N. moschatus* has also been observed in historic cemeteries in Georgia and South Carolina.

In eastern Texas historic African American cemeteries reflect a reliance on the fragrant jonquils *N. jonquilla* and *N. × odorus,* and the rare to occasional *N. pseudonarcissus* and "Twin Sisters." Other flowers found in cemeteries in the region include the white tazettas 'Grand Primo Citronière' and *N. italicus.* Piedmont, South Carolina, has its own array of memorial daffodils found in historic cemeteries. These include *N. × tenuior* ("Silver jonquil"), two strains of *N. pseudonarcissus* (a long neck or pedicil strain and a short neck strain), *N. medioluteus,* 'Butter and Eggs,' and 'Orange Phoenix'. The most commonly observed flowers are *N. × tenuior* first, followed by *N. pseudonarcissus,* probably the most common historic daffodil found in the uplands.

Last is a small site. The plantation of Valley View in northeast Georgia dates to 1850 and has remained in the Sproull-Fouché-Norton family hands ever since, each generation guarding the additions of the prior. The burial grounds for family members and for slaves and slave descendents are relatively close to each other. As expected the plantation owners' graves have full granite headstones, but no ornamental plants have been identified at these graves by the current owners. The graves of the slaves and their descendents were simply marked by a row of mortared river cobbles. While it is known who of the slave families are buried in the area, it is no longer known who is in which grave or where everyone is. In 2009 five clumps of dwindled daffodils (likely *N.* × *medioluteus* based on foliage morphology) were found around one grave in the slave and slave-descendent burial ground. Though the plants are no longer of blooming size because of shade from the tree canopy, the bulbs still return to bear witness and keep company.

Conclusion

Many a cemetery, large and small, still contains daffodils, although the number has dwindled precipitously with the advent of the gas-powered weed eater, allowing for the clear-cutting of many a far-afield cemetery and family plot. But as the daffodil was once one of the symbols to remember the dead, it has now become a symbol of remembering the living and struggling, through its adoption by the National Cancer Society. Instead of the white of paperwhites blooming in the dead of winter symbolizing resurrection, now yellow trumpets symbolize the hope of rebirth through arduous survival. It is the resiliency and beauty possessed by few, if any other, spring bulbs that continue to draw people to choose the daffodil as a sign for the hope of a new life.

6.

Daffodils in Historic Gardens

The following case studies are gardens containing period garden remnants with daffodils. All were visited by the author from 2009 to 2012, with the exceptions of Chantilly, and Bartram's Garden, which was reviewed in loose concert with the site curator, Joel Fry. I am indebted to site owners who graciously offered their hospitality and assisted my research, loaning images and researching ownership histories. Numerous other newly made acquaintances took time off to explore the byways in search of old gardens, sharing their knowledge and introducing me to their friends and neighbors and their gardens, all in the thrill of the hunt for the old and undiscovered. Their collective zeal for the hunt and passion for old gardens and old garden plants is really why this book exists.

Analyzing garden remnants is a bit like archaeology, but with certain classes of plants, rather than ceramics, as guideposts. As expected, surviving antebellum gardens with more than just boxwood or large trees are now few and far between. Those maintained past the Civil War often present a muddled picture to decipher. Some sites reflect opposite ends of the landscape methodologies of the time. While it is impossible to know if these case study gardens are truly representative for their respective periods, they are what remain and so must serve.

As with archaeology, it is ideal to find a "capped" site—one where a catastrophic event ended its occupation, so anything surviving at the site can be reasonably assumed to pre-date the catastrophe. For old houses and their gardens, fire is the main culprit, with abandonment from economic collapse a strong second. Then the method must become old-fashioned archival research, looking for period photographs, family records, and general histories.

In regard to the daffodils themselves, their dates of introduction and their styles of planting can quickly give a date range, albeit sometimes of decades. But a hybrid introduced in 1888 is an indicator a Victorian gardener worked in the garden—or a more modern "liberator" of bulbs who happened to like old flowers. Thus hybrid daffodils, coupled with the ownership history, often can yield the name of a likely responsible gardener.

One of the most interesting sources of plants in old gardens are the books produced by state garden clubs in the 1920s and 1930s. The level of effort varies greatly from project to project, as does the scholarship, and they leave one at the mercy of fading memories, personal preferences of the writers, and confusion as to the true age of hybrid cultivars, and with poor to no archival document citations. But when taken with a broad view, these gardens are very interesting indeed. Many poetic garden descriptions of swaths of daffodils in pre–Civil War landscapes become suspect. Banks of daffodils on ravines, creek beds, mixed with other bulbs along the drive, all begin to sound like "wild garden" naturalized bulb plantings of the late 1890s to 1920s. This becomes very apparent when authors swoon over the "ancient" 'Golden Spur,' "Lady of Leeds" and 'Stella'—all of which appeared in the American market in the 1880s or 1890s.

Another problem with period discussions of daffodils irrespective of source is local terminology. A narcissus isn't necessarily a narcissus, and neither is a jonquil, never mind the swirl of "what flower exactly is your 'Butter and Eggs'"? In 1909 A. M. Kirby weighed in on daffodil common idioms, indicating "narcissus" was still popularly applied to small-cupped flowers namely poets, tazettas, and jonquils. Elizabeth Lawrence remarked about southerners and their plant names; in the 1923 *Historic Gardens of Virginia* discussion of the Burwell, the writer lumps a yellow trumpet, a small white daffodil, and a double all as "jonquils." By the time of the garden club ladies, in general, "narcissus" in the Deep South had become the catchall term for any and all tazettas. In the 1700s and 1800s, "narcissus" was usually a *N. poeticus* spp. especially in the North (and tazettas were polyanthus narcissus), but when Fanny Kemble wrote of silvery narcissus blooming in February 1838 in coastal Georgia, there is no way botanically she's referring to any poet—the earliest of the poeticus clan blooms in mid-March, and not a month sooner. Conversely "narcissus" in New England may still refer to poets, as they are a much more dominant flower (preferring cool summers), and cold-tender tazettas are simply annuals. "Jonquil" poses a similar issue. In the country a "jonquil" can be either a member of the jonquil clan, or it could be any small yellow daffodil, including *N. pseudonarcissus*. A daffodil is usually a trumpet, and one suspects *N. pseudonarcissus* as it is the most common trumpet (particularly in the South), but this really is just supposition. And "Butter and Eggs" can be one of at least three if not four doubles, as it became the catchall term for any double, these being 'Butter and Eggs,' 'Orange Phoenix,' 'Sulphur Phoenix,' and 'Telamonius Plenus'. Thus without specific names or detailed flower descriptions, one must tread with care, and this is why period catalogs, and actual garden survivors, become so important.

Last, there is the confounding issue of general importance of the daffodil as reflecting the biases of the writers. One suspects that daffodils appeared in more gardens than

N. moschatus.

they are credited for, harkening back to Breck's comment that daffodils were so well known as to obviate the need for description.

Federal Gardens

Contrary to expectation there is a smattering of archaeological house and garden sites containing daffodils that likely date to the federal era. Not so surprising, the two identified here are both in Virginia, and fire ended habitation at both sites. That both are Lee family sites (Chantilly and Leesylvania) only adds to their glamour. Doubles are the surviving flower at both sites. Slightly more shade tolerant than jonquils, and with larger bulbs, these showy flowers possess the fortitude necessary to weather the vagaries of the ages. Unfortunately neither garden was much described in the archival record, so how the doubles were planted in the gardens is unknown.

Even more surprising, the surviving doubles (particularly at Leesylvania) are not 'Orange Phoenix' or 'Butter and Eggs,' the more respectable flowers grown by London nurserymen by the late 1780s. Instead it is the lowly common double yellow of Bartram's irritation, 'Telamonius Plenus,' that proves to be the hardiest of them all. ('Orange Phoenix' and/or 'Butter and Eggs' are still to be confirmed at Chantilly as of 2012.) One may presume other daffodils of more fashionable status were planted; but that the lowly crept into the gardens of the wealthy suggests that one did not turn away a sturdy flower when such were hard to come by (if much was lost in transatlantic ships, would gardeners have been willing to accept a lesser flower if it were at hand?).

'Telamonius Plenus,' The Forest, Natchez, Mississippi, 2012.

It is possible more federal-era garden sites survive (one suspect survives at the Goodale House in Augusta, Georgia, as of 2012; the side area where a formal garden may have existed has nothing but 'Telamonius Plenus' left), but as development pushes ever onward, the chances to find other gardens dwindle.

Chantilly, Virginia

Chantilly is an archaeological site with little archival documentation of its garden, so understanding it must be from afar through secondhand sources. Chantilly was constructed around 1763 by Richard Henry Lee and was his residence until his death in 1794. A signer of the Declaration of Independence, Richard Henry was one of six sons of Thomas Lee of nearby Stratford Hall.

Archaeological evidence indicates the house was either shelled and/or partially burned around the time of the War of 1812. It is thought the damaged structure was then dismantled for reuse elsewhere, and the site abandoned. Its land was kept more or less intact for farming, and at some point in the nineteenth century another house was built nearby.

An eyewitness account of the house site in 1871 describes the mournful site but makes no mention of another dwelling on the property:

Not a vestige of the old edifice remains save a rude mound of stones, half-concealed beneath briars and weeds. The plow has long since turned the walks, yard and garden into furrows and now the corn waves above the thresholds of the mansion. . . .

A few paces distant from the kitchen [marked by a large fireplace and chimney], under shelter of the hill, are still standing a group of aged and decaying plum and cherry trees. Near by are also a number of very large apples. . . . On that part of the hill which slopes toward the river, in a lovely alcove formed by nature near the margin of the valley, are several stately locusts. . . . In this vicinity too are trampled mounds and numerous flowers peering up from their neglected hiding places, and showing that this section of the grounds, overlooking the river and commanding the most enchanting prospect, was once handsomely laid off and adorned with terraces and flower-pots.[1]

Descriptions of the site in the twentieth century mention the site as marked by daffodils.

Daffodils were rescued from Chantilly by Stratford Hall staff and planted on the Stratford property. Also a former caretaker of the Chantilly property was given bulbs in the 1990s by the property owners. As access to the site has been curtailed, no actual site visit was possible by the author, so it was not possible to "ground truth" the presence or absence of any other daffodils.

According to the former caretaker, the property has long been leased out for farming, and the fields sprayed with herbicide before planting, presumably including former garden areas. Near the old house site is a nineteenth-century house, which sits at a slightly different elevation. According to the caretaker, all daffodils from the Chantilly house site area were doubles, while those taken from the nineteenth century house were all *N. pseudonarcissus*. (Confirmation of *N. pseudonarcissus* and 'Telamonius Plenus' was made in spring 2012 when bulbs shared with the author from the caretaker came into bloom. The two types of phoenix doubles [by her description] did not bloom.) Those daffodils taken to Stratford Hall as a representative sample were all 'Telamonius Plenus'. No other kinds of flowers have apparently survived at the site.

Leesylvania, Virginia

A better-known site than Chantilly, and under a more watchful eye as the land is now a Virginia state park, the garden of Leesylvania is similarly poorly recorded. But like Chantilly the common double daffodil of the colonial era grows at the site of the old garden. Thus what the flower lacked in perceived status it more than made up for in longevity and fortitude (and why it was probably allowed into the garden in the first place).

Leesylvania was the home of Henry Lee II, whose uncle was Thomas Lee of Stratford Hall and cousin of Richard Henry Lee of Chantilly. (Henry Lee II had eight children, including Henry "Light Horse Harry" Lee III, who grew up at Leesylvania; he in turn was the father of Robert E. Lee.) Henry Lee II lived at Leesylvania from 1749

Leesylvania, looking upslope at terrace remnants and 'Telamonius Plenus,' 2012. a. uppermost terrace. b. second terrace.

until his death in 1787; his wife Lucy Grymes died five years later, and shortly after her death the house burned. In 1825 the property passed into the Fairfax family's hands. The Fairfax house, built circa 1825, was located roughly five hundred yards away; it burned in 1910. The property essentially had a rough life after the Civil War, suffering logging disputes, bootlegging, and general neglect for much of the time.

Over the decades visitors have taken note of the site's daffodils. One visitor was the noted *Narcissus* disease expert (and past president of the American Daffodil Society) Willis Wheeler; his interest in the site's 'Telamonius Plenus' was not only in that they were very old but, more important, also in that they were virus free: "by what has been found on old abandoned estates [in Virginia] such as Leesylvania Plantation. There, on the shores of the Potomac River in Prince William County, old daffodil Van Sion found a home on the estate first lived on by the owners in 1747. It was apparently sometime between that date and 1790 that the plantings were made since the house burned on the latter date and was not rebuilt. The descendants of those early immigrant bulbs still flower there although not too vigorously since forests now cover what was once cleared land."[2] In 1972 a rose bush was noted on the south side of the house foundation ruins, and on the northwest slope of the site grew a mass of spring-blooming flowers, including "old-fashioned double daffodils."[3] The Lees were buried on the adjacent north ridge, overlooking the lower garden to the south and a view of the Neabsco Creek and Potomac River to its north.

Extremely little remains of the house site; in the 1950s a road was cut through the ridge, taking the house ruins with it. However, the abandoned road bed then curves,

View across second terrace and downslope, 2012.

missing the garden site. By the spring of 2012, the original garden footprint was gener-ally discernible. The garden was laid out to the west of the house site between two ridges descending from the ridge line on which the house was constructed. The narrow ravine between the two was terrace; from a narrow top, the entire garden area appears to have fanned out. The first level seems to have directly abutted the foundation, at about six feet below the current house ridge grade. The second level terrace is roughly four feet lower. From the second terrace is a graded slope, which becomes a long gentle slope down to what appears to be a man-made pond or canal bed roughly fifty yards distant. It is on the graded slope of the second terrace to the gentle grade (or possibly an eroded third terrace) that most of the 'Telamonius Plenus' still grow. Scattered plants may be found downslope, their arrangement suggesting deposition by erosion (say from uprooted tree root balls due to logging similar to a large downed tree at the time of the site visit). Interestingly a few 'Telamonius Plenus' are scattered down the adjacent ridge top south of the garden. No other ornamentals were observed, but this may be due to the time of year. Park staff appear to be keeping the garden area clear of understory growth.

Antebellum Gardens

Most antebellum gardens were comparatively simple affairs when it came to bulbs, at least in counterpoint to many of the fancy designs. Some gardens fell into disarray after the Civil War or later. Others kept gardeners busy for decades after the war, scrambling

One of first *N.* × *odorus* in the jonquil hedge to rebloom, 2010.
Courtesy of Barrington Hall Garden Archives.

the early plants and planting schemes. The gardens here reflect a cross-section of styles, and most have some supporting archival documentation.

The traditional fieldstone parterre garden of Mountain Shoals in South Carolina saw nearly a century of busy gardeners, who left stylistic landscape designs and intermittent archival signposts along the way. Barrington Hall in Georgia is a simple affair, with only a single line of archival documentation, yet as such it does not follow the landscaping literature's dictates of the day. Bartram's Gardens in Philadelphia poses a conundrum all its own; the ownership history indicates an antebellum time frame, while the landscape methods suggest a planting style of decades later. Barrington Hall and Bartram's Garden strongly intimate gardeners were more creative in their use of bulbs in the 1850s than one would believe from reading the literature of the time.

Many a tantalizing site proves too opaque to fathom. Menokin, the home of Francis ("Frank") Lightfoot Lee in Virginia, may qualify as preservation by poverty for the garden, but the same poverty in the end distressingly caused the loss of the house. Built as the wedding house of Francis Lee (son of Thomas Lee of Stratford Hall, brother of Richard Henry Lee of Chantilly) and his bride, Rebecca Tayloe, the property was abandoned around 1935, suggesting a "capped" site. But the history of the house and its uniquely asymmetrical terraced garden is too poorly documented from 1795 until its abandonment in 1935 to support any horticultural analysis past speculation. Its large swaths of obviously old *N.* × *medioluteus* growing on the tops as well as slopes of the terraces, kept company by a few *N. poeticus* and blue Roman hyacinths, serve only to tease the imagination with "what if's." The daffodils could date to the federal era as readily as to the Victorian.

Mountain Shoals, Enoree, South Carolina

Mountain Shoals is a complex garden, evidencing many a gardener's hand over many years. Its bulb garden rightly could be considered a showcase of three, if not four, major styles of gardening with bulbs over a hundred-year period, from roughly 1843 to the

1920s (antebellum, postbellum "ribbon," Victorian "wild garden," and to a lesser degree twentieth century vernacular). This garden and its long-gone daughter garden at Williamston forty miles away were documented in Ann Leighton's work *American Gardens of the Nineteenth Century "For Comfort and Affluence"* (1987). Teasing the layers of the garden to attribute to particular gardeners and time periods was based on planting styles, dates of introduction, and the presence or absence of bulbs in different parts of the garden.

It is surmised the garden was laid out by the second wife of James Nesbitt Jr., Caroline Brewton, shortly after their marriage in 1843. Both were of local Irish American families, and the house evidences signs of traditional Irish architecture (such as that the only stairway to the girls' upstairs bedroom was in the parents' room). As a traditional Piedmont region stone-lined garden, its geometric forms are strongly speculated to evoke marital love in the Irish tradition originating from the County Down. The circle represents eternity, the hearts love, and the diamonds success (thought to be based on Rune 22, Celtic for success in all new beginnings); the measurements of the forms are all multiples of three. The pattern beds were likely planted originally by Caroline in a formal, spare alternating pattern of *N. jonquilla* and plumed hyacinths (*Muscari comosum* 'Plumosum') for spring interest; in the summer the garden was kept in the swept dirt tradition. The hyacinths dwindled precipitously in the late twentieth century, but in the mid-1970s the alternating pattern was still evident in the side yard pattern beds. Meanwhile the *N. jonquilla* seeded across the side garden.

After the Civil War, the front garden was replanted in the ribbon style of alternating rows of cultivars that had first come into vogue in the 1850s and later promulgated by the southern horticulturist William White in the early 1870s. It seems likely this was done by Caroline's daughter Francis Nesbitt McClintock, who resided at Mountain Shoals from 1870 (if not sooner) until 1878. A number of bulbs planted also appeared in the garden of her older half-sister Nancy Narcissa Nesbitt Anderson at nearby Williamston. The plantings in the front beds best reflect Francis's hand, alternating rows planted with *Lycoris radiata, Leucojum aestivum,* and *N. pseudonarcissus.*

Alternatively the beds may have been planted by an early Hill family gardener, whose clan owned Mountain Shoals from 1878 to 1924. The presence of early hybrid daffodils in the side garden but absence in the front, and a spliced segment of 'Paper White Grandiflorus' (identified in 2013) in a row of 'Telamonius Plenus' in the Eternity circle bed, dictate a later planting date for these infill bulbs. It is posited here Francis McClintock planted the front ribbon patterns (the presence of Nancy's favorite *Leucojum* only in the front garden probably a key determinant) and an unknown Hill gardener then maintained the pattern some years on.

Layered over both Caroline's pattern gardens and Francis's ribbon plantings are swaths of daffodils planted as drifts or randomly spotted in, suggesting a late-Victorian method to early twentieth-century period. It is thought the likely gardeners were either Fay or Eva Hill. Daffodils such as 'Sir Watkin,' 'Stella Superba,' 'Queen of the North,' and 'Paper White Grandiflorus' appear, as well as Byzantine gladiolus, heavy plantings of *Lycoris radiata,* and *N.* × *medioluteus* or "Twin Sisters." The flower bed by the side

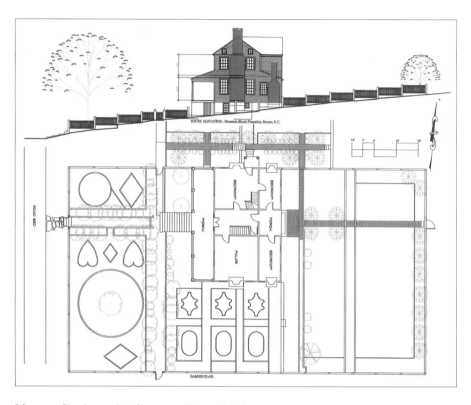

Mountain Shoals site plan. Courtesy of Martin Meek.

The Hill Family, ca. 1900. Courtesy of Martin Meek.

Front garden (from roof), 1976. Courtesy of Martin Meek.

Side garden (from roof), 1976. Courtesy of Martin Meek.

Side garden, 1976. Courtesy of Martin Meek.

Side garden, 2010.

door has some of the greatest variety in added bulbs, probably chosen as this bed is the most readily viewed both from the porch and the ground floor. Drifts and dependency foundation plantings of 'Telamonius Plenus,' 'Sulphur Phoenix,' and *N.* × *odorus* reflect twentieth-century planting styles.

The midtwentieth-century owner Josephine Biddleman Irby (1924–1973) was known for her flamboyancy rather than aggressive gardening (although she did add spirea and azaeleas), which helped preserve the preceding gardeners' handiwork. And all owners and gardeners have preserved Caroline's pattern of love.

Barrington Hall, Roswell, Georgia

Barrington Hall in Roswell, Georgia, was constructed in 1842 by city founder Barrington King. King's wife, Catherine, designed the pleasure garden shortly after they moved in. It is thought she used the services of English stoneworker and landscape designer Frances Minhinnett. The house remained in family-related hands (many of whom were gardeners and probably added daffodils around the property but alas were not terribly diligent in writing about their activities) until 2003, when it was taken over by the city of Roswell. It was opened as a historic site in 2005.

Although terraced with a formal parterre, Barrington Hall's garden does not closely comport with the landscape recommendations in the midnineteenth century. Yet its 1854 documentation is solid, suggesting gardeners were more creative with their garden plans and bulb plantings. Of note, Thomas King mentions in the mid-1850s visiting Miss Terrell in Sparta, Georgia. The Terrell gardens were legendary in Georgia for the unusual plants and garden design based on the latest trends in Europe.

Fortuitously one of the more anomalous planting locations described in an antebellum letter survives to the present day, originating from the pen of a lodger of the Kings. In an 1854 letter, George Camp mentioned a "hedge of jonquils" but neglected to indicate where said hedge grew on the premises. Camp rented an upstairs room for nine years from the Kings, its two windows providing an ideal view over the formal East Garden.

The East Garden lies before the formal parlor and dining room windows. It was a three-terrace form, the upper and middle terraces bordered by hedges on the north and south. The upper level contained a circular design framed by boxwood, some of which survives. (The current garden pattern was reimplemented following the design illustrated in *Gardens of Colony and State*.) The lower two terraces were simple squares, bisected by a straight path. The lowest-level terrace's simple pattern form has been recreated by current staff, based on surviving documentation. Granite fieldstone edging along the outer and inner border hedge beds for the upper and middle terraces remains for both hedge lines, in keeping with the Piedmont gardening tradition.

The north hedge was originally English hawthorn, replaced at some point by bridal wreath spirea. When the staff moved a section of the bridal wreath spirea hedge down to the third terrace in order to create a side opening to the garden for visitor access, they unwittingly took daffodil bulbs along. The daffodils *N.* × *odorus* and 'Telamonius Plenus' grow both within the spirea hedge's stone borders and outside it on the

Jonquil Hedge, 2012.

front lawn side. Two sections of daffodils were moved out into the front lawn at some point, and the bulbs still are in lines. These bulbs were identified by the staff and author in 2007 and finally started blooming in 2010. In the outer remnant of hedge line, one *Hyacinthoides* (Spanish bluebells) and one dwindled clump of *Leucojum aestivum* were identified. A few *Hyacinthoides* grow within the spirea, within the original granite-lined beds.

The south hedge was originally English dogwood. It was later removed by a family gardener and has since been replaced by city staff. Of the original south hedge, 'Telamonius Plenus' and *N. × odorus* remain only along the upper terrace level. A few blades of possible Byzantine gladiolus (known to have survived from family ownership but now almost completely gone from the property) were also found along the original stone edging. To date, the East Garden has not been thoroughly researched and documented, so which gardener moved what segment of hedge when, added what bulbs when, and even reconfigured the boxwood parterre inner circle remain conundrums.

That Camp made no other mention of spring bulbs suggests there weren't other bulbs in the jonquil hedge at the time. It could be that the other spring ephemerals didn't make enough of an impression on him to warrant mentioning, or that successive gardeners broadened the hedge's palette. The jonquil hedge's composition of two sorts of daffodils is unexpected, as the prevailing landscape literature of the day recommended planting single varieties in clumps in the herbaceous border or in designated parterre beds. Both daffodils do comport with antebellum preferences—fragrant jonquils and showy doubles. (It is not until the 1860s that ribbon planting designs using bulbs appear in the literature.) The closest this motif comes to is Juvenis's article in 1852 suggesting the edging of the borders with *Narcissus* alternated with hyacinths and edged with a low-growing bulb (and could possibly explain the Spanish bluebells). The lining of parterre beds with bulbs as per Hovey in 1854 could be another source of inspiration for Catherine King, but one would not expect the entire formal garden to be so "lined." Alternatively the Terrell gardens may have been a conduit for the latest

View from attic, 2012.

ribbon planting schemes from Europe to Barrington Hall. Whatever the inspiration, Camp's hedge of jonquils amazingly still survives.

John Bartram House and Garden, Philadelphia, Pennsylvania

For many in the gardening world, John Bartram needs little introduction. After his death his property and business eventually passed to his granddaughter Ann and son-in-law Colonel Robert Carr. While the Carrs were able to make a go of the business for awhile, eventually they had to sell. The property was bought in 1850 by the Philadelphia industrialist Andrew M. Eastwick, who sought to "preserve" the property and its legacy. One might argue his "preservation" was not necessarily so, given the vast changes he made, mostly in the early 1850s under the noted horticulturist Thomas Meehan. Not only were new trees and shrubs planted, but formal gardens, garden ornaments, and an elaborate path system were added, all befitting a wealthy industrialist's estate. The general suggestion is that Eastwick hit the financial skids by 1859 and tried selling the property in the early 1860s to the Pennsylvania Horticultural Society. By the first photographs of the property in the early 1870s, neglect of the property is evident; after Eastwick's death in 1879, neither his widow nor children had any interest in the gardens or much in the way of funds.

The property and house was eventually bought in 1891 by the city of Philadelphia for a city park. While the widow and descendents of Andrew Eastwick had remained on the property up to that point, after his death the grounds had been let go into a dreadful

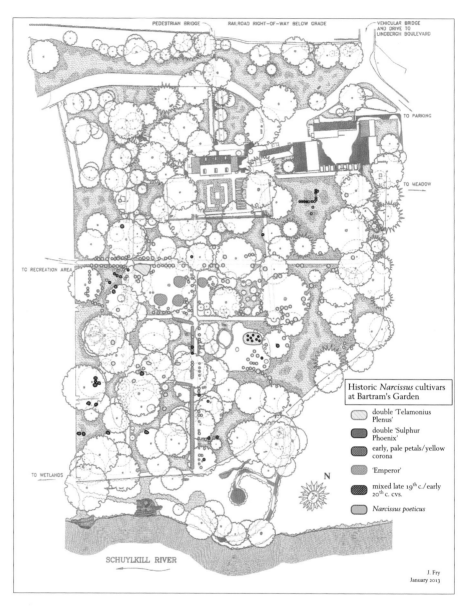

Plot of historic *Narcissus* cultivars at Bartram's Garden. Daffodil data and overlay plot courtesy of Joel Fry, The John Bartram Association, Bartram's Garden, Philadelphia. Base map courtesy of the HALS PA-1 documentation project, drawing by David Calderon, National Park Service, HABS/HAER/HALS/CRGIS Division.

state of neglect, to the point of suffering plant theft. The city eventually embarked on restoration plans, such that the Meehan paths were restored sometime between 1904 and 1907; new paths were built in 1918, and the garden extensively replanted in 1926.

Photographs from 1884, 1892, and again in 1900 clearly document daffodil foliage along the walkways in the original Bartram garden. Today there grow relatively large clumps of 'Telamonius Plenus' and 'Sulphur Phoenix' along the walk—rather ironic given John Bartram's complaint of the common yellow double. (Of note, the 1807, 1814, and 1819 Bartram's Garden catalogs listed the common *N. pseudonarcissus* but no doubles of any sort). It is thought that the daffodil-lined path to the great tree became a shortcut during Eastwick's tenure, as it is off Bartram's original line, thus implying the bulbs could not have been planted during the Carr family's ownership. During the path repaving projects of the early twentieth century, sections of the original daffodil lines were lost. It is thought an as-yet unidentified early-season yellow trumpet, planted to fill gaps in the 'Telamonius Plenus' and 'Sulphur Phoenix,' dates to the city's restoration efforts, along with the 'Emperor,' *N. poeticus,* and early-form bicolor hybrids as yet unidentified.

Given Eastwick's precarious financial state starting around 1860, it seems doubtful he would have spent money on daffodils along the paths after 1855. The likelihood of his widow or children planting daffodils in the 1880s is remote. Thus the daffodils pose a quandary; as to date the first landscape tome recommending daffodils for paths appears to be William Robinson's *Hardy Flowers: Descriptions of Upwards of thirteen hundred of the most ornamental species* (1871). For Narcissus incomparabilis, Robinson recommended: "Borders, fringes of shrubberies, and naturalized by wood-walks in ordinary soil."[4]

So the question becomes who was more likely to line paths with daffodils, the Carrs, from 1810 to 1850, who did experiment in unorthodox hedge plantings, or Thomas Meehan, fresh from Europe and well in tune with the new horticultural trends (including ribbon planting) of the 1850s. Meehan doubtless was keeping up on all the British landscape literature as editor of *Gardener's Monthly* (1859–1888), among his many horticultural endeavors (as nurseryman, landscape consultant, botanist, and so on). Too, Mehan undoubtedly read Andrew Downing's *Horticulturist,* which ran the Juvenis article in 1852. Despite the Carrs' general unconventionality for their day, to break so strongly with the tradition of bulbs in designated beds seems a far stretch. It becomes Meehan who might be the missing link to this early example of lining woodland walks with daffodils, expanding on Juvenis's and Hovey's work, twenty years before his time.

Postbellum, Antebellum Revival, and Victorian Gardens

As daffodils found greater favor in the gardening world, both highbrow and common, their chances of survival also increase—more gardens were planted, more gardens survive somewhat intact, and it is a shorter length of time for bulbs to survive. Gardens from this time period evidence great changes in gardening styles—some embrace new

"Bartram House from East," April 5, 1884. Courtesy of the Harvard University Herbaria and the Botany Libraries.

"W. M. Bartram and Bald Cypress, ca. 1900." Courtesy of the Harvard University Herbaria and the Botany Libraries.

The yellow trumpets 'Emperor' and a second early season trumpet (at left) were added in the twentieth century to fill in gaps of 'Telamonius Plenus' (at right). Courtesy of the John Bartram Association, Bartram's Garden, Philadelphia.

styles, some adapt new plant material to old motifs, and others press old plant material into the new motifs.

This urge to create new gardens after the old ways but with new plants appears widely, but to date no supporting documentation in the horticultural literature has been found. The late Jim Cothran lamented this state of affairs; in the South gardeners, often women, were recreating the antebellum glory days, but how they came to decide to do such things remains a mystery.

Some gardeners decided to give the old gardens a modern facelift. They kept the bones (boxwood parterres) but added the vogue plants du jour—bulbs. New hybrid narcissus, *Iphieon, Lycoris radiata, Hyacinthoides, Leucojum aestivum* or *vernum, Muscari, Ornithogalum ubellatum* or *nutans,* Dutch hyacinths, and Roman hyacinths all enlivened old parterres. Others planted new "old" boxwood parterre gardens, recycling favorite patterns of yore, but with the twist of modern plants. These new old gardens have been dubbed "antebellum revival" by Suzanne Turner, neatly summing up all the emotional baggage one suspects was involved.

Others wanted to create an "old-fashioned" garden more closely hewing to their childhood memories, usually of an old family garden. One such example is at the Henry Clay estate of Ashland in Lexington, Kentucky. At the turn of the twentieth century, Clay's granddaughter Anne Clay McDowell set about re-creating her grandparents'

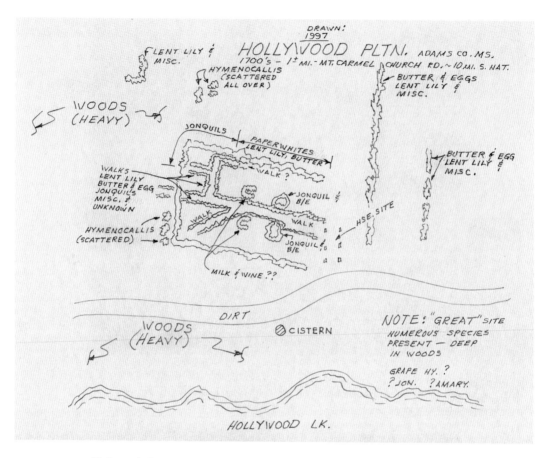

Hollywood plantation, circa 2002. Courtesy of David Atkins. Key: Lent—*N. pseudonarcissus*; Jonq.— *N. × odorus*; Paper—Paperwhites and bicolor tazettas; B&E—Doubles.

antebellum garden, but on a smaller scale; jonquils and roses from the vegetable borders of the first garden still bloomed in 1905.

Of the garden sites here, a few illustrate recommended period landscape motifs (Oakton, Magnolia Vale), some are adding new bulbs to old gardens (Hermitage, Wye House), and some are creating new gardens in the old ways with the new plants (Hargreaves, the Oaks, Wideman-Hanvey).

Magnolia Vale, Natchez, Mississippi

Naturalized spring bulbs can be one of the most tenacious survivors of old gardens; daffodils regularly survive the bulldozer if the scraping is not too aggressive. So while none of the gardens of Magnolia Vale survive, one of Natchez's most famous, at least some of its inhabitants survived into the twenty-first century. When comparing historic photographs of the garden, one may conjure a sense of the variety in grand old gardens.

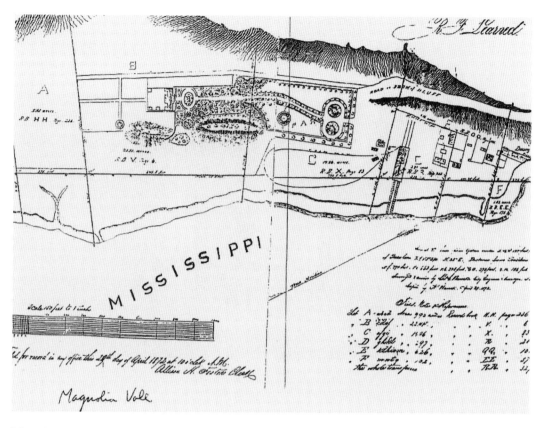

Magnolia Vale deed map, 1872. Courtesy of Dr. Elizabeth Boggess.

Built around 1845–1846, Magnolia Vale became an internationally renowned garden under the ownership of Scotsman and sawmill owner Andrew Brown and his wife, Louisa. Nestled below the bluffs of Natchez along the Mississippi river, the gardens in short order became a whistle-stop for passengers traveling on the Mississippi. "Brown's Garden" even warranted glowing praise in English gardening magazines. A number of photographs of the gardens with their railed or boarded beds before their destruction survive. One undated early spring image shows ornamental trees going into bloom and boarded flower beds lined with *Narcissus* foliage, and long, gangly tazetta foliage at that.

In 1872 Magnolia Vale's new owner, R. L. Learned, had the property surveyed and mapped, from which the garden plan in 1934 is an embellishment illustrating the placement of more plant materials. The original house burned in 1946, replaced by the current residence. Sadly the garden was bulldozed off the plateau and down the embankment to the river in the 1950s. Worse, the destruction of the garden remnants was completed in 2011, when the embankment was bulldozed to raise the elevation of the road to withstand annual spring floods from the river.

Magnolia Vale with Young Women, ca. 1880. Thomas H. and Joan Gandy Photograph Collection, Mss. 3778, Louisiana and Lower Mississippi Valley Collections, LSU Libraries, Baton Rouge, La.

In 2010 many of the bulbs still clung to the embankment below the house, overlooking the river. The lower elevation of the embankment was regularly flooded and so covered in debris, logs, and kudzu. Ornamentals included daylilies, white Roman hyacinths (called "baby whites" locally), blue Roman hyacinths, a few pink Roman hyacinths, Spanish bluebells, "itsy-bitsies," Star of Bethlehem, and *Lycoris radiata.* Daffodils were predominantly tazettas; survivors included three strains of *N. papyraceus* paperwhites, *N. italicus,* a small white hybrid, a small yellow trumpet and 'Emperor'.

The multiple strains of paperwhites, with small cups and pointed petals, suggest they were purchased and planted before 'Paper White Grandiflorus' overwhelmed the market in the late 1880s and 1890s. In other gardens in the coastal South, these small paperwhites have appeared only in gardens with an antebellum component. So it is possible these bulbs are antebellum too, but the site is too destroyed to support more than conjecture.

Also it is speculated that *N. italicus* was sold in America as "paperwhites" in the nineteenth century, as it has never appeared under its own name in an American catalog—but it had to have gotten here somehow. This cold-tender tazetta is ubiquitous across the coastal South, but its origin to date has been hazy. That Natchez gardeners call it "paperwhite" (and that it was remarked in Curtis's magazine in 1827 as sold in

Magnolia Vale garden, ca.1900. Courtesy of the Historic Natchez Foundation.

Mississippi River embankment, 2011.

Magnolia Vale embankment with 'Emperor,' 2011.

England with *N. papyraceus* as paperwhites) along with other near-white tazettas, may be the linguistic key to its arrival in American southern gardens.

Wye House, Easton, Maryland

A landmark plantation dating to the 1650s with a venerable family in residence since its founding, the Wye House gardens have seen many gardeners. The present Wye House is the third house on the property, finished around 1790 by Edward Lloyd IV (who married Elizabeth Tayloe) and oriented south to north. The second house, built circa 1660, was dismantled to erect the third, save the old kitchen wing (now the Captain's House). This second house was oriented east to west; the famous Orangery and original (east) garden align on its old east-west axis. Behind the Orangery lies the two-acre family cemetery; its wall serves as the south boundary to the formal garden space. To the west the garden space was bounded by a ditch and embankment; sometime in the late nineteenth century, the feature became a Lovers' Walk. The northern garden boundary is the present house.

Two boxwood gardens were created over time—one behind the second house and so on the east side of the present house, and the other to the west side of the present house, abutting the Lovers' Walk. Between the two is a grass bowling green, flowing from the present house's back porch to the Orangery. Descriptions of the east garden seem to vary; some suggest more of a cut-work parterre while others suggest an older pattern of rectangular beds. According to a family member, in the 1920s new plantings were added to the east garden, including a narrow rectangular cutting bed of peonies and a bed of daffodils. Many of the hybrid daffodils planted at that time in the east garden were removed by gardening staff in the recent past. In the 1960s all the boxwood in both gardens succumbed to disease (save the few variegated in the east garden).

The west garden may have been planted sometime after 1790 and comprised sets of long rectangular beds running north-south from house to the cemetery wall. Photographs of the Wye House gardens circa 1908 show a well-established garden. Family members recollect flowers planted within the beds. A midtwentieth-century map indicates fruit trees and vegetables filled other beds.

In the modern plantings where the west garden beds were located are large numbers of *N. moschatus* (interplanted with hostas), found nowhere elsewhere on the property. Given the approximate location of the new bed to where the old beds were aligned, it is quite possible the dainty white trumpets were simply collected and rearranged with new hostas in one of their same old beds after the boxwood succumbed.

The raised Lovers' Walk is thought to originally have been a ha-ha in the 1600s. A photograph published in 1923 illustrates part of the walk to have become a very overgrown affair. The embankment is now completely cleared, save for large trees and spring bulbs. Along the north section of the walk remain rows of 'Telamonius Plenus' and patches of *N.* × *medioluteus;* closer to the house at the south end, along the outside of the embankment, remains a large planting of *Leucojum vernum.*

Wye House, the west panel garden, ca. 1908.

Wye House Lovers' Walk looking north to cemetery wall, 2010. 'Telamonius Plenus' line the edge of the path, while *N.* × *medioluteus* grow on the slope.

Wye House Lovers' Walk looking south, 2010.

There is a strong division of daffodils—those found in the west garden are not found elsewhere (save 'Telamonius Plenus' planted along the cemetery wall behind the Orangery by gardening staff). No daffodils in the east garden (including *N. pseudonarcissus*) are planted in the west garden. Given the segregation of the varieties between the garden features and conspicuous lack of hybrid flowers, it is possible the Lovers' Walk bulbs and possibly the west garden *N. moschatus* are both antebellum plantings. More likely they are Victorian (particularly the less robust *N. moschatus*) and prior to the 1890s, in keeping with the period's romanticism and love of white trumpets.

Oakton, Marietta, Georgia

The notion of planting daffodils along a walk for all to admire has held on for over a hundred years since B. K. Bliss & Sons' catalog suggested planting *Narcissus* along the carriage drive. The downside to this simple touch of beauty is the ease of replacing one walkway border plant, or entire landscape plan, for another, such as when a house changes owners. Thus finding long-standing pathway borders can be challenging.

Oakton, built in Marietta, Georgia, around 1838, was purchased as a summer retreat from the sweltering, disease-laden air of Savannah by Joseph John Wilder, a wealthy Savannah shipping merchant in 1854. The house eventually passed to his granddaughter Anne Page Wilder Anderson. In 1939 the property was sold to Robert M. Goodman Sr., whose family has since held the house for three generations. The history recounted by *The Garden History of Georgia 1733–1933* suggests the garden is antebellum, but the current Goodman owners, who reviewed now-lost original Wilder correspondence to the gardener, date the garden to the 1870s. Furthermore the garden remained a work-in-progress into the twentieth century.

After the Civil War, the Wilder family decided to spend more time at Oakton, embarking on a major renovation of the house and grounds. In 1868 William Annandale, a Scottish gardener, was retained as farm manager. Elaborate cast iron urns imported from Italy by way of Mexico, and a demi-lune rose garden parterre were added to the front lawn. To the rear are the partial remains of a six-square kitchen garden bordered in boxwood. But it is a small garden feature to the side of the house where the surviving daffodils bloom. A thin line of daffodils leads from the house to acreage now developed, along the path to the pecan orchard and cow barn.

The line is a mix of daffodil varieties—doubles, trumpets, and others—some growing very close together. Based on a photograph from the 1930s, these bulbs are all that remain of a two-foot-wide border planting. The description in 1933 states that "a path bordered by bulbs and Louis Phillippe roses [leads] to the orchard."[5] By the late twentieth century, the path had been lost and the roses too; the current owner, Will Goodman, reinstated the gravel path (modifying it for the new property boundaries) and relocated the surviving peonies to a sunnier spot.

Comparing the location of the daffodils to the 1930s photograph, the daffodils were planted right along the edge, in front of the border bed. By 2012 the surviving daffodils of flowering size are primarily the doubles 'Orange Phoenix,' 'Sulphur Phoenix,' and 'Telamonius Plenus'; two clumps of *N. pseudonarcissus* hold on further down the

path, and two 'Emperor' and one 'Stella Superba' are scattered in. The presence of 'Emperor' could easily coincide with an early 1880s date for the installation of the border, as it appeared in American catalogs by 1883 (Peter Henderson & Co.). However, 'Stella Superba' appears in catalogs in the early 1900s (well eclipsed by 1920), suggesting a much later date for the border. Given how closely planted it is to other bulbs, alternatively it could have been added to the daffodil row sometime later, suggesting an ever-busy gardener.

Oakton orchard path, ca. 1935. Courtesy of Will Goodman.

The Hermitage, Nashville, Tennessee

The garden of Rachael Jackson, beloved wife of President Andrew Jackson, has known many hands since her passing in 1828, especially during the twentieth century. A traditional Tennessee variant of the Virginia four-square with a small circular bed in the center, the pattern of the garden is antebellum, as are the edging bricks placed on end. Andrew Jackson deeded a small corner of the garden to a family cemetery, alongside his wife's rotunda. Opposite, in a flower bed, is buried the faithful servant known simply as Uncle Alfred.

The house passed from Andrew Jackson to his adopted son Andrew Jackson Jr. and his wife, Sarah, in 1849. A few written records survive of Jackson's gardening directives to his daughter-in-law before his death in 1845; afterward the couple added the brick edging to the flower beds. In 1889 the house was taken over by the Ladies' Hermitage Association. Little in the way of substantive documentation exists for the association's oversight of the garden, although they did consult with granddaughter Rachel Jackson Lawrence.

In her history of the Ladies' Hermitage Association, Mrs. Dorris (a founding member) discussed the need for a caretaker and gardener early on in their management of the site:

> It became necessary to engage a caretaker to superintend the premises and protect it from all dangers. A suitable man, one who understood horticulture, for there was great need in that direction, was engaged. It was very necessary, with the limited income of the Association, that the caretaker be also a man who could give a good day's work on the grounds or house if needed. The new caretaker did good work in the garden, which was a perfect wilderness and overgrown with weeds, and improved its appearance not a little. He transplanted bulbs, moved shrubs, cut down trees which had voluntarily sprung up, dug up sprouts, and otherwise brought

Oakton orchard path with 'Emperor,' 'Telamonius Plenus,' and 'Orange Phoenix,' 2012.

order out of chaos. He remained at the Hermitage two years and performed a wonderful amount of very much needed work.[6]

By 1915 Dorris observed of the garden: "The early breath of spring calls from their slumbering beds hyacinths, lilies of the valley, jonquils, narcissi, purple shades, and the violet odored bluebottles."[7] In 1945 the association recorded planting one thousand old-fashioned jonquils, presumably the *N. × odorus*. These have been moved around over the intervening decades by various gardeners and survive to this day.

By 2010 the garden's daffodils fell into three categories: obviously modern (including the circa 1945 *N. × odorus*); Victorian; and possibly period/family. Many of the bulbs in the garden should be considered "modern," including the *Ipheion,* white and blue Roman hyacinths, and *Muscari* (which also appears at odd isolated areas of the property) based on placement and variety. Two Victorian-period daffodils are present. The most obvious is a very large clump of 'Stella Superba' (RHS date of pre-1899) planted just below the footstone of Uncle Alfred. Uncle Alfred died at the tender young age of ninety-eight in 1901. 'Stella Superba' was essentially off the American catalog market by the late 1910s and so here is considered a period planting. Over the burial of Sazie Lawrence Winn (d. May 6, 1882), is a surviving clump of *Muscari*.

The other Victorian-era daffodils are dwindled from the shade of boxwoods and thus easily missed, being four small clumps of the white trumpet *N. moschatus*. Two of the white trumpets appear on either side of a box planting on the south border (the size

The Hermitage garden, ca. 1909. Courtesy of the Hermitage: Home of President Andrew Jackson, Nashville, Tenn.

Uncle Alfred and 'Stella Superba,' 2010.

'Orange Phoenix,' the Hermitage, 2010.

of the box suggests a more Ladies' Association–era planting than a family planting of a shrub); the third is simply in the border mix—with a dwindled matching planting on the other side of the west entrance gate area. Thus both make paired plantings at the ends of the central cross walk. *N. moschatus* appeared in general bulb catalogs until 1915 and a specialty catalog to 1925.

The daffodils that could be "family" or antebellum are: *N. pseudonarcissus*, 'Telamonius Plenus,' and 'Orange Phoenix'. These bulbs appear in somewhat oddly placed clumps, as if they were originally between now-removed shrubbery and other plants. Early midtwentieth-century photographs of the garden show daffodil foliage where some of these clumps still grow, while other large plant material is conspicuously absent, giving the garden a very barren appearance. Thus, while it is quite possible the doubles were planted by the caretaker in the early 1890s, it is also possible these bulbs are some of the few plants to predate the Ladies' Hermitage Association.

Wideman-Hanvey House, Troy, South Carolina

Family oral history of the Wideman-Hanvey house, a small plantation house south of a prosperous town, dates it back to Buffalo Baptist Church, founded in 1776. The house was updated in 1888 when acquired by the Hanvey family; one of its charms is that the front columns supporting the rain porch are simply cedar trees pressed into service, branch stubs and all.

Rows of daffodils outline two triangles in front of the house, pointing southward to the original front gate and roadbed. Robert Hanvey (born in 1928), uncle of the current

N. moschatus, the Hermitage, 2010.

owner, recalls there were once triangular flower beds in front of the house. A separate row of daffodils leads from the front porch into the side yard. A back row of daffodils follows along a lost path from the rear yard to the vegetable garden. Last, drifts of daffodils alongside the old roadbed stand sentinel to the past every spring.

The beds are right triangles with their twenty-four-foot-long bases running parallel to the front porch and extending out past the corners of the house. Perpendicular to the bases and extending along the front path to the old roadbed and fence line are the thirty-six-foot-long second sides of each triangle. Interestingly the bed rows are not uniform in cultivars. The jonquil *N. × odorus* comprise the base and second side along the front path of the east bed, while the base and second side of the west bed are *N. pseudonarcissus*. At some point the base line of *N. pseudonarcissus* was relocated to accommodate a *Camellia japonica* 'Pink Perfection'. One small clump of *Iphieon* survives in the east bed. The hypotenuse line of both beds are planted with *N. × medioluteus*—called "May Narcissus" by the owner's mother, who also grew up in the house. A few 'Sulphur Phoenix' appear in the hypotenuse row of the right bed, providing some bloom interest to the line when the later-season daffodils were not in bloom.

The side row of doubles are also 'Sulphur Phoenix'. Behind the row of doubles are a few scattered daffodils, Spanish bluebells, and *Lycoris radiata*. The daffodils along the vegetable garden path are also *N. × medioluteus*. The drifts of daffodils along the original roadbed are all *N. pseudonarcissus*. Fortuitously, on March 21, 1910, the white and African American families who lived on the property posed for photographs in front of the house, in the same spot. Bricks set on an angle edge a flower bed behind the families in front of the house, and a narrow sandy strip borders the brick. To the Hanvey family's right appear daffodil foliage and a double daffodil flower on a bent stem. Supporting the notion of the beds being planted after the 1880s house renovations and porch additions is the alignment of the triangular beds to the house. The beds align with the later-added cedar columns, and not the earlier-constructed square porch columns.

The drift of *N. pseudonarcissus* along the old road is very Victorian in sensibility and may have been inspired by family friend Miss Jennie Wideman of Ivy Gates and her ill-fated plan to grow daffodils commercially. Jennie was employed by the Marshall Field family as the children's nurse and accompanied them to their various houses in and around Chicago and New York City in the early 1900s. Seeing the flower peddlers selling daffodils for great sums, Jennie wrote to her sister Clara at Ivy Gates, to tell her they could make a fortune doing the same thing. Apparently Miss Clara simply collected and planted daffodils from the area. Her surviving rows are dominated by *N. pseudonarcissus* and *N. × odorus,* with a smattering of 'Telamonius Plenus,' phoenix doubles, *Leucojum,* and a partial row of one hybrid. Alas Ivy Gates is not near a railroad line, so the inability to quickly ship flowers to market ensured Miss Wideman's project would not succeed.

Hargreaves House, St. Catherine's Creek National Wildlife Refuge, Mississippi

Not all gardens of the late 1800s strictly followed the new vogues; many adapted the garden designs of their childhoods to their new homes using new styles and trendy

Hanvey family, courtesy of private collection.

Wideman-Hanvey house, courtesy of private collection.

plants. One such abandoned house and garden south of Natchez, Mississippi, was of the traditional formal garden of a quincunx motif but planted in bulbs. The house belonged to Sophy Hargreaves by 1902 (it is unclear if she inherited the house in 1891 with her allocation of land or if she built afterward); it changed hands once in the 1950s before its donation to the wildlife refuge. Along the way the house became home to threatened Rafinesque's big-eared bats; when a pine tree fell into it, wildlife rangers installed a large bat house in the middle of the garden to encourage the bats to move in. By 2010 some semblance of the garden's original design and bilateral symmetry remained. (The oil drilling rig was luckily installed in the backyard.)

The Hargreaves house is situated on a slope facing east, downhill. The garden was gently terraced, stepping down an embankment to the drive and roadway. The front garden area was rectilinear, in scale with the front of the house. According to rangers with the St. Catherine's Creek National Wildlife Refuge, the garden at the time of its acquisition was sufficiently intact to tell the center circles and outer border lines were color coordinated—white around the garden edges and yellow circles in the middle. By 2010 no hardscape or evidence of fencing remained; it is standard local custom for all brick to be scavenged from abandoned structures for reuse.

The front walk was lined at least halfway with the venerable tazetta 'Grand Primo Citronière,' ubiquitous to the area, with clumps of *N. italicus* (called "paperwhites" by the locals—a catch-all term for any white tazetta) almost at the base of the front porch steps. Each "side" of the front garden area was full of *N. × odorus* and the double 'Butter and Eggs'. Some 'Grand Primo Citronière' was scattered about the front garden, no longer in a discernible pattern. More *N. italicus* was planted around the base of a cedar tree on the east line and the large oak on the south line. On the south side outer border, a double row of "Campernelli" remained distinct. Also two clumps of white Roman

Hargreaves garden. 'Grand Primo Citronie' along the central path and the back fence line, and *N.* × *odorus* in the center, 2010.

Hargreaves garden. 'Grand Primo Citronire' along front path, 2010.

hyacinth remain along the north line, near more *N. italicus*. Scattered about the middle of the two front garden areas were a few rose bushes; a popcorn spirea bush remained along the north front line as well as a ligustrum.

While the front garden, particularly if envisioned as fenced in, was of a formal nature, outside the fencing the plantings were much more in keeping with the Victorian drift style. On the south side was a large area of iris. On the north side were large clumps of the double 'Butter and Eggs,' and in line with the chimneys were plantings of *Lycoris radiata* (called September or Spider lilies) in a lawn drift planting.

The Oaks, Winnsboro, South Carolina

Some gardeners recreated the old in the cloth of the new. And such seems to be at the Oaks. Built around 1835 by R. A. Rapley Hallem, the Oaks was purchased in 1856 by John Montgomery Lemmon (1829–1906) and his wife, Mary Yonge. A now-lost photograph of the Lemmon family in front of their home was taken circa 1870 by a circuit-riding photographer. Father, children, a servant, and the house with front garden are documented. One of the girls was Belle, who lived at the Oaks with her sister Jaime into spinsterhood into the 1940s and 1950s. But fortuitously photocopies of the original image survive, and it is the house that holds the crucial clue.

Between the back porch and the location of the original kitchen are the erratic lines of a pattern bed of daffodils and spider lilies (*Lycoris radiata*), situated under a now large oak, pushing up through the sod. Lines of 'Telamonius Plenus,' *N. × odorus*, paperwhites, Phoenix-type doubles (around an old pear tree since removed), and *Lycoris* define long-lost geometric beds of diamonds, triangles, and circles. To the opposite side of the backyard (left, if standing on the back porch) is a very large crepe myrtle encircled by a large bed of *Lycoris radiata*, with a few jonquils and one hyacinth representing another circle. This circular bed is matched on the right in the pattern bed by a circle of dwindled jonquils (probably *N. × intermedius* often called "Texas Stars") complemented by an inner circle of hyacinths—both encircling a volunteer crepe myrtle to pair with the left. These circles, in turn, are framed in part by a corner of 'Telamonius Plenus'. Where the kitchen is thought to have been located lurk two or three 'Golden Spur'—a Victorian-era hybrid trumpet daffodil, first appearing in American catalogs around 1888. A single clump of bicolor tazettas bloomed along the outer fence line.

In the front garden, the trumpet *N. pseudonarcissus* borders the front walk and side fence lines but interestingly is not present in the pattern garden. In the fall *Lycoris radiata* follow the same paths. Outside the original fence lines around the house, on the west side, is a drift planting of daffodils alas not of blooming size. Given the pattern bed's location in the "working" area, likely the area was a swept yard at its inception. Daffodils and swept yards were also a well-fitted landscape match two counties north at Mountain Shoals.

Now to return to the 1870 photograph of the house. On the front porch was strung string or wire for vines to grow up on, thus providing shade. However, this wire is more a scaffold than the traditional simple single run; attached to the center of the second story porch, the wires are intertwined to form a pattern of diamonds. It is this pattern

The Oaks back garden, 2011. Multiple diamond patterns are evident across the garden. At far left is remnant of a diamond in 'Sulphur Phoenix,' in middle a large diamond of *N.* × *odorus* around a replaced tree, and along the left side from the far back to the fence post are diamond remnants in *Lycoris radiata* and *N.* × *odorus*.

Lycoris radiata, ca. 2010. Courtesy of Carol Cooke, current owner of the Oaks.

N. × *odorus*, 2011.

of diamonds from their childhood that Belle and Jaime later recreated in *Lycoris radiata* and *N.* × *odorus* across the backyard and in 'Sulphur Phoenix' around an old fruit tree. Determining when the garden the Oaks could have been planted depends on knowing when Belle and Jaime Lemmon came of age to plant a garden, and whether that was before or after the death of their father in 1906, when they became mistresses of the house.

Colonial Revival Gardens

For daffodils Colonial Revival gardens fall into two broad categories. For some the gardeners set out to re-create a colonial-era garden as they understood it to appropriately complement their colonial-era houses, and the use of daffodils and other popular bulbs was simply part of the overall broader palate of "old fashioned" flowers. Others, possibly swept up in the patriotic mood, desired a fashionable garden of the current vogue. In part this was helped along by Colonial Williamsburg; many an old boxwood garden (including Nancy Narcissa Nesbitt Anderson's Williamston) was dug up and sold to help create the historic site and gardens we now know.

But for every "this is so" case—such as the reimagined colonial gardens found in Virginia and New England, and the fashionable gardens such as at Reynolda in North Carolina, there is the exception. And for daffodils in Colonial Revival gardens, the exception is the Chafee garden in Augusta, Georgia.

N. × *medioluteus* near Westover Plantation cemetery along the James River, 2010.

Reynolda, Winston-Salem, North Carolina

The gardens at Reynolda were begun even before the house was built in 1917 by Katharine Smith Reynolds (her husband, Richard Joshua, founded the R. J. Reynolds Tobacco Company). She began with the landscape architecture firm of Buckenham and Miller in 1912 but in 1915 changed firms to that of the Philadelphian Thomas Warren Sears. Sears designed the four-acre Greenhouse Garden composed of four intricate, color-coordinated parterres within an encompassing border garden in the Colonial Revival style. Two parterres were designated primarily for roses, the third was the Blue and Yellow Garden, and the fourth was the Pink and White Garden. Reynolds ordered by the train car load from nursery sources including Henry A. Dreer's of Philadelphia. Reynolds was not without her wild garden, however. Drifts of daffodils were naturalized in the trees along the estate's entrance drive to the house, many of which still grace the property.

Daffodils and crocuses were the early spring bulbs of choice by Sears. The plantings of the daffodils themselves were of irregular, curved forms within the rectilinear beds. A limited palate of daffodils was employed, spanning from early season to midseason —'Golden Spur,' 'King Alfred,' 'Sir Watkin,' 'Conspicuus' (often called "Barri Conspicuus"), with 'Ornatus' and *N. poeticus* "grandiflorus" the last to bloom. Interestingly these are the two midseason poets usually available, so no flowers past late March were selected.

The Blue and Yellow Garden plants list called for two hundred "Barri Conspicuus" and four hundred 'Sir Watkin' as pale yellow flowers, and the Pink and White

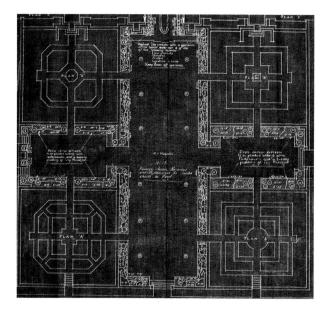

"Planting Plan for Greenhouse Garden. Estate of Mrs. R. J. Reynolds, Winston-Salem, N.C.—Plan C," by Thomas W. Sears. September 25, 1917. Courtesy of Reynolda House Museum of American Art.

Garden called for fifty "Poeticus Grandiflorus" and an undetermined quantity of 'Ornatus' as white flowers. The solid yellow daffodils were destined for the inside border beds or "Sunken Garden" —two hundred 'Golden Spur' and two hundred "Narcissus major," along with four hundred 'Sir Watkin'. No daffodils were called for in the outer border or shrubbery beds.

The current gardens were re-created from the original plantings lists given on the garden blueprint plans. A multitude of perennials were planted atop the daffodils. In the modern garden, staff have not noticed a problem from summer rot thanks to the irrigation system, likely, as the perennials absorb sufficient water to keep the dormant bulbs below dry and safe from rot.

Daffodil drifts behind Lake Porch, ca. 1920. Courtesy of Reynolda House Museum of American Art.

Pink and White Parterre and west end of greenhouse, ca. 1920. Courtesy of Reynolda House Museum of American Art.

Chafee Bulb Garden, Augusta, Georgia

One of the most enticing gardens (for a bulb enthusiast) encountered is that attributed to an early settler of Augusta by the name of Mistress Hannah Howard, in *Garden History of Georgia, 1733–1933*. The history was set out in glowing romanticism, presumably narrated in part by the then-owner, Maisie Chafee, a direct descendant of Hannah Howard. Regrettably the book's research notes have been lost to the vagaries of time, so there is no way to ascertain what data was originally collected from what source.

However, for all the images of the garden accepted by the Archives of American Gardens at the Smithsonian Institution, the garden did not warrant mention in Lockwood's *Gardens of Colony and State*. An image of the bulb parterre is given prominence at the beginning of the chapter on Georgia gardens, but no written discussion is included past the image's caption. And an interesting pithy caption it is, noting that the design was used extensively in a garden movement of around 1800, with no explanation of what that garden movement was.

Reportedly a woman of modest means, Hannah Howard purchased an existing cabin and five acres around 1785 outside of Augusta, Georgia, fleeing the uprising against the British in North Carolina. Lore has her busily setting out to improve the property with gardens, including a formal parterre bulb garden, described as in "the

The Chafee Garden, ca. 1933. Courtesy, Georgia Archives, Vanishing Georgia Collection, RIC-128.

old Dutch style." Oddly the current parterre is laid out behind the original detached kitchen and not the main house, possibly because the land is a bit flatter there than the gentle slope behind the house.

In 1933 the property was still in family ownership, with descendent Maisie Chafee an industrious gardener (she inherited the property when a young child in the 1880s). Period photographs show the center bed was solid with trumpets, and "phoenix"-type doubles were planted in the corner beds, bordered by low-growing bulbs. Purportedly the original tulips, being tulips in the South, did not survive, and the pinks used as bed borders similarly died out, having been replaced with the now-present aggregate concrete coping (suspected to date to the 1920s).

By 2009 the garden form had survived, but not many of the daffodils. Many beds were tilled up to make way for roses around 1999 by a past owner, and a subsequent owner relocated more bulbs to convert the parterre into a summer perennial garden. The granite paths were turned to sod (which the current owners have begun removing). Fortuitously a few back beds were not tilled and are still filled with a few paperwhites, snowflakes (*Leucojum aestivum*), jonquils (*N.* × *odorus*), a very uncommon all-white tazetta (as yet unidentified), lots of the tazettas 'Grand Monarque' and 'Silver Chimes,' the bicolor trumpet 'Empress,' and a very few gladiolus. Many of the border Spanish bluebells survived, as well as a few Roman hyacinths and many of the center bed's trumpets—the bicolor 'Empress'. Sadly only one original 'Butter and Eggs' survived in the four surrounding beds. A row of the yellow trumpet 'Unsurpassable' mixed with paperwhites still leads to a lost section of the far side garden.

Thus instead of the garden being a quick flush of early color, the garden actually started blooming in December with paperwhites, then transitioned to early spring with 'Grand Monarque,' *N. × odorus,* and Roman hyacinths. In March came the 'Butter and Eggs' and 'Orange Phoenix,' the bicolor trumpet 'Empress,' and Spanish bluebells. Late midseason daffodils bloom from mid-March to early April, including the pink and white 'Mrs. R. O. Backhouse,' a white-orange similar to 'Croseus' or 'Franciscus Drake,' the popular white 'Queen of the North,' and a large dose of the late-blooming tazetta 'Silver Chimes,' closing out with the robust poet 'Actaea' with *N. × medioluteus* the last.

Annely Hayes (now Klingensmith) lived with her gardening husband, Bert, at the Howard-Chafee house from 1956 until 1976. Their daughter Patience helped her father in the garden and still adores the "bulb maze" of her childhood. One of her most favorite games was to count all the kinds of bulbs in the maze—thirty-two or thirty-three. It is through Patience's mind's eye that Maisie's work can be traced through time. Bert Hayes thinned overcrowded clumps of bulbs, but he never overplanted the bulbs for the summer nor added any new kinds. The white gravel paths remained intact during the Hayes's tenure, but the small box shrubs at the ends of the beds were long gone and the sundial had already been replaced. Patience vividly remembers the distinctive 'Mrs. R. O. Backhouse,' as well as the doubles daffodils being both the yellow and white kinds. As time has progressed, it appears many of the missing daffodils were spotted around property when the parterre was converted into a perennial garden—and many of the thirty-two or thirty-three types still survive.

The Chafee Garden, 2012.

The Chafee Garden, center bed of 'Empress,' 2012.

The Chafee Garden, 'Silver Chimes,' 'Empress,' and kitchen, 2012.

The nagging question regarding this garden is whether it is a pre–Civil War parterre or if it is a good Colonial Revival garden. Just down the road, another quincunx garden was installed in 1856. A very close reading of the original garden history reveals only two bulbs were "family" or attributed to Hannah Howard by Maisie Chafee—the "Butter and Eggs" and the bluebells/blue Roman hyacinths. Thus it is plausible these bulbs were relocated by Maisie when she created her garden masterpiece in the Colonial Revival style.

Maisie was an energetic and proud gardener, fond of bulbs and iris. She may have reworked an older quincunx parterre, adding the not-so-traditional side runner beds. Or she could have created the bulb maze completely from scratch, providing her familial bulbs a new showcase home. The parterre's location is difficult to reconcile; given its placement behind the kitchen it seems more likely Maisie is responsible for the existing parterre. However, it is tempting to speculate that Maisie, dutiful to family and house-proud, relocated or recreated an earlier family garden to conform with her grand designs for overhauling the property, as avid gardeners are wont to do.

Bulb Lawns—Wild Gardens

Drifts of naturalized daffodils as an intentional landscape motif are only of late gaining recognition—which is a good thing, as they lurk about more than one realizes. Wild gardens or bulb lawns are as varied as their original gardeners. They run every gamut imaginable—large swaths to modest patches, wealthy estates to modest homeowners, long periods of bloom to one glorious flush, a wide array of bulbs to a simple handful.

Some bulb lawns have predominant colors in different areas, others a mixture. All are planted to have some successional bloom, some longer than others, and some even a successional color scheme. One is even planted in a fair percentage of jonquils for wafting fragrance. Some are mixed in with other bulbs, such as winter aconite, *Leucojum aestivum,* freesia, *Lycoris radiata,* and *Ipheion,* while others are not. Many pair in with blue flowers such as Roman hyacinths, Spanish bluebells, *Muscari neglectum* or purple violets. All follow the natural topography to some degree or other major natural feature such as a tree drip line, service road, ridge top, wood line, and so on. The earliest plantings identified to date were begun in the 1880s, while a number of large estates were planted around 1917.

A number of public gardens across the country still are graced with surviving "wild garden" bulb plantings. These include Filoli Mansion and Gardens near San Francisco, California; Goodwood Museum and Gardens in Tallahassee, Florida; Blithewold Mansion, Gardens and Arboretum in Bristol, Rhode Island; and Krippendorf Lodge—Lob's Woods in Cincinnati, Ohio (Carl Krippendorf's correspondence with Elizabeth Lawrence was the basis for her book *The Little Bulbs*). McLaughlin Daffodil Hill in Volcano, California, is a private ranch that opens for the season to the public. Historic gardens dating from the late 1920s to the 1940s tend to showcase only daffodils; public gardens include Cypress Gardens near Charleston, South Carolina; Shaw Nature Reserve of the Missouri Botanical Garden; and Daffodil Hill at Lake View

The Old Hill Place, planted by Jane Hill (d. 1913), Washington, Georgia, 2008.

Cemetery in Cleveland, Ohio. Two of the gardens discussed here are open to the public year-round—Reynolda House and Winterthur—and Tuckahoe is open regularly during Virginia Garden Week as well as to group tours by appointment.

Tuckahoe, Richmond, Virginia

In the early 1920s, one of Richmond's favorite old homes was awash in daffodils:

> Below the schoolhouse, jonquils have spread into a veritable Cloth-of-Gold field, flinging high their April trumpets above a mass of periwinkle blue as the sky. These signals of spring that dance so joyously leave the memory of their beauty throughout the garden year. And there are so many varieties of daffodils and narcissi at this charming old place. Beginning with the short-stemmed Obvallaris the beautiful Stellas follow in profusion. These bulbs were planted long before the days of the Olympia as the Gold Spur and the double sorts—Orange and Golden Phoenix, familiarly known as Butter and Eggs and Eggs and Bacon—will attest. But, daintiest of all the daffodil family which blooms at Tuckahoe, is the delicate, old-fashioned, little white flower known as "The Lady of Leeds."
>
> Scattered about the garden, and all over the lawn, are four varieties of narcissi —the Polyanthus, which, though in the minority, compensates in its bright yellow flowers; the white Biflorus, and, most pleasing of all, Ornatus and Poeticus.[8]

The history of the pleasure garden of Tuckahoe, best-known as the childhood home of Thomas Jefferson, begins much later than his residence there. Mrs. Richard (Mary) Allen moved to Tuckahoe sometime between 1860 and 1865. Her husband's parents bought Tuckahoe in 1850; Mary and Richard in turn sold the plantation in 1898. Allen had a penchant for bulbs, and for writing letters to the editor to "gently" correct erroneous information published about her gardening work. In one letter she invited the ladies of Richmond out to admire her eight hundred hyacinths she bought and planted in a row from Thomas Jefferson's schoolhouse to the garden gate, bordering *her* box maze (not planted in colonial times, thank you very much, as she clearly delineated in another such letter). (The maze was lost to disease in the midtwentieth century.)

She planted daffodils and other bulbs along the edge of the grass and down the slopes to the canal and ice pond on the south (front) of the house, as well as near the ice house and along the ice pond slope edge. The ravine behind the school was the slope alongside Allen's prized box maze. Period photographs in the possession of the current owners show daffodil foliage across the lawn around the turn of the twentieth century. By 2010 primarily two daffodils remained—'Telamonius Plenus' and a single trumpet. Fortuitously for restoration efforts to replant the daffodils, Edith Tunis Sale's detailed descriptions in *Historic Gardens of Virginia* (1923) came from firsthand knowledge—at the time of writing and editing the book, she resided at Tuckahoe as a caretaker.

The daffodils along the (now) front walk and lawn suffered losses in the late twentieth century. Planted around huge American elms lost to Dutch elm disease, some of

Tuckahoe, circa 1900. Courtesy of Sue Thompson.

Tuckahoe, 2013.

the bulbs lining the drive were inadvertently destroyed when the stumps were ground out. Once this was determined, the remaining stumps have been left to rot naturally, preserving the bulbs. Historic images of the house and lawn document the daffodils lauded by Edith Tunis Sale, but alas these too have gone.

Of the flowers listed, four are Victorian-era introductions, and thus not of Greek mythological antiquity. The small (and comparatively early-blooming) poet 'Ornatus' was offered by Grant Thorburn by 1882. The wildly popular 'Stella' was offered by Peter Henderson in 1888, along with the earliest "Leedsii"-type flowers. The Dutch foundling 'Golden Spur' appeared in Dingee & Conard's 1889 catalog. If Allen was ordering from European catalogs, then these dates are easily too late—pushing her daffodil plantings to the early to mid-1880s.

Allen seems to have planted areas of the garden with a bit of a color scheme in mind. The now-shaded slope from the schoolhouse to the water was once predominantly yellow, with a light accenting of white. Conversely her mid- to late-season lawn planting was predominantly white, with a light accent of yellow. The lawn planting would have bloomed after the predominantly white Stellas under the elms. And as the current owners are dedicated to preserving the property, its buildings, and its landscape, Mrs. Allen's Stellas will be greeting visitors for some time to come.

Winterthur, Delaware

The well-known du Pont estate of Winterthur is possibly the best-known example of William Robinson's "wild garden" in America—not surprising as Henry Francis du Pont (a noted amateur horticulturist in his own right who bought his bulbs from

George Heath) met with both Robinson and Gertrude Jekyll along the way. Du Pont commenced planting his March Bank in 1902 and started with daffodils. When one now reads gardening articles on the naturalized plantings, much attention is paid to the incredible range of plants over the entire growing season, with daffodils just a relatively small part of the palate. However, du Pont's own articles, if not just the sheer volume he planted over the decades, belie his interest in daffodils. While articles on the March Bank wax poetic over the woody spring ephemerals and wildflowers, du Pont himself couched his start in bulbs: "but it was not until 1902 that I laid out and planted my first narcissi garden on a gentle slope in front of our house where the lawn faded into the woods."[9]

When he began planting in 1902, there were already a few small patches of daffodils about the estate. Apparently he started with straight-line rows, which he soon dispensed with. Finding a gentle slope with a background of evergreen shrubs ideal, he laid his paths five and a half feet in width. He wrote of his landscaping methods in 1915 and again in 1930, updating in 1961 after he had opened Winterthur to the public. His palate of daffodils broadened over the decades as well. His first dependable flowers were the bicolor trumpet 'Horsfieldi' accented by the yellow trumpets 'Golden Spur,' *N. obvallaris,* and 'Santa Maria,' complemented by 'Ornatus,' 'Mrs. Langtry,' and 'Conspicuus'. The small daffodils *N. minor, N. nanus,* and *N. minor* var. *minimus* he paired with crocus, *Chionodoxas, Muscari,* and other small bulbs. His daffodil list eventually grew to thirty by 1925 and around 280 cultivars by the time he was done.

Du Pont's updated article serves well for anyone desirous of artistic drifts of daffodils to fill large spaces. He found that usual recommendations of simply tossing bulbs and planting where they fall to be functionally impractical. Instead he settled on laying out actual beds first, outlined with branches and sticks found in the woods, to be ideal. The curves formed naturally by working with the found branches created appealing forms, giving "all the regularity or irregularity of contour one could desire."[10] The daffodil cultivars he recommended were chosen not only for durability and length of blooming time but also for compatibility and contrast of color. "For naturalizing in large groups one must have deeper and lighter shades and many types of blooms,"[11] as one takes care to overlap blooming times to assure a working continuity of color. All daffodils selected were first trialed for two to three years in his designated cutting beds to assess their suitability. Interestingly, while many home gardeners planted their drifts of daffodils with accenting color bulbs of white (*Leucojum*) and blue (*Muscari, Hyacinthoides,* Dutch and Roman hyacinths, *Ipheion*), du Pont makes no such references. This is in spite of his other spring ephemerals (squills and glory-in-the-snow create the main flush, accented with lavender crocus, lavender Italian windflowers, and Virginia bluebells) creating an extended blue phase.

While most gardeners mixed their daffodils in their drifts to extend the season, du Pont counseled against it. "An excellent rule to follow in all bulb planting is to have the earlier bulbs in an entirely separate locations from the others; as with our sudden heat waves they spoil the main effect by their early fading, and no late blooming bulb is too late to put with the mid-season varieties as the very hot early days make them

The March Bank with daffodils, early twentieth century. Courtesy of the Winterthur Library: Winterthur Archives.

overlap invariably."[12] "The secret of a successful big planting of narcissi is: first, only have varieties that bloom at about the same time—never more than one week's difference; have them of contrasting forms and shades, and have your patches of pleasing shapes and sizes."[13] He strongly advised against the cheap mixtures of bulbs, finding the mish-mash of different forms of trumpets, doubles, poets, and so on to be a "perfect nightmare."[14]

In 1925 du Pont began planting daffodils in the permanent pastures and meadows (and later golf course). He found a new set of constraints to be negotiated, resulting from the no-mow requirements of the foliage. "Hence avoid planting them too close to lawns or flower beds, or in front of neat shrubberies, where long grass in May or June would be unsightly."[15] (After Du Pont installed the golf course, a golfer whose ball landed in the daffodil beds had to take a penalty shot as playing through the beds was not allowed.) Though by 2012 many of the early March Bank daffodils were suffering from shade creep as the mature trees expand, those daffodils in brighter spots and the sunny fields continue to delight the visiting public.

Postscript

The presence or absence of common daffodils in period gardens presents interpretive challenges. *N. pseudonarcissus* is a conundrum. It is one of the most commonly encountered heirloom daffodils, particularly in the Piedmont region of South Carolina and

Winterthur, former golf course. Courtesy of the Winterthur Library: Winterthur Archives.

Clenny Run with 'Queen of the North'. Courtesy of the Winterthur Library: Winterthur Archives.

Cutting bed, unidentified poets, 2012.

Georgia, and grows in old gardens and home sites from Virginia to Florida to Texas. Yet in gardens with federal or antebellum components, namely Chantilly, Leesylvania, Mountain Shoals, Bartram's Garden, and Barrington Hall (and possibly the Wye House), no *N. pseudonarcissus* is present in the earliest garden areas. (The Hermitage could be an exception.) Known as a commoner's flower in the colonial period, was *N. pseudonarcissus* still truly a commoner's in the antebellum period, contrary to current assumptions?

At home sites of persons of lesser means across the South, *N. pseudonarcissus* is very common and was added postbellum to gardens such as Mountain Shoals and Wideman-Hanvey. Even at Wye House, with its unknown dates of planting, *N. pseudonarcissus* is found in the 1920s-era addition planting, but not in the earlier planting in the west parterre nor as part of the Lovers' Walk planting. What then changed in gardeners' attitudes to accept *N. pseudonarcissus* after the Civil War? Was it simply by dint of presence—no one had money, so if someone had a new flower to share, then receiving gardeners thankfully accepted them?

Similarly *N.* × *medioluteus*, "Primrose Peerless," was another commoner's flower but may have somehow gotten a "pass" if the conundrum at Menokin is any indication (and the Wye House Lovers' Walk bulbs *may* be very old). Joseph Breck led with *N.* × *medioluteus* in his discussion of common garden daffodils in 1851; albeit a Boston nurseryman, Breck was well traveled, and his determinations of commonality were likely based on observations across the country. The 1766 garden list for John Mercer's Malborough

South Georgia fence with collected paperwhites, 2008.

may bolster the argument for this flower's tacit acceptance in the gardens of the wealthy at least in the colonial era.

In contrast was the "common double" 'Telamonius Plenus' more accepted in high-style gardens as it was a double, its hardy constitution then giving it the staying power for succeeding generations? The preponderance of double daffodils in the federal gardens parallels the federal period gardeners' notes of Middleton, Skipwith, and LeConte of planting predominantly doubles. Do these garden sites echo the notion of double varieties as preferred for a garden of means, while *N. pseudonarcissus* was a commoner's flower and thus generally not planted?

Jonquils held prominence in antebellum gardens as expected and continue to command high esteem from modern gardeners. Double jonquils, of more delicate constitution, have not survived the centuries, nor have *N. triandrus, N. minor*, "Albus Plenus Odoratus," and others. *N. poeticus* survives in upper South and northern gardens but as yet has not been found in a definitively antebellum context. Older strains of paperwhites or *N. papyraceus* such as those at Magnolia Vale support Fanny Kemble's observations of silvery tazettas in coastal antebellum gardens. Whether or not surviving *N. italicus* and differing strains of 'Grand Primo Citronière' date as far back remains speculation for now. More surviving old garden sites may be sans daffodils because the bulbs were given new homes in the twentieth century, often just down the road.

Appendix A: Gallery

There are four kinds of unnamed daffodils lurking in American gardens—those whose names have simply been forgotten (or were never known to begin with); those that are natural hybrids created by insects pollinating and seeds dropping (often discernible to a trained eye); those that are differing botanical "strains" resulting from original species populations from different areas of Europe being dug up and sold (or brought over by immigrants); and those "clones" resulting from intentional hybridizing and then raised from seed (so two of the same named varieties cross-pollinated and seeds grown on to increase stock, resulting in more of the same by name but actual slight genetic variations having occurred). Some of these flowers never had proper names by their first owners—particularly if they just bought "mixed sorts." Some went under catch-all names; others went by a local common name as they became pass-along flowers. But all confound to distraction modern gardeners trying to save, compare, and name these dwindling garden inhabitants.

Old strains of old species flowers have been sleuthed by gardeners for decades. One of the better-known sleuths was garden writer Elizabeth Lawrence, who documented many a strain held by gardeners she corresponded with across the country. In *The Little Bulbs* (1957), Lawrence enumerated strains of *N. jonquilla* (about four), *N. moschatus* (four strains, two of which she'd found in Southern gardens, plus two other old, no-name white, presumably species, trumpets), and possible variations of *N. × tenuior*. The proper identification of white swan's-neck trumpets has vexed gardeners for decades; the only rough consensus seems to be that the "Silver Bells" strain of *N. moschatus* or *N. alpestris* is no more—outside of American gardens.

Today two "heirloom" strains of *N. jonquilla* are commercially available in limited quantities, one from Louisiana but originating from family stock from antebellum Virginia (introduced as "Early Louisiana") and the other rescued from a now-obliterated farmstead in Texas ("Pine Mills"). Modern garden sleuths also have identified a number of types of *N. bulbocodium* in Louisiana and Arkansas, and two forms of *N. pseudonarcissus* in upstate South Carolina.

It is thought multiple strains of double *N. poeticus* (a.k.a. "Albus Plenus Odoratus") survive in northern American gardens. Commercial growers in Cornwall, England, have identified upward of four strains, two of which have been formally recognized and named by the RHS ('Spalding Double White,' 'Tamar Double White'), in addition to those flowers known by the general catch-all name 'Plenus'. Thus it is not surprising that an heirloom double poet in Ohio brought from Jeffersontown, Kentucky (the home of Luther Clay Owings, 1857–1920), looks suspiciously like 'Spaulding Double White'. Representative flowers of clones resulting from intentional hybridizing (Dutch) and then raised from seed may well explain variants of bicolor tazettas found across the South. One such candidate is again from Louisiana and is speculated to be a form of 'Grand Primo Citronière'.

Early named hybrid daffodils present their own problems. Usually deprived of adequate micronutrients for decades, even after years of "fattening up" they can still be difficult to identify; early small white forms are notoriously difficult. To make matters worse, early hybrids are far more weather-sensitive than hybrids developed later. Flowers that have pale yellow petals up north turn white after three days in the far South. Or, depending on the number of cold hours at the exact time the red color chemicals are developing in the flower bud, the cups can have a red rim ring one year and the next none at all. Furthermore flowers appear in old gardens that apparently were never sold in American catalogs, but *were* common in the wholesale catalogs (raising the specter of "substitution").

In the coastal South, one of the more intractable problems of old *Narcissus* lurks, namely the survival of old tazettas without names. Most of the hybrid tazettas sold by the Dutch prior to 1920 have little in the way of useful descriptions, be it flower form, season of bloom, size of plant, and so on, and they were not photographed for catalogs. What little descriptions there are consist of basic petal and cup color, maybe a fade pattern, and in rare instances a comment regarding plant height or early blooming season. Further, with the problems of "true to name" stock being provided by Dutch wholesalers, and American nurserymen perchance not being as attentive as they might otherwise be, early catalog descriptions can be quite contradictory. So then one must tease apart various descriptions, and determine if any nurseryman could be considered more reliable than average.

One of the more widespread unknown bicolor tazettas was registered as 'Nat Williams,' in honor of Nat Williams of Thomasville, Georgia—who was very interested in saving daffodils he found in old gardens. It has been only in the past few years with the availability of period catalogs that sufficient cultivar descriptions have been gathered to suggest its possible original name, including "States General" ('Staaten Generaal') and 'Grootvorst'. Another old flower renamed is 'Early Pearl,' thought to be 'French Monarque'. Elizabeth Lawrence, in *A Southern Garden* (1942), discussed the elusive 'White Pearl,' considered by then to be obsolete. By around 1960 George Heath had discovered and rescued a stock of said 'White Pearl' from an old garden in Norfolk, Virginia, and brought it back to market.

All-yellow tazettas are not nearly as common; it is possible that coming from more arid regions of the Mediterranean they are not as robust in the soggy climate of the coastal South. A few have been discovered over the years, but identification remains frustrating. While not an illustrious flower (other than being a legacy back to the barbarous host of tazettas in the florist's parterre—is it a species or is it a hybrid?), *N.* × *intermedius* warrants inclusion here as it is a very common heirloom garden flower across the Deep South. Sold under its old name "Etoile d'Or," it appeared regularly in catalogs from the 1860s to around 1901, when it was finally dropped from the listings of tazettas with so many other flowers.

Orange-cupped tazettas are the most elusive of all, save for "Chinese Sacred Lily" and its double. It is tacitly agreed by tazetta species experts that both 'Romanus' and 'Constantinople' are double forms of *N. cypri*. However, neither perennializes in the southern United States and California. That double, which is found in old coastal South and California gardens dating back to around 1900 or so, is the double of "Chinese Sacred Lily," which did make it into the commercial trade. Meanwhile there are scads of strains of paperwhites, many humble in form, but one dwarf form in particular (called "Snowflake" in south Georgia) is quite refined. Discussions of heirloom species variations across the South may be found in Van Beck and Van Beck, *Daffodils in Florida: A Field Guide to the Coastal South* (2003).

It is not practical to include images of all the flowers discussed in this text. Readers are referred to identification materials provided on the American Daffodil Society's website. Early hybrid daffodils warrant their own identification textbook. A few generalizations of early flower forms are provided here as quick diagnostic field tools. In very old flower forms, particularly those hybridized prior to 1900, the petals are narrower and more pointed, giving a star-shape form to the flower. Often the petals twist or curl at the edges, so the petals do not overlap much if at all. The petals often seem thin or translucent, and many are ridged or lined. Cups are often very ridged and unsymmetrical (out of round), and rims crinkled or serrated. The cup color is often more staining or bleeding from the rim into the cup, and not a solid, saturated color.

With trumpets the petals may cup or surround the trumpet, instead of being held perpendicular to the trumpet. The greater the petal overlap and the greater the petal substance (thickness), the more recent the flower's hybridization date. With yellow trumpets, the green of the stem often bleeds up toward the backs of the (yellow) petals, and the petals are often a paler yellow than the trumpet (giving a two-tone effect). The foliage can be narrower, closer to the species' parents' form, while modern daffodils often have wide foliage (this is particularly apparent on trumpets, but even jonquils can have noticeably wider leaves). The bulbs are often smaller, again closer to the originating species' size.

The flowers shown here were chosen as they are either strains found in American gardens in some quantity or are rare but currently commercially available from specialty growers (*N. minor* and *N. pseudonarcissus* 'Plenus'; *N. bicolor* is on occasion available to the dilettante from UK sources). The American Daffodil Society has numerous Internet (http://daffseek.org) and electronic identification tools available providing vetted images of historic daffodils to help gardeners play the old favorite game of "pin the name on the flower."

Commonly found garden strains are illustrated here, unless otherwise noted; most images from rescued stock or gardens and are identified when the specific location is known. Commercially obtained flowers are *N. minor,* 'Orange Phoenix,' double *N. jonquilla,* and double *N. pseudonarcissus.*

N. pseudonarcissus subsp. *psuedonarcissus* var. *pseudonarcissus.* A historic form found in South Carolina, Georgia, Florida and Alabama.

N. minor var. *minor.*

N. bicolor var. *bicolor*. Courtesy of Ian Tyler, England.

N. moschatus. Rescued flowers from north Georgia.

N. jonquilla var. *jonquilla.*
Courtesy of Drew McFarland.

N. × *odorus.* The historic Southern form.

N. poeticus. A historic form found in Missouri, Indiana, Ohio, and elsewhere. Courtesy of Drew McFarland.

'Telamonius Plenus.' A well-opened flower from Bartram's Garden. Courtesy of the John Bartram Association, Bartram's Garden, Philadelphia.

'Butter and Eggs'. At Historic Oakland Cemetery, Atlanta.

'Orange Phoenix'.

'Sulphur Phoenix'. At Jones Floral Farm, Calhoun, Georgia.

'Plenus'. Double *N. pseudonarcissus*. Rarely available. Courtesy of Ron Scamp, Quality Daffodils, Cornwall.

'Plenus.' Double *N. poeticus.*
"Albus Plenus Odoratus" form
from the Owings farmstead in
Kentucky. Courtesy of Drew
McFarland.

'Flore Pleno'. Double *N. jonquilla.* Courtesy of Hein Meuusein.

'Plenus'. Double *N.* × *odorus.* At the Ward cut flower field, Atlanta.

N. × *medioluteus.* At Westover, Virginia.

N. bulbocodium subsp. *bulbocodium* var. *conspicuus*. From an old Arkansas garden.
Courtesy of Keith Kridler.

N. × *intermedius*. A common southern form. At Historic Oakland Cemetery, Atlanta.

N. italicus. From a Texas farmstead. Courtesy of Keith Kridler.

'Paper White Grandiflorus'. The common coastal South form.

N. tazetta subsp. *lacticolor.* "Chinese Sacred Lily."

Double *N. tazetta* subsp. *lacticolor.* Double "Chinese Sacred Lily."

Appendix B: Catalogs

These are the autumn bulb catalogs up to 1941 that were relied on in the creation of this work. The year given is for the fall of that year—so a 1924 catalog was issued in the fall of 1924 for the spring 1925 season. Catalogs readily available on the Internet have been included—sources are the Internet Archive (www.archive.org) and Google Books (books.google.com). Catalogs at the Cherokee Garden Library, Kenan Research Center at the Atlanta History Center (Atlanta, Georgia) fall into two primary categories. Those up to 1860 are held in the James R. Cothran Collection of the Cherokee Garden Library and are photocopies Mr. Cothran made of original catalogs held at the National Agricultural Library. Catalogs from 1861 and after are located across a number of collections at the library. Recently, additional catalogs have been made available on the American Daffodil Society website: http://DaffLibrary.org.

Special thanks are due to Scott Kunst (Old House Gardens), Jim Kibler (the Pomaria Collection), Joe Hamm (former Historics Committee chair, American Daffodil Society), and Jason Delaney (curator, Missouri Botanical Garden), who kindly provided photocopies of catalogs from their collections. The remainder is the author's collection, to be donated to the Cherokee Garden Library. In the interest of space, only company, location, and year are provided; botanic gardens referred to in the main text are not included.

1800–1860 Catalogs

A. & F. Starr—Piasa Nursery (Alton, Illinois): 1856–1857, Cherokee Garden Library.

Agricultural Warehouse and New England Seed Store (Boston, Massachusetts): 1836, Cherokee Garden Library.

Arthur Bryant & Son—Persimmon Grove Nursery (Princeton, Illinois): 1858, Cherokee Garden Library.

Bartram's Botanical Garden (Philadelphia, Pennsylvania): 1814, Cherokee Garden Library.

Bernard M'Mahon (Philadelphia, Pennsylvania): pre-1804, Cherokee Garden Library.

David and Cuthbert Landreth (Philadelphia, Pennsylvania): 1824, Cherokee Garden Library, Google Books.

Ellwanger & Barry—Mount Hope Nurseries (Rochester, New York): 1845 & 1846, Cherokee Garden Library; 1846 & 1847, Cherokee Garden Library.

John Bartram & Son (Philadelphia, Pennsylvania): 1807, Cherokee Garden Library.

Michael Floy (New York City): 1816, Cherokee Garden Library.

R. Buist (Philadelphia/Moyamensing, Pennsylvania): 1844–1845, Cherokee Garden Library; 1846, Google Books.

Thomas Learmont (Columbia, South Carolina): 1860, Pomaria Collection.

William Booth (Baltimore, Maryland): 1810, Cherokee Garden Library.

William Prince, Jr. (Flushing, New York): 1822, Google Books.

William R. Prince & Co. (Flushing, New York): 1845, Archive.org; 1846 & 1847, Archive.org, Google Books; 1847, Archive.org; 1860, Cherokee Garden Library.

Catalogs 1861–1941

American

B. K. Bliss & Sons (New York City): 1880.

B. T. Wells (Boston, Massachusetts): 1882.

C. E. Allen (Brattleboro, Vermont): 1890.

Christopher Reuter (New Orleans, Louisiana): 1924.

Commercial Nurseries (Jacksonville, Florida): 1889 (Dorothy Dodd Collection, Florida State Library).

Conley's Blossom Farm (Eugene, Oregon): 1940.

Delkin Bulb Farm (Bellevue, Washington): 1941.

The Dingee & Conard Co. (West Grove, Pennsylvania): 1889, 1906.

D. M. Ferry & Co.: 1879, 1882, 1888, 1895, 1901, 1911, 1914, 1916, 1919, 1933.

F. Lagomarsino & Sons (Sacramento, California): 1944.

Fottler, Fiske, Rawson Co. (Boston, Massachusetts): 1911, 1920.

Frederick. H. Horsford (Charlotte, Vermont): 1923.

Fruitland Nurseries (Augusta, Georgia): 1867, (Hargarett Library, University of Georgia) Cherokee Garden Library.

Gardenville Bulb Growers (Tacoma, Washington): 1938.

George Lawler (Tacoma, Washington): 1931.

George W. Park (Fannettsburg, Pennsylvania): 1887.

Henry A. Dreer (Philadelphia, Pennsylvania): 1870, 1890, 1896, 1904, 1917, 1920, 1924, 1933.

H. G. Hastings & Co. (Atlanta, Georgia): 1901, 1920, 1921, 1923, 1925, 1927, 1934, Cherokee Garden Library.

Holland-American Seed Co. (Grand Rapids, Michigan): 1931.

James M. Thorburn & Co. (New York City): 1882, 1896, 1901, 1909, 1913, 1914.

James Vick (Rochester, New York): 1868, 1869, 1870, 1871, 1872, 1881, 1884, 1904.

J. H. Parsons & Co. (Savannah, Georgia): 1875, Cherokee Garden Library.

John Lewis Childs (Floral Park, New York): 1886, 1891, 1892, 1894, 1897, 1904, 1907, 1915, 1917, 1922.

John Scheepers, Inc. (New York City): 1922, 1925, 1927, 1928, 1929, 1931, Cherokee Garden Library.

Joseph Breck & Sons (Boston, Massachusetts): 1922.

Joseph W. Vestal & Son (Little Rock, Arkansas): 1905, 1922, Cherokee Garden Library.

J. R. McLean (Elma, Washington): 1939.

Peter Henderson & Co. (New York City): 1883, 1888, 1889, 1892, Cherokee Garden Library; 1895, 1899, 1900, 1901, 1904, 1907, 1913, 1914, 1916, 1924.

Phebe J. Marshall (Hibernia, New York): 1901.

R. & J. Farquahar & Co. (Boson, Massachusetts): 1904, 1915.

S. S. Berry (Redlands, California): 1936, 1838, Cherokee Garden Library.

Stassen Floral Gardens, Inc. (Roslyn Heights, Long Island, New York): 1932.

The Storrs and Harrison Co. (Painesville, Ohio): 1903, 1904, 1909, 1914.

Trivett's Tested Seeds, Inc. (New York City): 1937, Cherokee Garden Library.

T. W. Wood & Sons (Richmond, Virginia): 1915, Cherokee Garden Library.

Van Bourgondien Brothers (Babylon, Long Island, New York): 1932, Cherokee Garden Library.

Vaughn's Seed Store (Chicago and New York): 1913, 1916, 1923, 1938.

W. Atlee Burpee Co. (Philadelphia, Pennsylvania): 1925, 1931, 1934, 1936, 1938, 1939, 1941, Cherokee Garden Library.

W. W. Rawson & Co. (Boston, Massachusetts): 1907.

The Wayside Gardens Co. (Mentor, Ohio): 1932, 1933, Cherokee Garden Library; 1937, 1938.

Zandbergen Brothers (Oyster Bay, Long Island, New York): 1929, Cherokee Garden Library.

Z. DeForest Ely & Co. (Philadelphia, Pennsylvania): 1892.

Dutch Catalogs

Anthony C. van der Schoot (Hillegom): 1923.

Anthony Roozen & Son Bulbgrowers (Overveen): 1895, 1904.

E. H. Krelage (& Son) (Haarlem): 1827, Cherokee Garden Library; 1846 (Collection: Antiquariaat FORUM BV 't Goy-Houton, The Netherlands), 1888 (KAVB Library), 1906.

Flora Nurseries (Oegstgeest): 1893.

Groenewegen & Co. (Amsterdam): 1897.

Grube and Nieuwland (New York office): 1872.

Segers & Co./Segers Brothers, Ltd. (Lisse): 1892, (Pomaria Collection), 1931.

British Catalogs

Barr and Sons (Covent Garden—London): 1886, Cherokee Garden Library; 1891, 1893, 1895, 1906, 1907, 1908, Google Books; 1909, 1911, 1912, 1913, 1917, 1918, 1920, 1924, 1926, 1928, 1930, 1934, Cherokee Garden Library.

Charles Turner (Royal Nursery—Slough): 1853.

Conrad Loddiges & Sons (Hackney—London): 1820, Google Books.

James Carter (London): 1842, 1846, 1847, 1852, 1853, 1854, Google Books.

William Baylor Hartland (Cork, Ireland): 1885, 1887, 1897, Cherokee Garden Library.

W. Masters (Canterbury—London): 1831, Google Books.

Notes

Chapter 1—A Brief History of Daffodils in Britain and the Netherlands

1. "Narcissus," 181.

2. This difference in origins is neatly summed up in Carolus Clusius's 1576 work on the plants of the Iberian Peninsula, *Rariorum alioquat stirpium per Hispanius....* Chapter 1 of the second book addresses *Narcissus,* including paperwhites, jonquils, and fall-blooming species (along with bulbs now known not to be *Narcissus*); chapter 2 is a short entry for *N. pseudonarcissus.* In the appendix, however, Clusius discusses tulips, muscari, anemones, and ranunculus he had obtained from Constantinople, reflecting the newly forged trade links between Turkey, Austria, and the Netherlands, just twenty years after Dodoens.

The double tazetta from Constantinople elicited a long explanation from John Gerard in his 1636 herbal: "The double white Daffodill of Constantinople was sent into England unto the right honourable the Lord Treasurer, among other bulbed flowers.... It is called of the Turkes, *Giul Catamer lale,* that is, Narcissus with double flowers" (Gerard, *The Herball* [1597], 111). The Turkish name is interesting as "lâle" is the Turkish word for the tulip. Later Gerard elaborates, "(Giul Catamer lale), which name they generally give unto all double flowers" (Gerard, *The Herball* [1597], 114). Just to keep the name-game going, in his own garden catalog of 1596, Gerard listed this flower as "Narcissus albus Bizantinus multiplex" (Jackson, *A Catalogue of Plants Cultivated in the Garden of John Gerard,* 12), while its Latin name in *The Herball* was "*Narcissus albus Polyanthos*" in the 1597 edition and "*Narcissus albus multiplex*" in the 1633 edition (or the double white daffodil of Constantinople).

Parkinson observed, "This beautifull and goodly Daffodill (wherewith all Florists greatly desire to bee acquainted, as well for the beauty of his double form, as also for his superabounding sweete smell, one stalk with flowers being instead of a nosegay)" (Parkinson, *Paradisi in sole,* 84).

By 1831 a reported French name for tazettas was "le narcisse de Constantinople" (Kent and Hunt, *Flora Domestica,* 265).

3. This new interest may be found in Matthias L'Obel in his *Kruydtboeck* (1581). He discussed numerous *Narcissus* or "Janetten," as he was from the Flemish province of Nord-Pas de Calais, and mentions from where they came, such as the "Narcisse oft Spaesche Jennette geel inde middel" (tazettas with yellow cups) that came to the Netherlands from Languedoc in 1561, the double white narcissus of Constantinople, and jonquils from the Barbary Coast of Africa, the "Geel Narcisse van Afriken." The opposite of Dodoens, who was interested only in the medicinal, L'Obel writes up every different *Narcissus* known, detailing where it grows and who (illustrious folk of the day such as Clusius) said what about it, and providing a woodcut illustration for most. L'Obel illustrated twenty *Narcissus,* compared to Dodoens's mere handful, just twenty-seven years later.

4. This great divide between the truly educated lover of the goddess *Flora* and those interested only in the opulence of novelty lasted into the early 1700s and warranted by van Oosten a chapter entitled "Of the Difference between a true Florist, and an ignorant Pretender" (van Oosten, *The Dutch gardener*, 166–68).

5. Rea, *Flora*, 80.

6. Sweert was in charge of Rudolph II's gardens in Vienna, as well as a bulb merchant. In the 1647 edition, six of its sixty-seven pages of bulbous flowers were devoted to the genus *Narcissus*. Of the twenty-nine *Narcissus* illustrated, nine are trumpets, four poets, nine tazettas, and five doubles, along with a smattering of others. His *Florilegium* eventually went into six editions and is credited with contributing to the delinquency of the Dutch in their tulipmania.

7. van de Passe, *Hortus Floridus*, n.p.

8. Parkinson, *Paradisi in sole*, 67. Daffodil name confusion as an intellectual sport began very early on; Parkinson began his section on the Narcissus thus: "There hath beene great confusion among many of our moderne Writers of plants, in not distinguishing the manifold varities of Daffodils; for every one almost, without consideration of kinde or forme, or other speciall note, giveth names to diversly one from another, that if any one shall receive from severall places the Catalogues of their names (as I have had many) as they set them down, and compare the one Catalogue with the other, he shall scarce have three names in a dozen to agree together, one calling that by one name, with another calleth by another, that very few can tell what they meane" (Parkinson, *Paradisi in sole*, 67). And so it goes . . .

An early and influential nurseryman was Pierre Morin of Paris, renowned for his tulips. Issuing his first catalog in 1651 with his brother, Morin supplied the English gardener John Tradescant for the Cecil garden at Hatfield. Morin's treatise cum catalog, *Remarques Necessaires pour la Culture des Fleurs* (1658) was a gardener's guide and nursery catalog combined. Although *Narcissus* receive no attention in the monthly gardener's almanac, "Narcisses à bouquets du Levant" are mentioned for the garden of the second degree of cold (32); for the earth "graffe et humide" one was to plant "Narcisse blanc double" and "Narcisse iaune double à molette d'éperon" (40). While tazettas from the Levant were to bloom in January and tazettas of various sorts through March and April, "Ionquille simple à grand calice" was to bloom in March, along with the yellow common double, the yellow double of Angleterre (England) and the yellow double of "Tradesque" (Tradescant); lastly was "Trobous d'Espagne, qui est une espece de Ionquille" (58–59). The vulgar yellow double, the Trombon double of England, the white with orange cup, and the double white appeared in April (60). Interestingly all the tazettas are from the Levant, suggesting those of the western Mediterranean were not of much value; and perchance hinting at these sorts' French origins, as the French were notable raisers of tulips at this time.

France as a source of *Narcissus* appears sporadically in the literature. In discussing the double Narcissus from Constantinople, Gerard goes on to explain "Not withstanding we have received from beyond the seas, as well from the lowe Countries, as also from Fraunce, another sort of greater beautie, which from yeere to yeere doth yeeld foorth most pleasant double flowers, and great encrease of rootes, very like as well in stalks as other parts of the plant, unto the other sorts of Daffodils" (Gerard, *The Herball* [1597], 111).

9. J. H. Krelage, "On Polyanthus Narcissus," 341.

10. Johannes Commelin, director of the Amsterdam Physic Garden, issued the *Catalogus Plantarum Horti Medici Amstelodamensis* (1689). As expected, of the thirty-three plants listed under Narcissus, the first sixteen are tazettas, followed by poets, jonquils, and trumpets. He provides the original citations for flowers, such as "Eystet.," Clusius and Parkinson. What is particularly noteworthy for those interested in old names is the listing of each plant's common

name in "Belg." (presumably "Belgian")—"tasset" for many tazettas, "tydeloos" for trumpets and "gemeene" for poets—the same terms used by L'Obel in his *Kruydtboeck*. Many of the tazettas indicate their place of origin in their names—Argiers (Algeria), Africanus, Constantinople, Pisa, Orientalis, and Italicus, reflecting where the original species daffodils were dug. Commelin followed the nomenclature laid out by Caspar Bauhin, the Swiss botanist, in *Pinax Theatri Botanici* (1671), then giving the other reference, then the common name in Belg. Commelin did not follow the arrangement order of Bauhin, thus strongly suggesting the rank of perceived importance of the daffodils in the physic garden—tazettas first, then poets, with jonquils and trumpets following. The use of the term "tasset" seems to confound the source of the word Tazetta being Italian for "small cups."

11. van Oosten, *The Dutch Gardener*, 71–72.

12. Ibid., 75.

13. Ibid., 76. Typically, flowers are presented in order of importance. Van Oosten devotes the first thirty chapters to the Tulip (and later include another treatise on the French method of manuring tulips), chapters 31–33 to Narcissus (tazettas only), chapters 34–37 to Jonquils, chapters 38–43 to Hyacinths, chapters 44–46 to tuberoses, and from thereon flowers warrant one to three chapters from crown imperials and crocus (one) to anemonies and ranunculus (three to four).

This comment regarding the passé status of the "Joncquille," and yet the French being fond of it, is a direct translation of 1703 Dutch edition and brings to mind the great enthusiasm the double jonquil occasioned in the early 1600s for Clusius's nephew.

In the 1711 English edition, van Oosten indicates another word for polyanthus narcissus was "jenet" in English but "jenetten" in the 1703 Dutch edition. The Spanish occupation of the Netherlands evidences in early herbals and botanical works in the citations of the "Spaensche" or Spanish-Dutch term for a given flower. In Lyte's 1578 translation of Dodoens, "jennettekens" was the Spaensche term for "Narcissus." John Gerard in 1597 and 1633 gives "Jennetten" as Spanish for Narcissus. Abraham Munting, in *Waare oeffening der planten, waar in de rechte aart, natuire en verborgene. . . .* (1682), indicates Narcissus in Spanish Dutch is called Jenette. By the *Lexicon Plantarum Polyglotton Universale,* by Christiani Mentzelii, (1715) "Jenetten" is given as "Belgian" for Narcissus. By 1885, "Spanish jenetten" is given as an old folk name in *Flora Batava* (1885).

By 1831 a reported French name for the poet's narcissus was "janette des contois" (Kent and Hunt, *Flora Domestica,* 265).

14. van Oosten, *The Dutch Gardener,* 82.

15. Ibid., 96.

16. Ibid., 161. John Evelyn comments on this difference with the Flemings, stating, "The Holanders, with lesse ceremonie, have (when their *Tulips* are in perfection.) an Annuall *Festivitie,*" simply appointing a single judge for a year (Evelyn, *Elysium Britannicum,* 349).

17. van Kampen, *The Dutch Florist,* 80.

18. *Journal of Horticultural Tour through . . . Flanders,* 182.

19. In 1817, members of the Scottish Caledonian Horticultural Society took a jaunt through the bulb district around Haarlem, Leyden, and so on (a "bloemistry" being a bulb-nursery):

All around the little village of Overveen, the soil is admirably adapted to the raising of bulbous-rooted plants, consisting of a light vegetable mould resting on fine sand; and in this favourable situation, we now found, have been established the most extensive bulb-nurseries. Above a hundred English acres, Mr Eldering thinks, are in this neighbourhood occupied in producing the different kinds of bulbous and tuberous flower-roots. All of these, it is to be understood, require nursing for several successive years, some of them for not less than six or seven, before they become ready for the market. The gardens of the florists on the south side of Haarlem are chiefly for show, and contain only bulbs which have attained maturity, or are in a flowering condition. These florists frequently purchase supplies of bulbs from the growers at Overveen. The most extensive cultivators are Messrs Veen and Co., and Mr Eldering. (*Journal of a Horticultural Tour,* 182)

He Very obligingly offered to walk with us through part of his nursery-grounds; and as he was not only well informed in this branch of Dutch horticulture, but spoke English fluently, we found him, in more respects than one, an interesting acquaintance. He had begun replanting his bulbs about a week before; and we observed that the polyanthus-narcissus is the first committed to the ground. We saw several workmen engaged in this operation. The bulbs are brought to the field in large wheel-barrows. They are planted in beds, between four and five feet broad, and of great length. The surface-soil, to the depth of six or seven inches, is taken oft' the first bed, and removed to the neighbourhood of the last one, in the compartment to be planted. The bulbs being placed in cross rows on the beds, are arranged merely by guess of the eye, and slightly pressed into the soil with the fingers. The surface-earth of the next bed is then thrown as equally as possible over the bulbs;—and this process is repeated, till all the beds be filled. This mode is evidently much superior to planting with any sort of dibble: it is not only much more expeditious, but all risk of leaving hollows below or around the bulbs is effectually avoided. Twelve persons, men and boys, were engaged in planting; and although they have begun thus early, Mr Eldering signified, that he would be glad to find that all his roots were safely lodged in the ground, by the middle, or even the end of November. He has more than twenty English acres occupied with the culture of flower-bulbs of different kinds, in various stages of progress. But it is to be observed, that all these twenty acres are not, at one and the same time, employed in this sort of cultivation. On the contrary, the places in which the finer flowering hyacinths and tulips are planted, are here changed every year; crops of various culinary vegetables being taken for two or three years in succession after the bulbs, and manure (almost always from the cow-house) added, as judged necessary, along with these grosser feeding plants. We noticed rows of very luxuriant pease and beans, now nearly past. It thus happens, that, for every acre of choice bulbs, not fewer than five or six acres of ground must be continually in a state of preparation; and in this way, a very fine, rich, and yet light soil is gradually prepared for receiving the hyacinth and tulip bulbs. The Crocuses, flowering very early, and soon perfecting their new bulbs, a good crop of potatoes is often raised, the same season, on the ground from which they are removed. (Ibid., 183–84)

20. For all the French love of jonquils in the 1600s and 1700s, by the late 1800s things were very different.

A propos of the essentially English associations of the daffodil, I have been told by Mons. H. L. de Vilmorin, of the great French firm of seedsmen and florists, that the venture of growing it on a large scale for the Paris market failed entirely. The more fanciful and fickle Parisian tires of a continuance of one flower, liking here a bit of white lilac, there a spray of mimosa or a bunch of Riviera anemones, but only now and then a daffodil. In France, too, there has never prevailed, as in England, what may be termed *intensive* gardening, the loving and exhaustive study of some one particular flower in all its phases and potentialities. The sight is inconceivable in France, which may be witnessed any April at a Royal Horticultural Society's gathering, of four men standing rapt and abstracted, their heads in close contact over a match-box containing a single "pip" or floweret of a new auricular seedling. (Engleheart, "The Daffodil in Cornwall," 328–29)

21. Rev. Joseph Jacobs remarked in 1910, "Old Dutchmen have told me they can very well remember the time when no one thought of growing any Narcissi or Daffodils but these [Polyanthus types] except on the very smallest scale, for there was no sale for them. How different it must have been from the sight I saw this spring at Messrs. Van der Schoot & Son's bulb fields at katwijk, where there were more Sir Waktins than I thought were to be found in the world!" (Jacob, *Daffodils,* 14). A delightful period book on the Dutch bulb world through British eyes may be found in *Dutch Bulbs and Gardens* (1909) by Una Silberrad and Sophie Lyall, with paintings by Mima Nixon.

22. Robert Sydenham attributed the lack of Dutch hybridizing in flowers other than trumpets to their soils, "as their soil seems to light to produce colour and substance" (Sydenham, *All about Daffodils and Narcissi,* 23). After commenting how a number of English trumpets were still priced very dear after years on the market, he commented about the Dutch approach: "At Hillegom, in Holland, I saw in 1896, the finest Trumpet Narcissus I had ever seen, it measured six inches across the perianth, which was of grand form and substance, each segment being about two inches broad; the trumpet, which was deep *yellow,* and perfect in form, was fully two and a half inches across the mouth; this variety had nine blooms in 1897, and twenty blooms in 1898, over thirty bulbs and blooms in 1899, and 69 blooms in 1900. The raiser put it on the market as *Waveren's Giant,* at £10 each, but now bulbs may be had at about 5/- each" (ibid., 23). In Peter Barr's 1906 Barr's Gold Medal Daffodils catalog, 'Van Waveren's Giant' listed at £7 7s. Registered as 'Van Waveren's Giant,' this flower went on to be a stalwart in American catalogs in the 1910s and 1920s (first appearing in Peter Henderson & Co.'s specialty catalog around 1913), even grown in American fields during the narcissus embargo of 1926–1938. This also demonstrates the length of time it took from the first appearance of a flower to make it to the commercial market.

23. Esther Singleton provides a translation from the Latin:

A garden should be adorned on this side with roses, lilies, the marigold, molis and mandrakes; on that side with parsley, cort, fennel, southernwood, coriander, sage, savory, hyssop, mint, rue, dittany, smallage, pellitory, lettuce, cresses, ortulano, and the peony. Let there also be beds enriched with onions, leeks, garlic, melons, and scallions. The garden is also enriched by the cucumber, which creeps on its belly, and by the soporiferous poppy, as well as by the daffodil and the acanthus. Nor let pot-herbs be wanting, if you can help it, such as beets, herb mercury, orache, and the mallow. It is useful also to the gardener to have anise, mustard, white pepper, and wormwood. (Singleton, *The Shakespeare Garden,* 7)

The Latin:

Cap. CLXVI.
   De herbis et arboribus et floribus horto crescentibus.
   Hortus ornari debet hinc rosis et liliis, solsequio, violis, et mandragoris, inde petrosilino, et costo, et maratro, et abrotano, et coriandro, salvia, et satureia, hysopo, menta domestica, ruta, ditanno, apio, piritro, lactuca, nasturtio hortolano, pionia. Fiunt et areae ditatae cepulis, porris, alliis, peponibus, ahinnulis. Nobilitant etiam hortum hinc in ventrem crescens cucumis, et stuporiferum papaver, inde narcissus et acanthus.
   Nec tibi desunt olera, si suppetit tibi facultas, betae, mercurialis, atriplicis, et acedularum, et malvae.
   Anisum, et sinapis, et piper album, et absinthium, nonnullam hortolano conferunt utilitatem. (Neckam, *De Naturis Rerum,* 274)

24. Early garden expert John H. Harvey, in "The First English Garden Book," posits the true author likely was a leading master gardener of the time, with connection to either the palace at Westminster or Windsor Castle during the reign of Edward III, and suggests the most likely person to be John de Standerwy of London (d. 1345), who knew John de Wyndesores of Windsor Castle (master gardener from 1336 to around 1350).

25. Dodoens, *A nievve herball . . . Lyte,* 210.

26. Ibid., 212.

27. Ibid., 214. At this time, "jonquils" were still spelled in deference to their Spanish origin— "iunquillias" ("as the Spaniardes call it"), the "j" appearing somewhat later. He further gives the common names for *N. pseudonarcissus* of "yellow crow bels" in English and "conquelourde" in French (Dodoens/Lyte, *A niewe herbal,* 214).

28. Fitter, *London's Natural History,* 98. Clusius reiterates this in 1601, observing N. Pseudo-narcissus "tanta abundátia in pratis, Londino satis vicinis, crescera certú est, ut in celebri illo vico vulgo *Ceapside* nuncupato Martio mése rusticæ mulieres maximâ copiâ flores venales proponent, & omnes tabernæ eo flore exornatæ conspiciantur" (Clusius, *Rariorum plantarum historia,* 164).

29. Gerard, *The Herball* [1597], 109.

30. Ibid., 115.

31. Ibid., 115.

32. Ibid., 114.

33. Ibid., 115.

34. Gerard's Double Daffodil is *N. pseudonarcissus* 'Plenus,' also called the "English double daffodil." William Cecil, a.k.a. Lord Burghley (1520–1598), employed John Gerard to supervise his gardens in London around 1577–1578. Lord Burghley was the chief advisor to Queen Elizabeth during most of her reign and served as secretary of state (twice) and Lord High Treasurer.

35. By 1896 garden historian Alicia M. T. Amherst observed: "Bulb culture is a favourite pursuit in the manufacturing districts of north-west England. It is thought the taste was carried thither by the Flemish weavers, who in earlier times brought the love of these plants with them from the Low Countries, when they first settled in East Anglia, Essex and Kent" (Amherst, *A History of Gardening in England,* 331).

36. Lawson, *A new orchard,* 88.

37. Ibid., 90.

38. Gerard gives the English names for daffodil as "Daffodilly, Daffodowndilly, and Primrose peerelesse" (Gerard, *The Herball* [1597], 114). None of these names appear in Henry Lyte's translation of Dodoens.

39. Parkinson, *Paradisi in sole,* 100.

40. Ibid., 103.

41. Rea, *Flora* [1665], 9.

42. Ibid., 73.

43. Ibid., 83.

44. John Evelyn (1620–1706) was a founding member of the Royal Society, a bibliophile, a noted diarist, wrote the first work on London's growing smog problem, as well as on trees and horticulture, translated numerous varied works from French, and was an all-round renaissance man.

45. Hanmer, Lord John, *A memorial,* 133. Rea, *Flora* [1665], 2.

46. Hanmer, Lord John, *A memorial,* 138–39.

47. Ibid., 140.

48. Ibid., 141.

49. Basilius Besler included 'Narciss de Argiers' (Narcissus of Algeria) in Plate 63, plant II, in his *Hortus Eystettensis* in 1613, which some believe to be *N. aureus.*

John Evelyn, in his unpublished manuscript *Elysium Britannicum, or The Royal Gardens* (1650s–1660s), devoted a chapter to imparting cultivation knowledge of all important garden flowers. As Eveyln modified and expanded his original manuscript he inserted numerous references to see notes from Sir Hanmer on specific flowers, including tulips, hyacinths, iris, anemones, and daffodils, reflecting Hanmer's status in the gardening world and Evelyn's respect for his knowledge. Under the entry for Narcissus, Evelyn stated there were sixty kinds, and like Hanmer included the Virginian, Indian, and Sea daffodils. In a nod to the herbals, Evelyn noted that water distilled from the Narcissus may be used "against *Epilepsia* by washing the head therewith; but the chemicall Oyle is much superior to it"; and that jonquils "yielding a rare essence for the Ladies" (*Elysium Britannicum, or The Royal Gardens,* 372).

50. Aubrey, *The Natural History of Wiltshire,* 112.

51. Harvey, "The English Nursery Flora," 89.

52. Philip Miller, *The Gardeners Dictionary* [1733], Crocus.

53. Woolridge, *Systema horti-culturae,* 98–99.

54. Bradley, *New improvements in planting and gardening,* 121.

55. Liger, *The Compleat Florist,* 211.

56. Ibid., 293.

57. Philip Miller, *The Gardeners and Florists Dictionary,* 156.

58. Philip Miller, *The Gardeners Dictionary* [1754], Narcissus. In the 1768 edition, Miller changes his terminology from "agreeable prospect" to a "good appearance" before the trees come out in leaf. (Miller, *The Gardeners Dictionary* [1768], Narcissus.)

59. Miller's list:

These have yellow petals and Orange, yellow or sulphur-coloured cups or nectariums.

The Great Algiers	The Most Beautiful
The Ladies Nosegay	The Golden Star
The Greater Bell	The Mignon
The Golden Royal	The Zeylander
The Golden Scepter	The Madouse
The Triumphant	The Golden Sun

The following have white petals, with yellow or sulphur-coloured cups or nectariums.

The Archdutchess	The Greater Bozelman
The Triumphant Nosegay	The Czarina
The New Dorothy	The Grand Monarque
The Passe Bozelman	The Czar of Muscovy
The Superb	The Surpassante (Miller, *The Gardeners Dictionary* [1768], Narcissus)

60. Miller, *The Gardeners Dictionary* [1768], Narcissus.

61. Burchell, *A Catalogue of Trees, Shrubs, and Plants,* 55.

62. "The English Florist," 346.

63. Ibid., 347.

64. Ibid., 233–34.

65. Ibid., 68. This is very similar to the recommendations of *Every man his own gardener* (1767) by Thomas Mawe and John Ambercrombie. Choice sorts were to be planted in narrow beds, all of a kind, to facilitate care against inclement weather, as well as to show best sorts to advantage; for commoner sorts, they recommended planting in the border in well-spaced clumps, each a circle of five or six roots, one in the center the rest around the edge.

66. The prices for these vary from 2 pence (2*d.*) to 1*s*. 8*d.* (1 shilling 8 pence) for the bicolors 'Primo Calliard' and 'Reine de Perou,' followed by the yellow 'Lion of Orange' at 1*s*. 6*d.* The three all-white varieties, 'Primo Geerens,' 'Souvereign,' and 'White Queen,' were cheap at 3*d* and 4*d*. At the cheapest end of the scale were at 2 pence were two yellows still grown today—the "Etoile d'Or" (*N.* × *intermedius*) and 'Soleil d'Or.' In comparison, anemones somewhat comparably priced, same with crocus. Hyacinths, which had their own "mania" in the early 1730s, were the most pricey, ranging from a few pence up to 1, 2 and 3 pounds. Tulips vary widely by type and color, from a few pence to up to a pound or so. In modern currency, 12 pence = 1 shilling, 20 shillings = 1 pound; 1 pence = 83¢, 1 shilling = $10.00; 1£ = $2.00.

None of the varietal names in Weston's catalogue are the same as those given by Sir Hanmer in either his preface or his Garden Book, but there is similarity between Miller's anglicized names of 1768 and the French names listed by Weston. However, Miller lists "The Great Algiers," while Hanmer in his Garden Book lists "The Great Yellow Narcissus of Argiers or of Africke," and the "great white Argiers" and "yellow Argiers narcissus" growing in his garden.

67. H., "Eighteenth Century Gardening," 129.

68. Miller, *The Gardeners Dictionary* [1754], Narcissus.

69. "Narcissus Biflorus. Two-Flower'd Narcissus," in Curtis, *The botanical magazine*, Plate 197.

70. "Narcissus Odorus. Sweet-Scented, Great Jonquil," in Curtis, *The botanical magazine*, Plate 78.

71. "Narcissus Incomparabilis. Peerless Daffodil," in Curtis, *The botanical magazine*, Plate 121.

72. "Narcissus Major. Great Daffodil," in Curtis, *The botanical magazine*, Plate 51.

73. "Narcissus Tenuior. Slender Narcissus," in Curtis, *The botanical magazine*, Plate 379.

74. "Narcissus Triandrus. Reflexed Daffodil," in Curtis, *The botanical magazine*, Plate 48.

75. Sowerby "Narcissus Pseudo-narcissus. *Common Daffodil*," English Botany, Plate 17.

76. "Narcissus Bulbocodium. Hoop Petticoat Narcissus," in Curtis, *The botanical magazine*, Plate 88. In 1841, Mrs. Loudon commented *N. bulbocodium* "is so common in gardens as scarcely to need description.... The exact year of its introduction is not known, but it was before 1620, and after 1597, as it is not mentioned by Gerard" (Mrs. Loudon, *The Ladies' Flower-Garden*, 169–70).

77. Herbert, "Hybrid Narcissi," Plate 38.

78. Per Peter Barr about Leeds's first published hybrids, "Nothing was made public as to the new seedlings Leeds raised until in Moore and Ayre's *Gardener's Magazine of Botany* (1850–1851) six varieties were figured, namely, one Leedsii, three Incomparabiilis, a yellow Trumpet, called Major Superbus, and a large handsome bicolor trumpet called Bicolor Grandis. Of these, only the last named is still in cultivation" (Peter R. Barr, "The Renaissance of the Daffodil in Britain," 23–24).

79. Barr, "The Renaissance of the Daffodil in Britain," 23.

80. "Plate 58. Narcissus Tazetta-Luna."

81. Barr, "The Renaissance of the Daffodil in Britain," 25.

82. Barr's exposure to and interest in daffodils may have been piqued by the influx of daffodils, particularly tazettas, into the Covent Garden cut flower market around 1865. The first lot of cut flowers was shipped from the Scilly Isles and realized about one pound;

> the trade grew gradually until 1885, when about 65 tons of cut flowers were dispatched to the principal towns in England and Scotland; in 1887 this trade increased to 100 tons; in 1890 it had increased to nearly 250 tons, and the trade has developed considerably each year since, and it is calculated that in the season the enormous quantity of 5,000 to 6,000 boxes are often sent away in one day. Mr. T. A. Dorrien Smith, the proprietor of these islands, told me that he alone sent about 12,000 boxes to England every season, each box averaging 500 blooms, or some 6,000,000 flowers in all: but this is already much exceeded by some of the Lincolnshire growers, as mentioned above. In the Spring of 1913, one firm in Lincolnshire reported shipping 35,000 boxes of cut flowers, or nearly 20 million flowers. (Sydenham, *All About Daffodils and Narcissi*, 12–13)

T. A. Dorrien Smith is credited with the introduction of the robust tazetta 'Avalanche'.

83. Burbidge, *The narcissus: its history and culture*, 2.

84. Kirby, *Daffodils*, 158.

85. Ibid., 99.

86. Only nine hybridizers were acknowledged by the Conference Committee to have raised "New Daffodils": William Backhouse, Peter Barr, S. A. de Graaff, Dr. Horsfield, Edward Leeds, Rev. John G. Nelson, (?) Pickstone, Max Leichtlin (Germany), and Rev. A. Rawson, with nearly all coming from the late William Backhouse of Weardale and the late Edward Leeds of Longford Bridge.

Barr's seminal *Ye narcissus or daffodyl flowere: containing hys historie and culture, &c., with a compleat liste of all the species and varieties known to Englyshe amateurs* (1884) combines his talk at the RHS meeting with an annotated version of his catalog. Barr found he had so many seedlings (reportedly 360 varieties) he had named that he needed a system to classify them with. He enlisted the assistance of J. G. Baker for the catalog; flowers are grouped by long, medium, and short coronas, with doubles in their own class. With species are listed hundreds of hybrid cultivars from Leeds and Backhouse, the hybridizer denoted by an "L" or "B" respectively (only a handful are not attributed to either man). The fluidity of cultivars warranting separate names, or similar seedlings being split apart or lumped together, is evidenced in Barr's catalogs. A copy of his 1884 book in the RHS collection appears to be annotated in Barr's own hand, indicating select cultivars "absorbed into" another named variety. Most of the "absorbed" names are then absent from Barr's following catalog.

87. William Baylor Hartland, *Hartland's Original Little Book of Daffodils*, n.p.

88. Peter Barr, "Early Days of the Daffodil" [June 2, 1906], 297.

89. Kirby, *Daffodils*, 9–10.

90. Engleheart, "Seedling Daffodils," 93.

Chapter 2: Daffodils in Early America, 1735 to 1820

1. Gerard, *The herball* [1636], 132.

2. Parkinson, *Paradisi in sole*, 108.

3. Ashe, *Carolina*, 10.

4. Sarudy, *Gardens and Gardening in the Chesapeake*, 66.

5. Earle, *Old Time Gardens*, 21.

6. Brickell, *The Natural History of North Carolina*, 22.

7. Ibid., 24.

8. Berkeley and Berkeley, eds., *The Correspondence of John Bartram*, 59.

9. Ibid., 126.

10. Collinson's favorites were polyanthus narcissus. On March 16, 1767, Collinson wrote to Carl Linneaus: "The 16th March, plenty of Hyacinthus, Coeruleus et albis in the open Borders & Anemonies & now my Favourites, the Great Tribe of Narcissus & Polyanthos Shew all over the Garden & Fields. Wee have Two Species Wild in the Woods that now begin to Flower. Next the Tulipa precox are Near Flowering, & so Flora Decks the Garden with Endless Variety (Ever Charming)" (Collinson, *Forget not mee & my garden,* 272). Collinson's letters also discuss Narciss of Naples (*N. papyraceus? N. italicus?* 'Romanus'?) and China Narciss (N. orientalis?). Are these some of the rare ones he wouldn't share? And what would the wild daffodils be? *N. pseudonarcissus* and *N. × medioluteus* ("Primrose Peerless") were thought to be wild, the former by Sowerby, the latter by Gerard and Parkinson.

The issue of names is confounded by that everyone operated by common names, and many plants were poached from the wild, so with variations in species populations from location to location, what was being dug and sold could quite easily not be the same exact species strain from year to year.

11. Berkeley and Berkeley, eds., *The Correspondence of John Bartram*, 126.

12. Ibid., 155–56.

13. Moly major, flore purpureo was listed with other Molys (Alliums) as a June bloomer in *Traité des Fleurs et Oignons* by the Harlem florist Nicolas van Kampen in 1760. An interpretation of "Geele Franse Roos" is "yellow French Rose" narcissus, which could be either "Robinus His Daffodil" ('Eystettensis') or "The Great Double French Daffodil" a.k.a. "Gallicus Major Flore Pleno." The "campanelle" is possibly *N. triandrus,* which has both yellow and white strains.

14. Collinson, *Forget not Mee,* 156–57.

15. If "guise," interpreted as "gause" in the transcription by Emma B. Richardson, is a term related to white tissue, it is tempting to speculate she was requesting paperwhites. Fifty years later, Louis LeConte grew two strains of the species paperwhite *N. papyraceus,* and paperwhites have been part of the coastal Southern garden repertoire ever since.

16. Berkeley and Berkeley, eds., *The Correspondence of John Bartram*, 523.

17. Ibid., 500.

18. Ibid., 506.

19. Ibid., 522.

20. Ibid., 508.

21. Ibid., 523.

22. Salisbury, Richard, "On the Cultivation of Rare Plants," 353.

23. Ibid., 349.

24. Ibid., 359–60.

25. Berkeley and Berkeley, eds., *The Correspondence of John Bartram*, 602.

26. Ibid., 611.

27. Ibid., 619.

28. Hanmer, *The Garden Book,* 26.

29. Many pre-1700s English colonists came from near the southern and western British port towns of London, Bristol, and Liverpool. Also, the earliest immigrants to the Philadelphia area were actually the Germans who founded Germantown in 1683, home of Dr. Witt, so the flower may conceivably have German origins.

The Royal Horticultural Society's date of introduction/registration for "Albus Plenus Odoratus" ('Plenus') is pre-1861; however, there are questions as to what strain was running around when, or what double of which species poet. Recently two different strains have been recognized—'Tamar Double White'(back dated to 1880) and 'Spalding Double White'. Interestingly, the *Lady's Magazine* in 1787 listed three doubled varieties for "The Poet's Daffodil, or Common White Narcissus"—semi double-flowered, full double-flowered, and double purple-cupped ("The English Florist," 345). Philip Miller in *The Gardeners Dictionary* 1735 and 1754 editions recognized only one "double white daffodil, or *Narcissus.*" Granted the *Lady's Magazine* is not now a known authority, but it does reflect what was an opinion at the time.

30. Berkeley and Berkeley, eds., *The Correspondence of John Bartram,* 517.

31. Ibid., 594.

32. The common Double Daffodil of gardens and orchards, in many sequestered parts of the country, is a much larger plant, with deep green leaves, and the great rose-like flowers are of a much deeper golden yellow colour. This is a double form of Haworth's N. Telemonius, and well deserves culture as one of the most effective of the monstrous kinds. This is the plant alluded to by Parkinson at p. 102 of his before mentioned work (*Paradisi in sole*), as Pseudo-Narcissus aureus Anglicus maximus, or Mr. Wilmer's Great Double Daffodil, who adds that himself and "Mr. Wilmer, of Stratford, Bowe, Esq." received it from "Vincent Sion, borne in Flanders, dwelling on the bank's side in his lives time, but now dead; an industrious and worthy lover of faire flowers"(Burbidge, *The Narcissus,* 28). Sir John Hanmer begins his section on Narcissus: "OF DOWBLE NARCISSUS *with* ONLY ONE FLOWER *on a* STALKE, there are *Tradescant,* the greatest dowble Narcissus wee have, of a good yellow color, grows very thicke of leaves, and round like a rose; *Willmers,* or the common dowble yellow, like the former, but not soe round and large" (Hanmer, *The Garden Book,* 26).

33. Stetson, "John Mercer's Notes on Plants," 44.

34. In 2010 the last week of April saw much *N.* × *medioluteus* from the Tidewater to the Northern Neck and the foothills, but all the poets were long-finished blooming.

35. Frankland, *Diary,* n.p.

36. The early American nurseryman Grant Thorburn recounted his fateful decision to sell pots for indoor plants in his grocery store window in 1802, which set him on his singular path of plantsman:

About this time the ladies in New York were beginning to show their taste for flowers; and it was customary to sell the empty flower-pots in the grocery stores; these articles also comprised part of my stock....

In the fall of the year, when the plants wanted shifting, preparatory to their being placed in the parlor, I was often asked for pots of a handsomer quality, or better make. As I stated above, I was looking round for some other means to support my family. All at once it came into my mind to take and paint some of my common flower-pots with green varnish paint, thinking it would better suit the taste of the ladies than the common brick-bat colored ones. I painted two pair, and exposed them in front of my window. I remember, just as I had placed the two pair of pots in front of my window on the outside, I was standing on the sidewalk, admiring their appearance, a carriage came along, having the glasses let down, and one lady only in the carriage. As the carriage passed my shop, her eye lit on the pots; she put her head out at the window, and looked back, as far as she could see, on the pots. Thinks I, this will take; and it did take—for these two pots were the links of a chain by means of which Providence was leading me into my extensive seed establishment. They soon drew attention, and were sold. I painted six pair; they soon went the same way. Being thus encouraged, I continued painting and selling to good advantage: this was in the fall of 1802. (Thorburn, *Fifty Years' Reminiscences,* 61).

37. Emmett, "Kirk Boott and the Greening of Boston," 27–28.

38. Rafinesque, "A Journal of the Progress of Vegetation," 79.

39. Salisbury, "On the Culture of Rare Plants," 364.

40. Frankland, *Diary,* n.p.

41. Ibid., n.p.

42. Burke, "Garden Adventures," 395.

43. Frankland, *Diary,* n.p. The region around Caen, France, appears to have been a center of daffodil growing in the 1700s. Raoul A. Fréard du Castel in 1767 commented regarding double jonquils, "Quand ils sont ronds ils portent bien plus de Fleurs: on en éléve beaucoup à Bayeux. Les Marchands de Caen les y viennent chercher pour les vendre à Paris" (Fréard du Castel, *L' École du Jardinier Fleuriste,* 13). (Bayeux is 30km northwest of Caen.) Castel discusses only three tazettas—the yellow/golden yellow "Le Narcisse d' Alger a Bouquet Jaune," a white and citron bicolor "Le Narcisse de Constantinople a Bouquet Blanc," and the double "Le Narcisse de Constantinople Double" (ibid., 13). Thus Frankland getting his tazettas from Caen means only he was buying tazettas from Caen, and not necessarily a specific species or hybrid variety.

44. Schöpf's biased preference for European flowers surfaces in his description of Charleston in early 1784:

During these cold days of January and February, in the neighborhood of Charleston not an indigenous plant was to be seen in bloom; for in this climate spring does not really come before the middle of March or the beginning of April. But in sundry gardens the following European plants might be found greening and blooming:—*Alsine media*—Lamium *amplexicaule,*—*Leontodon Taraxacum,*—*Rumex crispus & Acetosa,*—*Poa annua,*—*Vitica dioica* and *Sonchus arvensis.* Of garden-flowers there were blooming at this time narcissuses and jonquils. Also the orange-trees, which are everywhere in the houses and in the open in gardens, seemed to be standing the severe weather pretty well; they were full of fruit and burgeons. But often they are frozen, and this is not seldom the case even to the south, at Pensacola in Florida. (Schöpf, *Travels in the Confederation, 1783–1784: Pennsylvania,* 171).

Given the time of bloom, these "narcissus" are tazettas.

45. Schöpf, *Travels in the Confederation. . . New Jersey . . . ,* 93.

46. Ibid., 95.

47. John Faris, *Old Gardens in and about Philadelphia,* 155.

48. Burbidge, "Double Daffodils and Narcissi," 297.

49. "Henry Middleton," 76.

50. Edwards, *The New Flora Britannica,* 316.

51. Richardson, *The Heyward-Washington House,* 12.

52. Briggs, *Charleston Gardens,* 20.

53. White, *Vanishing Gardens,* 165.

54. Wright, *Colonial Garden at Stenton,* n.p.

55. Laurens, *The Papers of Henry Laurens,* 458–59.

56. This business practice held well into the early 1800s. From the Scottish horticulturalists on their trip through the Netherlands comes this passing comment: "Before bidding adieu

to the bloemistries, we may mention, that the principal florists commonly unite in publishing yearly a general catalogue of their bulbous and tuberous rooted flowers. This is entitled, 'Groote Hollandsche Catalogus van de aller voortreffelljkste Bol-Bloemen.' Hyacinths take the lead, and are followed by Tulips, Ranunculuses, Anemones, and Polyanthus-Narcissus" (*Journal of a Horticultural Tour*, 196).

57. Berkeley and Berkeley, eds., *The Correspondence of John Bartram,* 509.

58. Miller, *The Gardeners and Florists Dictionary,* Narcissus's. Liger is more detailed, indicating that mixing ones bulbs (albeit planted in lines) in parterre or in beds will ensure the garden is adorned with flowers for several months.

59. Miller, *The Gardeners Dictionary* [1754], Narcissus.

60. Berkeley and Berkeley, eds., *The Correspondence of John Bartram,* 376.

61. Ibid., 440.

62. On February 16, 1761, Thomas Lamboll of Charleston wrote to John Bartram, detailing how his wife (the noted gardener Mrs. Lamboll) prepared her raised beds for Dutch bulbs:

> The manner Mrs. Lamboll manages her Ranunculas & Anemonies every Year, is thus: She prepares Beds of good Rich Mould at least Two Months before she takes up the Flower Roots; that the Earth may be well settled by Rain. Wherever the Ground is low, she raised the Flower Beds, at lest half a foot in heighth, and where high flattens them. In Summer time, the leaves of the Flower Roots being thoroughly dry, immediately after a Shower of Rain happens, she takes up the said Roots, divides & cleanses them (but not by washing) from Insects, then makes slight holes with the Fingers on the Tops of the prepared Beds, places the Roots about four inches asunder and covers them over with Dirt, Scrap'd from the paths, about half an Inch deep; strewing it over with the Fingers. And if the Rain fails she afterwards causes the Beds of the Flower Roots to be Watered gently, such Water having first stood a Convenient time in the Sun. In Cold Weather she causes the Flower Beds to be Cover'd and Shelter'd; especially when they have begun to Sprout.
>
> I have at length Got a Box of Earth, containing the under mentioned Roots, Plants and Herbs vizt. A small Root Winter Savory: a Root Winter Sweet Marjoram; a Root blew Flagg, two Roots white Iris; two Roots Grape Hyacinths, a few Roots Early white Spanish Hyacints; a Root of white Feather'd Hyacinths; a Root of Starry Hyacints; a few Plants of Water Oak; a few Ditto live-Oak; two Plants white Broom; two Ditto Oleander; Six Roots Narcissus, wch you call Pancratium, and a few Plants of Great Garden Cresses; for as to Seed we were prevented from Saving any last summer. (Berkeley and Berkeley, eds., *The Correspondence of John Bartram,* 492)

63. M'Mahon, *The American Gardener's Calendar,* 71–72.

64. Cothran, *Gardens of Historic Charleston,* 17.

65. As regards Dutch florists' bulbs, Annapolis innkeeper and nurseryman William Faris of Annapolis sold tulips and hyacinths from his own garden from 1792 to 1801; one of Faris's great joys was hybridizing his own tulips. Henri Stier also sold tulips and other bulbs out of his garden. The men would open their gardens during the blooming season, and visiting customers would mark their selections with a stick for summer lifting. Stier had fled Antwerp to end up near Annapolis in 1794, where he remained until 1803. Upon leaving Annapolis, Stier sold his Dutch bulb stock; when back home, he ordered and shipped bulbs to his former neighbors.

66. The rise of the American seed merchant coincides with the rise of the U.S. Postal Service. You cannot order and receive, or base a business on getting product to far-flung customers,

without reliable shipping. In 1775 Postmaster Benjamin Franklin established a mail route from Boston to Savannah; in the same year, biweekly mail service was established between New York City and Boston.

67. In 1790 the florists John Chalvin & Co., Florists and Gardeners of France, placed an advertisement in the Charleston paper *South Carolina Gazette* announcing their arrival from France bearing flowering trees, lily roots, hyacinths, crows feet, roses and herb seeds. Le Rougetel, *A Heritage of Roses*, 21.

68. Lockwood et al., *Gardens of Colony and State*, 12.

69. Hedrick, *A History of Horticulture in America*, 165–66.

70. Richard Stockton is cited as writing in 1766 from England to his wife at their beautiful home Morven, in Princeton, New Jersey: "I am making you a charming collection of bulbous roots, which shall be sent over as soon as the prospect of freezing on your coast is over. The first of April, I believe, will be time enough for you to put them in your sweet little flower garden, which you so fondly cultivate" (Earle, *Old Gardens Newly Set Forth*, 30).

71. "Minton Collins," 52.

72. John Bartram & Son, *Catalogue of trees*, 32.

73. "William Booth," 141.

74. Ramsey, *The History of South Carolina*, 348.

75. Susanin, *Grumblethorpe*, 40–41.

76. "The Garden Notes . . . Part II," 10.

77. Faris, *The Diary of William Faris*, 182.

78. Ibid., 311.

79. Ibid., 298.

80. "Fross Nercess" present a true mystery. No word even close to "Fross" appears in the 1797 edition of Samuel Johnson's *A Dictionary of the English Language*. As Faris got the bulbs from a Belgian, then possibly with his phonetic spelling the word he was trying to spell was either Dutch, French, or Belgian. A contender comes from Nicolas van Kampen's *Traité des Fleurs et Oignons* (1760). The entry for "Les Narcisses en Bouquet" gives "tros narcissen" in the alternate nomenclature. A long-standing term in Dutch (and probably Spaensch) for tazettas, it translates to "spray narcissus."

81. Letzer and Russo, eds., *The Diary of William Faris*, 285.

82. Faris's garden flowers included tuberoses, white roses, India pinks, Chinese asters, tulips, hyacinths, and jonquils for the necessary path beds; main walk beds—tuberoses, tulips, anemones, Chinese asters, crown imperials, globe amaranthus, and larkspur. A third bed—Job's tears, satin flowers, India pinks, snapdragons, tulips, and flowering beans. Quartered circle bed— polyanthus, tuberoses, wall flowers, India pinks, Chinese asters, hyacinths, jonquils, and tulips.

83. Betts, *Thomas Jefferson's Garden Book*, 4.

84. Ibid., 94.

85. Ibid., 562.

86. Sale et al., *Historic Gardens of Virginia*, 281.

87. Hatch, "Restoring the Monticello Landscape," 6.

88. "I wish we had more detail on the bulbs that appeared in the early 20th century. We now have a lot of the tasseled hyacinth and the species Florentine tulip, *T. sylvestris*, naturalized in quantities. Plus, lots of crocus. Maybe some Narcissus in other nearby parts of the property. The star of Bethlehem is still around as well. But that's it. Henry Mitchell used to say there were naturalized colonies of the lady tulip, *T. clusiana*, but I haven't seen them." Peter Hatch, personal correspondence, 2010.

89. Charleston Botanic Society and Garden, *Catalogue of Plants*, n.p.

90. Ibid., 7.

91. Ibid., 9.

92. Ibid., 12.

93. Per Burbidge,

The true double-flowered N. PseudoNarcissus has been lost to cultivators for years, and was only reintroduced to our collections by Mr. P. Barr, who obtained a few bulbs from the Isle of Wight in the spring of 1874. This is the Pseudo-Narcissus Anglicus flore-pleno of Parkinson's "Paradisus," p. 103, n. 5, who says it "is assuredly first naturell of our own country, for Mr. Gerard first discovered it to the world, finding it in a poor woman's garden in the west parts of England, where it grew before the woman came to dwell there, and as I have heard since is naturell of the Isle of Wight." M. Henri Lecoq has some interesting notes on this plant in his "De la Fecondation et del'Hybridation," and at page 383 of this interesting work it is stated, that the normal form of N. PseudoNarcissus is "less often seen in the environs of Grasse and in the larger portion of Provence than the double-flowered form," and this is also the case in other continental localities. (Burbidge, *The narcissus,* 26–27)

Also, per Rev. S. E. Bourne, "Gerard's Double Daffodil" is *N. pseudonarcissus* 'Plenus'.

94. Stritikus, "An Early (1813–1815) List," 4–5.

95. Gordon, "Notices of some of the principal Nurseries and Private Gardens," 287.

96. Anderson, *LeConte,* 883.

97. Ibid., 892.

98. Holmes, *The Annals of America,* 522. Abiel was father of Oliver Wendell Holmes Sr., and grandfather of the Supreme Court justice.

99. Christian Gottlieb Reuter was assigned as surveyor of the Wachovia tract in North Carolina, settled 1753. Reuter noted daffodils in 1759 and 1760, and specifically yellow daffodils in his 1764 survey. Further, he commented there were no white daffodils in the garden in 1760—so were their white daffodils elsewhere about Bethabara?

100. "Narcissus Orientalis. Cream-coloured Narcissus of the Levant," in Curtis, *The botanical magazine,* Plate 948.

Chapter 3: Daffodils in America, 1820 to 1860

1. Fraser, "Gardening," 179.

2. This English taste for the bold and showy was detailed by Andrew J. Downing in his influential 1844 landscape treatise:

In the English flower garden, the beds are either in symmetrical forms and figures, or they are characterized by the irregular curved outlines. The peculiarities of these gardens, at present so fashionable in England, is, that each separate bed is planted with a single variety, or at most two varieties of flowers. Only the most striking and showy varieties are generally chosen, and the effect, when the selection is judicious, is highly brilliant. Each bed, in its season, presents a mass of blossoms, and the contrast of rich colours is much more striking than in any other arrangement. No plants are admitted that are shy bloomers, or which have ugly habits of growth, meager or starved foliage; the aim being brilliant effect, rather than the display of a great variety of curious or rare plants. To bring about this more perfectly, hyacinths and other fine bulbous roots occupy a certain portion of the beds, the intervals being filled with herbaceous plants, permanently planted, or with flowering annuals and green-house plants renewed every season. (Downing, *A treatise,* 400)

3. Squibb, *The Gardener's Calendar,* 3.

4. The unnamed author(s) of "The Flower Garden," a noted addition in 1827 to Charleston nurseryman Robert Squibb's original 1787 gardening calendar directed for November: "The soil of the whole garden should now be renewed and turned. Hyacinths planted in beds prepared for them; (Tulips, Colchicums, Martagons, Crown Imperials Anemonies, Fritillaries) we are obliged to exclude on account of climate for they only bloom one year.—. . . Lilies of all sorts set out either for the garden or green-house—Polyanthus's divided and set out in shady situations; Tube Roses taken up and dried; Tuberous roots separated and set out, Dahlias divided and the soil changed in order to make them bloom spring and fall" (Squibb, *The Gardener's Calendar,* 4). This is an early documentation of tazettas as good garden flowers for the far South (the author and later publishers lived in Charleston), and how other bulbs that were favorites of the day were in actuality problematic in hot climates.

5. Hibbert and Buist, *The American Flower Directory,* 320.

6. Bridgeman, *The young gardener's assistant,* 42.

7. Sayers, *The American Flower Garden Companion,* 68.

8. Downing, *A treatise on the theory and practice of landscape gardening,* 404–5.

9. British journals repeatedly warned their gardening readers of the perils of being cheap. In 1837 and again in 1843, gardeners were warned away from auctions:

> The period has arrived when the Dutch bulbs make an appearance in all the seedshop windows, and at which, those who bloom them in glasses or borders, should be looking out to make their purchases; but there is a description of persons who, instead of going to respectable dealers, lay by for sales, give for a few lots as much as they would have to pay at a first-rate shop, and run the greatest risk, or incur a certainty of disappointment and loss. The London seedshops, unquestionably, have the picked roots from all the Dutch houses, and Hyacinths never came over finer than they have the present season. After the prime roots are all gone, the refuse is offered to a lower grade of dealers, who pick the best of the bad, and the remainder, consisting of bulbs internally diseased, externally damaged, imperfectly ripened, cankered, or otherwise affected, are packed in boxes, and consigned to persons in London, for sale by auction. They are generally put up in lots of half a dozen, and bought at a higher price than would be charged by a respectable dealer for proper sound bulbs. Persons, therefore, cannot be too strongly cautioned against purchasing at auctions; we are going against our own interests in discouraging them, for they are always advertised, while the general dealers do not always advertise. Nevertheless, we are quite certain of two things, which are well worth people's consideration before they buy at auctions. First, that they cannot meet with sound and faultless bulbs at all; and second, that they must pay as high as the City shopkeepers would charge for first-rate picked bulbs of the same varieties. We were offered in the City, at sixpence each, the finest roots we ever saw of Waterloo, Groot-voorst, and other established favourites, and we found all things reasonable in proportion. It is a strange fancy to run after auctions, where any thing like a warranty is desirable, and particularly as we have seen Crocuses bringing eighteen pence a lot, fifty in a lot, when the best of the London dealers where charging but half-a-crown a hundred. ("Bulb Purchases," 269)

10. Prince, *A Short Treatise on Horticulture,* 159–60.

11. Ernest Heinrich Krelage, *Drie eeuwen bloembollenexport,* 80.

12. Winter, *A Guide to Floriculture,* 195.

13. Ibid., 195–96.

14. The *Farmer's Register* of Richmond, Virginia, 1836, reprinted an article on indoor hyacinth flowering from the *American Gardener's Magazine:*

> Select good large solid bulbs, especially for glasses; we have often seen it stated in the communications of experienced growers, that "small bulbs are worse than useless;" it is labor lost, to cultivate those which are sold at auction; they are the mere refuse of the Dutch florists, such as would be thrown away as worthless; the roots are weak, and would fail to flower well if put in their natural element, the earth; much more so if in an artificial one of water. How frequent we have heard complaints that bulbs start well, make a rapid growth of an inch or two, and then stop; the flower stems dying ere a flower opens. This is from the cause that there is not sap enough stored in the bulb the preceding year; and it must consequently make a premature and sickly growth the blowing one. Unless attention is paid to the selection of first rate bulbs, disappointment must certainly ensue. All complaints arise from this cause; and if cheap bulbs are cultivated, cheap looking flowers must also repay amateurs for their care. ("On the Cultivation of Hyacinths in Glasses and Pots," 499).

When one reads how the Dutch actually grew their bulbs in the early 1800s, it isn't a surprise Dutch bulbs dwindled in American gardens. Great care was taken in the composition of the compost in which bulbs were grown, and replaced annually for each year's crop, as at the seedling bulb nursery of Eldering of Overveen: "The natural vegetable earth of the country receives an additional proportion of fine white sand, sometimes collected from ruts on the by-roads, or from the margins of ditches; and rotten tree-leaves, particularly oak-leaves, and well decomposed cowdung, which has lain in store not less than two years, are added in equal quantities. Sometimes, but not very often, a small proportion of old tanners'-bark, such as comes from an exhausted hot-bed, is likewise introduced" (*Journal of a Horticultural Tour,* 184). With this rich a growing medium, no regular garden, even if manured, can compete.

15. Breck, *The Flower-Garden,* 67.

16. Juvenis, "On the Culture of the Narcissus," 422. "Juvenis" is Latin for "youth"; conceivably this pen name was for a known horticulturist.

17. Ibid., 424–25.

18. Nurseryman R. Buist in 1854 readdresses the general problem with polyanthus narcissus in the garden: that although they require a richer soil than lilies, "even then they do not bloom so finely in a few years as they do when first imported; but they are cheap, and can be annually procured." This problem did not apparently plague the single and double jonquils—only that they did not bloom well the first year as in the second and third years, and so should be lifted every three years (Buist, *American flower-garden directory,* 118).

19. Hovey, "Art. IV. Flower and Bulb Gardens," 325–26.

20. Ibid., 328–29.

21. The Tennessee home of Clinchdale was built by Judge James T. Shields in 1850 for his bride, Elizabeth Simpson; it remained in the Shields family into the 1930s. "Beyond the office building an old-fashioned flower garden once flourished. In the center was a large circular bed of two tiers, filled with pinks, daffodils, phlox, lilies, poppies, sweet william, and other such favorites, while long borders of bridal wreath, lilacs, moss roses, japanese quince, and sweet shrubs made their contribution to the beauty of the place" (Moore et al., *The History of Homes and Gardens of Tennessee,* 45).

22. Rion, *Ladies' Southern Florist,* 59.

23. Winter, *A Guide to Floriculture,* 194.

24. "Ladies Department," 349. In his 1851 original edition of *Breck's Book of Flowers*, the illustrious Joseph Breck neglected the culture of indoor plants. This was pointedly rectified in the second edition, issued in 1858: "One great omission was, a chapter on the cultivation of plants in the parlor, of which the author has very often been reminded by female amateurs from every part of the country" (Breck, *The Flower-Garden* [1858], vi).

25. Sayers, *The American Flower Garden Companion*, 72.

26. Sayers's 1838 list is echoed by Bridgeman's list in *The young gardener's assistant* (1837), albeit with better color descriptions of the flowers: "Grand Monarque de France" white/yellow, 'Belle Liegeoise' white/yellow, 'Glorieux' yellow/orange, 'Luna' white/citron, 'Reine Blanche' entirely white, 'Morganstern' entirely white, "Double Roman." Double jonquils warrant mention for indoor forcing; polyanthus are suitable for the open border; but the only daffodils mentioned are the two doubles—Incomparable ('Butter and Eggs') and the white fragrant double. Interestingly, most of the tazettas Bridgeman recommended, and the largest category carried by Prince 1842 and 1843, were bicolors (twenty-seven); yellow-floret flowers came second (fourteen), and all whites a noticeably distant third (eight).

Hovey & Co. in the *Magazine of Horticulture, Botany and All Useful Discoveries and Improvements in Rural Affairs,* 1837, ran their entire fall bulb catalog as an advertisement, listing sorts and prices. The customer was assured of their bulbs' quality: "Hovey & Co., In addition to a large collection which they cultivate, import direct from one of the oldest and most celebrated establishments in Holland, every season, a fine assortment of the most choice and superb varieties. The following are such as can be relied on, they having grown and observed them carefully, for the remarkable size of their bulbs, their beautiful shape, and the vividness and delicacy of their colors. Those which are annually sold at auction, are the poorest softs, the refuse of the Dutch florists, the bulbs weak and unfit for flowering well; good ones being worth in Holland ten times what those generally sell for" (Hovey & Co., "Catalogue of Bulbous and Tuberous Flower Roots," n.p.). After hyacinths and tulips were listed narcissus, doubles at 12 cents each/$1.00/dozen, and polyanthus narcissus at 25 cents each/$2.00/dozen. Double sorts offered were Incomparable, 'Orange Phoenix,' 'Sulphur Phoenix,' and "Van Sion;" tazettas were 'Bouquet Royal,' 'Grand Soleil d'Or,' "Grand Primo," 'Grootvoorst," "Grand Monarque de France," and 'Staaten General'.

In 1854 J. M. Thorburn ran an advertisement in the *Country Gentleman* of Albany, New York. He promised his stock to be "all of the best qualities, imported to order, from the oldest and most extensive Flower Nursery in Holland, warranted sound, true to name and color, and at prices as low as are usually paid for inferior roots at auction—can be packed and safely sent to any part of the United States" for both retail and wholesale customers (J. M. Thorburn & Co., "Fresh Imported Dutch Bulbous Roots," 290). Thorburn ran the same advertisement in the fall of 1854 in issues of the *Ohio Cultivator.*

27. Juvenis, "On the Culture of the Narcissus," 424.

28. Jewel of Harlaem (white with orange cup, 25 cents apiece) was offered by William R. Prince & Co. in 1842–1843 and 1844–1845 catalogs, but the only tazetta beginning with letter "I" is Illustre. Interestingly Prince & Co. offered "States General" in 1822 and in 1860–1861, but not in the 1842–1845 catalogs—at least by name (fifteen bicolor varieties were offered nameless, in addition to twelve by name); it was offered wholesale by E. H. Krelage in 1846. "States General" (its true name 'Staaten Generaal') became a stalwart tazetta for decades, appearing in American catalogs until around 1900. Prince 1822 has 'Passetout' as a bicolor. Regrettably the names of Smith's daffodils are vague, given only as jonquil, single white narcissus (a poet), single yellow narcissus, and so on.

A recounting of the trials of indoor gardening comes from Juliana Horatia Ewing (1841–1885), who lived in Frederickton, New Brunswick, Canada. In February 1869 she wrote her friend back home in England detailing her woes and successes. Ordering from Carter and Sons, much was lost to mold in transit, but the hyacinths and 'Soleil d'Or' tazettas survived the voyage. She potted her bulbs in leaf mold and sand and placed them in her dress closet. Later she moved the pots to the stair landing window, next to the "dumb stove," an iron box surrounding the vent pipe from the downstairs hall stove, used to warm the second floor. In her northern climate Mrs. Ewing had to remain vigilant to move her pots away from the windows at night in case a hard freeze set it. The three 'Soleil d'Or' bulbs she treated herself to flowered well, sending up four stems with twenty-nine florets total.

29. Shoberl, *The Language of Flowers,* 64.

30. Johnson, *Every Lady Her Own Flower Gardener,* 47–48.

31. Wirt, *Flora's Dictionary, by a Lady,* n.p.

32. The double 'Plenissimus,' a.k.a. "Tratus Cantus," presents another mysterious disappearance from American catalogs with no ready explanation. It was offered by Peter Barr in his 1891 catalog (but not in his 1906?). However, in 1884 Peter Barr indicated, "This Daffodil is not much known, the one usually sold for it, viz., *lobularis grandiplenus,* is dwarfer" (Peter Barr, *Ye narcissus,* 46.) A. M. Kirby in 1907 noted it as being sold, but it is quite likely that the substituted flowers were in play. By 1934 even the great E. A. Bowles (*A Handbook of Narcissus,* 88) indicated "so if anyone still grows this heavy-headed," suggesting it had faded from British view and gardens by then. It likely simply faded from favor, particularly as the new forms overtook the gardening public's attention, and then dwindled away for good.

33. Breck, *The Flower-Garden,* 67–68.

34. In the 1822 Prince catalogue, tazettas ranged from 25 cents to 50 cents a bulb, double daffodils were 12 cents each, jonquils were 12 cents (double jonquils 13 cents each), and single daffodils ranged from 12 cents to 25 cents. In the 1842–1843 catalog, tazettas ranged from 20 cents to 35 cents apiece, doubles were 10 cents, and most singles were 12 cents, with poeticus at 10 cents and triandrus and bifrons (*N. × intermedius*) at 25 cents. Jonquils were 10 cents to 12 cents each. For comparison, in the 1842–1843 Prince catalogue, in order of appearance: Hyacinths ranged from 20 cents to $3.50 (only one variety so priced); Tulips ranged from 10 cents to $1.75; Crown Imperials were 20 cents to 75 cents; Fritillaries were 20 cents to 50 cents; Lilies were 10 cents to $2.00; and Martagons were 31 cents to 45 cents. Narcissus came next; Crocus, listed after Narcissus, ranged from 5 cents to 10 cents, but most were at 6 cents apiece.

35. Minor, "Fruit, Trees, Plants, &c." 176.

36. The reach of these seedsmen and their catalogs can be seen in the election of Robert Buist (along with A. J. Downing) as an honorary member of the Chunnannugee Ridge Horticultural Society Alabama in 1847.

37. William A. Gill & Co., "Fresh Bulbous Roots," 352.

38. Cothran, *Gardens and Historic Plants of the Antebellum South,* 94.

39. In *Gardens of Colony and State,* the garden of Indian Hill Farm in West Newbury, Massachusetts, provides an anecdote of someone ordering *Narcissus* from Thorburn. The book was written by the owner, F. S. Moseley, and she indicates the garden description actually came from Miss Ellen Poore. Miss Poore was sister to Benjamin Poore, who, in 1833, hired James Lowe, an English gardener, to make a new garden: "The flowers in the garden were the crocus, tulip, narcissus, daffodil, princes' feather, tassel flowers (little bunches of red tassels), ladies' delights, that became almost like weeds, single zinnias, all kinds of marigolds, wild chandelier lilies, balsam (touch-me-not), single asters, and many others. The seeds and bulbs for the garden were supplied by Thorburn of New York, while the trees and plants were, in most cases, imported from England" (Lockwood et al., *Gardens of Colony and State,* 101).

40. Jenkins, Jenkins Papers, Diary 1841–1844 (n.p.).

41. Sykes, "Gardening with Mrs. Balfour," 6.

42. Ibid., 6.

43. Elder, "The Pleasures of Bulb Culture," 299.

44. Ibid., 299.

45. Ward, "The Winter in Georgia," 132.

46. Ward, "Editorial Correspondence," 144–45.

47. Gray, "Ornamental Gardening in the South," 53.

48. Gray, "The Gardens of the South," 83.

49. McDonald, "Alabama Farming," 296.

50. "Flowering of Fruit-Trees in 1857," 91.

51. Stuart, *Three Years in North America*, 66.

52. Devens, *Sketches of Martha's Vineyard*, 103–4.

53. Northend, *Historic Gardens of New England*, 9.

54. Earle, *Old Time Gardens*, 416.

55. Sale et al., *Historic Gardens of Virginia*, 175.

56. Ibid., 176.

57. Cooney et. al., *Garden History of Georgia*, 50.

58. Owen and Owen, *History of Alabama*, 601.

59. Stritikus, "Forest Home," 3.

60. "The Stryker Mansion," 191.

61. "Some Old Grave-Yards," n.p. The house was also called Rosevale for the gardens and its roses (and peacocks); the land was eventually purchased by the city of New York to form part of DeWitt Clinton Park and then in turn part of the New York Passenger Terminal.

62. The mixed border garden, per Downing:

The *mingled* flower-garden, as it is termed, is by far the most common mode of arrangement in this country, though it is seldom well effected. The object in this is to dispose the plants in the beds in such a manner that, while there is no predominance of bloom in any one portion of the beds, there should be a general admixture of colours and blossoms throughout the entire garden during the whole season of growth.

To promote this, the more showy plants should be often repeated in different parts of the garden, or even the same parterre when large, the less beautiful sorts being suffered to occupy but moderate space. The smallest plants should be nearest the walk, those a little taller behind them, and the largest should be the farthest from the eye, at the back of the border, when the latter is seen from one side only, or in the centre, if the bed be viewed from both sides. A neglect of this simple rule, will not only give the beds, when the plants are full grown, a confused look, but the beauty of the humbler and more delicate plants will be lost amid the tall thick branches of sturdier plants, or removed so far from the spectator in the walks, as to be overlooked. (Downing, *A treatise*, 406)

63. Howitt, *Our Cousins in Ohio*, 61.

64. *Old Homes and Gardens of North Carolina*, 44.

65. Flowers, "The Garden at Flowery Dale Plantation," 7.

66. Garden flowers, along with garden designs, left Virginia for Tennessee. Per Moore:

Of course, many women of the frontier did not neglect such a wealth or fail to make it contributory to the beautification of their surroundings. The front walk was bordered with some of these. Of flowers brought from old homes, free exchanges were made among neighbors; and, after the manner of the Virginians, a part of the vegetable garden was given over to flowers and shrubs, the front and the sides of the walkways. The lilac was a favorite as it deserved to be. The snowball claimed recognition, where all could not find space. Lavender and the damask rose in their fragrance were reminders of the old home and of loved ones left behind. (Moore et al., *The History of Homes and Gardens of Tennessee,* 22)

67. Ibid., 35.

68. Ibid., 151.

69. Elizabeth Patterson Thomas, *Old Kentucky Homes and Gardens,* 147.

70. Flint, *Recollections of the last ten years,* 334.

71. Flint, *The History and Geography of the Mississippi Valley,* 66.

72. Wellford, "A Nosegay in Fredewicks," 396.

73. Woodson, "My Recollections of Frankfort," 197.

74. Kemble, *Journal of a Residence on a Georgia Plantation,* 136.

75. Ibid., 160.

76. Owen and Owen, *History of Alabama,* 602.

77. Espy, "Diary," n.p.

78. Ibid., n.p.

79. West, *A History of Methodism in Alabama,* 475.

80. Mackie, *From Cape Cod to the Dixie and the Tropics,* 106–7.

81. Ibid., 97.

82. Ibid., 90.

83. Ely, *A Woman's Hardy Garden,* 154.

Chapter 4: Rise of American Daffodils, 1860 to 1940

1. "A City Back Yard," 192.

2. Sale et al., *Historic Gardens of Virginia,* 298.

3. Physicians took note as well. Conventional wisdom held indoor plants were detrimental to the sick and so were to be kept out of the sickroom if not the bedroom in general; some thought house plants contributed to malaria. In 1886 Dr. J. M. Anders, a determined physician, set out to test and demonstrate the beneficial effects of plants on atmospheric levels of carbonic acid (carbon dioxide), oxygen, and humidity—both to help cure the sick and to promote general health, as well as to advocate for indoor gardening (with some help from Thomas Meehan).

4. Grube & Nieuwland, *Wholesale Catalog,* 10.

5. Vick when listing Dutch bulbs suitable for winter blooming listed in order hyacinths, tulips, crocuses, snowdrops, and narcissus, as well as oxalis and the cyclamen particularly desirable.

6. British catalogs continued to offer named tazettas well into the 1900s; William Robinson's 1933 (15th) edition of *The English Flower Garden* discussed seven varieties, some likely never offered in America—Luna, 'Czar de Muscovie,' 'Grand Sultan,' 'Her Majesty,' 'Queen of the Netherlands,' 'Lord Canning,' and Golden Era.

7. Henderson, *Garden and Farm Topics,* 25–26.

8. Peter Henderson & Co., *Peter Henderson and Co.'s 1883 Catalogue of Bulbs for Fall Planting,* 25–26.

9. Peter Henderson & Co., *Autumn 1889 Bulbs and Plants,* 15.

10. Ibid., 13.

11. Henderson, *Handbook of Plants and General Horticulture,* 269.

12. A visitor to Hawaii in the late 1880s commented on the Chinese growing their favorite tazettas for the lunar new year: "They also grow plants of narcissus so as to have them in bloom at that time, and the china pots and dishes full of the yellow and white flowers, look very sweet and fresh" (Grant, *Scenes in Hawaii,* 68–69).

13. "The Chinese plant them in season to have them bloom on their New Year. The bulbs are all brought from China. The Chinese say that there is but one place where they grow wild and naturally. . . . They say it will only grow and blossom well for the good, and have many super-stitions about it. The Chinese laundrymen frequently present these plants to their customers. . . . To forbid the importation of these bulbs would probably drive all the Chinamen out of the country. It might be tried if all other means fail. To deprive 'John' of his beloved lily would surely make him quite sick at heart" ("The Chinese National Flower," 84).

14. F. A. Miller, "The Bulb Season," 367.

15. James Vick, *Vick's Floral Guide Autumn 1881,* 126.

16. Shinn, "An Early Winter Garden in California," 85.

17. Deland, "Jonquils," 163.

18. Ibid., 164.

19. Ibid., 165.

20. H. G. Hastings & Co., *Bulbs and Roses,* 5.

21. Barr & Sugden, *Barr & Sugden's Autumnal Catalogue,* 10.

22. Rand, *Bulbs,* 29.

23. Henderson, *Practical Floriculture,* 122.

24. Rand, *Seventy-Five Popular Flowers,* 45.

25. Ibid., 47.

26. Scott, *The art of beautifying suburban home grounds of small extent,* 247.

27. "Notes on Spring Flowering Bulbs," 316.

28. William N. White, "The Flower Garden," 177.

29. Ibid., 410.

30. William N. White, "Bulbs," 301–2.

A very pretty effect may be had where one has a large number of bulbs, by selecting the different colors and planting each color in a row by itself, so that when they blossom, there will be ribbon-lines of red, white, blue, or yellow, as the case may be. Or, if one has a large number of beds of different shapes, cut so as to form a design of some kind, each season may be planted with a different color (hyacinths are the best for this work), and when all come into bloom in April, the effect will be most charming. We tried this "massing" of the differ-ently colored bulbs one year, in a "design" of one hundred different sections of all conceivable shapes, planting the bulbs so that when in blossom, the whole would present a harmonious effect. It would be hard to conceive of a more attractive sight than that presented by all those bulbs in full bloom in early April, when every thing else looked barren and cheerless. They were admired by every one who saw them. Bulbs of this character bloom and pass away in season to allow room for other plants to be set out. These may be set between the rows of bulbs, and not disturb them in the least. (Sheehan, "Fall or Holland Bulbs," 423)

The *Rural Carolinian* was devoted to agriculture and domestic arts, with only one or two orna-mental gardening articles in each monthly issue. In 1871 *The Rural Carolinian* ran an article attempting to nudge its readership into the newer, tasteful flower bed designs. Modifying an article from the *Horticulturist,* it touted first circular beds planted in the ribbon style, and second more "fanciful" shapes. These were given in the context of summer flowers, although passing mention was made of extending their flowering seasons with bulbs.

> We have among us too much Dutch gardening, with its "rectangular formality" and its stiff unnatural looking trees and shrubs. It is certainly an expensive kind of adornment, if adornment it be, and to our eye it is ugly. We do not speak against art. We believe in it, and love it, but let it be that kind of art which cooperates with Nature instead of contravening all her laws. Here are some plans which illustrate imperfectly what may be called the natural style of ornamental gardening. We copy them from an old volume of the Horticulturist, with the accompanying remarks:
>
> Circle groups in small plots of ground where little labor, and that of a common laborer, is expected to be given, are pleasingly satisfactory, and from their simplicity can always be kept in form. Fig 3 show and arrangement of circles that, with the list of plants accompanying, which are always easily and cheaply attainable, presents during the whole of summer a succession, or rather constancy off flowers most effective and satisfactory, and may be used on one corner of a lawn, or as a regular lawn garden, where the grounds are less extensive. ("Plans for Flower-Beds," 285).

31. Michigan State Horticultural Society, *Sixteenth Annual Report,* 454.

32. Variations of this become very popular in the 1890s and early 1900s in the planting of intricate multicolored patterns of all tulips or hyacinths.

33. Conversely Peter Barr in 1884 indicated the arrangement of all flowers should be beneficial to the amateur to help him select for planting in the garden or in the grass.

34. W. Robinson, *The Wild Garden* [1881], 15–16.

35. Ibid., 19.

36. Ibid., 151.

37. W. Robinson, *The Wild Garden* [1903], 18.

38. Ibid., 20.

39. "The Wild Garden," 500.

40. Shinn, "Future Gardens of California," 155.

41. "The Day of the Daffodil," n.p.

42. Ellwanger, *The Garden's Story,* 89.

43. Ibid., 95.

44. Ibid., 101.

45. In the early 1900s, educators began encouraging New York City teachers to grow Dutch bulbs in "window gardens" as classroom teaching modules for life studies as well as a general beautification project (Julien, "Window Gardens for City Schools," 50). Others encouraged rural and village school teachers to plant small "bulb gardens" on school grounds, for nature and agriculture studies, with the hope that it might encourage children to then force bulbs at home for winter and early spring blooming.

46. Kirby, *Daffodils,* 152.

47. Ibid., 90.

48. Ibid., 81.

49. A review of Kirby's book in the Chicago-based magazine *Gardening* commented, "'Naturalizing in the Grass' is a point on which many are seeking information and the subject is very well handled. A table of varieties suitable for this purpose, with their time of flowering and other

peculiarities, is not the least useful part of this excellent chapter and we are glad to see the author standing up for a natural method of planting" ("New Books: Daffodils and How to Grow Them," 379).

Gardening continued advocating for the planting daffodils in grass:

> No apology is needed for the frequent advocacy of the practice of planting daffodils in grass, and in the wilder parts of the garden where an annual digging is not considered essential, for though the progress made in the method of dealing with some bulbous plants is great, the opportunities offered are much greater still, and there are yet large spaces in the surroundings of many gardens where the grass and other herbage is allowed to grow away at will until say mid-July. . . . Personally I think they look best in informal groups, . . . avoiding anything in the way of formal outline or any attempt to plant them [daffodils] in lines. ("Daffodils in Grass," 50)

> "I give below a selection of varieties that have been found most successful, but refrain from including any of the newer, higher-priced varieties, as these can only be tested in bulk when they become cheaper, and are not yet subjects for wholesale planting." The recommended cultivars were: 'Horsfieldii,' 'Empress,' Rubilobus, 'Emperor,' N. cernuus (*N. moschatus*), 'Princeps,' 'Telamonius Plenus,' 'Sir Watkin,' 'Frank Miles,' 'Autocrat,' 'Minnie Hume,' 'Conspicuus,' 'Figaro,' 'Duchess of Westminster,' 'Sulphur Phoenix,' 'Orange Phoenix,' Yellow Phoenix ('Butter and Eggs') and all the poets. Written by a northerner, this list is fairly applicable to as far south as north Georgia, with the exception of the poets. ("Daffodils in Grass," 51).

50. Kirby, *Daffodils*, 81.
51. Rathbone, "Our Hardy Flowers," 51.
52. Earle, *Old Time Gardens*, 318.
53. Ibid., 381.
54. Ibid., 71–72.
55. Rexford, *Amateur Gardencraft*, 121. A similar landscaping point of view came from a California garden writer:

> Garden-Places for Bulbs.—Although scattered clusters of bulbs can be effectively used in borders of mixed flowers or put in singly here and there as you like, the most rational way is to grow them in beds or borders by themselves so that you can arrange for their rest or activity without compromising with other growths in some way. Of course you can make a great front-lawn display with bulbs in succession or you can transplant other plants to take the places of bulbs as they mature and to conceal their decrepitude when they are necessarily in the sere and yellow leaf, but unless you have an unusual amount of leisure you will have to hire a gardener, and that throws you out of our class of working amateurs.

> Our choice is to locate the bulb-areas in the rear yard or at the side and not to rely upon them to please the passer on the highway, except as he may catch vistas of them between and beneath the trees—although we have had very good success with them along the secondary walks through the fruit trees, just back of the violet edgings. In this way they stray into and out of sight from the street and do not flash boldly into view.

> In their own areas we prefer to grow bulbs in straight rows—not less than a foot and a half between the rows, so that one can freely hoe up and down the rows; or in curves, if you like, providing good hoeing space is given. It is a mistake to put them in fantastic figures or

to jumble them up and thus make cultivation always dangerous, if not impossible. (Wickson, *California Garden-Flowers*, 118)

Tabor's book went into three printings then was picked up by another press. Its reissue by Countrywide Press (dropping her credit as author) bears some important changes. Tabor's bulb garden plan was rectangular, entered under an arbor, and graced with a wide array of bulbs—crocus, colchicum, fritillaries, a wide array of iris and lilies, and *N. jonquilla* and *N. poeticus*. The bulb garden plan in Countrywide Press version is a square plan layout similar to Earle's, but without the expense of sinking it below grade and adding a brick wall, and (unsurprisingly) it is dominated by tulips.

    56. In Henry A. Dreer's catalog for 1871, Narcissus came after hyacinths, tulips, crocus, iris, and Lily of the Valley.

    57. James Vick, *Vick's Illustrated Catalogue of Hardy Bulbs* [1872], 4.

    58. Wisconsin, "The Narcissus," 317.

    59. Elder, "Plant Hardy Bulbs," 294.

    60. James Vick, *Vick's Illustrated Catalogue of Hardy Bulbs 1872*, 4. B. K. Bliss & Sons similarly reassured their customers in the fall of 1880:

Our present stock of bulbs was selected by our senior *personally*, while visiting Holland this past summer, and can be confidently recommended. In making our selections we have strived to present to our patrons only such varieties as are of the greatest merit, so that while we offer under each section new and expensive roots, we have at the same time selected among the cheap and old varieties, those kinds only which possess sufficient beauty to entitle them to a prominent place in the flower garden. Young amateurs may therefore commence their floral career among the cheaper sorts, while the experienced will find new and valuable varieties worth adding to their collections. (B. K. Bliss & Sons, *Autumn Catalogue*, 4)

    61. Peter Henderson & Co., *Peter Henderson and Co.'s 1883 Catalogue of Bulbs for Fall Planting*, 1.

    62. James Vick, *Vick's Floral Guide Autumn 1881*, 126.

    63. Other horticultural tidbits found in responses to letters to the editor include what to do about the large quantity of nonblooming Narcissus in a reader's old New Bedford, Massachusetts, garden; in addition to lifting and replanting, "a thin dressing of lime and ashes a few weeks before planting would do good" ("Narcissus" [1880], 152). In 1878, R. S. of Lehi, Utah, asked how to "preserve Tulip, Hyacinth and Narcissus bulbs through the summer" (S., "Preserving Dutch Bulbs during Summer," 184).

    64. B. K. Bliss & Sons, *Autumn Catalogue*, 22.

    65. James M. Thorburn & Co., *Annual Descriptive Catalogue*, 10.

    66. Park, "Narcissus! Narcissus!," 194.

    67. George W. Park, *Park's Bulb Catalogue*, 7.

    68. C. E. Allen, *1890 Bulb and Plant Catalogue*, 8.

    69. Peter Henderson & Co., *Catalogue of Bulbs, Plants and Seeds for Autumn Planting 1895*, 16.

    70. Henry A. Dreer, *Dreer's Autumn Catalogue 1896*, 10.

    71. John Lewis Childs, *Illustrated Catalogue of Bulbs and Plants Fall 1891*, 1.

    72. John Lewis Childs, *Illustrated Catalogue of Bulbs and Plants Fall 1892*, 1.

    73. In his 1894 catalog, Childs simply lumped all his stock together and boldly stated: "For fifteen years we have made a leading specialty of these Bulbs, and have brought them prominently

to the attention of all lovers of rare and beautify flowers. We grow and sell them by the million—more even than is sold by all other Fall Catalogues issued in the United States combined. We offer only the highest grade Bulbs, those which are grown and selected especially for us, hence the unequalled reputation which our Hyacinths, Tulips, Crocus, Narcissus, Lilies, Freesias and other Bulbs enjoy" (John Lewis Childs, *John Lewis Childs Fall Catalog for 1894*, 2).

74. Kirby, *Daffodils*, 10–11.

75. W. W. Rawson, *Rawson's Bulb Handbook*, 1.

76. Tridymus hybrids were novel but not well received by the gardening public, quickly falling into obscurity. Other flowers besides yellow trumpets were used in their hybridization. Few were really ever introduced in England, and even fewer appeared in mainstream American catalogs. Two flowers are now found on the show bench and have remained in commerce—Peter Barr's 'White Owl' and 'Cloth of Gold'.

77. In his 1896 catalog, Henry A. Dreer Co. offered university color hyacinth mixes for many of the leading universities including Yale, Pennsylvania, Cornell, Columbia, and Harvard. All customers need do was provide the size and shape of the bed, and Dreer's would provide an estimate. By 1913 Peter Henderson & Co. was selling size and color combinations in tulips for belted circular beds and square beds with triangle, and a round bed with a star. By 1916 an entire page was devoted to pattern bed combinations for tulips and hyacinths, illustrating intricate patterns.

78. Henry A. Dreer, "Dreer's Old-Fashioned Hardy Garden Plants," 89.

79. Thomas Meehan & Sons, Inc., "Hardy Plants Worth Owning," 89.

80. H. G. Hastings Co., *70th Catalog Fall 1925*, 42.

81. Thomson, "Third Size Tuberose Bulbs," 127.

82. Thomson, "Exchange," 92.

83. The *Southern Cultivator and Dixie Farmer* commented: "Mrs. J. S. R. Thomson, of Spartanburg, S. C., is contributing some very interesting articles on floriculture to the *Gardeners' Monthly*, of Philadelphia. She is one of the most successful florists and versatile writers in the South, and has often contributed to The Cultivator articles that were highly appreciated. We hope to have her again in our list of contributors." She was state vice president of the Society of American Florists, and she wrote for horticultural magazines on topics such as celery growing and edging flower beds with pinks and native flora for the garden, and she collaborated with Liberty Hyde Bailey on perfumery gardening ("Editorial Buds," 496).

84. Mrs. Kersey at Haywards in Alameda County, who once sang in the opera, grew an array of daffodils in her pear orchard on a warm, sunny slope, carefully guarding her fertilizing regimen. She went to England in the early 1890s and fell in love with the yellow trumpet 'Ard Righ,' bringing a goodly quantity home for her own garden. She studied all the Dutch literature she could lay her hands on, becoming a daffodil expert on bulbs in her own right. What once started as a small passion grew into substantial commercial enterprise, consisting of bulbs by the ton and cut flowers by the hundred thousand by 1900. She supplied the local florists with cut flowers starting in December, likely her cherished 'Ard Righ' trumpets, considered the finest on the market in 1903. By coming into bloom a full month sooner than the other area growers, her flowers garnered top dollar. As her competitors came to market later in the season, the prices of cut daffodils sold by the San Francisco street flower boys dropped to a penny. At this point Kersey then focused on selling bulbs to East Coast florists who needed an annual supply of bulbs for their forcing cut flower trade.

85. Local cut flower farms popped up near many major American cities. Around World War I in Illinois, farmers delved into the cut flower trade to diversify their income as other edible crops developed disease problems. Near Alma, the enterprising farmer William Slutz Ross

imported 'Emperor' bulbs from Holland sometime before World War I. Soon other farmers followed suit; by planting a variety of cultivars they were able to extend the blooming season. In addition to 'Emperor,' farmers grew 'Bersheeba,' 'Mrs. R. O. Backhouse,' 'King Alfred' and a poeticus on upward of sixty-five to seventy-five acres. Forty-five to fifty children picked the stems before school (a nickel for a morning's work), and around one hundred women bundled the stems, thirteen to a bunch, and packed them for daily rail shipment to the Water Street Market in Chicago. The locals called 'King Alfred' "Easter Flowers" and the poeticus "Mother's Day Flowers" (Joy, "Daffodils, Pears, Melons and More," 10). Some farmers maintained daffodil fields into the 1970s. The decline of street peddlers, the unwillingness of high schoolers to pick flowers, and the passing of the local railroad spelled the doom of the Alma daffodil business.

86. One large-scale cut flower industry got its start in a rather unusual fashion. In early 1900s Hugh MacRae, a real estate developer in Wilmington, North Carolina, embarked on an interesting agricultural and rural development plan. He decided to bring Europeans from various countries to settle new farming communities, the communities based on nationality and functioning as cooperatives. His first community was St. Helena, founded with seven Italian families in 1905, which quickly grew. His second community was Castle Hayne, in which MacRae settled forty Dutch and ten Hungarian families. Hollanders were also settled at Van Eeden; Germans and Hungarians at New Berlin; Poles at Artesia; and Greeks at Marathon. All told, MacRae settled upward of three hundred immigrants to eastern North Carolina.

At the outset MacRae's plan was for families to intensively farm ten-acre plots. Farming equipment was held in common by the community to reduce capital costs to the farmers. Three-room houses were provided to the families, with the expectation the families would expand them as needed. By 1926 MacRae's colonies had consolidated down to two stable communities, St. Helena and Castle Hayne.

As might be expected, the Dutch farmers grew florists' flowers—paperwhites, daffodils, tulips, iris, peonies, and gladiolus. Castle Hayne grew into a 6,000-acre development. A happy accident befell the community, when some of the bulbs were accidentally refrigerated, causing the bulbs to bloom early. This early bloom provided the farmers a niche to exploit, as they could now get their cut flowers to the Northern markets sooner than competitors from other regions (particularly the Pacific Northwest). By 1939 the farmers of Castle Hayne were shipping eight to ten thousand cartons of cut flowers each season.

87. David Fairchild is the namesake of Fairchild Gardens in Miami, Florida.

88. T. K. Godbey (1858–1940) came to Waldo, Florida, by way of Cooper County, Missouri, in 1882. An innovator, he became renowned for his business acumen in the world of commercial agriculture for his ability to spot a new money maker and the intuition to exit that crop at its peak of monetary return (he was dubbed the "Burbank of Florida" by the *Florida Grower* in 1926). When Godbey signed up, he had already observed paperwhites and "Chinese Sacred Lily" growing in dooryards in north Florida and so reasoned them to be a potential cash crop. By 1910–1911, Godbey was in full scale commercial production of 'Paper White Grandiflorus' and "Chinese Sacred Lily" and became the first in Florida to commercially grow gladiolus. In 1918 Godby pioneered the commercial growing of Easter lilies.

Godbey sold both bulb stock and cut flowers of cannas, narcissus, gladiolus, Japanese iris, and amaryllis, shipping primarily to Philadelphia, New York, and Boston. Close proximity to rail lines was essential to supply the northern floral trade. By 1926 Godbey ascertained the peak had been reached with paperwhites, unloaded all of his paperwhite bulbs, and shifted to ten acres of "Chinese Sacred Lily" (with double the flower stems, and treble the bulb increase as well as treble the price, per acre, of paperwhites). He reportedly thus cornered the market on "Chinese Sacred Lily." Flower stems were cut with two florets open and shipped in sphagnum moss, and bulbs were sold for forcing. Approximately 25 percent of each year's primary bulb crop was retained for replanting (along with the offsets), the rest sold. One acre required fifty thousand bulbs to be set, so ten acres yielded approximately half a million bulbs. In comparison Godbey grew thirty-two varieties of cannas on fifteen acres, selling five hundred cases of 250 plants each.

89. A letter sent in 1909 to the annual Convention of the Society of American Florists and Ornamental Horticulturists by O. W. D'Alcorn of Portsmouth, Virginia, may be from the same operation. Apparently an English florist who immigrated to America in the 1890s, he wrote his letter to plead his case of growing daffodils for the cut flower market as an up-and-coming flower:

OUTDOOR BULB GROWING FOR CUT FLOWERS.

When we first came to this country we went to West Twenty-eighth street, New York, and heard the worst of news. One wholesale man said, "You may be able to sell the bulbs, but don't send the flowers here, for we couldn't sell them." It may have been the truth, but when each spring he sees more and more arriving and getting sold, I wonder if he thinks of the party he told they could not be sold in New York! We were discouraged at every turn. Our friend, the late Mr. Allen, of Floral Park, well meaning enough, advised us to go to Tampa, and we booked to Raleigh, but could not find suitable soil nor climate within fifty miles, but struck it here all right, this season in particular, as we've had a regular English season. Probably we are even later than the old country, as at this day our Emperor are nothing like ready to lift, and the longer the tops stay on the better the bulbs in all respects. To show the increasing popularity of the so-called jonquils, retail customers place their orders with us as early as May, being afraid they should forget in the fall. Again, they ask for them by their proper name, and do not miscall them jonquils, but then they have been educated up to it here, there being two bulb farms for ladies of Norfolk and Portsmouth to roam about at will, with the privilege of plucking their own purchases. What has been done here can be done all over the country, and florists I beg of you to remember this most important fact of all, that we are increasing your trade and not detracting your customers from carnations, roses, etc. It is safe to say that 50 per cent of the buyers of our flowers would not be buyers at all were it not that they can get good, clean, fresh flowers at a price within their reach, and the vendor is still able to get his little 100 per cent. We consider $4 per 1,000 good for Poeticus or Barri, and at 10 cents a dozen this leaves the florist 100 per cent profit. Our great confidence in the business is our belief in the love of flowers by Americans being greater than it is in Great Britain.

I want florists to see the great future to this industry. Those that shut their eyes to it will regret it when the boom comes. We don't anticipate a tulip boom again, but we do think the next great boom in this country will certainly be in this line. (D'Alcorn, "Outdoor Bulb Growing," 48–50)

90. Some local bulb growers stepped up their promotion of bulbs as a viable cash crop to encourage a new agricultural industry that would get a leg up in the marketplace with the quarantine. One in particular was Dr. G. M. Randall of Volusia County, Florida, who went so far as to self-publish *Dutch and French Bulb Culture in Florida Also Diversified Farming* in 1926. As president of the Halifax District Growers Association and executive director for Agriculture of the Daytona Beach Chamber of Commerce, he had testified before Congress to urge the quarantine based on the eighty-two diseases introduced from Holland and France.

91. Van Waveren & Sons had a long relationship with the area, as Charles Heath purchased his starter stock from them when starting business on the old estate of Auburn.

92. The Kress department stores in South Carolina had their own paperwhite farms down in the coastal plain to supply their stores, but they sold to other department stores as well. Claude W. Kress owned Buckfield Plantation, better known as Kress Narcissus Farm, which was the Kress family's winter residence as well as a commercial venture.

93. Some of the flowers on the farm were *N. jonquilla, N. × odorus,* 'Flore Pleno,' *N. bulbocodium, N. pseudonarcissus,* 'Butter and Eggs,' *N. radiiflorus, N. moschatus,* 'Sir Watkin,' 'Franciscus Drake,' 'Laurens Koster,' 'Trevithian,' and 'Klondyke'.

94. One such consolidator operated in Florida, focusing on the small paperwhite crops across the Gulf Coast. In 1928 W. V. (William Vincent) Stephenson, an accountant and part-time potato farmer in Doctor's Inlet, Florida, was approached by Dutchman Leo Allbersberg, vice president and sales manager United Bulb Company, with a proposition to go into the narcissus business. At the time, three acres of paperwhites fetched more than the four acres of vegetables. Stephenson and Allbersberg embarked on a program to buy all the small farms they could from Florida to Texas, usually around five acres, and consolidating the bulb stock. In six years, through the depths of the Depression, the farm grew to 250 acres as they bought the stock of those whose ventures failed, giving some idea of the number of failed ventures. Allbersberg provided guidance in his business, and the United Bulb Company remained Stephenson's preferred wholesale buyer for bulbs. In 1934 Stephenson relocated to a 350-acre bulb farm in Hastings, Florida. In addition to employing migrant workers to pick bulbs (after the potato season), he built six houses for the farmhand families who picked the flowers (mostly the women and children), housing about thirty people. He sold out in 1942 a wealthy man, as the war made both gasoline and fertilizer scarce and bulbs were not essential to the war effort.

95. As the Dutch disease containment system had been severely impaired during the war between loss of equipment and loss of chemicals, it took until 1951 for an agreement between the Netherlands Ministry of Agriculture/Plant Protection Service, the Dutch bulb exporters' association (KAVB—Royal General Bulb Growers' Association), and the USDA to be worked out to provide reliable inspections. Once inspection procedures were in place, the floodgates opened.

96. Sale et al., *Historic Gardens of Virginia,* 345.

97. In the description of Hickory Hill, jonquils do make a brief appearance in the approximately four-acre extensive gardens. "On the two terraces or falls (as they are preferably called), at the lower end of the garden, box-trees, still higher, cast their cool shadows on the thirty-foot stretch of grass and fragrant shrubbery. These are closed in by fences covered with climbing roses, yellow jasmine and honeysuckle, at the bottom of which nestle long stretches of iris, syringes, jonquils and periwinkle" (Sale et al., *Historic Gardens of Virginia,* 96). Interestingly some roses were brought from Shirley plantation in 1820 by the young bride Anne Carter; more roses were planted in 1848 by the then young bride Mrs. W. C. Wickham, whose daughter continued the tradition eighteen years later when she took flowers to Annefield.

98. Sale et al., *Historic Gardens of Virginia,* 24–25.

99. Lockwood et al., *Gardens of Colony and State,* 216.

100. Hitchcock, *Dungeness Historic District Cultural Landscape Report,* 125.

101. When the Gertrude Jekyll garden was finally installed and many of the flowers could not be found or did not do well in Connecticut, substitutions were made—hence the choices of the 1950s and 1960s of 'Ice Follies,' 'Actrice,' 'Actaea,' and 'Thalia'.

Amy L. Cogswell was principal in the Lowthorpe School for Women Landscape Architects (a vocational school, later absorbed into the Rhode Island School of Design) in Groton,

Massachusetts, from 1916 to 1923, when she moved to Norwich, Connecticut, and continued in private practice. Cogswell's peak productive period appears to be the 1920s; in 1921 she was hired to design the Colonial Revival gardens at the Webb House, now Webb-Deane-Stevens Museum), in Wethersfield, Connecticut, which have recently been restored.

Chapter 5: Daffodils in Cemeteries

1. John Claudius Loudon, *On the Laying Out, Planting, and Managing of Cemeteries,* 21–22.

2. *The Topological, Statistical, and Historical Gazatteer of Scotland,* 650.

3. "Sketches from Munich, No. 3," 193.

4. John Hill Martin, *Historical Sketch of Bethlehem in Pennsylvania,* 83.

5. Olmstead, *A Journey in the Seaboard Slave States,* 406.

6. Ingraham, *The sunny South,* 265–66.

7. Dearborn, *A concise history of, and guide through Mount Auburn,* 16.

8. Poughkeepsie Rural Cemetery, *The Poughkeepsie Rural Cemetery,* 30.

9. Crafts, *Forest Hills Cemetery,* 153.

10. Espy, "Diary," n.p.

11. "Flowers for a Grave," 25.

12. In 1864 the *Canada Farmer* published a similar directive calling for floral restraint:

> In the planting of flowers and flowering shrubs, we notice in our cemeteries a great variety, greater than seems to us to be in keeping with the place or its true associations. Flowers of gaudy hues, flowering in scarlet or flashing in gold, may be attractive adornments of home, but more modest colours seem to us to be most in harmony with the dwellings of the dead. We would plant largely of such shrubs and plants as bear pure white flowers, and if we admitted any others they should be of the most modest tints. The plum-leaved Spirea, the Mock Orange, Deutzia Scabra, Deutzia Gracilis, White Lilac and Mountain Ash-leaved Spirea are some of our hardiest white flowering shrubs, to which might be added a few white flowering herbaceous plants, as the Double White Daisy, Feverfew, White Campanula, Spirea Tilipendula, Lily of the Valley, and the like. With these tastefully planted and properly cared for, our rural cemeteries will soon become what they ought to be, pleasant spots where we sow in hope that the seed we bury in sorrow shall come forth at the last in beauty and vigor immortal. ("Rural Cemeteries," 204)

13. Despite what readers may have been told, a desire for bright colors seems to have lingered for some time.

> We are beginning to use more bright flowers in cemetery lots. Until quite lately we saw mostly white ones there, because most persons associate the idea of death with something as far removed from gayety and brightness as possible, and also because white typifies purity, and the memory of our dead makes them pure to us, for the change blots out all faults and defects, and we think of them as having become "white of soul." Therefore, the white flower is full of suggestiveness for this use. But I consider any flower appropriate, for if we read the lesson of the flowers aright we see the beauty and wisdom of God's character in it, and such lessons are appropriate for any place or time. The flowers we plant upon graves are tributes of affection and remembrance, and any flower can transmit to them the message of our love. Let the cemetery be made bright and beautiful. Take away from it all suggestions of the

"cold, chill grave," and let it typify the "summer-land of God," where the flowers are fadeless, and there are no graves.

I am asked by a correspondent to give a list of some plants suitable for cemetery use, hardy plants which require but little care, and from which a succession of bloom can be obtained through the season.

One of the best shrubs for such use is the Deutzia. It is an early bloomer, and its long, slender branches, with their profusion of white flowers are attractive anywhere. It is quite hardy, and given a good soil and an occasional pruning to remove old and broken branches, is about all the attention it will require. D. gracilis is the best variety for small lots, as it is a dwarf grower.

The Spiraeas are beautiful plants of the easiest culture. S. Billardi is rose color; S. callosa alba is pure white, and S. prunifolia, with its double, Daisy-like flowers, is one of the finest.

For large lots I know of nothing finer than Hydrangea paniculata grandiflora. It is perfectly hardy without any protection whatever, standing our most severe winters without the loss of a bud. That is more than can be said of many native plants. It blossoms in August and September, when most shrubs have ceased to bloom. Its individual flowers are small, but so many of them are borne in a cluster that it has the most massive effect of any shrub I know, and this without any appearance of stiffness or clumsiness. The flowers are waxy white, and last for a long time.

The best Rose for cemetery use, if white is desired, is Madame Plantier. This Rose is not a large one, but the flowers are borne in clusters, and the effect is fine. It is a pure white, a very profuse bloomer and a graceful grower.

An excellent evergreen shrub, growing low and spreading considerably, is Daphne Cneorum. It has pale rose colored flowers, which are very fragrant. It blooms quite profusely in spring and at intervals thereafter during the season. It is perfectly hardy.

Among herbaceous plants we have no white one more beautiful than the Astilbe. It blooms early, and bears its little flowers in great profusion in clustered spikes, which have a feathery grace and delicacy quite charming and unusual among herbaceous plants.

I know of no more beautiful white flowers for the cemetery than some of our Lilies, especially longiflorum and candidum. They are hardy, and planted in good soil where water does not stand in spring, they will give increasing satisfaction year after year and require but little care.

For a vine to train about the enclosure of a lot, one cannot do better than to have our American Ivy. It is so hardy, so robust a grower, so beautiful at all seasons, that it occupies the same place in my regard with the English Ivy, which may be more desirable in some ways, but which has not the beauty of color which its American namesake takes on in fall.

All the plants I have named are robust, self-reliant ones, and they will give pleasure which does not have to be paid for with a great deal of labor.

The Lily of the Valley is a beautiful plant for the cemetery. It blooms early, and no flower has more charms for us. Its purity, its fragrance, its grace makes it a favorite everywhere. It ought to be raised more than it is. It will do well in shade, and can be used where large evergreens would make it useless to try to raise many other flowers. (Rexford, "Flowers for the Cemetery," 299–300)

14. McCandless, *Allegheny Cemetery*, 126.

15. B. T. Wells, *Catalogue and Price-List of Dutch Bulbs and Flower Roots*, 1.

16. "Lily for Grave," 310.

17. Lichen, "My Old Kentucky Home," 603.

18. Shoberl, *The Language of Flowers*, 69.

19. Shoberl included a "Calendar of Flowers;" the chosen Narcissus are presented here for general interest:

The Roman Catholic Monks, or the observers of the Roman Catholic ritual, have compiled a Catalogue of Flowers for every day in the year, and dedicated each flower to a particular saint, on account of its blooming about the time of that saint's festival. These appropriations form a complete Calendar of the Flowers. The figures attached express the year in which the saint died.:

February

6. Narcissus Roman, *Narcissus Romanus*. St. Apollonia, 249.

March

6. Lily, Lent, *Pseudo narcissus multiplex*. St. Colette, bishop, [no date given, author]

7. Daffodil, early, *Narcissus simplex*. St. Perpetua, martyred under the emperor Severus, 203.

8. Jonquil, great, *Narcissus lætus*. St. Felix, 646.

9. Daffodil, hoop-petticoat, *Narcissus bulbocodium*. St. Catherine of Bologna, 1463.

16. Daffodil, nodding, *Narcissus nutans*. St. Julian of Cilicia.

23. Daffodil, peerless, *Narcissus incomparabilis*. St. Alphonsus Turibius, archbishop of Lima, 1606.

27. Jonquil, sweet, *Narcissus odorus*. St. John of Egypt, hermit, 394.

30. Daffodil, lessor, *Narcissus minor*. St. Zosimus, bishop of Syracuse, 660.

April

13. Narcissus, green, *Narcissus viridiflorus*. St. Hermenegild, martyr, 586.

18. Narcissus, musk, *Narcissus moschatus*. St. Apollonius, 186.

21. Narcissus, cypress, *Narcissus orientalis albus*. St. Anselm, Archbishop of Canterbury.

27. Daffodil, great, *Narcissus major*. At. Anastsius, Pope, 401.

May

3 Narcissus, poetic, *Narcissus poeticus*. The discovery of the Cross, 326.

October

29 Narcissus, green autumnal, *Narcissus viridiflorus*. St. Narcissus, bishop of Jerusalem, second century.

This was a reprint from the earlier 1832 *Flora's Dictionary*, by Elizabeth Washington Wirt, who in turn had abstracted it from the 1826 edition of William Hone's *The every-day book, or everlasting calendar of popular amusements, sports. . . .*

20. Gierlow, "The Language of Flowers," 224–25.

21. Tyas, *Language of Flowers*, 215.

22. Surprisingly one of the earliest examples of flowers on gravestones comes from Puritan Cape Cod, Massachusetts, in the early 1700s (1703–1714), where a few headstones and footstones have been documented with the iconography of wilting tulips. Ever intent on reminding the living that death was to be prepared for, the Puritans' illustrations of the demise of the popular tulip seems more pleasant than the better-known images of winged skulls and crossed bones; they were also a reminder that those popular tulips in the strict Puritan world were going to die too.

23. Marion, "Flowers for Cemetery Planting," 126. Gardeners from around the country wrote to their favorite nurseryman's journal, providing lists of suitable cemetery plant material. A more expansive list was provided by a reader in Kentucky in 1894:

I GIVE a list of hardy white flowers, both plants and bulbs, for those who desire only white ones for the cemetery. Where one lives some distance from the cemetery, they will find much more satisfaction in these hardy plants and bulbs than in the tender ones that require constant care and attention. Try always to have flowers of some kind on your loved ones' graves, but never the artificial monstrosities. The list I give will bloom for years without any attention, after they are once started. I give a list of the hardiest kinds only, that require no protection. Do not plant tall shrubs, or spreading plants; that would be an annoyance to the owners of neighboring lots.

First of all comes the Snow Drop, the flowers pure white, with the exception of a margin of green around the centre. Next the Crocus, which are very pretty and sweet, and also very cheap. They are priced at sixty cents per hundred in most of the catalogues. None are too gay for cemetery planting, but if you prefer pure white, Mt. Blanc is an excellent variety, one of the purest whites and a very large flower. The Crocus bloom from eight to ten days, and bloom in this locality about the middle of February or 1st of March.

Next the Narcissus Poeticus, pure white, both single and double. Then the Polyanthus Narcissus, Aurora, Paper White and double Roman are the best. All are white with very little color.

A little later the Hyacinths and Tulips. Of the single Hyacinths, large kinds, all pure white, Albertine, La Franchise and Mozart, are the best, and double Boquette Royal, Jenny Lind and La Virginiate. You can also procure the bulbs of pure white sorts, in both the Grape and Roman Hyacinths. The last named are small, but as sweet as they can be. These will give flowers until the middle of April. Then comes the Lily of the Valley, than which there is nothing sweeter or more suitable for a grave.

The pure white Peonies Iris Kempferi (Gold Bound and J. C. Vaughn) bloom in May and June.

I also give a list of hardy hybrid perpetual Roses and only the best white ones. They will commence to bloom in May or June and bloom through the Summer. Coquette des Alpes, Mad. Fanny de Forest, Coquette des Blanches, Lady Emily Peel, Mad. Francois Pettit, Mad. Plantier (best), Perfection des Blanches and Perle des Blanches.

For August there is the white Plantian or Day Lily; then the old-fashioned Candidum or Annunciation Lily, which is an emblem of purity. Could anything be more appropriate? Speciosum Rubrum, Longiflorum, Album, are all good white Lilies.

The Perennial Phlox blooms from Midsummer until frost, the best white ones being Richard Wallace and White Queen.

Will only give the names of the best early Chrysanthemums: Miss Kate Brown, Lady Shelbourne, Lady St. Clair, Jessica, all excellent varieties, of the purest white, bloom about the middle of October. (Laura Jones, "A List of White Flowers for the Cemetery," 25).

24. Henderson, *Henderson's Handbook of Plants,* 269.

25. George W. Park, "Only a Few Bulbs Left," 218.

26. "Report from Allegheny Cemetery," 118.

27. "The City of Atlanta," 40.

28. "Flowers for Graves," 1.

29. Malone, *History of the Atlanta Ladies Memorial Association,* 48.

30. Spring Grove Cemetery, *The Cincinnati Cemetery of Spring Grove,* 33.

31. Ragan, *Transactions of the Mississippi Valley Horticultural Society,* 273.

32. Mobile, *The Charter and Code of Ordinances,* 54.

33. Harrison, "Mrs. Harrison Again in Florida," 96.

Chapter 6: Daffodils in Historic Gardens

1. Beale, "Chantilly," 2410–11.

2. Wheeler, "Daffodil Bulb Trade," 185–87.

3. Virginia Historic Landmarks Commission Survey Form 76-45, n.p. (continuation sheet/sheet 4).

4. William Robinson, *Hardy Flowers,* 181–82.

5. Cooney et al., *Garden History of Georgia,* 116.

6. Dorris, *Preservation of the Hermitage,* 79–80.

7. Ibid., 200.

8. Sale et al., *Historic Gardens of Virginia,* 118.

9. du Pont, "Naturalized Narcissi at Winterthur," 42.

10. Ibid., 42.

11. Ibid., 45.

12. Ibid., 42.

13. Ibid., 43.

14. Ibid., 43.

15. Ibid., 45.

Bibliography

Many of these works are now available on the Internet. Source websites include the Internet Archive (www.archive.org), Google Books (books.google.com), the Missouri Botanical Garden (www.botanicus.org), the Biodiversity Heritage Library consortium (www.biodiversitylibrary .org), the Digital Library del Real Jardín Botánico CSIC (Consejo Superior de Investigaciones Científicas; the Royal Botanic Garden, Spain) (http://bibdigital.rjb.csic.es/ing/index.php), JSTOR (www.jstor.org), and the HathiTrust Ditigal Library (www.hathitrust.org).

Adams, Denise Wiles. *Restoring American Gardens: An Encyclopedia of Heirloom Ornamental Plants, 1640–1940*. Portland, Ore.: Timber Press, 2004.

Allen, C. L. *Bulbs and Tuberous-Rooted Plants: Their History, Description, Methods of Propagation and Complete Directions for Their Successful Culture in the Garden, Dwelling and Greenhouse*. New York: Orange Judd, 1893.

Amherst, Alicia M. T. (Mrs. Evelyn Cecil). "A Fifteenth Century Treatise on Gardening. By "Mayster Jon Gardener." "In *Archaeologia, or, Miscellaneous Tracts Relating to Antiquity*, vol. 54, pt. 1, 157–72. London: By Society of Antiquaries of London, 1894.

———. *A History of Gardening in England*. London: B. Quaritch, 1896.

Anders, James Meschter. *House-Plants as Sanitary Agents; or, the Relation of Growing Vegetation to Health and Disease. Comprising also a Consideration of the Subject of Practical Floriculture, and of the Sanitary Influences of Forests and Plantations*. Philadelphia: J. B. Lippencott, 1887.

Anderson, Richard LeConte. *LeConte History and Genealogy: With Particular Reference to Guillaume Leconte of New Rochelle and New York and His Descendants*. Vol. 2. Macon, Ga.: R. L. Anderson, 1981.

Andrews, Karin. "The Daffodils of Gloucester." *House and Home Magazine* 1, no. 7 (March/April 2009): 52–58.

Ant. Roozen & Son. *Ant. Roozen & Son's Catalogue of Choice Dutch, Cape and Exotic Bulbs and Herbaceous Plants, Together with General Cultural Directions and flowering Periods for all classes of bulbs, and plants*. Overveen, Holland: Ant. Roozen & Son, 1904.

Ashe, Thomas. *Carolina; or a Description of the Present State of that Country, and the Natural Excellencies thereof, viz. The Healthfulness of the Air, Pleasantness of the Place, Advantage and Usefulness of those Rich Commodities there plentifully abounding, which much encrease and flourish by the Industry of the Planters that daily enlarge that Colony*. Tarrytown, N.Y. Reprint, William Abbatt, 1917. Being Extra Number 59 of the Magazine of History with Notes and Queries.

Aubrey, John. *The Natural History of Wiltshire*. Middlesex: Echo Library, 2006.

Bacon, Francis. *On Gardens An Essay. With Introduction by Helen Milman and Frontispiece and Cover Design by Edmund H. New*. London: John Lane, 1902.

Bailey, Liberty H., and William Miller. *Cyclopedia of American Horticulture, comprising suggestions for cultivation of horticultural plants, descriptions of the species of fruits, vegetables, flowers and ornamental plants sold in the United States and Canada, together with geographical and biographical sketches.* New York: Macmillan, 1904.

Barr, Peter. "Early Days of the Daffodil." *Garden* 69, no. 1799 (May 12, 1906): 255–56.

———. "Early Days of the Daffodil." *Garden* 69, no. 1802 (June 2, 1906): 297.

———. *Ye narcissus or daffodyl flowere: containing hys historie and culture, &c., with a compleat liste of all the species and varieties known to Englyshe amateurs.* London: Solde by Barre & Sonne, 1884.

Barr, Peter R. "The Renaissance of the Daffodil in Britain." In *The Daffodil Year-Book 1933* 4, London: Royal Horticultural Society (1933): 23–24.

Barr & Sons. *Barr's "Gold Medal" Daffodils.* London: Barr & Sons, 1906.

Barr & Sugden. *Barr & Sugden's Autumnal Catalogue, comprising choice selections of Dutch, Cape flowering bulbs, &c.* London: Barr & Sugden, 1861.

Bauhin, Caspar. *Caspari Bauhini Pinax Theatri botanici: sive Index in Theophrasti, Dioscoridis, Plinii et botanicorum qui à seculo scripserunt opera : plantarum circiter sex millium ab ipsis exhibitarum nomina cum earundem synonymijs & differentiis methodice secundum genera & species proponens : opus XL. annorum summopere expetitum ad autoris autographum recensitum.* Basileæ: Impensis Joannis Regis, 1671.

Beale, George William. "Chantilly, the Home of Richard Lee." *Northern Neck of Virginia Historical Magazine* 23, no. 1 (December 1973): 2409–12.

Bemiss, Margaret Page, and Roger Foley. *Historic Virginia Gardens: Preservation Work of the Garden Club of Virginia, 1975–2007.* Charlottesville, Va.: University of Virginia Press, 2009.

Bender, Steve. "Love Forever, Annie Lou. (Sisters' Bulb Farm in Gibson, Louisiana, Which Grows Legacy-Type Daffodils and Jonquils.)" *Southern Living* 32, no. 3 (March 1997): 146–49.

Berkeley, Edmund, and Dorothy Smith Berkeley, eds. *The Correspondence of John Bartram, 1734–1777.* Gainesville, Fla.: University Press of Florida, 1992.

Besler, Basilius. *The Book of Plants: The Complete Plates.* Edited by Klaus Walter Littger and Werner Dressendörfer. Köln: Taschen, 2007.

Betts, Edwin Morris, ed. *Thomas Jefferson's Garden Book 1766—1824, with Relevant Extracts from His Other Writings.* Memoirs of the American Philosophical Society 22. Philadelphia: American Philosophical Society, 1944.

Betts, Edwin M., and Hazlehurst Bolton Perkins. *Thomas Jefferson's Flower Garden at Monticello.* 2nd ed. Charlottesville, Va.: University Press of Virginia, 1971.

B. K. Bliss & Sons. *B. K. Bliss & Sons' Autumn Catalogue and Floral Guide, 1880–1881.* New York: B. K. Bliss & Sons, 1880.

Blight, Robert, ed. "Among the Plants: Garden Field and Forest—California Daffodils." *Current Literature, A Magazine of Record and Review* 29 (July–December, 1900): 468–70.

Bourne, Stephen Eugene. *The Book of the Daffodil.* London, New York: John Lane, 1903.

Bowles, Edward Augustus. *A Handbook of Narcissus.* London: Martin Hopkinson, 1934.

Bradley, Richard. *New improvements of planting and gardening, both philosophical and practical; explaining the motion of the sapp and generation of plants.* London: printed for W. Mears, 1718.

Breck, Joseph. *The Flower-Garden, or, Breck's Book of Flowers, in which are described all the various hardy herbaceous perennials, annuals, shrubby plants, and evergreen trees, desirable for ornamental purposes, with directions for their cultivation.* Boston: John P. Jewett, 1851.

———. *The Flower-Garden: or, Breck's Book of Flowers; in which are described the various hardy herbaceous perennials, annuals, shrubby plants, and evergreen trees, desirable for ornamental purposes, with directions for their cultivation.* New ed., rev. and enlarged. New York: A. O. Moore, 1858.

Brickell, John. *The Natural History of North Carolina, with an account of the trade, manners, and customs of the Christian and Indian inhabitants. Illustrated with Copper-Plates, whereon are engraved the Map of the Country, strange Beasts, Birds, Fishes, Snakes, Insects and Plants, &c.* Dublin: Printed by James Carson for the Author, 1737.

Bridgeman, Thomas. *The young gardener's assistant: containing a catalogue of garden & flower seeds, with practical directions under each head, for the cultivation of culinary vegetables and flowers; also directions for cultivating fruit trees, the grape vine, &c.; to which is added, a calendar, showing the work necessary to be done in the various departments of gardening in every month of the year.* New York: Mitchell & Turner, Printers, 1837.

Briggs, Loutrell Winslow. *Charleston Gardens.* Columbia: University of South Carolina Press, 1951.

Brinkley, M. Kent, and Gordon W. Chappell. *The Gardens of Colonial Williamsburg.* Williamsburg, Va.: Colonial Williamsburg Foundation, 1996.

Broker, Stephen P. *Death and Dying in Puritan New England: A Study Based on Early Gravestones, Vital Records, and other Primary Sources Relating to Cape Cod, Massachusetts.* Yale–New Haven Teachers Institute. Yale National Initiative, Curriculum Unit 03.02.01, 2003.

B. T. Wells. *Catalogue and Price-List of Dutch Bulbs and Flower Roots Imported by B. T. Wells.* Boston: B. T. Wells, 1882.

Buist, Robert. *American flower-garden directory: containing practical directions for the culture of plants in the flower-garden, hot-house, green-house, rooms, or parlour windows. . . .* 5th ed. Philadelphia: A. Hart, late Carey and Hart, 1854.

"Bulbous Flowers for Autumn Planting." *American Agriculturist* 16, no. 10 (October 1857): 230.

"The Bulb Growing Industry." *Success with Flowers, a Floral Magazine* 3, no. 5 (February 1893): 133.

"Bulb Purchases." *Gardener and Practical Florist* 2 (1843): 296.

Burbidge, Frederick William "Double Daffodils and Narcissi." *Garden* 25 (April 12, 1884): 296–97.

———. "The Narcissus." *Journal of the Royal Horticultural Society* 11 (1889): 70–92.

———. *The narcissus: its history and culture: with coloured plates and descriptions of all known species and principal varieties. By F. W. Burbidge, to which is added by kind permission, a scientific review of the entire genus, by J. G. Baker.* London: L. Reeve, 1875.

Burchell, William. *A Catalogue of Trees, Shrubs, and Plants; also Fruit-Trees and Flowers; which are propagated for sale, by William Burchell, Nursery-Man, at Fullham in Middlesex.* London, 1764.

Burke, Anna M. "Garden Adventures." *Art World* 2 (July 1917): 394–96.

Bynum, Flora Ann L. *Cultivated Plants of the Wachovia Tract in North Carolina 1759–1764. Christian Gottlieb Reuter's Lists of Plants Grown at Behabara, in the Vegetable Garden, the Medicinal Garden, and in the Fields.* Winston-Salem, N.C.: Old Salem, 1979.

———. "Old World Gardens in the New World: The Gardens of the Moravian Settlement of Bethabara in North Carolina, 1753–72." *Journal of Garden History* 16, no. 2 (1996): 70–86.

Camp, George Hull, Connie M. Cox, and Darlene M. Walsh, eds. *Providence: Selected correspondence of George Hull Camp, 1837–1907: son of the North, citizen of the South: including letters from the Camp, King, Atwood and Dunwoody families. . . .* Macon, Ga.: Indigo Publishing, 2008.

Capen, Oliver Bronson. *Country Homes of Famous Americans.* New York: Doubleday, Page, 1905.

Carr, William, and Robert Carr. *Catalogue of trees, shrubs, and herbaceous plants, indigenous to the United States of America: cultivated and for sale at Bartram's Botanical Garden, Kingsess, near Philadelphia, to which is added a catalogue of foreign plants, collected from various parts of the globe.* Philadelphia: William and Robert Carr, 1814. James R. Cothran Papers, 1771–2006, Mss. 989, Cherokee Garden Library, Kenan Research Center at the Atlanta History Center.

C. E. Allen. *Bulbs and Plants for Winter Culture. Small Fruits.* Brattleboro, Vt.: C. E. Allen, 1890.

Charleston Botanic Society and Garden. *Catalogue of Plants in the Botanick Garden of South-Carolina, Charleston, S.C.* Printed for the Botanick Society, by E. Morford, Willington, 1810.

"Chat about Flowers." *Vick's Monthly Magazine* 2, no. 10 (October 1879): 308.

"The Chinese National Flower." *Vick's Monthly Magazine* 1, no. 3 (March 1878): 84.

"Circulation." *Mayflower* 14, no. 10 (October 1898): 405.

"A City Back Yard." *Park's Floral Magazine* 45, no. 12 (December 1909): 192.

"The City of Atlanta." *Harper's New Monthly Magazine* 60, no. 355 (December 1879): 30–43.

Clare, Henrietta Ramsy. *Plans for Restoration of the Kincaid-Anderson Gardens, c.1789, Jenkinsville, South Carolina.* M.A. thesis, Clemson University, 1976.

Clusius, Carolus. *Caroli Clusi Atrebatis, Impp. Caess. Augg., Maximiliani II, Rudolphi II, aulae quondam familiaris, Rariorum plantarum historia: quae accesserint, proxima pagina docebit.* Antverpiae: Ex officina Plantiniana: Apud Ioannem Moretum, 1601.

———.*Caroli Clusii Atrebat Rariorum alioquot stirpium per Hispanias observatarum historia: libris duobus expressas....* Antverpiae: Ex officina Christophori Plantinus, 1576.

———. *Rariorum alioquat stirpium per Hispanius....* Antverpiae: Ex officina Christophori Plantinus..., 1576.

Collinson, Peter. *Forget not Mee & My Garden, Selected Letters 1725–1768 of Peter Collinson F.R.S.* Edited and with introduction by Alan W. Armstrong. Philadelphia: American Philosophical Society, 2002.

Commelini, Johannes. *Catalogus Plantarum Horti Medici Amstelodamensis. Pars Prior.* Amstelodami: Ex typographia Commeliniana, Sumptibus Arnoldi Oosaen, 1689.

Commission of Fine Arts. *The National Commission of Fine Arts, Ninth Report, July 1, 1919–June 30, 1921.* Washington, D.C.: Government Printing Office, 1921.

Cooney, Loraine Meeks, Hattie C. Rainwater, Florence Nesbit Marye, and Phillip Thorton Marye. *Garden History of Georgia, 1733–1933.* Atlanta: Peachtree Garden Club, 1933.

Cothran, James R. *Gardens and Historic Plants of the Antebellum South.* Charleston: University of South Carolina Press, 2003.

———. *Gardens of Historic Charleston.* Charleston: University of South Carolina Press, 1995.

Coulter, John Merle, John Gaylord Coulter, and Alice Jean Patterson. *Practical Nature Study and Elementary Agriculture: A Manual for the Use of Teachers and Normal Students.* New York: D. Appleton, 1909.

Crafts, William August. *Forest Hills Cemetery: Its Establishment, Progress, Scenery, Monuments, Etc.* Boston: Damrell & Moore and George Coolidge, 1860.

"C.R.C." (Lieutenant Condor). "The Rose of Sharon." In *Palestine Exploration Fund. Quarterly Statement for 1878,* January 1878, 46. London: Palestine Exploration Fund, 1878.

Curtis, William. *The botanical magazine, or, Flower-garden displayed: In which the Most Ornamental Foreign Plants, Cultivated in the Open Ground, the Green House, and the Stove, Will be Accurately Represented in Their Natural Colours: to which Will be Added, Their Names, Class, Order, Generic and Specific Characters, According to the Celebrated Linnaeus; Their Places of Growth, and Times of Flowering: Together with the Most Approved Methods of Culture: a Work Intended for the Use of Such Ladies, Gentlemen, and Gardeners, as Wish to Become Scientifically Acquainted with the Plants They Cultivate.* London: Printed for W. Curtis by Fry and Couchman, 1787–1800.

Dabney, Edith. "Quaint Houses of the South, III: Wye House." *House and Garden* 12 (July 1907): 24–26.

"Daffodil Garden Club Holds First Flower Show." *Atlanta Constitution* (1881—2001): March 24, 1929; ProQuest Historical Newspapers Atlanta Constitution (1868–1929), p. E9.

"Daffodils in Grass." *Gardening* 17, no. 388 (November 1, 1908): 50–51.

D'Alcorn, O. W. "Outdoor Bulb Growing for Cut Flowers." In *Proceedings of the Twenty-fifth Convention of the Society of American Florists and Ornamental Horticulturists.* Held at Cincinnati, Ohio, August 17, 18, 19 and 20, 1909, 48–50. N.p.: Society of American Florists and Ornamental Horticulturists, n.d.

"The Day of the Daffodil." *New York Times,* April 30, 1893. New York Times Article Archives, http://select.nytimes.com/gst/abstract.html?res=F30EIEFE3F5515738DODA90B94DC405B8385F0D3.

Dearborn, Nathaniel. *A concise history of, and guide through Mount Auburn: with a catalogue of lots laid out in that cemetery, a map of the grounds, and terms of subscription, regulations concerning visitors, interments, &c., &c.* Boston: N. Dearborn, 1843.

de Graaff, Jan. "Daffodils—A Review and Preview." In *The 1960 American Daffodil Yearbook,* edited by Carey E. Quinn, 10–20. Frederick, Md.: Frederick News-Post, 1960.

De Jong, Eric. *Nature and Art: Dutch Garden and Landscape Architecture.* Philadelphia: University of Pennsylvania Press, 2000.

Deland, Margaret. "Jonquils." *Good Housekeeping* 39, no. 2 (August 1904): 162–66.

Devens, Samuel Adams. *Sketches of Martha's Vineyard and Other Reminiscences of Travels at Home, etc.* Boston: James Munroe, 1838.

Dickinson, Emily. *Emily Dickinson's Herbarium.* Cambridge, Mass.: Belknap Press of Harvard University Press, 2006.

Dictionary of Trade, Commerce and Navigation: Explanatory of the Objects, Terms, Statistics, Laws and Regulations of the Excise, Customs, Public Affairs, Banking, Monies, Weights, Shipping, Fisheries, Imports, Exports, Book-Keeping, Commercial Geography, National Flags, the General Affairs of Business, Corrected up to the Latest Period. Brittain, Paternoster Row: Berger, Hoylwell Street, 1844.

Dodoens, Rembert. *A nievve herball, or, Historie of plantes: wherein is contayned the vvhole discourse and perfect description of all sortes of herbes and plantes: their diuers and sundry kindes . . . and that not onely of those whiche are here growyng in this our countrie of Englande but of all others also of forrayne realmes commonly used in physicke. First set foorth in the Doutche or Almaigne tongue/by that learned D. Rembert Dodoens . . . and now first translated out of French into English, by Henry Lyte, Esquyer.* London: Mr. Gerard Dewes, 1578.

Donn, James. *Hortus Cantabrigiensis, or a Catalogue of Plants, indigenous and foreign, cultivated at the Walkerian Botanic Garden, Cambridge.* 2nd ed. Cambridge: John Burges, 1800.

———. *Hortus Cantabrigiensis, or A Catalogue of Plants indigenous and foreign, cultivated in the Walkerian Botanic Garden, Cambridge.* Cambridge: Printed by John Burges, and sold by James Donn, 1796.

Dorris, Mary C. *Preservation of the Hermitage, 1889–1915: annals, history, and stories; The Acquisition, Restoration and Care of the Home of General Andrew Jackson by the Ladies' Hermitage Association for over a Quarter of a Century.* Nashville, Tenn.: Smith and Lamar, 1915.

Downing, Andrew J. *A treatise on the theory and practice of landscape gardening, adapted to North America; with a view to the improvement of country residences. Comprising historical notices and general principles of the art, directions for laying out gardens and arranging plantations, the description and cultivation of hardy trees, decorative accompaniments to the house and grounds, the formation of pieces of artificial water, flower gardens, etc., with remarks on rural architecture.* New York: Wiley and Putnam, 1844.

du Pont, H. F. "Naturalizing Narcissi." *The Daffodil Year-Book 1915,* 67–68. London: Spottiswoode, 1915.

———— "Naturalized Narcissi at Winterthur." *The Daffodil and Tulip Year Book 1961*, no. 26, 41–46. London: Royal Horticultural Society, 1961.

————. "Dutch Catalogues." *The Gardeners' Chronicle. A Weekly Illustrated Journal of Horticulture and Allied Subjects* 4 (August 28, 1875): 274.

Earle, Alice Morse. *Old Time Gardens, Newly Set Forth by Alice Morse Earle; a Book of the Sweet O' the Year.* New York: Macmillan; London: Macmillan, 1901.

"Editorial Buds." *Southern Cultivator and Dixie Farmer* 44, no. 12 (December 1886): 496.

Edwards, Sydenham. *The New Flora Britannica, illustrated with one hundred and thirty-three plants, engraved by Sansom, from the original pictures, and coloured with the greatest exactness from drawings by Sydenham Edwards.* London: Printed for John Stockdale, by T. Bensley, 1812.

E. H. Krelage & Son. *No. 411 1st August 1888. Catalogue of Dutch Flowers Cultivated for Sale by E. H. Krelage & Son, American Edition.* Haarlem, Holland: E. H. Krelage & Son, 1888.

————. *Preis-Verzeichniss von Allen Gattengen (sp) Blumenzwiebeln.* Welche in den schonsten und auserlesensten Sorten, zu bekommen sind bei E. H. Krelage, Blumist zu Haarlem in Holland, (Kleine Houtweg, No. 148). 1846. Collection: Antiquariaat FORUM BV 't Goy-Houton (Netherlands).

Elder, Walter. "Plant Hardy Bulbs." *Gardener's Monthly and Horticultural Advisor, Devoted to Horticulture, Arboriculture, Botany and Rural Affairs* 2, no. 10 (October 1869): 294–95.

————. "The Pleasures of Bulb Culture." *Gardener's Monthly. Devoted to Horticulture, Arboculture, Botany and Rural Affairs* 5, no. 10 (October 1863): 299.

Ellwanger, George Herman. *The Garden's Story, or Pleasures and Trials of an Amateur Gardener.* New York: D. Appleton, 1889.

Ellwanger and Barry. *1845 & 1846. Descriptive Catalogue of Fruits, Ornamental Trees, Flowering Shrubs and Plants, cultivated and for sale by Ellwanger & Barry, at the Mount Hope Botanic Garden and Nurseries, Saint Paul-Street, Nearly Opposite the Cemetery, Rochester, N.Y.* Rochester: Printed by Canfield & Warren, Under the Museum, 1845. James R. Cothran Papers, 1771–2006, Mss. 989, Cherokee Garden Library, Kenan Research Center at the Atlanta History Center.

————. *1846 & 1847. Descriptive Catalogue of Fruits, Ornamental Trees, Flowering Shrubs and Plants, cultivated and for sale by Ellwanger & Barry, at the Mount Hope Botanic Garden and Nurseries, Saint Paul Street, Nearly Opposite the Cemetery, Rochester, New-York.* Rochester: Power Press of the Daily Advertiser, 1846. James R. Cothran Papers, 1771–2006, Mss. 989, Cherokee Garden Library, Kenan Research Center at the Atlanta History Center.

El-Shimy, M. "Preparation and Use of Perfumes and Perfumed Substances in Ancient Egypt." In *Molecular and Structural Archaeology: Cosmetic and Therapeutic Chemicals*, edited by Georges Tsoucaris and Janusz Lipkowski, 29–50; Spring 2003, Proceedings of the NATO Advanced Research Workshop on Molecular and Structural Archaeology: Cosmetic and Therapeutic Chemicals, Erice, Sicily, Italy, May 23–27, 2002. Dordrecht, Netherlands: Kulwer Academic Publishers, 2003.

Ely, Helena Rutherfurd. *A Woman's Hardy Garden.* New York: Macmillan, 1903.

Emmet, Alan. "Kirk Boott and the Greening of Boston, 1783–1845." *Arnoldia* 47, no. 4 (Fall 1987): 24–34.

Encyclopaedia Americana. A Popular Dictionary of Arts, Sciences, Literature, History, Politics and Biography, Brought Down to the Present Time; Including a Copious Collection of Original Articles in American Biography; on the Basis of the Seventh Edition of the German Conversations-Lexicon. Vol. 5. Edited by Francis Lieber, Edward Wigglesworth, and Thomas Gamaliel Bradford. Philadelphia: Carey and Lea, 1831.

Engleheart, George. "The Daffodil in Cornwall." *Cornish Magazine* 1: 322–32.

———. "Seedling Daffodils." *Journal of the Royal Horticultural Society* 11 (1889): 93–100.

"The English Florist: Description and Culture of Bulbous-Rooted Flowers." *Lady's Magazine* 17 (1787): 345–48.

Epstein, Susan. "1810 Catalogue of Plants in the Botanick Garden of South-Carolina." *Magnolia* 25, no. 3 (Summer 2012): 6–7.

Espy, Sarah R. "Diary Kept by Sarah Espy from 1859 to 1868, While Living in Cherokee County, Alabama." Alabama Department of Archives and History, Montgomery, Alabama. ADAH Digital Archives: http://digital.archives.alabama.gov/cdm/compoundobject/collection/voices/id/3607/rec/1.

Estienne, Charles. *L'Agriculture et Maison Rustique.* Paris: Jaques du Puis, 1564.

Estienne, Charles, et. al. *Maison rustique, or The countrey farme. Now newly reuiewed, corrected, and augmented with diuers large additions . . . and the husbandrie of France, Italie, and Spaine reconciled and made to agree with ours here in England.* London: Printed by Adam Islip for John Bill, 1616.

Evelyn, John. *Elysium Britannicum, or The Royal Gardens.* Edited by John E. Ingram. Philadelphia: University of Pennsylvania Press, 2001.

Ewing, Juliana Horatia. "Juliana Horatia Ewing 1869." In *Garden Voices, Two Centuries of Canadian Garden Writing,* edited by Edwinna von Baeyer and Pleasance Kaufman Crawford, 224–28. Toronto: Random House of Canada, 1995.

"Experiments in Bulb Culture." *Gardening* 15, no. 343 (December 15, 1906): 99.

Faris, John T. *Old Gardens in and about Philadelphia and Those Who Made Them.* Indianapolis: Bobbs-Merrill, 1932.

Faris, William. *The Diary of William Faris, the Daily Life of an Annapolis Silversmith.* Edited by Mark B. Letzer and Jean B. Russo. Baltimore: Press at the Maryland Historical Society, 2003.

Federal Writers' Project (N.C.). *North Carolina: A Guide to the Old North State.* Chapel Hill: University of North Carolina Press, 1939.

Fessenden, Thomas G. *The New American Gardener, containing practical directions on the culture of fruits and vegetables; including landscape and ornamental gardening, grape-vines, silk, strawberries, &c. &c.* Boston: J. B. Russell, 1835.

Fitter, Richard Sidney Richmond. *London's Natural History.* New Naturalist 3. London: Collins, 1945.

Fitzpatrick, John T. "Plants Recorded by Jacob Smith, 1844 through 1859." *Magnolia* 6, no. 4 (Spring 1990): 9.

Flint, Timothy. *A Condensed Geography and History of the Western States, or the Mississippi Valley.* Cincinnati: E. H. Flint, 1828.

———. *The History and Geography of the Mississippi Valley: to which is appended a condensed physical geography of the Atlantic United States, and the whole American continent.* Cincinnati: E. H. Flint; Boston: Carter, Hendee, 1833.

———. *Recollections of the last ten years, passed in occasional residences and Journeyings in the Valley of the Mississippi . . . from Pittsburg and the Missouri to the Gulf of Mexico, and from Florida to the Spanish frontier, in a series of letters to the Rev. James Flint, of Salem, Massachusetts.* Boston: Cummings, Hilliard, 1826.

"Florida's Burbank Specializes in Bulbs Pioneer Plant Breeder of Alachua County Is a Benefactor of State-Wide Agriculture for He Has Developed New Crops and Found Profitable Pathways to Market." *Florida Grower* 33, no. 12, Whole No. 909 (March 20, 1926): 1, 14.

"Flowering of Fruit-Trees in 1857." In *American Almanac and Repository of Useful Knowledge for the Year 1858,* 91. Boston: Crosby, Nichols; London: Turner; Paris: Bossange, 1857.

Flowers, John Baxter. "The Garden at Flowery Dale Plantation, Eastern North Carolina, 1835–1878." *Magnolia* 2, no. 3 (Winter 1986): 8–9.

"Flowers for a Grave." *American Agriculturist for the Farm, Garden and Household* 25, no. 1 (January 1866): 25.

"Flowers for Graves." *Constitution*, August 23, 1879, 1.

"Flower Trade." In *The Popular Encyclopedia; Being a General Dictionary of Arts, Sciences, Literature, Biography, History and Political Economy*, vol. 3, pt. 1, 217. Glasgow: Blackie and Son, 1835.

Frankland, Charles Henry. *Charles Henry Frankland, Diary, 1755–1767.* Reel 4, vol. 4.4. Pre-Revolutionary Diaries at the Massachusetts Historical Society (Guide to the Microfilm Edition). Call number P-363, Massachusetts Historical Society, Boston.

Fraser, Charles. "Gardening." In *The Charleston Book, A Miscellany in Prose and Verse*, edited by William Gilmore Simms, 165–81. Charleston, S.C.: Samuel Hart, 1845.

Fréard du Castel, Raoul-Adrien. *L'École du Jardinier Fleurist.* A Yverdon, 1767.

Fruitland Nurseries. *Dutch Bulbs and Other Flowering Roots.* Augusta, Ga.: P. J. Berckmans, 1867. Broadsides Collection, Hargrett Rare Book and Manuscript Library, University of Georgia Libraries, Athens, Georgia.

Fuller, Sarah E. "The Woman's Relief Corps." *New England Magazine* 2, no. 6 (August 1890): 633–39.

Galloway, B. T. "Bulb Growing in Washington." *Gardening* 16, no. 373 (March 15, 1908): 200.

Gandy, Joan W., and Thomas H. Gandy. *Natchez: City Streets Revisited.* Charleston, S.C.: Arcadia Publishing, 1999.

"The Garden Notes of Lady Jean Skipwith. Part I." *Garden Gossip* 10, no. 2 (February 1935): 9–10.

"The Garden Notes of Lady Jean Skipwith. Part II." *Garden Gossip* 10, no. 4 (April 1935): 3–4.

Gentil, François, and Louis Liger. *Le Jardinier Solitaire, The solitary or Carthusian gard'ner, being dialogues between a gentleman and a gard'ner . . . ./written in French by François Gentil . . . ; also The Compleat Florist, or; The universal culture of flowers, trees and shrubs . . ./by the sieur Louis Liger d'Auxerre. . . .* London: Printed for Benjamin Tooke, 1706.

George W. Park. "Bulbs for Cemetery Planting." *Park's Floral Magazine* 42, no. 9 (September 1906): n.p.

———. "Bulbs for the Cemetery." *Park's Floral Magazine* 32, no. 11 (November 1896): n.p.

———. "Narcissus! Narcissus!!" *Park's Floral Magazine* 22, no. 12 (December 1886): 194.

———. "Only a Few Bulbs Left." *Park's Floral Magazine* 45, no. 12 (December 1909): 218.

———. *Park's Bulb Catalogue. For 1887.* Fannettsburg, Pa.: George W. Park, 1886.

Gerard, John. *The Herball, or, Generall historie of plantes/gathered by John Gerarde of London, master in chirurgerie.* London: John Norton, 1597.

———. *The herball or Generall historie of plantes. Gathered by John Gerarde of London master in chirvrgerie; Very much enlarged and amended by Thomas Johnson citizen and apothecarye of London.* London: Printed by Adam Islip[,] Joice Norton and Richard Whitakers, 1636.

The Gertrude Jekyll Papers. Seabury Society for the Preservation of the Glebe House. Woodbury, Connecticut.

Gierlow, John. "The Language of Flowers. According to the Oriental Interpretation inscribed to the Ladies of the South. By John Gierlow, of Macon, Ga." *Southern Cultivator* 14, no. 7 (July 1856): 224–25.

Goldgar, Anne. *Tulipmania: Money, Honor and Knowledge in the Dutch Golden Age.* Chicago: University of Chicago Press, 2007.

Gordon, Alexander. "Notices of some of the principal Nurseries and Private Gardens in the United States of America, made during a Tour through the Country, in the Summer of 1831; with some Hints on Emigration." *Gardeners' Magazine*, June 1832, 277–89.

Grant, M. Forsyth (Mrs. Minnie Caroline Robinson Grant). *Scenes in Hawaii, or Life in the Sandwich Islands.* Toronto: Hart, 1888.

Gray, Andrew. "Ornamental Gardening in the South." *Magazine of Horticulture, Botany and All Useful Discoveries and Improvements in Rural Affairs* 51 (May 1855): 223–25.

———. "The Gardens of the South." *Magazine of Horticulture* 21, no. 2 (February 1855): 83.

Green, Roland J. *A treatise on the cultivation of ornamental flowers: comprising remarks on the requisite soil, sowing, transplanting, and general management: with directions for the general treatment of bulbous flower roots, green house plants, &c.* Boston: John B. Russell; New York: G. Thorburn & Son, 1828.

Grube & Nieuwland. *Wholesale Catalogue, of Superior Dutch Bulbs, and Other Flowering Roots.* New York: Washington Hull, Steard Book and Fine Job Printing Establishment, 1872.

H. "Eighteenth Century Gardening. Border Flowers." *Journal of Horticulture and Home Farmer* 56, no. 1441 (February 6, 1908): 129.

Hampden, Mary. *Bulb Gardening.* New York: C. Scribner's Sons, 1922.

Hanmer, Lord John. *A Memorial of the Parish and Family of Hanmer in Flintshire, out of the Thirteenth and into the Nineteenth Century.* London: Chiswick Press, 1876.

Hanmer, Sir Thomas Bart. *The Garden Book of Sir Thomas Hanmer, Bart.* Introduction by Eleanour Sinclair Rohde. Mold, Clwyd (Wales): Cyngor Sir Clwyd County Council Library and Information Service, 1991.

Hannibal, Lester H. "Tazettas." *Daffodil Handbook: A Special Issue of the American Horticultural Magazine* 45, no. 1 (1966): 137–40.

Harbour, J. L. "A Flower Loving Author." *Success with Flowers* 8, no. 7 (April 1898): 132.

Harkness, Deborah E. *The Jewel House: Elizabethan London and the Scientific Revolution.* New Haven: Yale University Press, 2007.

Harrison, Mrs. "Mrs. Harrison Again in Florida; Japonicas; Southern Cemeteries; Bees Visiting Cut Flowers." *Gleanings in Bee Culture, A Journal Devoted to Bees, Honey and Home Interests* 26, no. 3 (February 1, 1898): 96.

Hartland, William Baylor. *Hartland's "Original" Little Book of Daffodils."* Cork: Printed by Purcell Printers, 1885.

Harvey, John H. "The English Nursery Flora, 1677–1723." *Garden History* 26, no. 1 (Summer 1998): 60–101.

———. "The First English Garden Book: Mayster Jon Gardener's Treatise and Its Background." *Garden History* 13, no. 2 (Autumn 1985): 83–101.

———. *The Nursery Garden.* London: Museum of London, 1990.

Hatch, Peter J. "Restoring the Monticello Landscape, 1923–1955." *Magnolia* 23, no. 1 (Fall 2009–Winter 2010): 1–8.

Hedrick, U. P. *A History of Horticulture in America to 1860.* New York: Oxford University Press, 1950.

Henderson, Peter. *Garden and Farm Topics.* New York: Peter Henderson, 1884.

———. *Gardening for Pleasure: a guide to the amateur in the fruit, vegetable, and flower garden, with full directions for the greenhouse, conservatory, and window-garden.* New York: Orange Judd, 1875.

———. *Handbook of Plants and General Horticulture.* New York: Peter Henderson, 1890.

———. *Handbook of Plants and General Horticulture.* New York: Peter Henderson, 1904.

———. *Henderson's Handbook of Plants.* New York: Peter Henderson, 1881.

———. *Practical Floriculture; a Guide to the Successful Cultivation of Florists' Plants, for the Amateur and Professional Florist.* New York: Orange Judd, 1869.

Hendrick, Burton J. *The Lees of Virginia, Biography of a Family.* Boston: Little, Brown, 1935.

Henry A. Dreer. *1870–1871. Dreer's Descriptive Catalogue of Bulbs and Other Flower Roots.* Philadelphia: Collins, Printer, 1870.

———. *Dreer's Autumn Catalogue 1896 Bulbs, Plants, Seeds.* Philadelphia: Henry A. Dreer, 1896.

———. "Dreer's Old-Fashioned Hardy Garden Plants." *Garden Magazine* 3 no. 2 (March 1906): 89.

"Henry Middleton's Seed and Plant Order (circa 1800)." In *Southern Plants List,* edited by Gordon W. Chappell, 73–76. Southern Garden History Society and the Colonial Williamsburg Foundation, 2000. http://southerngardenhistory.org/PDF/SouthernPlantLists.pdf.

Herbert, William. *Amaryllidaceæ, preceded by an attempt to arrange the monocotyledonous orders, and followed by a treatise on cross-bred vegetables, and supplement.* London: James Ridgway and Sons, 1837.

———. "Hybrid Narcissi." *Edwards's Botanical Register* 29 (August 1843): Plate 38.

H. G. Hastings Co. *70th Catalog Fall 1925.* Atlanta: H. G. Hastings Co., 1925.

———. *Bulbs and Roses, H. G. Hastings & Co.* Atlanta: H. G. Hastings Co., n.d.

Hibbert, Thomas, and Robert Buist. *The American Flower Directory: containing practical directions for the culture of plants in the hot-house, garden-house, flower garden, and rooms or parlours, for every month in the year. With a description of the plants most desirable in each, the nature of the soil and situation best adapted to their growth, the proper season for transplanting, &c. Instructions for erecting a hot-house, green-house, and laying out a flower garden. Also, Tables of Soils most congenial to the Plants contained in the Work. The whole adapted to either large or small gardens, with lists of annuals, biennials, and ornamental shrubs, contents, a general index, And a Frontispiece of Camellia Fimbriata.* Philadelphia: Adam Waldie, 1832.

Hitchcock, Susan L. *Dungeness Historic District Cultural Landscape Report.* Cultural Resources, Southeast Regional Office, National Park Service, 2007.

Hobhouse, Penelope. *Plants in Garden History.* London: Pavilion Books, 1992.

———. *The Story of Gardening.* London: DK Publishing. 2002.

Hogg, James. "Bulbous Roots." *Magazine of Horticulture, Botany and All Useful Discoveries and Improvements in Rural Affairs* 13 (October 1847): 4.

———. "On the Cultivation of Bulbous Roots in Pots and Glasses." *American Farmer* 2, no. 5 (November 1846): 150–52.

Holmes, Abiel. *The Annals of America, from the Discovery by Columbus in the Year 1492, to the year 1826.* Cambridge: Hilliard and Brown, 1829.

Hone, William. *The every-day book, or everlasting calendar of popular amusements, sports. . . .* London: Hunt and Clarke, 1826.

Hosack, David. *Hortus Elginensis, or A catalogue of plants, indigenous and exotic, cultivated in the Elgin Botanic Garden, in the vicinity of the city of New-York: established in 1801.* New York: Printed by T. & J. Swords, 1811.

Hovey, Charles Mason. "Art. IV. Flower and Bulb Gardens. By the Editor." *Magazine of Horticulture, Botany and All Useful Discoveries and Improvements in Rural Affairs* 20, no. 7 (July 1854): 324–29.

Hovey & Co. "Catalogue of Bulbous and Tuberous Flower Roots, comprising the most splendid varieties hyacinths, tulips, narcissus, crown imperials, lilies, crocuses, paeonies &c. for sale by Hovey & Co." *Magazine of Horticulture, Botany and All Useful Discoveries and Improvements in Rural Affairs* 3 (1837): n.p.

Howard, McHenry. "Wye House, Talbot County, Maryland." *Maryland Historical Magazine* 18, no. 4 (December 1923): 293–99.

Howett, Catherine M. *A World of Her Own Making: Katharine Smith Reynolds and the Landscape of Reynolda.* Amherst: University of Massachusetts Press, 2007.

Howitt, Mary. *Our Cousins in Ohio.* London: Darton, 1849.

How to Make a Bulb Garden, Illustrated and with Planting Tables. Harrisburg, Pa.: Countryside Press, 1915.

Hutteman, Anne Hewlett. *Wilmington, North Carolina.* Charleston, S.C.: Arcadia Publishing, 2000.

Ingraham, Joseph Holt. *The sunny South, or, The southerner at home; embracing five years' experience of a northern governess in the land of the sugar and the cotton.* Philadelphia: G.G. Evans, 1860.

Irvin, Hilary Somerville. "Through the Allees: The French Influence." In *The Southern Heirloom Garden,* edited by William C. Welch and Greg Grant, 29–38. Dallas: Taylor, 1995.

Jackson, Benjamin Daydon. *A Catalogue of Plants Cultivated in the Garden of John Gerard, . . .* London: Privately printed, 1876.

Jacob, Rev. Joseph. *Daffodils.* Preface by Rev. W. Wilks. Present-Day Gardening series. London: T. C. & E. C Jack, printed by Ballantyne, Hanson, Edinburgh and London. 1910.

James M. Thorburn & Co. *Annual Descriptive Catalogue of Bulbs and other Flowering Roots.* New York: James M. Thorburn & Co., 1882.

James Vick. *Vick's Floral Guide Autumn 1881.* Rochester, N.Y.: James Vick, 1881.

———. *Vick's Illustrated Catalogue of Bulbs for the Autumn of 1868.* Rochester, N.Y.: James Vick, 1868.

———. *Vick's Illustrated Catalogue of Hardy Bulbs.* Rochester, N.Y.: Benton and Andrews, Book and Job Printers, 1869.

———. *Vick's Illustrated Catalogue of Hardy Bulbs.* Rochester, N.Y.: James Vick, 1872.

———. *Vick's Illustrated Catalogue of Hardy Bulbs and Floral Guide.* Rochester, N.Y.: James Vick, 1870.

Jansma, Harriet. "Jacob Smith—A Biographical Sketch." *Magnolia* 6, no. 4 (Spring 1990): 3.

Jean Rosenkrantz et fils. *Grand catalogue Hollandois de fleurs.* Heemstede: Jean Rosenkrantz et fils, 1791.

Jefferson-Brown, Michael. *Narcissus.* Portland: Timber Press, 1991.

———. *The Daffodil: Its History, Varieties and Cultivation.* London: Faber and Faber, 1951.

Jenkins, John C. Jenkins (John C. and Family) Papers (Mss. 141, 142, 184, 187). Louisiana and Lower Mississippi Valley Collections, Special Collections, Hill Memorial Library, Louisiana State University Libraries, Baton Rouge, Louisiana State University.

J. M. Thorburn & Co. *Bulbs for Fall Planting.* New York: J. M. Thorburn & Co., 1901.

———. *Catalogue of Bulbs and Flowering Roots for Fall Planting.* New York: J. M. Thorburn & Co., 1909.

———. "Chinese Chrysanthemums &c." *Cultivator* 7, no. 10 (October 1850): 350.

———. "Fresh Imported Dutch Bulbous Roots." *Country Gentleman, A Journal for the Farm, the Garden, and Fireside* 4, no. 18 (November 2, 1854): 290.

———. "Fresh Imported Dutch Bulbous Roots." *Ohio Cultivator* 9, no. 20 (October 15, 1854): 319.

John Bartram & Son. *Catalogue of trees, shrubs, and herbaceous plants, indigenous to the United States of America: cultivated and disposed of by John Bartram & Son, at their botanical garden, Kingsess, near Philadelphia. To which is added a Catalogue of Foreign Plants, collected from various parts of the globe.* Philadelphia: Bartram and Reynolds, 1807. James R. Cothran Papers, 1771–2006, Mss. 989, Cherokee Garden Library, Kenan Research Center at the Atlanta History Center.

John Lewis Childs. *Illustrated Catalogue of Bulbs and Plants Fall 1891.* Floral Park, N.Y.: John Lewis Childs, 1891.

———. *Illustrated Catalog of Bulbs and Plants Fall 1892.* Floral Park, N.Y.: John Lewis Childs, 1892.

———. *John Lewis Childs Fall Catalog for 1894.* Floral Park, N.Y.: John Lewis Childs, 1894.

Johnson, Louisa. *Every Lady Her Own Flower Gardener.* New Haven, Conn.: S. Babcock, 1844.

Jones, Celia. "Sweetly Scented Heirloom Daffodils Signal Spring's Arrival." *Fine Gardening* 58 (November/December 1997): 24–29.

Jones, Laura. "A List of White Flowers for the Cemetery." *Success with Flowers, a Floral Magazine* 5, no. 2 (November 1894): 25.

Jordan, James C. "Recreating a Federal Period Garden in Eastern North Carolina." *Magnolia* 5, no. 2 (Autumn 1988): 4–5.

Joseph Breck & Sons. *1822—1922 Breck's Summer and Autumn Catalogue.* Boston: Joseph Breck & Sons, 1922.

Journal of a Horticultural Tour through Some Parts of Flanders, Holland and the North of France, in the Autumn of 1817. By a Deputation of the Caledonian Horticultural Society. Edinburgh: P. Neill for Bell & Bradfute, 1823.

Joy, Judith. "Daffodils, Pears, Melons and More." *Illinois Steward* 16, no. 1 (Spring 2007): 9–13.

"J.R.S.C." "Notes on Early English Horticulture." *Journal of Horticulture, Cottage Gardener and Home Farmer* 21, no. 529 (August 14, 1890): 155.

Julien, Fanny. "Window Gardens for City Schools." *New York Teachers' Monographs* 4, no. 1 (March 1904): 45–53.

Julius Roehrs Co. "How to Have a Complete Dutch Bulb Garden." *Garden Magazine* 34, no. 2 (October 1921): 111.

Juvenis. "On the Culture of the Narcissus." *Horticulturist, and Journal of Rural Art and Rural Taste* 7 (1852): 422–25.

Kemble, Francis Ann. *Journal of a Residence on a Georgia Plantation in 1838–1839.* New York: Harper and Brothers, 1864.

Kent, Elizabeth, and Leigh Hunt. *Flora Domestica, or the Portable Flower-garden, with directions for the treatment of plants in pots and illustrations from the works of the poets.* London: Printed for Taylor and Hessey, 1823.

Kirby, Arthur Martin. *Daffodils, Narcissus and How to Grow Them as Hardy Plants and for Cut Flowers, with a Guide to the Best Varieties.* New York: Doubleday, Page, 1907.

Krelage, Ernest Heinrich. *Drie eeuwen bloembollenexport: de geschiedenis van den bloembollenhandel en der hollandsche bloembollen tot 1938.* 'S-Gravenhage: Rijksuitgeverij, Dienst van de Nederlandsche Staatscourant, 1946.

Krelage, J. H. "On Polyanthus Narcissus." *Journal of the Royal Horticulture Society* 12 (1890): 339–46.

"Ladies Department." *American Farmer, containing original essays and selections on agriculture, horticulture, rural and domestic economy, and internal improvements, with illustrative engravings and the prices of country produce* 10, no. 44 (January 16, 1829): 349.

"The Language of Flowers." *Favourite* 1 (1854): 13–17. London: Partridge, Oakey.

Laurens, Henry. *The Papers of Henry Laurens,* vol. 3, *January 1, 1759–August 31, 1763.* Edited by Phillip M. Hamer and George C. Rogers. Columbia: University of South Carolina Press, 1972.

Lawrence, Elizabeth. *The Little Bulbs: A Tale of Two Gardens.* New York: Criterion Books, 1957.

———. *A Southern Garden: A Handbook for the Middle South.* Chapel Hill: University of North Carolina Press, 1942.

Lawson, John, Fred A. Ols, and William Byrd. *History of North Carolina.* Charlotte: Observer Printing House, 1903.

Lawson, William. *A new orchard, and garden; or, The best way for planting, grafting, and to make any ground good, for a rich orchard: particularly in the north, and generally for the whole kingdome of England . . . With the country housewifes garden for hearbes of common use . . . As also the husbandry of bees, with their severall uses and annoyances, all being the experience of 48 yeares labour, and now the second time corr. and much enl. Whereunto is newly added The art of propagating plants. . . .* London: Printed by Nicholas Okes for John Harison, 1631.

Lea, Grady F., Lois Wright, and Katherine Stumbaugh. "St. Michael's Cemetery Plant Identification." Survey in conjunction with *The Search for the Hidden People of St. Michael's Cemetery Project,* the University of West Florida Geography (GeoData Center—Geographic Information System) and the Escambia County Extension Service—Master Gardener Program. 2001–2002. http://www.uwf.edu/gis/research/smc.

Leighton, Ann. *American Gardens in the Eighteenth Century: For Use or for Delight.* Boston: Houghton Mifflin, 1976.

———. *American Gardens of the Nineteenth Century "For Comfort and Affluence."* Amherst: University of Massachusetts Press, 1987.

———. *Early American Gardens: For Meate or Medicine.* Amherst: University of Massachusetts Press, 1986.

Lelièvre, J. F. *Nouveau Jardinier de la Louisiane.* New Orleans: J. F. Lelièvre, 1838.

Le Rougetel, Hazel. *A Heritage of Roses.* Owing Mills, Md.: Stemmer House Publishers, 1988.

Lichen. "My Old Kentucky Home." *Arthur's Home Magazine* 49, no. 10 (October 1881): 603–4.

"Lily for Grave." *Vick's Illustrated Magazine* 2, no. 10 (October 1879): 310.

Link, Helen. "The History and Evolution of the Daffodil." *Daffodil Journal* 28, no. 3 (1992): 182–83.

Littlewood, A. R. "Ancient Literary Evidence for the Pleasure Gardens of Roman Villas." In *Dumbarton Oaks Colloquium on the History of Landscape Architecture, X,* edited by Elisabeth Blair Macdougall, vol. 1984, 7–30. Washington, D.C.: Dumbarton Oaks Research Library and Collection, 1987.

L'Obel, Matthias de (Lobelius). *Kruydtboeck oft beschrÿuinghe van allerleye ghewassen, kruyderen, hesteren, ende gheboomten/deur Matthias de L'Obel. . . .* t'Antwerpen: By Christoffel Plantyn, 1581.

Lockwood, Alice G. B., and Garden Club of America. *Gardens of Colony and State: Gardens and Gardeners of the American Colonies and of the Republic before 1840.* New York: Smallwood and Stewart for the Garden Club of America, 2000.

Lodewijk, Tom. *The Golden Spade: The Story of a Flowerbulb Company, 1793–1953.* Lisse, Holland: Royal Flowerbulb Co., H. de Graaff & Sons, 1953.

Long, John Dixon. *Pictures of Slavery in Church and State: Including Personal Reminiscences.* Philadelphia: John Dixon Long, 1857.

Loudon, Mrs. (Jane). *The Ladies' Flower-Garden of Ornamental Bulbous Plants.* London: W. Smith, 1841.

Loudon, John Claudius. *Encyclopaedia of Gardening; comprising the Theory and Practice of Horticulture, Floriculture and Arboriculture, and Landscape-gardening, including All the latest Improvements; A general history of gardening in all countries; and a statistical view of its present state; with suggestions for its future progress in the British Isles.* A new edition. London: Longman, Hurst, Reess, Orme, Brown, Green and Longman, 1835.

———. *On the Laying Out, Planting, and Managing of Cemeteries, and on the Improvement of Churchyards.* London: Longman, Brown, Green and Longmans, 1843.

Mackie, J. Milton. *From Cape Cod to the Dixie and the Tropics.* New York: G. P. Putnam, 1864.

Maddock, James. *The florist's directory; or a treatise on the culture of flowers; to which is added a supplementary dissertation on soils, manures, &c.* London: Printed for the author, & sold by B. White & Sons; G. G. J & J. Robinson; and T. & J. Egerton, 1792.

Malone, Alberta. *History of the Atlanta Ladies Memorial Association, 1866–1946: Monuments and Markers.* N.p.: 1946.

Marion. "Flowers for Cemetery Planting." *Western Garden and Poultry Journal* 5, no. 6 (June 1894): 126.

Martin, Chlotilde R. *Northern Money, Southern Land, the Lowcountry Plantation Sketches of Chlotilde R. Martin.* Edited by Robert B. Cuthbert and Stephen G. Hoffius. Columbia: University of South Carolina Press, 2009.

Martin, John Hill. *Historical Sketch of Bethlehem in Pennsylvania: With Some Account of the Moravian Church.* Philadelphia: John L. Pile, 1873.

Martin, Peter. *The Pleasure Gardens of Virginia, from Jamestown to Jefferson.* Princeton, N.J.: Princeton University Press, 1991.

Massey, W. F. "Commercial Bulb Culture in North Carolina." In *North Carolina Agricultural Experiment Station, Bulletin No. 96,* 62–63. Raleigh: N.C. College of Agricultural and Mechanical Arts, North Carolina Agricultural Experiment Station, 1894.

———. "Report of the Horticulturist." In *North Carolina Agricultural Experiment Station, Fifteenth Annual Report,* 32–36. Raleigh: N.C. College of Agricultural and Mechanical Arts, North Carolina Agricultural Experiment Station, 1893.

Mawe, Thomas, John Ambercrombie, and other gardeners. *Every man his own gardener: Being a new, and much more complete, gardener's Kalendar than hitherto published . . . . The Second Edition, Corrected, Enlarged and very much Improved.* London: W. Griffin, 1767.

McCandless, Wilson. *Allegheny Cemetery: historical account of incidents and events connected with its establishment, charter and supplemental acts of legislation; reports of 1848 and 1857; proceedings of corporators, June 21, 1873; rules, regulations, &c.; list of officers, managers and corporators to date; remarks on the ornamentation and arrangement of cemeteries; funeral oration of Wilson McCandless, esq., on Commodore Barney and Lieut. Parker; illustrated with sixteen photographic views.* Pittsburgh: Bakewell & Marthens, 1873.

McCoy-Massey, Debra P. "The Life of Mary Catherine Rion." *Magnolia* 17, no. 2 (Winter 2001–2002): 9–13.

McDonald, Alexander. "Alabama Farming." *American Farmer* 1, no. 10 (April 1846): 296.

McFarland, Kenneth M. "Old Salem Conference Examines Women and Southern Gardens." *Magnolia* 12, no. 1 (Fall 1995): 1–9.

McGahee, Susan H., and Mary W. Edmonds. *South Carolina Cemetery Preservation Guideline.* Columbia: South Carolina Department of Archives and History, State Historic Preservation Office, 1997.

McLean, Teresa. *Medieval English Gardens.* New York: Viking Press, 1980.

M'Connell, Marion Daniel. "Women Who Earn. The Woman of New Occupations." *Alkahest, the Literary Magazine of the South* 7, no. 1 (July 1900): 33–38.

Meager, Leonard. *The English gardner: or, A sure guide to young planters & gardeners. In three parts. I. Shewing the way and order of planting and raising all sorts of stocks, fruit-trees, and shrubs . . . II. How to order the kitchin-garden, for all sorts of herbs, roots, and salads. III. The ordering of the garden of pleasure. . . .* London: Printed by J. Rawlins, for M. Wotton . . . and G. Conyers . . . 1688.

Mellen, William P. "Flowering of Trees, Shrubs, &c., at Natchez, Miss., in 1848." In *American Almanac and Repository for Useful Knowledge, for the Year 1849,* 94. Boston: Charles C. Little and James Brown, 1848.

Mentzelii, Christiani. *Lexicon Plantarum Polyglotton Universale. Ex diversis, Europaeorum, Asiaticorum, Africanorum et Americanorum, Antiquis et modernis Linguis, earumque dialectis variis, quotquot ex probatis Autoribus excerpi potuerunt, juxta Alphabeti seriem operose concinnatum; In quo Plantarum Genera, Species, Colorum et Quarumvis Partium differentiae, ab eruditis hactenus adnotatae, legitimo ordine collocantur, adductis cujusque Linguae autoribus antiquis et recentioribus Berolini, apud Christoph.* Gottlieb Nicolai, 1715.

Michell's Bulb Growing Guide: A Complete Treatise on the Culture and Uses of All Bulbs Offered in Our Fall Catalog. Philadelphia: Henry F. Michell, 1911.

Michigan State Horticultural Society. *Sixteenth Annual Report of the Secretary of the State Horticultural Society of Michigan. 1886.* Lansing: Thorp & Godfrey, 1887.

Miller, F. A. "The Bulb Season." *California Horticulturist and Floral Magazine* 5, no. 12 (December 1875): 367–68.

Miller, Philip. "An Account of some Experiments, relating to the Flowering of Tulips, Narcissus's, &c. in Water, by placing their Bulbs upon Glasses of Water, made by Mons. Triewald, Director of Mechanicks at Stockholm, and F.R.SS. of England and Sweden, and read before the Royal Society May the 7th, 1730, as they were tried the next Season by Philip Miller, F.R.S. Gardiner to the worshipful Company of Apothecaries, at their Botanick Garden in Chelsea." *Philosophical Transactions. Giving some account of the Present Undertakings, Studies, and Labours of the Ingenious, in many Considerable Parts of the World.* 37 (1731, 1732): 81-84.

———. *The Gardeners Dictionary. containing the best and newest methods of cultivating and improving the kitchen, fruit, flower garden, and nursery, as also for performing the practical parts of agriculture: including the management of vineyards, with the methods of making and preserving wine, according to the present practice of the most skilful vignerons in the several wine countries in Europe. Together with directions for propagating and improving, for real practice and experience, all sorts of timber trees.* 8th ed. London: Printed for the author, 1768.

———. *The Gardeners Dictionary. containing the methods of cultivating and improving all sorts of trees, plants and flowers for the kitchen, fruit, and pleasure gardens; as also those white are used in medicine. With directions for the culture of vineyards, and making of wine in England. In which likewise are included the practical parts of husbandry. Abridged from the last folio ed., by the author, Philip Miller. . . .* 4th ed. London: Printed for the author, 1754.

———. *The Gardeners Dictionary: containing the methods of cultivating and improving the kitchen, fruit and flower garden, as also the physick garden, wilderness, conservatory, and vineyard.* Abridged from the Folio Edition. . . . London: Printed for the Author, and sold by C. Rivington, 1735.

———. *The Gardeners Dictionary: containing the methods of cultivating and improving the kitchen, fruit and flower garden, as also, the physick garden, wilderness, conservatory, and vineyard; according to the practice of the most experienc'd gardeners of the present age.: Interspers'd with the history of the plants, the characters of each genus, and the names of all the particular species, in Latin and English; and an explanation of all the terms used in botany and gardening . . . : Adorned with copper plates.* 2nd ed. London: Printed for the author; and sold by C. Rivington, 1733.

Minor, Charles. "Fruit Trees, Plants, &c." *Tennessee Farmer* 1, no. 11 (October 1835): 192.

"Minton Collins. *Virginia Gazette and Richmond Daily Advertiser*, November 5, 1792." In *Southern Plants List,* edited by Gordon W. Chappell, 51–52. Southern Garden History Society and the Colonial Williamsburg Foundation, 2000. http://southerngardenhistory.org/PDF/Southern PlantLists.pdf.

M'Mahon, Bernard. *The American Gardener's Calendar, adapted to the climates and seasons of the United States. Containing a complete account of all the work necessary to be done . . . for every month in the year; with ample practical directions for performing the same. . . .* Philadelphia: Printed by B. Graves, 1806.

———. *The Gardener's Calendar, Adapted to the seasons of the United States: containing a complete account of all the work necessary to be done . . . for every month in the year: with ample practical directions for performing the same. . . .* 11th ed., greatly enlarged, improved and illustrated. Philadelphia: Lippincott, 1857.

Mobile. *Annual Reports submitted at the annual meeting of the general council of the city of Mobile, March 15, 1899, together with a historical sketch of Mobile.* Mobile, Ala.: W. J. Patterson. 1889.

————. *The Charter and Code of Ordinances of the City of Mobile.* Mobile, Ala.: G. Matzenger. 1889.

Moore, Mary Brown Daniel, Roberta Seawell Brandau, and the Garden Study Club of Nashville. *The History of Homes and Gardens of Tennessee.* Nashville: Parthenon Press, 1936.

Morin, Pierre. *Remarques Necessaires pour la Culture des Fleurs.* Paris: Chez Charles de Sercy, au Palais, dans la Salle Dauphine, à la Bonne-Foy couronnée, 1658.

Morton, Hugh M., and William Friday. *Hugh Morton, North Carolina Photographer.* Chapel Hill: University of North Carolina Press, 2006.

Mott, Hopper Striker. *The New York of yesterday: a descriptive narrative of old Bloomingdale, its topographical features, its early families and their genealogies, its old homesteads and country-seats, its French invasion, and its war experiences considered, in their relation to its first religious society, the Bloomingdale Reformed Church, organized in 1805, incorporated in 1806 as the church at Harsenville.* New York: G. P. Putnam's Sons, 1908.

Munting, Abraham. *Waare oeffening der planten, waar in de rechte aart, natuire en verborgene. . . .* Amsterdam: Jan Rieuwertsz Boekverkoper, 1682.

Murrin, John M., Paul E. Johnson, James M. McPherson, Alice Fahs, Gary Gerstle, Emily S. Rosenberg, and Norman L. Rosenberg. *Liberty Equality Power: A History of the American People,* vol. 1, *To 1877.* Boston: Wadsworth, Cengage Learning, 2012.

"Narcissus." *Vick's Illustrated Monthly Magazine* 6, no. 6 (June 1878): 181.

"Narcissus." *Vick's Monthly Magazine* 3, no. 5 (May 1880): 152.

National League of American Pen Women, Birmingham Branch. *Historic Homes of Alabama and Their Traditions.* Birmingham: Birmingham Publishing, 1969.

National Park Service. Historic America Landscape Survey of John Bartram House and Garden. HALS No. PA-1. http://www.loc.gov/pictures/item/PA3904/.

Neckham, Alexander. *Alexandri Neckham De Naturis Rerum libri duo. With the poem of the same author "De laudibus divinae sapiteinae."* Edited by Thomas Wright. London: Longman, Roberts and Green, 1863.

————. *De Naturis Rerum et De Laudibus Divinæ Sapientiæ.* Edited by Thomas Wright. In *Rerum Britannicarum Medii Aevi Scriptores, or Chronicles and Memorials of Great Britain and Ireland during the Middle Ages.* London: Longman, Roberts, and Green, 1863.

Nestor, Bradley Alexander. *Paradise Rediscovered: An Archival Restoration of the Horticultural and Design Elements of Barnsley Gardens, Georgia.* M.A. thesis, University of Georgia, 1995.

Nestor, Bradley A., and William A. Mann. "An Archival Restoration of the Horticultural and Design Elements of Barnsley Gardens, Georgia." *Landscape and Urban Planning* 42 (1998): 107–22.

Newberry, Percy E. "On the Vegetable Remains Discovered in the Cemetery of Hawara." In *Hawara, Biahmu and Arsinoe, with Thirty Plates,* edited by W. M. Flinders Petrie, 46–53. London: Field and Tuer, Leadenhall Press, 1889.

"New Books: Daffodils and How to Grow Them." *Gardening* 15, no. 360 (September 1, 1907): 379.

Nichols, Rose Standish. *English Pleasure Gardens.* New York: Macmillan, 1902.

Northend, Mary Harrod. *Historic Gardens of New England.* New York: Mentor Association, 1916.

"Notes on Spring Flowering Bulbs." *American Agriculturist, for the Farm, Garden and Household* 24, no. 10 (October 1865): 316–17.

O'Dell, Jeffrey M. "1972 Excavation at the Chantilly Manor House Site, Westmoreland County, Virginia." *Northern Neck of Virginia Historical Magazine* 23, no. 1 (December 1973): 2413–26.

Old Homes and Gardens of North Carolina. Photographs by Bayard Wootten, historical text by Archibald Henderson, compiled by Mrs. Charles A. Cannon, Mrs. Lyman A. Cotten, Mrs.

James Edwin Latham. Published under the auspices of the Garden Club of North Carolina. Chapel Hill: University of North Carolina Press, 1939.

Olmsted, Frederick Law. *A Journey in the Seaboard Slave States: With Remarks on Their Economy.* New York: Dix & Edwards; London: Sampson Low, Son & Co., 1856.

O'Mara, Patrick. "The Late Arthur Martin Kirby." *American Florist* 48, no. 1505 (April 7, 1917): 641.

"On the Cultivation of Hyacinths in Glasses and Pots." *Farmer's Register, A monthly publication devoted to the improvement of the Practice, and support of the interests of agriculture* 3, no. 8 (1835): 498–500. Edited by Edmund Ruffin, Petersburg, Virginia: Edmund Ruffin.

Owen, Thomas McAdory, and Marie Bankhead Owen. *History of Alabama and Dictionary of Alabama Biography.* Vol. 1. Chicago: S. J. Clarke, 1921.

Park, George W. "About Narcissus." *Park's Floral Magazine* 21, no. 5 (May 1885): 73.

Parkinson, John. *Paradisi in sole Paradisus terrestris, or, A garden of all sorts of pleasant flowers which our English ayre will permit to be noursed vp: with A kitchen garden of all manner of herbes, roo-tes, & fruites, for meate or sause vsed with vs: and An orchard of all sorte of fruitbearing trees and shrubbes fit for our land together with the right orderinge planting & preseruing of them and their vses & vertues.* London: Printed by Humfrey Lownes and Robert Young, 1629.

———. *Theatrum Botanicum The Theater of Plants. Or, An Herball of a Large Extent . . . ,* London: Printed by Thomas Cetes, 1640.

Parsons, Samuel, Jr. *Landscape Gardening: notes and suggestions on lawns and lawn planting, laying out and arrangement of country places, large and small parks, cemetery plots, and railway-station lawns, deciduous and evergreen trees and shrubs, the hardy border, bedding plants, rockwork, etc.* New York: G. P. Putnam's Sons, 1891.

Pavord, Anna. *The Tulip.* New York: London: Bloomsbury. Distributed by St. Martin's Press, 1999.

Peter Henderson & Co. *Autumn 1889 Bulbs and Plants.* New York: Peter Henderson & Co., 1889.

———. *Autumn Bulb Catalogue.* New York: Peter Henderson & Co., 1901.

———. *Catalogue of Bulbs, Plants and Seeds for Autumn Planting.* New York: Peter Henderson & Co., 1895.

———. *Henderson's Autumn Catalogue.* New York: Peter Henderson & Co., 1907.

———. *Henderson's Autumn Catalogue.* New York: Peter Henderson & Co., 1913.

———. *Henderson's Autumn Catalogue.* New York: Peter Henderson & Co., 1916.

———. *Peter Henderson and Co.'s 1883 Catalogue of Bulbs for Fall Planting, Plants for Winter Flowering, Seeds for Fall Sowing.* New York: Peter Henderson & Co., 1883.

Phipps, Amanda W. "Gardens of Old Natchez." In *Pioneer American Gardening,* edited by Elvenia Slosson, 100–103. New York: Coward-McCann, 1951.

Pieters, A. J. "Home Grown Bulbs." *Gardening* 13, no. 307 (June 15, 1905): 297.

"Plans for Flower-Beds." *Rural Carolinian, an Illustrated Magazine, of Agriculture, Horticulture, and the Arts* 2, no. 5 (February 1871): 285–87.

"Plate 58. Narcissus Tazetta-Luna—Tazetta-Intermedius—and Juncifolius." *Floral Magazine. Figures and Descriptions of the Choicest New Flowers for the Garden, Stove or Conservatory* 12, no. 15 (March 1873): Plate 58.

Potter, Elisabeth Walton, Beth M. Boland, and National Register of Historic Places. *Guidelines for Evaluating and Registering Cemeteries and Burial Places,* National Register Bulletin 41. Washington, D.C.: U.S. Dept. of the Interior, National Park Service, Interagency Resources Division, National Register of Historic Places. 1992.

Poughkeepsie Rural Cemetery. *The Poughkeepsie Rural Cemetery, Its By-laws, Rules and Regulations: And the Dedication Ceremonies, with Appendix.* Poughkeepsie: Platt & Schram, 1854.

Pregill, Philip, and Nancy Volkman. *Landscapes in History: Design and Planning in the Western Tradition.* New York: Van Nostrand Reinhold, 1993.

Prince, William. *Catalogue of fruit and ornamental trees and plants, bulbous flower roots, green-house plants, &c. &c., cultivated at the Linnaean Botanic Garden, William Prince, Proprietor, Flushing, Long Island, near New York. To which is added a short treatise on their cultivation, &c.* 21st ed. New York: T. and J. Swords. 1822.

———. *A Short Treatise on Horticulture: embracing descriptions of a great variety of fruit and ornamental trees and shrubs, grape vines, bulbous flowers, greenhouse trees and plants, &., nearly all of which are at present comprised in the collection of the Linnaean botanic garden, at Flushing, near New York. With directions for their culture, management, &c.* New York: T. and J. Swords. 1828.

Rafinesque, Constantine Samuel. "A Journal of the Progress of Vegetation near Philadelphia, between the 20th of February and the 20th of May, 1816, with occasional Zoological Remarks." *American Journal of Science, &c.* 1 (1818): 77–82.

Ragan, W. H. *Transactions of the Mississippi Valley Horticultural Society.* Indianapolis: Carlon & Hollenbeck, Printers and Binders, 1884.

Ramsey, David, M. D. *The History of South Carolina, from Its First Settlement in 1670, to the Year 1808.* Charleston: David Longworth, 1808.

Rand, Edward S. *Bulbs: A Treatise on Hardy and Tender Bulbs and Tubers.* Boston: J. E. Tilton, 1866.

———. *Flowers for the Parlor and Garden.* Boston: J. E. Tilton, 1863.

———. *Seventy-Five Popular Flowers and How to Cultivate Them.* Boston: J. E. Tilton, 1870.

Randall, G. M. *Dutch and French Bulb Culture in Florida Also Diversified Farming.* De Land, Fla.: E. O. Painter Printing, 1926.

R. and J. Farquahar & Co. *Bulb Catalogue.* Boston: R. & J. Farquahar & Co., 1904.

Rathbone, Alice M. "Our Hardy Flowers." In *How to Make a Flower Garden: A Manual of Practical Information and Suggestions,* edited by Wilhelm Miller, 39–51. New York: Doubleday, Page, 1910.

R. Buist. *Eighth Edition of R. Buist's Catalogue of Green-House Plants, Ornamental Trees, Shrubs, Roses, Herbacious Plants, &c.* Philadelphia: Nursery in Moyamensing, 1844–1845. James R. Cothran Papers, 1771–2006, Mss. 989, Cherokee Garden Library, Kenan Research Center at the Atlanta History Center.

Rea, John. *Flora: seu, De florum cultura, Or, A complete florilege, furnished with all requisites belonging to a florist. The second impression corrected, with many additions, and several new plates. In III. books.* London: printed by T[homas]. N[ewcomb]. for George Marriott, 1676.

———. *Flora: seu, De florum cultura. Or, A complete florilege: furnished with all the requisits belonging to a florist. In III books.* London: Printed by J. G. for Thomas Clarke, 1665.

Reed, Wallace Putnam, ed. *History of Atlanta, Georgia: With Illustrations and Biographical Sketches of Some of Its Prominent Men and Pioneers.* Syracuse, N.Y.: D. Mason, 1889.

Reinberger, Mark, and Elizabeth McLean. "Isaac Norris's Fairhill: Architecture, Landscape, and Quaker Ideals in a Philadelphia Colonial Country Seat." *Winterthur Portfolio* 32, no. 4 (Winter 1997): 243–74.

Reisem, Richard O., and Frank A. Gillespie. *Mount Hope: America's First Victorian Municipal Cemetery.* Rochester, N.Y.: Landmark Society of Western New York, 1994.

"Remodeling a Neglected Cemetery." *Park and Cemetery and Landscape Gardening* 24, no. 7 (September 1914): 228–29.

"Report from Allegheny Cemetery, Allegheny PA." *Park and Cemetery and Landscape Gardening* 14, no. 7 (September 1904): 118.

Rexford, Eben Eugene. *Amateur Gardencraft: A Book for the Home-Maker and Garden Lover.* Philadelphia: J. B. Lippincott, 1912.

———. "Flowers for the Cemetery." *Vick's Monthly Magazine* 7, no. 10 (October 1884): 299–300.

Richardson, Emma B. *The Heyward-Washington House Garden.* Charleston Museum Leaflet No. 15. Charleston, S.C.: Charleston Museum, 1941.

Rinz, Jac. "Holland and the Netherlands." *Gardener's Magazine* 6 (1830): 592–96.

Rion, Mary Catherine. *Ladies' Southern Florist.* Columbia, S.C.: Printed by Peter B. Glass, Co., 1860.

Robert and William Carr. *Catalogue of trees, shrubs, and herbaceous plants, indigenous to the United States of America: cultivated and for sale at Bartram's Botanical Garden, Kingsess, near Philadelphia. To which is added a Catalogue of Foreign Plants, collected from various parts of the globe.* Philadelphia: Robert and William Carr, 1807. James R. Cothran Papers, 1771–2006, Mss. 989, Cherokee Garden Library, Kenan Research Center at the Atlanta History Center.

Robinson, Ednah. "The Commerce of Blossom Land: A Brief Study of the Development of Trade in Flower Products in California." *Sunset* 11, no. 5 (September 1903): 444.

Robinson, William. *The English Flower Garden: style, position, and arrangement: followed by a description, alphabetically arranged, of all the plants best suited for its embellishment, their culture and positions suited for each.* London: J. Murray, 1883.

———. *The English Flower Garden and home grounds of hardy trees and flowers only.* Fifteenth edition. London: John Murray, 1933.

———. *Hardy Flowers: Descriptions of Upwards of thirteen hundred of the most ornamental species.* . . . London: Frederick Warne, 1871.

———. *The Wild Garden or, Our Groves & Shrubberies Made Beautiful by the naturalization of hardy exotic plants: with a chapter on the garden of British wildflowers.* London: John Murray, 1870.

———. *The Wild Garden or, Our Groves Made Beautiful by the naturalization of hardy exotic plants: being one way onwards from the Dark Ages of Flower Gardening, with suggestions for the Regeneration of the Bare Borders of London Parks.* London: Garden Office; New York: Scribner and Wellford, 1881.

———. *The Wild Garden or the Naturalization and Natural Grouping of Hardy Exotic Plants with a Chapter on the Garden of British Wildflowers.* London: J. Murray, 1903.

Rockwell, Frederick Frye. *The Book of Bulbs: a guide to the selection, planting, and cultivating of bulbs for spring, summer, and autumn flowering—and to winter-long beauty of bulbs indoors.* New York: Macmillan, 1927.

Rome Sponsoring Committee for Daffodil Debut. *Welcome to Bray Gardens at Daffodil Farm.* N.p., n.d. Collection of the author.

"Rural Cemeteries." *Canada Farmer; A Fortnightly Journal of Agriculture, Horticulture and Rural Affairs* 1 (July 15, 1864): 204.

S., Mrs. R. "Preserving Dutch Bulbs during Summer." *Vick's Monthly Magazine* 1, no. 6 (June 1878): 184.

Sale, Edith Tunis, and James River Garden Club. *Historic Gardens of Virginia.* Richmond: William Byrd Press, 1923.

Salisbury, Richard Anthony. "On the Cultivation of Rare Plants, especially such as have been introduced since the death of Mr. Philip Miller. Read January 6, February 4 and March 3, 1812." *Transactions of the Horticultural Society of London* 1 (1812): 261–366.

Salisbury, William. *Hortus Paddingtonensis: or, a Catalogue of Plants Cultivated in the Garden of J. Symmons, Esq. Paddington-house.* London: Printed by S. Couchman for Shepperson and Reynolds, 1797.

Sanborn, Nathan Perkins. *The Fountain Inn, Agnes Surriage and Sir Harry Frankland: A Paper Read before the Marblehead Historical Society, December 8, 1904.* [Marblehead, Mass.:] Marblehead Historical Society, 1905.

Sarudy, Barbara Wells. *Gardens and Gardening in the Chesapeake 1700–1805.* Baltimore: Johns Hopkins University Press, 1998.

———. "South Carolina Seed Merchants and Nurserymen before 1820." *Magnolia* 8, no. 3 (1992): 6–10.

Sayers, Edward. *The American Flower Garden Companion. Adapted to the Northern States.* Boston: Joseph Breck; New York: G. C. Thorburn, 1838.

Schaffer, Edward Terry Hendrie. *Carolina Gardens; the History, Romance and Tradition of Many Gardens of Two States through More Than Two Centuries.* Foreword by DuBose Heyward. New York: Huntington Press, 1937.

Schnare, Susan E., and Rudy J. Favretti. "Gertrude Jekyll's American Gardens." *Garden History* 10, no. 2 (Autumn 1982): 149–67.

Schöpf, Johann David. *Travels in the Confederation, 1783–1784: New Jersey, Pennsylvania, Maryland, Virginia.* Translated and edited by Alfred J. Morrison. Philadelphia: William J. Campbell, 1911.

———. *Travels in the Confederation, 1783–1784: Pennsylvania, Maryland, Virginia, the Carolinas, East Florida, the Bahamas.* Translated and edited by Alfred J. Morrison. Philadelphia: William J. Campbell, 1911.

Scott, Frank Jessup. *The art of beautifying suburban home grounds of small extent; the advantages of suburban homes over city or country homes; the comfort and economy of neighboring improvements; the choice and treatment of building sites; and the best modes of laying out, planting, and keeping decorated grounds. Illustrated by upwards of two hundred plates and engravings . . . With descriptions of the beautiful and hardy trees and shrubs grown in the United States.* New York: D. Appleton, 1870.

Sheehan, Thomas. "Fall or Holland Bulbs." *American Agriculturist for the Farm, Garden and Household* 43, no. 10 (October 1884): 423.

Sherman, Conger. *Guide to Laurel Hill Cemetery, near Philadelphia. With illustrations.* Philadelphia: C. Sherman, 1847.

Shinn, Charles Howard. "An Early Winter Garden in California." *American Garden* 11, no. 2 (February 1890): 84–85.

———. "Future Gardens of California." *Californian A Western Monthly Magazine* 2 (1880): 153–56.

———. "Garden Art in California." *American Gardening* 11, no. 1 (January 1890): 23–25.

———. "Wizards of the Garden. (Third Paper.) Carl Purdy and the Native Bulbs." *Land of Sunshine The Magazine of California and the West* 14, no. 4 (April 1901): 276–89.

Shoberl, Frederic. *The Language of Flowers: with illustrative poetry; to which are now added The Calendar of Flowers and The Dial of Flowers.* Philadelphia: Lea & Blanchard, 1839.

Silberrad, Una L. and Sophie Lyall. *Dutch bulbs and gardens.* London: A. and C. Black, 1909.

Sims, John. *Curtis's Botanical Magazine, or, Flower-Garden Displayed: In Which The most Ornamental Foreign Plants, cultivated in the Open Ground, the Green-House, and the Stove, are accurately represented in their natural Colours. To Which Are Added, Their Names, Class, Order, Generic and Specific Characters, according to the celebrated Linnaeus; their Places of Growth, and Times of Flowering: Together with the Most Approved Methods of Culture: a Work Intended for the Use of Such Ladies, Gentlemen, and Gardeners, as wish to become scientifically acquainted with the Plants they cultivate. Continued by John Sims, M.D. Fellow of the Linnean Society.* London: Printed by Stephen Couchman for T. Curtis, 1801–1844.

Singleton, Esther. *Dutch New York.* New York: Dodd, Mead, 1909.

———. *The Shakespeare Garden.* New York: Century, 1922.

"Sketches from Munich. No. 3." *Catholic Weekly Instructor, or Miscellany of Religious, Instructive and Entertaining Knowledge,* no. 17 (Saturday, October 5, 1844): 151.

Smith, John P. "Bulb, Root or Hyacinth Vases in the 18th and 19th Centuries." *Journal of the Glass Association* 7 (2004): 29–38.

"Some Old Grave-Yards, Homes of the Dead Still Found within City Limits." *New York Times,* May 18, 1879. New York Times Article Archives, http://query.nytimes.com/mem/archive-free/pdf?res=F40712FD385A137B93CAA8178ED85F4D8784F9.

Sowerby, James. *English Botany: Or, Coloured Figures of British Plants, with their essential characters, synonyms, and places of growth. To which will be added, occasional comments.* London: J. Davis, 1790.

"The Spring Garden." *Magazine of Horticulture, Botany and All Useful Discoveries and Improvements in Rural Affairs* 34, no. 11 (November 1868): 321–26.

Spring Grove Cemetery. *The Cincinnati Cemetery of Spring Grove, Report for 1857.* Cincinnati: C. F. Bradley, 1857.

Squibb, Robert. *The Gardener's Calendar for the States of North-Carolina, South-Carolina, and Georgia, with an Appendix, Containing a variety of particular and general information on husbandry and horticulture.* Charleston, S.C.: published by P. Hoff, No. 10, and E. Gibbs, No. 48, Broad-Street. P. Hoff, Printer, 1827.

Stephenson, Theodore "Teddy," Ouida Trammell Stephenson, and John C. Van Beck. "Paper White Farming in Florida 1928–1942: A Bit of History." *Daffodil Journal* 31, no. 3 (March 1995): 162–65.

Stetson, Sarah P. "John Mercer's Notes on Plants." *Virginia Magazine of History and Biography* 61, no. 1 (January 1953): 34–44.

Stritikus, George R. "The 1858 Herbarium of Fannie A. Nelms, Marion Female Seminary, Perry County, Marion, Alabama (PMI #44)." George Stritikus Papers, Mss. 983, Cherokee Garden Library, Kenan Research Center at the Atlanta History Center.

———. "Caroline Frances Smith's *Scrapbook of Pressed Flowers,* Lowndesboro, AL, cir. 1830–1850 (PMI # 21)." George Stritikus Papers, Mss. 983, Cherokee Garden Library, Kenan Research Center at the Atlanta History Center.

———. "An Early (1813–1815) List of Bulbous Plants associated with the LeConte Plantation at Woodmanston, Georgia (GSA #6)." *George Stritikus Papers, 1979–1998,* Mss. 983, Cherokee Garden Library, Kenan Research Center at the Atlanta History Center.

———. " "Forest Home" described in *The Annuals of Ann Fennel Davis* by Mary Davis Henry (PMI #23)." George Stritikus Papers, Mss. 983, Cherokee Garden Library, Kenan Research Center at the Atlanta History Center.

———. "Minute Book of the Chunnannuggee Ridge Horticultural Society (PMI #4)." George Stritikus Papers, Mss. 983, Cherokee Garden Library, Kenan Research Center at the Atlanta History Center.

———. "Miss Betty Roper's Herbarium, 1853, Rocky Mount, Al., Lower Montgomery County (PMI #20)." George Stritikus Papers, Mss. 983, Cherokee Garden Library, Kenan Research Center at the Atlanta History Center.

"The Stryker Mansion." *Appleton's Journal of Literature, Science and Art* 8, no. 191 (Saturday, November 23, 1872): 562.

Stuart, James. *Three Years in North America.* New York: J. & J. Harper, 1833.

Studebaker, Russell. "Cherokee Daffodils." *Horticulture* 100, no. 2 (April 2003): 32.

Susanin, Jay Stephenson. *Grumblethorpe: An Historic Landscape Report.* M.A. thesis, University of Pennsylvania, 1990.

Sweert, Emmanuel. *Florilegium Amplissimum et selectissimum, quo non tantum varia diversorum florum praestantissimorum et nunquam antea exhibitorum genera, sed et rarae quamplurimae Indicarum plantarum, et radicum formae, ad vivum partibus duabus, quatuor etiam linguis offeruntur et delineantur.* Amstelodami: apud Joannem Janssonium: 1647–1654.

Sweet, Robert. *Hortus suburbanus Londinensis: or a catalogue of plants cultivated in the neighborhood of London; arranged according to the Linnaean system: with the addition of the Natural Orders to which they belong, References to Books where they are described, their native Places of Growth, when introduced, Time of Flowering, and Reference to Figures.* London: James Ridgway, 1818.

Sydenham, Robert. *All about Daffodils and Narcissi.* 3rd ed. Self-published [Birmingham]: 1913.

Sykes, John. "Gardening with Mrs. Balfour: An Antebellum Vicksburg Gardener." *Magnolia* 17, no. 3 (Spring 2002): 1–9.

Tabor, Grace. *Making a Bulb Garden.* New York: McBride, Nast, 1912.

Taliaferro, Tevi. *Historic Oakland Cemetery.* Charleston, S.C.: Arcadia, 2001.

Thick, Malcolm. "Market Gardening in England and Wales." In *The Agrarian History of England and Wales*, vol. 5, *1640–1750*, edited by Joan Thirsk, 503–32. Cambridge: Cambridge University Press, 1985.

Thomas, Bernice L. *America's 5 & 10 Cent Stores, the Kress Legacy.* New York: John Wiley and Sons, 1997.

Thomas, Elizabeth Patterson. *Old Kentucky Homes and Gardens.* Louisville, Ky.: Standard Print. Co., 1939.

Thomas Meehan & Sons, Inc. "Hardy Plants Worth Owning." *Garden Magazine* 3 no. 2 (March 1906): 89.

Thomson, Mrs. J. S. R. "Exchange." *Park's Floral Magazine* 21, no. 6 (June 1885): 92.

Thomson, R., Jr. "Third Size Tuberose Bulbs." *American Florist, a Semi-monthly Journal for the Trade* 1, no. 8 (December 1, 1885): 127.

Thorburn, Grant. *Fifty Years' Reminiscences or New-York, or Flowers, from the Garden of Laurie Todd: Being a collection of fugitive pieces which appeared in the newspapers and periodicals of the day, for the last thirty years; including tales of the sugar-house [prison] in Liberty-Street; the yellow-fever in New-York, from 1798 to 1822; traditions and anecdotes of the war of the revolution, &c., &c., &c., &c. Obtained from actors in the scenes.* New York: Daniel Fanshaw, 1845.

Tilghman, J. Donnell. "Wye House." *Maryland Historical Magazine* 48 (1953): 89–108.

The Topographical, Statistical, and Historical Gazetteer of Scotland. First volume, A–H. Glasgow: A. Fullarton, 1842.

Triewald, Marten. "A Letter from Mr. Triewald, Director of Mechanicks to the King of Sweden, and F.R.SS. of England and Sweden, to Sir Hans Sloane, Bart. Pref. R.S. relating to an extraordinary Instance of the almost freezing of Water; and giving an Account of Tulips, and such bulbous Plants, flowering much sooner when their Bulbs are placed upon Bottles filled with Water, as in TAB. II. than when planted in the Ground." *Philosophical Transactions: Giving some account of the Present Undertakings, Studies, and Labours of the Ingenious, in many Considerable Parts of the World* 37 (1731, 1732): 79-81.

"A Trip to Cuba and the Southern States. Number 10. Natchez, Mississippi." *Horticulturist and Journal of Rural Art and Rural Taste. Devoted to horticulture, landscape gardening, rural architecture, botany, pomology, entomology, rural economy, etc.* 8 (March 1858): 126–27.

Troubetskoy, Ulrich. "F.F.V. of Old Dominion Gardens." *Virginia Cavalcade* 9, no. 4 (Spring 1960): 44.

Tucker, Arthur O. "Delmarva: A Wasteland or Unexplored Wilderness of Horticulture?" *Magnolia* 8, no. 3 (Winter 1992): 4–6.

Turnbull, Martha Barrow. *The Sixty Year Garden Diary of Martha Turnbull, Mistress of Rosedown Plantation 1836 to 1896: The Legendary Gardens of Rosedown as Viewed through the Words of Their Creator.* St. Francisville, La.: Rosedown Plantation and Historic Gardens, 1996.

Turnbull, Martha Barrow, Suzanne Turner, and William Seale. *The Garden Diary of Martha Turnbull, Mistress of Rosedown Plantation.* Baton Rouge: Louisiana State University Press, 2012.

Tyas, Robert. *Language of Flowers, or, Floral Emblems of Thoughts, Feelings and Sentiments.* London; New York: George Routledge and Sons, 1869.

Untitled. *Vick's Illustrated Monthly* 1, no. 10 (October 1878): 289–91.

Van Beck, Linda M., and Sara L. Van Beck. *Daffodils in Florida: A Field Guide to the Coastal South.* Tallahassee: for the authors, 2003.

Van Beck, Sara L. "Daffodils in Georgia's Landscapes." *Magnolia* 21, no. 4 (Spring 2008): 1–9.

———. "Gardening with Bulbs: Mountain Shoals, 1838 to Present." *Magnolia* 24, no. 1 (Winter 2011): 1–7.

———. "The Lost Narcissus Farms of Florida." *Florida Gardening* 14, no. 4 (April/May 2009): 22–24.

———. "Louis LeConte's Bulb Garden, 1813-1838." *Magnolia* 27, no. 1 (Winter 2014). In press.

———. "A Token of Remembrance—Daffodils in Cemeteries." *Magnolia* 18, no. 2 (Spring 2003): 7–9.

Van de Passe, Crispijn. *Hortus floridus: The first [-second] book contayninge a very lively and true description of the flowers of the springe.* Preface by Eleanour Sinclair Rohde and calligraphy by Margaret Shipton. London: Cresset Press, 1928–1929.

Van Eeden, Frederik Willem. *Flora Batava, Afbeelding en beschrijving der nederlandsche gewassen, aangevangen door wijlen Jan Kops, voortgezet door F.W. Van Eeden, zeventiende deel.* Leiden: De Breuk & Smits, 1885.

Van Kampen, Nicholas, and Son. *The Dutch Florist: or, True Method of managing all Sorts of Flowers with Bulbous Roots. To which is added, The particular Method of Treating the Guernsey Lily.* London: R. Baldwin, 1764.

Van Kampen, Nicolas, et fils. *Traité des Fleurs et Oignons: Contenant tout ce qui est nécessaire pour les bien cultiver, sonde sur une Expérience de plusieurs Années.* Harlem, Holland: C. H. Bohn, 1760.

Van Oosten, Henrik. *The Dutch gardener, or, The compleat florist: containing the most successful method of cultivating all sorts of flowers: the planting, dressing, and pruning of all manner of fruit-trees: together with a particular account of the nursing of lemon and orange trees in northern climates/written in Dutch, by Henry Van Oosten . . . ; translated into English.* London: Printed for D. Midwinter, 1711.

Vaughan's Seed Store. *Fall Edition of Vaughan's Gardening Illustrated.* Chicago: Vaughan's Seed Store, 1913.

Virginia Historic Landmarks Commission Survey Form File No. 76-45, Leesylvania Site. Richmond: Virginia Department of Historic Resources, n.d.

Virginia Historic Landmarks Commission Survey Form File No. 76-74, Fairfax House Site. Richmond: Virginia Department of Historic Resources, n.d.

Ward, Malthus A. "Editorial Correspondence." *Horticultural Review and Botanical Magazine* 4 (1854): 144–45.

———. "The Winter in Georgia." *Magazine of Horticulture, Botany, and All Useful Discoveries and Improvements in Rural Affairs* 13 (1847): 132.

Waterman, Catharine H. *Flora's Lexicon.* Philadelphia: Hooker and Claxton, 1839.

Weeks, Christopher. *Where Land and Water Intertwine: An Architectural History of Talbot County, Maryland.* Baltimore: Johns Hopkins University Press, 1984.

Welch, Dr. William C., and Dr. Greg Grant. "Blumen Auf Dem Grab (Flowers on the Grave): Round Top Cemetery." *Magnolia* 9, no. 3 (Spring 1993): 6–8.

Wellford, Charles C. "A Nosegay in Fredewicks, in Virginia, Feb. 6—." *Gardeners' Magazine* 4 (1828): 396.

West, Anson. *A History of Methodism in Alabama.* Nashville, Tenn.: Methodist Episcopal Church South, 1893.

Weston, Richard. *The English Flora: Or, a Catalogue of Trees, Shrubs, Plants and Fruits, Natives as well as Exotics, Cultivated, for Use or Ornament, in the English Nurseries, Greenhouses and Stoves, Arranged according to the Linnaean System, with The Latin Trivial, and common English Names. Also, A General Catalogue of Seeds, for the Kitchen-Garden, Flower-Garden, Grass-Lands, Etc. Usually Raised for Sale, and Those annually imported from America.* London: Printed for the author: and sold by J. Millan, Whitehall; Robson and Co. New Bond-Street; T. Carnan, St. Paul's Church-Yard; E. and C. Dilly, in the Poultry; and by all the nurserymen and seedsmen in England, 1775.

———. *The Universal Botanist and Nurseryman: Containing Descriptions of the Species and Varieties of All the Trees, Shrubs, Herbs, Flowers, and Fruits, Natives and Exotics: at present cultivated in the European Nurseries, Greenhouses, and Stoves, or described by Modern Botanists; arranged according to the Linnaean system, with their names in English. To which are Added a Copious Botanical Glossary, Several Useful Catalogues and Indexes. Illustrated with Elegant Engravings.* Volume the third. London, J. Bell, 1772.

Whately, Thomas. *Observations on Modern Gardening, Illustrated by Descriptions.* London: Printed for T. Payne at the Mews-gate, 1770.

W. H. Coe & Berry. *Illustrated Priced Catalogue of the Cut Flower Department, Floral Hill Nursery.* Lockhaven, Pa.: W. H. Coe & Berry, ca. 1870.

Wheeler, Willis H. "Daffodil Bulb Trade." *The Daffodil Handbook: a special issue of the American Horticulture Magazine* 45, no. 1 (January 1966): 185–94.

White, Sharon. *Vanishing Gardens (Finding Nature in Philadelphia).* Athens: University of Georgia Press, 2008.

White, William N. "Bulbs." *Southern Farm and Home: A Magazine of Agriculture, Manufacturers and Domestic Economy* 2, no. 8 (June 1871): 301–2.

———. "The Flower Garden." *Southern Farm and Home: A Magazine of Agriculture, Manufacturers and Domestic Economy* 1, no. 11 (September 1870): 410.

———. "The Flower Garden. For the Southern Farm and Home. Laying out a Flower Garden. Prepared from the unpublished Manuscripts of the late Wm. N. White." *Southern Farm and Home: A Magazine of Agriculture, Manufacturers and Domestic Economy* 1, no. 5 (March 1870): 176–77.

Wickson, Edward James. *California Garden-Flowers, Shrubs, Trees and Vines: Being Mainly Suggestions for Working Amateurs.* San Francisco: Pacific Rural Press, 1914.

Wilder, Louise Beebe. *Colour in My Garden.* Garden City: Doubleday, Page, 1918.

———. *My Garden.* Garden City: Doubleday, Page, 1916.

"The Wild Garden." *American Agriculturist, for the Farm, Garden and Household* 40, no. 11 (November 1881): 500.

Wilks, Rev. W. Preface to *Daffodils,* by Rev. Joseph Jacob. London: T. C. & E. C Jack, 1910.

William A. Gill & Co. "Fresh Bulbous Roots." *Ohio Cultivator* 9, no. 22 (November 14, 1853): 352.

"William Booth. A Catalogue of Kitchen Garden Seeds and Plants; Physical Seeds and Plants; and Seeds to Improve Land; Fruit Trees & Fruits; Annual, Biennial and Perennial Flowers; Herbaceous Plants and Bulbous Roots; Forest Trees, Flowering Shrubs and Evergreens;

Green-House and Stove Plants." In *Southern Plants List,* edited by Gordon W. Chappell, 116–59. Southern Garden History Society and the Colonial Williamsburg Foundation, 2000. http://southerngardenhistory.org/PDF/SouthernPlantLists.pdf.

William R. Prince & Co. *1842 & 1843. Catalogue of Bulbous and Tuberous Rooted Flowers, of the most choice and splendid varieties, cultivated at Prince's Botanic Garden and Nurseries, Flushing, Near New-York.* N.p.: n.p., 1842.

———. *1844 & 1845. Catalogue of Dahlias, and Bulbous and Tuberous Rooted Flowers, of the most choice and splendid varieties, cultivated at Prince's Botanic Garden and Nurseries, Flushing, Near New-York.* Flushing, N.Y.: Printed at the Office of the Flushing Journal by C. B. Lincoln, 1844.

———. *1846 & 1847. Catalogue of Bulbous and Tuberous Rooted Flowers, of the most choice and splendid varieties, cultivated at Prince's Botanic Garden and Nurseries, Flushing, Near New-York.* Jamaica, N.Y.: Printed at the Office of the Long Island Farmer, 1846.

———. *1860 and 1861. Prince's Select Catalogue of their Unrivaled Collection of Bulbous Flowers of Every Class.* . . . New York: Wynkoopo, Hallenbeck & Thomas, Printers, 1860. James R. Cothran Papers, 1771–2006, Mss. 989, Cherokee Garden Library, Kenan Research Center at the Atlanta History Center.

———. "Superior Bulbous Roots and Peonies." *Cultivator* 4 (November 1858): 385.

Williams, Henry T., ed. *Window Gardening. Devoted specially to the culture of flowers and ornamental plants, for In Door Use and Parlor Decoration.* New York: Henry T. Williams, 1872.

Winter, Thomas. *A Guide to Floriculture; containing instructions to the young florist, for the management of the most popular flowers of the day.* Cincinnati: Derby, Bradley, 1847.

Wirt, Elizabeth Washington. *Flora's Dictionary, by a Lady.* Baltimore, Md.: Fielding Lucas, Jr., 1832.

Wisconsin. "The Narcissus." *Vick's Monthly Magazine* 4, no. 10 (October 1881): 317–18.

Woodson, Mrs. Mary Willis. "My Recollections of Frankfort." *Register of the Kentucky Historical Society* 61, no. 3 (July 1963): 193–213.

Woolridge, John. *Systema horti-culturae, in three books. The I. Treateth of the excellency, scituation, soil, form, walks, arbours, springs, fountains, water-works, grotto's, statues, and other ornaments of gardens, with many rules, and directions, concerning the same. The II. Treateth of all sorts of trees planted for ornament of shade, winter-greens, flower-trees, and flowers, that are propagated or preserv'd in the gardens of the best florists, and the best way's and methods of raising, planting, and improving them. The III. Treateth of the kitchin garden, and of the variety of plants propagated for food, or for any culinary uses: with many general and particular rules, and instructions, for the making hot beds, altering and enriching any sort of garden ground, watering, cleansing, and adapting all sorts of earth to the various plants that are usually planted therein. To the great improvement of every sort of land, as well for use and profit, as for ornament and delight. Illustrated with sculptures, representing the form of gardens, according to the newest models.* London: William Freeman, 1700.

Wright, Letitia Ellicott Carpenter. *Colonial Garden at Stenton Described in Old Letters.* Philadelphia: Philadelphia Horticulture Society, 1916.

W. W. Rawson & Co. *Rawson's Bulb Handbook 1907.* Boston: W. W. Rawson & Co., 1907.

Yang, Linda. "Wild Wonder." *Winterthur Magazine* (Winter 2007): 21–23.

Zandbergen, Mathew. "The Windmill and the Daffodil." In *The Daffodil and Tulip Yearbook,* 34: 54–62. London: Royal Horticultural Society, 1968.

Index

For individual listings of flowers, see under *narcissus*

About the author

Sara L. Van Beck, horticulturist and plant historian, is an officer of the American Daffodil Society and serves on the board of the Cherokee Garden Library at the Atlanta History Center. Van Beck has worked as a museum curator with the National Park Service and is the former president of the Georgia Daffodil Society. She is co-author of *Daffodils in Florida: A Field Guide to the Coastal South* and has written articles for the *Daffodil Journal,* the *Magnolia* bulletin of the Southern Garden History Society, and *Florida Gardening.*